She Also Wrote Plays

Susan Croft has worked as a director, dramaturg, workshop leader and Lecturer in Creative and Performance Arts. In 1986 she founded the New Playwrights Trust. In 1996 she was awarded an Andrew W. Mellon Fellowship to pursue her research on women playwrights at the Harry Ransom Humanities Research Center at the University of Texas at Austin. Since 1997 she has been Curator of Contemporary Performance at the Theatre Museum in London. She is currently completing her *Critical Bibliography of Published Women Playwrights in the English Language 1360–1914* for Manchester University Press.

in the same series

GABRIELLA GIANNACHI/MARY LUCKHURST (EDS)
On Directing: Interviews with Directors

LIZBETH GOODMAN (ED.)
Mythic Women/Real Women: Plays and performance pieces for women

DAVID HARE
Acting Up

KEITH JOHNSTONE
Impro for Storytellers

WENDY LESSER
A Director Calls: Stephen Daldry and the Theatre

DAVID MAMET
True and False: Heresy and common sense for the actor

MICHAEL MCCALLION
The Voice Book

RICHARD NELSON AND DAVID JONES (ED. COLIN CHAMBERS)
Making Plays: The writer/director relationship in the theatre today

PETER REYNOLDS AND RICHARD HAHLO
Dramatic Events: How to run a successful workshop

DAVID WOOD WITH JANET GRANT
Theatre for Children: A guide to writing, adapting, directing and acting

ALEKS SIERZ
In-Yer-Face Theatre: British drama today

SHE ALSO WROTE PLAYS

An International Guide to Women Playwrights from the 10th to the 21st Century

SUSAN CROFT

faber and faber

Dedicated to the memory of my father

First published in 2001
by Faber and Faber Limited
3 Queen Square London WC1N 3AU

Published in the United States by Faber and Faber Inc
an affiliate of Farrer, Straus and Giroux LLC, New York

Typeset by Faber and Faber Limited
Printed in England by Clays Ltd, St Ives plc

A CIP record for this book is available from the British Library

ISBN 0–571–20602–6

10 9 8 7 6 5 4 3 2 1

Contents

Author's Note vii

How to Use this Book viii

Abbreviations Used ix

Acknowledgements xi

Playwrights A–Z 1

Appendix 1: Anthologies and Series 279

Appendix 2: Books on Women Playwrights and Women in Theatre 286

Appendix 3: Contact Addresses 290

Author's Note

For reasons of space, this book is, necessarily, a representative selection of women playwrights from the 10th to the 21st centuries. Exactly who to include and who to leave out is always a difficult decision, especially as part of the raison d'être for such a book is to make visible those who have been invisible. I have included writers whose work shows the spread of dramatic development in each English-speaking country over the centuries. In addition, I have tried to include a range of work from boulevard comedy to performance art. In the case of prolific playwrights, I have included a selection of their publications. Although there are a number of the earliest playwrights in the book, the emphasis is on the twentieth century and, in particular, the latter part. This last may seem a surprising decision in an era when communication is thought to be paramount and any notion of women's invisibility an outmoded view. But it is still true to say that there are far fewer productions of plays by women than by men and part of the purpose of this book is to guide people to the wealth of excellent material just waiting to be discovered or rediscovered.

How to Use this Book

As the aim of this book is to make the information quickly and easily available, I have followed certain rules:

- **Playwrights** are entered under their most commonly used name, whether real or assumed, for example, Dodie Smith rather than C. L. Anthony. Married names are used only where the writer is better known by the husband's name.
- **Nationalities** are given as simply as possible, for example, American rather than Asian-American. The more complex issues of identity are addressed within each entry.
- **Anthologies and Series** referred to in 'Plays include' are listed in full in Appendix 1.
- **Female and male parts** in casts are indicated by, for example, (4f,2m+), indicating 4 female, 2 male plus extras of either sex. Children are not indicated separately.
- **Further Reading** referred to in 'See also' is listed by author in Appendix 2.
- **Contact Addresses** for all major drama publishers are listed in Appendix 3.

Abbreviations Used

Standard abbreviations are used for American and Australian states.

ADS	Australasian Drama Studies
AFL	Actresses Franchise League (UK)
AT	American Theatre
BBC	British Broadcasting Corporation
BPP	Broadway Play Publishing
CEAD	Centre des auteurs dramatiques (CAN)
CBC	Canadian Broadcasting Corporation
CD	Canadian Drama
CTR	Canadian Theatre Review
CnTR	Contemporary Theatre Review (Harwood Academic Publishers)
DDF	Danske Dramatikeres Forbund (Denmark)
dp	doubling possible
DPC	Dramatic Publishing Company
DPS	Dramatists Play Service (US)
LCP	Lord Chamberlain's Plays (UK – manuscript collection of plays submitted for censor's approval)
ICA	Institute of Contemporary Arts (UK)
id	includes doubling
ITI	International Theatre Institute
JDTC	Journal of Dramatic Theory and Criticism
MD	Modern Drama
MP	Member of Parliament
n.d.	no date given
NEA	National Endowment for the Arts (US)
NHB	Nick Hern Books (UK)
n.p.	no publisher listed
NTQ	New Theatre Quarterly (UK)
NY	New York
PAJ	Performing Arts Journal (US)
PI	Plays International (UK)

P&P	Plays and Players (UK)
PiP	Plays in Process (US)
PM	Performance Magazine (UK)
RNT	Royal National Theatre (UK)
RSC	Royal Shakespeare Company (UK)
SAD	Studies in American Drama 1945–Present
SF	San Francisco
SSP	Scottish Society of Playwrights
TA	Theatre Annual (US)
TCG	Theatre Communications Group (US)
TDR	The Drama Review (US)
TiD	Themes in Drama (UK, ed. James Redmond, Cambridge UP)
T.I.E.	Theatre In Education
TJ	Theatre Journal (US)
UCal	University of California
UP	University Press (includes University of X Press)
W&P	Women and Performance (US)
WCP	West Coast Plays (US)
WP	Women's Project (US)
WPT	Women's Playhouse Trust (UK)
WSPU	Women's Social and Political Union (suffrage campaign,UK)
WTG	Women's Theatre Group (now 'The Sphinx', UK)

Acknowledgements

This book has gone through a long process to arrive in its present form. It would not exist without the support of many people, in particular my parents, Catherine and Peter Croft. My greatest sadness is that my father did not live to see it published. Also the rest of my family for their love, support and much-tried patience and my brother Simon for computer assistance. This book is also here because of the trust, feedback and listening ear of special friends: Sue Cohen, Hattie Naylor, April De Angelis, Lavender Aaronovitch, Alda Terracciano, Millicent Witherow, Susan Pfisterer, Tas Samuels, Penny McHale, Claire MacDonald, Nora Connolly, Nettie Scriven, Gabi Bail, Penny Ciniewicz, Diane Speakman, Janis Valdes, Steve Harris, Viv Gardner Margaret Beetham, Janet Weller and my Theatre Museum colleagues. Abroad I have been supported in tracking down obscure information or supplying accommodation by friends such as Chrissie Shaw and Sherry Engle, Jane Mont and Chris Mitchell, Abbie Ellicott, Cheryl Thornton, Kate Kelly, Emma Long and Pat Fox at the Harry Ransom Humanities Research Center at the University of Texas, whose research fellowship allowed me to pursue much of the work on the American section of the book. Among those institutions whose resources and staff have been invaluable are the British Library, Hertfordshire County Libraries and the London Library. Agents, playwrights' organizations, publishers and translators have gone out of their way to track down dates and cast sizes, send me copies, find addresses and out-of-print copies. Among them: Jodi Armstrong at Playwrights Canada, Alison Lyssa and Currency Press in Australia, Playmarket in New Zealand. Thank you also to my agent Harriet Cruickshank for continuing to believe in what must have seemed sometimes like a mirage. Finally this book is for all those women who contributed to the five International Women Playwrights Weeks till now and all those who contribute to the future ones . . . and to all those women playwrights who continue to give me such pleasure. Special thanks to my partner Peter Beringer who brought me through the final stages of the book delivery and to my son Luke who was delivered shortly afterwards!

Kathy Acker

American, 1948*–97

The queen of postmodern, plagiarized punk prose (*Blood and Guts in High School, Great Expectations, Empire of the Senseless*), the East Village art scene and body-building and tattoo as performance art, Acker also wrote and was adapted for performance (not always meeting with her approval). Richard Foreman, avant-garde director of the Ontological Hysteric Theatre, produced *The Birth of the Poet* as an opera and 'provocative, turbulent extravaganza'. Opening with the destruction of a nuclear power plant, it goes on to create a world of raw sexuality and violence that slips between the mean streets of New York and classical Rome.

A final section of *The Birth of the Poet*, in both English and Arabic, is reminiscent of the world of *Algeria*, one of several of her prose works peppered with dialogue passages. *Lulu* (cf. **Carter**) also began as such a section and became the basis for the experimental production in London of *Lulu Unchained* (1984), although collaborative problems led to much of the text being cut by the male director – ironic in a piece that explores female sexuality and attempts to release Wedekind's Lulu from male objectification.

In *Variety*, a young woman, desperate for work, takes a job in the box office of a porno-movie theatre. She develops an increasing fascination with the clientele and becomes a voyeur herself. *Eurydice in the Underworld* (1997) ends with a 'prose diary written by Eurydice when she's dead' and like *Requiem* remakes myth to investigate sickness and approaching death.

Plays include: *Lulu Unchained* (5f,3m) in PAJ 30 and *Don Quixote*, London: Paladin/NY: Grove, 1986; *Variety* (screen, directed Betty Gordon, 1983); *The Birth of the Poet* (6f,6m, 1987) in Marranca and Dasgupta 5 and with *Algeria* in *Hannibal Lecter, My Father*, NY: Semiotexte(e), 1991 and with *Eurydice in the Underworld* (2f, 2m,4f/m); *Requiem* (7f,7m) in *Eurydice in the Underworld*, London: Arcadia, 1997.

See also App. 2: Juno and Vale.

---

* Other sources give Acker's year of birth as 1944

Marianne Ackerman
Canadian, 20th century

A former theatre critic with the *Montreal Gazette* (1983–7), Ackerman is joint director of Theatre 1774. Her *L'Affaire Tartuffe* is a fascinating and acclaimed piece which explores the complex relationship of language, politics and national identity. Like Timberlake **Wertenbaker**'s *Our Country's Good*, the piece also explores the power of theatre to offer liberation. Using French, English and Gaelic it ingeniously juxtaposes the action of Molière's *Tartuffe* with the personal and political intrigues of its performers, as the British authorities, on the brink of the American colonies' rebellion, seek to appease French-Canadian demands for independence, with a performance in French as a goodwill gesture. The Catholic church opposes the anti-religious play but supports British efforts to stem demands for democracy; Gaelic-speaking Irish immigrants side with the Americans but are challenged by their Scottish counterparts. The eighteenth-century action is framed by a twentieth-century film-maker's search for the funding for a film on the same subject, as politicians and businesspeople, the counterparts of the historical characters, manoeuvre to gain advantage from financing the endeavour.

In *Céleste* Ackerman again creates a tri-lingual text in English, French and Yiddish examining memory, solitude and failures of communication between individuals and across cultural divides.

Plays include: *L'Affaire Tartuffe or The Garrison Officers Rehearse Molière* (3f,7/8m, 1993) and in CTR 67; *Woman by a Window* (3f, 1993) and *Céleste* (2f,2m, 1995) – all Montreal: Nuage Editions, 1996; *Meanwhile, Goodbye* (1f, 1996) in Brennan.

Kay Adshead
English, 1954–

Born in Manchester, Adshead trained as an actress at RADA and has had a comprehensive career in British stage, TV and film and is a published poet. *Thatcher's Women* (1987) was her first full-length play and grew out of hearing women from the English Collective of Prostitutes declaring how their situation was worsened by competition from trainloads of northern women who, driven by the tide of poverty and unemployment, had arrived in London to try to make money to feed their families and pay rent. Adshead's play focuses on three such women, mixing gritty realism with more poetic imagery and tries to capture the sense of the extraordinariness of her 'ordinary' characters, as they attempt to cope in the climate of 'caring capitalism'.

Plays include: *Thatcher's Women* (4f,2m, 1987) in Remnant 7; *Ravings, Dreamings* (MS, 1993); *Bacillus* (MS 1993); *The (Bogus) People's Poem* (MS, 1998); *Juicy Bits* (MS, 1998).

See also App. 2: Sierz.

Isidora Aguirre
Chilean, 1919–

Since the 1950s Aguirre has had more than thirty of her plays staged, many, like *The Flower Stand* (*La piegola de las flores*), throughout the Spanish-speaking world. She creates both popular political theatre, often drawing on Brechtian epic forms, and works on Chilean popular legends and folk traditions. Seeking to 'recapture historical events that are lessons and criticisms for the present and the future', Aguirre believes her work draws on a female language more attuned to express the humanity of suffering than would the abstractions of an index on poverty.

Altarpiece of Yumbel deals with the 'disappeared' of the Chilean regime under General Pinochet. In *The Pascualas* she draws on a folk legend of three women who drowned themselves in a lake for love. In telling the story of a mother, daughter and aunt, isolated in the country, who fall for a young botanist who stumbles on their estate, she creates a compelling, erotic and evocative piece that is both contemporary and timeless. *Express for Santiago* presents an ironic perspective on the same passion as a woman manipulates her ardent young admirer into returning to her flat to turn off the gas burner she's terrified she left lit.

Untranslated plays include: *Lautaro*; *Bolívar y Miranda*; *Diálogos del fin del siglo*.

Translated plays include: *Altarpiece of Yumbel* (8f,5m, 1987) tr. T. Salas & M. Vargas, in Salas and Vargas; *Express for Santiago* (2f,3m+) tr. Stanley Richards in *The Best Short Plays 1959–60* ed. Margaret Mayorga, Boston: Beacon Press, 1960; *The Pascualas* (6f,2m) tr. Willis Knapp Jones in *Poet Lore* 59, Sept. 1964.

3

Ama Ata Aidoo
Ghanaian, 1940–

Aidoo is one of Ghana's leading writers and the author of powerful and provocative novels and short stories as well as plays for theatre and radio. For years a member of the faculty in the Department of African Studies at University of Ghana, she has also served as Minister for Education. Her plays often draw on oral traditions incorporating poetry, chants and traditional sayings into the narrative. She dissects Western guilt and the impact of colonization on both the West and Africa with irony and humour. A recurrent theme is that of African 'been to's' – Africans who have visited Europe or the metropolis and observed the strange ways of Westerners and their reactions to Africa. Many of her works focus on the particular predicament of women caught between the demands of tradition and the desire for change. *Anowa*, based on a Ghanaian legend and set against a nineteenth-century backdrop of colonial defeat, is about a girl who defies her parents' wishes and marries the man of her choice – but her refusal to conform to the traditional behaviour of a wife brings tragic consequences. It has been widely performed. In *The Dilemma of a Ghost*, Ato brings a wife, Eulalie, home from America. She smokes, drinks and is careful not to get pregnant. Can the gulf between her and her new family be bridged?

Plays include: *Anowa* (1968, 8m,5f+, 1970) and in *Contemporary African Drama* ed. M. Banham and J. Plastow, Methuen, 1998; *The Dilemma of a Ghost* (9f,4m, 1965). Both London: Longman Drumbeat.
  See also: essays in *African Literature Today* No. 15 and No. 8; App. 2: James, Gilbert and Tomkins.

Joanne Akalaitis
American, 1937–

Akalaitis is a director, designer, performer and writer. She is also one of the founder members, with Lee Breuer, Ruth Maleczech and others, of the acclaimed New York-based Mabou Mines theatre group. Her performance pieces are constructed as collages, drawing on a range of different texts. *Dressed Like an Egg* is a homage to theatre, based on the life and work of the French writer, Colette, herself an actress at various periods of her life (cf. **Mueller**). As with all Akalaitis's pieces, visual images are as important as words in works of vivid theatricality – here, magically framed stage illusions, resplendently lit, mix with stand-up comedy and Kabuki-style puppet shows. In *Dead End Kids*, conjuring tricks are linked to scientific experiments and alchemical investigations in a piece that also draws on Goethe's *Faust*, 1950s instructions on building a nuclear fall-out shelter and accounts of the bombing of Nagasaki in a powerful anti-nuclear piece. *Green Card* draws on multiple accounts of the experience of immigrants to the USA, creating 'a barrage . . . of music and film, comedy, poetry and testimony' (Teich), in a piece that includes Balinese dance to celebrate the multiplicity of cultures in the USA, while also addressing immigrants' continuing encounters with alienation, exclusion and racism.

Plays include: *Dressed Like an Egg* (3f,2m, 1977) in Marranca and Dasgupta 4; *Dead End Kids* (c.7f,13m) in *Theater* 13.3, Summer/Fall 1982; *Green Card* (5f,6m) in *Theater* 18:2, Spring 1987 and BPP, 1991.

See also: Teich in *Theater* 18:2, Schechter in *Theater* 13:3, NTQ 52, Nov. 1997.

Zoë Akins
American, 1886–1958

Born in Missouri, Akins started her theatre career as an actress in New York while writing experimental poetic drama. Success came with her switch to a satirical vein with *Papa*, set among wealthy sophisticates, where two sisters compete for the glamour of claiming a romantic past – a fabulous affair with an opera singer; the illegitimate child of the union, meanwhile, gets passed from hand to hand. *The Greeks Had a Word For It* is a satirical commentary on, among other things, young women 'gold-diggers'.

Both *Déclassée* and *Greatness* (*The Texas Nightingale*) are built round bravura comic central characters. In *Greatness* Madame Canava is a highly strung opera singer with a chaotic personal life, while Lady Helen Haden of *Déclassée* is an impoverished, eccentric and charming English aristocrat, who is unfortunately killed off by her creator in a sentimental final scene. Akins's dramatization of Edith Wharton's *The Old Maid* won the Pulitzer Prize in 1935.

Plays include: *The Varying Shore* (MS); *The Greeks Had a Word For It* (MS, 1931); *Papa: an amorality* (5f,5m); *Déclassée* (6f,11m, 1919); *Daddy's Gone A-Hunting* (6f,5m, 1921), *Greatness* (3f,5m, 1922) NY: Boni & Liveright, 1923; *The Old Maid* (9f,5m) NY: Appleton-Century, 1935; *Little Miracle* (5+f) NY: Harper, 1936; *Mrs*

January and Mr X (9m,6f) French, 1948; *Christopher Strong* (screen, 1933); *Camille* (screen, 1936); *Showboat* (screen, from Edna **Ferber**, 1936); *Desire Me* (screen, 1947).

See also App. 2: Bradley in Schlueter; Shafer.

Lynne Alvarez
American, 1947–

Daughter of an Argentinian immigrant, Alvarez grew up in Oregon and Michigan. She began writing creatively after she was politicized by her experience as a journalist in Mexico in the late 1960s, where she witnessed the violent suppression of student revolt. *The Guitarrón* is loosely based on a period spent in Veracruz with her husband, attempting to live from fishing. Real characters are transmuted, taking on fabulaic and archetypal overtones in a piece that juxtaposes an old maestro cello player's ability to transform lives through his playing with the destructive machismo of the surrounding community. Strange, fantastical qualities imbue the short *On Sundays*, where a doll-like woman prepares for her day and combats a savage Beast in a transparent box, while a man pours out his unrequited love for her, as he gradually ages a lifetime.

Plays include: *The Guitarrón* (1f,6m, 1983) in Osborn; *The Reincarnation of Jamie Brown* (3f,5m) in Smith 1994; *On Sundays* (1f,1m) in Halpern; *Hidden Parts* (2f,2m, 1983) Maplewood, NJ: Waterfront Press, 1988; *Eddie Mundo Edmundo* in *New Plays from ACT's Young Conservatory*, Lyme, NH: Smith and Kraus, c.1996; *The Wonderful Tower of Humbert Lavoignet* (1f,4m, 1985) BPP, 1990. All, with *Don Juan of Seville* (tr. from Tirso de Molina) and *Thin Air: Tales from a Revolution*, in *Lynne Alvarez Collected Plays, Vol. 1* Lyme, NH: Smith and Kraus, 1998

Loula Anagnostaki
Greek, 20th century

Born in Thessaloniki, Anagnostaki is influenced by both European existentialism and by the Greek experience of exile, deracination and political instability. The threat which haunts her plays is both non-specific and suggestively historical – references to imprisonment and the Occupation abound. Her three one-acts were presented as one, billed as *The Town*. The image of the town that haunts all three, despite the confinement of each to the space of one room, is both dreamed or recollected, ideal and illusion – the 'real' town, not as it was remembered, is a disappointment, like every other town, and the characters take refuge in fantasy and isolation, hiding out in small rooms. The middle-aged man in *Overnight Stop* offers a young woman shelter for the night in order to see her leave again, reconfirming his escape from the world of human demands for food, conversation and explanations. In *The Parade*, while his sister placidly knits, a brother watches the preparations for a parade in the square below, until fascination turns to horror as an unveiled 'statue' is revealed as a guillotine. When the victim led out is revealed as their father, violence threatens to engulf them.

Untranslated plays include: *Antonio* (1971); *Nike* (1978); *I Kaseta* (1982).

Translated plays include: *The Town* (1f,2m, 1965) in *Chicago Review* 21:2, 1969; *Overnight Stop* (2f,1m, MS, 1965) – both tr. Aliki Halls; *The Parade* (1f,1m, 1965, MS tr. Halls), also extract tr. Christopher Robinson in Arkin and Shollar and tr. Anastasia Revi and Yiorges Glastra in *Contemporary Greek Theatre Vol. 1*, London: Arcadia, 1999.

See also: *Modern Greek Theater: Roots and Blossoms* by Halls Athens: Diogenis, 1982

Laurie Anderson
American, 1947–

Identified as a musician by musicians, a visual artist by visual artists, Anderson is one of the most successful performance artists. Her 'O Superman' from the album *Big Science* and the show *United States* broke into mainstream music after it went to number 2 in the British pop charts in 1982. Her work has continued to cross boundaries, using experimental text, invented instruments such as the tape bow violin and electronic drum sensors responding to her body movements, projections, computer graphics, storytelling and her own quirky stage presence. She has also developed work in new technologies, such as the CD ROM *Puppet Motel*.

Anderson's writing evokes a surreal America, a continually transforming landscapes of drive-in banks and shopping malls mutating into strange and ghostly presences. Eccentric angles of observation isolate and make strange familiar ritual social exchanges, juxtaposed with fantastic 'theories on motion, history and vision', encapsulating late twentieth-century urban alienation in a manner both disturbing and compelling. In her most political work, *Empty Places*, her oblique pointed observations criticize the censorship of artists by Jesse Helms *et al.*, US expansionism and the absurdities of US defence programmes. Her published books are at once production documentations, visual art works, meditations and texts.

Performance texts include: *United States* (1984), also extract in Champagne; *Empty Places* (1991); *Stories from the Nerve Bible* (all 1f, 1994) NY: Harper Perennial; *New York Social Life* (1f) in Russell. Recordings include: *United States*; *Big Science*; *The Ugly One with the Jewels*. Video/film: *Home of the Brave*.
  See also: TDR 86 & 154; PM 18, 1982; 23, 1983; 41, 1986; App. 2: Sayre.

The Anna Project
Created Canada, 1983

One of the key productions in Canadian feminist theatre history, *This Is For You Anna: a Spectacle of Revenge*, was collectively scripted and performed by Suzanne Odette Khuri, Patricia Nichols, Maureen White, Ann-Marie **MacDonald** and Banuta **Rubess**. It takes as its starting point the case of Marianne Bachmeier, a German woman who walked into the trial of the man who had raped and killed her 7-year-old daughter and shot him seven times; she was put on trial herself by the press for her sexual past. Using an episodic structure, it uses storytelling, snatches of music, multiple roles – all performers play Marianne. It also draws on other narratives of women's revenge, including fairy tales, the stories of Lucretia and of Agate, and subtle but powerful recurrent images such as the filling of a glass of milk for a child no longer there, which at the end overflows and splatters all over the floor.

Plays: *This Is For You Anna* (5f, 1983) in CTR 43 and Filewod.
  See also: Bartlett in PM 37, Oct./Nov. 1985; App. 2: Wilson in Brask.

Robyn Archer
Australia, 1948–

Archer, daughter of a popular entertainer father, was born in Adelaide and began singing in clubs and on TV as a teenager, honing a powerful performance style united to a resonant voice, an incisive wit and a committed feminism.

A number of her plays and shows re-create the lives of earlier women. *A Star is Torn* is a tribute to the struggles of eleven female performers, including Janis Joplin, Edith Piaf and Judy Garland, while *Poor Johanna* explores the life of a disfigured woman who, too 'ugly' to find work as a woman, disguised herself and worked as a male boundary rider in nineteenth-century Australia. *Café Fledermaus* uses songs and sketches and a range of styles from the cultural ferment of *fin de siècle* Vienna, from 'Secessionist elegance' to Expressionism, to portray a society in turmoil from the 1890s to the horrors of the First World War. Archer has also made a number of recordings of her songs, and those of Brecht and others, and published *The Robyn Archer Songbook* (1980).

Plays include: *The Conquest of Carmen Miranda* (MS, 1978); *Il Magnifico* (MS, 1980); *A Star is Torn* (documentation, 1f) Virago, 1986; *Cafe Fledermaus* (1f+ f band,2m) Currency, 1990; *Poor Johanna* (with Judith Rodriguez, 2f,3m,id) in Spender 1991.
See also App 2: Tompkins and Holledge; Tait.

Jane Arden
British, 20th century

Arden was an actress, playwright and screenwriter in the 1950s–70s. An early play, *The Party*, was conventional in form, but explored mental breakdown and the turmoil of adolescence. In 1966, with films such as *The Logic Game* (on the isolation of women in bourgeois marriages) and *Separation*, she began to address the political context of women's personal dilemmas. With the production (by Jim Haynes at London Arts Lab) of *Vagina Rex and the Gas Oven*, one of the first plays to come out of the post-war Women's Liberation Movement, she found a form reflecting the artistic as well as the political ferment of the Sixties. Anarchically imaginative, it uses surrealism, rock music, visual imagery, poetic language, characters who transform from role to role and a chorus of Furies to examine female rage and oppression and woman's position as social victim. Arden went on to establish a women's theatre group, Holocaust, in London.

Plays: *Conscience and Desire* (MS, 1954); *Dear Liz* (MS, 1954); *The Party* (3f,3m, 1958) in Trewin 18; *A New Communion – for Freaks, Prophets and Witches* (MS, 1971); *Vagina Rex and the Gas Oven* (1f, 1m + chorus) Calder & Boyars, 1971.
See also App. 2: Wandor, 1987, Sierz.

Linda Aronson
Australian, 1950–

Aronson's pieces are marked by lively humour and the creation of vivid female characters who refuse to conform. In *Reginka's Lesson*, Reginka is in her late sixties, a Jewish Holocaust survivor, settled in Australia and learning the recorder, described by her author as both cynical and idealistic, earthy and prudish. She's a woman who continues to struggle and survive despite old age, alienation from her neurotic daughter and whizzkid son, the sins of next door's cat and the machinations of the recorder trio that wants to exclude her. *Dinkum Assorted* is a boisterous comedy musical in which a group of women workers in wartime Warrabadanga fight to keep the biscuit factory open, in between organizing entertainments for the Yanks and conducting wonderfully chaotic air-raid training practices.

Plays include: *Kostas* (screen); *The Fall Guy* (4m) in *Theatre Australia*, June–July 1977; *Endangered Species* (MS, 1979); *Invitation to Eternity* (MS, 1982); *Reginka's Lesson* (1f, 1989) Currency; *Dinkum Assorted* (15f, musical, 1989) Currency; *A Night with Robinson Crusoe* (MS, 1990).

Liliane Atlan
French, 1932–

Born in Montpellier of a Jewish family, Atlan spent the war years in hiding. This experience and her study of the great Hebrew texts, Midrash and Kabbalah, are major influences on her work. She has worked in creating collective theatre in France and Israel, with drug addicts and with children, though the Holocaust remains her most persistent theme. In *Mister Fugue or Earth Sickness*, Grol, a German soldier, abandons his duties to accompany a group of ghetto children to their deaths. On the way they tell stories of marriage, courtship, success and failure, playing out the lives that will be taken from them. *The Little Carriage of Flames and Voices* focuses on a woman trying to heal her fragmented sense of self through eroticism, drugs, knowledge and revolt. *The Messiahs* watch the Earth from their planet lost in the immensity of space and dream of saving it. Many have already descended to Earth, but have been helpless to do anything. As Kristalnacht approaches and the Earth cries out, they prepare to act. The plays fuse Hebraic symbolism, film, video, and strong visual and theatrical imagery in exploring their disturbing subjects.

Atlan has created a number of experimental pieces for radio including *Some pages torn from the great book of dreams* (France Culture, 1994) and *An Opera for Theresienstadt*, simultaneously broadcast at Passover in France and Israel.

Untranslated plays include: *Leçons de Bonheur* (1982).

Translated plays include: *An Opera for Theresienstadt* (MS, 1980); *Mister Fugue or Earth Sickness* (2f,7m, 1967) also in Fuchs; *The Little Carriage of Flames and Voices* (2f,2m+, 1971); *The Messiahs* (4f,14m+, 1969). All three tr. Marguerite Feitlowitz in *Theatre Pieces* by Liliane Atlan, Penkevill Publishing, 1985. *The Passersby* (1f) tr. Rochelle **Owens**, NY: H. Holt, 1993.

See also: interview in *Theater*, Fall/Winter 1981; intro. to *Three Pieces*; App. 2: Isser; Patraka in Case ed.; Lamar; Betsko and Koenig.

Jane Austen
English, 1775–1817

While Austen did not write professionally for the stage, her work, especially *Pride and Prejudice*, has been much adapted since for theatre, screen and television, by writers who include Fay **Weldon** and Emma Thompson. A section of the central plot of *Mansfield Park* that revolves around the decision to present a performance of the play *Lovers' Vows*, by the German Kotzebue as adapted by Elizabeth **Inchbald**, might suggest Austen's apparent opposition to private theatricals. But she herself contributed to family charade-writing and performing and produced some juvenile plays. In 1977 a short play of hers was rediscovered: the central joke of *Sir Charles Grandison* is that Austen manages to get through the action of Samuel Richardson's enormous seven-volume novel of the same name in the space of five very short acts, with Harriet Byron abducted, fainting several times, rescued, loved and married by Sir Charles in double quick time.

Plays: *Jane Austen's Sir Charles Grandison* (15f,14m) ed. Brian Southam, Oxford UP, 1981; *The Visit* (4f,4m) and *The Mystery* (3f,5m), both c. 1787–93, in *The Juvenilia of Jane Austen and Charlotte Bronte*, ed. Frances Beer, Penguin, 1986; *Charades, written a hundred years ago*, London: Spottiswoode, 1895.

Mary Austin
American, 1868–1934

In 1888 Austin moved with her mother from Illinois to the Mojave Desert, where her lifelong interest in Indian culture was established. From an unhappy marriage to a fellow teacher she had one child, born mentally handicapped. Indian myths and rituals and a passionate feminism formed the basis for her stories, novels and plays. Among many theatrical activities she wrote scenarios and dance dramas for community production and worked to revive the Spanish folk plays of New Mexico. Her best-known play, *The Arrow-Maker*, written in 1911, was one of the earliest plays to represent American Indians as fully developed dramatic characters, rather than noble savages and loyal Pocahontases. Its heroine, the Chisera, is the shaman of the tribe, a position usually held by a man which she had inherited from her father. But where he could marry and be fully part of the tribe as well as have spiritual power, she is isolated by the women, feared by the men and manipulated by her secret lover, Simwa, who attempts to use her powers to reinforce his claim to become chief. Austin's is a complex and startlingly contemporary piece expressing a female dilemma which remains highly pertinent in the conflict between the demands of career and the desire for relationship.

Plays include: *The Arrow-Maker* (8f,7m) NY: Houghton and Mifflin, 1911; *Sekala Ka'ajma* (1f,3m+) in *Theatre Arts Monthly*, Apr. 1929.

See also: *Earth Horizon*: autobiography Boston: Houghton Mifflin, 1932. *Mary Austin: Song of a Maverick* by Esther Lannigan Stineman, New Haven: Yale UP, 1989.

Enid Bagnold
English, 1889–1981

As the daughter of an army officer father, Bagnold grew up in an artistic upper-class environment that is reflected in her plays. Characterized by strange ménages of odd aristocratic older women, quirky, slightly mad, younger ones and crusty, domineering old servants, they are also notable for finely wrought language. Drawing-room comedies with a difference, they meditate on their own artificial conventions and, unconventionally, sometimes feature characters who are homosexual or black.

Her best-known play, *The Chalk Garden*, makes a central symbol of the hard-to-cultivate soil which only begins to yield new growth to Miss

Madrigal, the eccentric stranger-with-a-past, hired as companion for a disturbed granddaughter. *The Chinese Prime Minister* nods towards Chekhov's *The Cherry Orchard* in the image of an old house, threatened by change and inhabited by an ageing actress and a faithful old butler and, intermittently, by her sons and their mismatched spouses. Offered the opportunity of a new life in Arabia when her oil tycoon husband reappears, the actress chooses instead a meditative old age. Bagnold's biggest theatrical success was her adaptation of her novel *National Velvet*, later filmed with Elizabeth Taylor.

Plays: *Lottie Dundass* (6f,7m, 1942) and *Poor Judas* (4f,6m, 1951) in *Two Plays*, Heinemann/NY: Doubleday, 1951; *Gertie* (alt. *Little Idiot*, MS, 1952); *The Chalk Garden* (7f,2m, 1955), *The Chinese Prime Minister* (3f,5m, 1964), *Call Me Jacky* (4f,4m, 1967) also in Trewin 34, *The Last Joke* (2f,7m, 1960) all in *Four Plays*, Heinemann/Boston: Little Brown, 1971; *A Matter of Gravity* (4f,4m), Heinemann, 1978; *National Velvet* (4f,7m, 1946) in *Embassy 2* and DPS, 1961.

See also: *Enid Bagnold: a Biography* by Anne Serra, London: Weidenfeld and Nicolson, 1986; App. 2: Gale; Taylor in Griffiths and Llewellyn-Jones.

Joanna Baillie
Scottish, 1762–1851

Born in Lanarkshire, daughter of a kirk minister, Baillie later settled in Hampstead, where she produced, at first anonymously, her *Plays on the Passions* from 1798 to 1826. Her aim was to write a tragedy and a comedy about each major human emotion: love, hatred, ambition, fear, hope, remorse, jealousy, pride, anger, joy, grief and religion. She left out revenge as it was such a common dramatic theme. She is unusual in her development of a detailed theory of drama, explained in prefaces accompanying each play, addressing its origins in Dionysian ritual, identifying various classes of comedy with their distinguishing features and expounding her belief in presenting the passions, not fully hatched, but in development throughout the play. Love, in *The Tryal*, becomes increasingly obsessive leading to betrayal and suicide. In one of the few of Baillie's plays to be produced, *De Monfort* (1800), the anti-hero's irrational hatred for the generous and hapless Rezenvelt, lover of his sister, escalates throughout the play.

Her plays form part of the Gothic tradition whose earlier exponents include the novelist Ann Radcliffe and then Mary Shelley with *Franken-*

stein. Characterized by dark atmospheric settings – castles full of secret dungeons and passageways, ruined abbeys and gloomy forests, ghostly figures, brooding passionate villains and heroines driven insane – Gothics provided admirable opportunities on stage for actresses such as Sarah Siddons, who played Jane De Monfort, to give bravura performances in electrifying mad scenes and for innovations in lighting and design to be exhibited, creating elaborate and terrifying settings. Among Baillie's most interesting plays are *Orra*, in which a young girl's mania for horror stories is used to drive her mad, and the sinister *Witchcraft*.

Plays include: Tragedies: *Basil* (3f,8m); *Rayner* (4f,11m); *De Monfort* (5f,7m) also in *Seven Gothic Dramas 1789–1825*, ed. Jeffrey Cox, Athens: Ohio UP, 1992; *Constantine Paleologus* (3f,10m); *Ethwald* (4f,11m); *Orra* (4f,8m). Comedies: *The Tryal* (4f,9m); *The Second Marriage* (4f,9m); *The Election* (5f,9m); *The Country Inn* (7f,6m). Dramas: *The Bride* (4f,6m); *The Martyr* (1f,9m) as *A Series of Plays 1799–1802*, reissued, Garland, 1977. All with: Tragedies: *Witchcraft* (7f,8m); *The Stripling* (2f,7m); *The Separation* (3f,9m). The *Homicide* (2f,7m); *The Family Legend* (3f,9m) also in Scullion. Comedies: *The Match* (4f,6m); *Enthusiasm* (5f,8m); *The Alienated Manor* (4f,7m). Musical dramas: *The Phantom* (5f,9m) in *The Dramatic and Poetical Works of Joanna Baillie*, London: Longman, 1851.

See also: *The Life and Work of Joanna Baillie* by Margaret S. Carhart, New Haven, CT: Yale Studies in English, 1923; *Closet Stages* by Catherine B. Burroughs, Philadelphia: Pennsylvania UP, 1997; App. 2: Donkin.

Elizabeth Baker
English, 1876–1962

Baker began work as a typist in a world where the options in paid work for women were severely constrained, especially for a Londoner from a lower-middle-class family such as herself. While many 'new women' writers explore women's struggle for useful employment, Baker, like **Hamilton**, explores the drudgery and monotony of dull and grinding work. Plays such as *Chains* or *Miss Tassey* draw, in harshly realistic detail, the stifling respectability of the petit bourgeoisie, the dullness of a safe job as a clerk in the city or a shop-girl with no prospects of escape except through marriage, and the struggle of individuals against their confinement. She also pictures the narrow conformism of respectable marriage which, for Charley in *Chains*, is a trap which prevents him realizing his dreams of emigration and a new life. Other plays present independent successful working women denied recognition by family assumptions of their incompetence (*Edith*)or the struggle for greater fulfilment in a world where the cost of success is to have no life outside the business (*Partnership*).

Plays include: *Chains* (5f,7m, 1909) in Fitzsimmons & Gardner and in Dickinson; *Miss Tassey* (5f, 1913) also in Clark; *Miss Robinson* (6f,5m, 1920); *Edith* (5f, 1912 published 1927) – all London: Sidgwick & Jackson; *Bert's Girl* (6f,6m) London: Benn, 1927; *Partnership* (6f,5m, 1917) French, 1921.

See also App. 2: Gardner and Rutherford; Stowell; Gale.

Charlotte Mary (Conner) Barnes

American, 1818–63

Charlotte Barnes, part of a New York theatrical family, became an actress, touring throughout America and to Britain. Her first play, an adaptation, appeared when she was seventeen and the following year she played the lead in *Octavia Bragaldi*, in which the heroine demands that her husband murder the man who tricked her into a false first marriage. Based on real events in Kentucky, Barnes's play transposes them to the more exotic setting of Renaissance Italy. *The Forest Princess* dramatizes the familiar romantic story of Pocahontas, the American Indian princess who saves Captain Smith and the English settlers.

Plays include: *The Forest Princess* (14m,4f+, 1844) in Kritzer; *Octavia Bragaldi* (2f, 13m+, 1837). Both in *Plays, Prose and Poetry*, Philadelphia: E. H. Butler & Co, 1848, NY: Scholarly Reprints, 1976.

Djuna Barnes

American, 1892–1982

Barnes, from upstate New York, became a newspaper columnist and drama critic, before settling in Paris, where she became a member of the expatriate artistic community, living with sculptress Thelma Wood and writing the innovative novel *Nightwood* (1936).

Her first short plays were produced at the Provincetown Playhouse (see **Glaspell, Boyce**) in the 1920s or published in magazines, sometimes under the pseudonym 'Lydia Steptoe'. They are bleakly satirical or, influenced by Strindberg, compulsively revisit images of antagonism between the sexes, featuring stormy, aristocratic heroines, rejected suitors, vampirism, doomed madonnas. Her major dramatic work, *The*

Antiphon, has largely defeated producers and been read as a closet drama, its dense, allusive, archaic language evoking Jacobean tragedy, clotted with metaphor, replete with grotesque masques, a doomed aristocratic lineage, hints of sexual sin and religious expiation (cf. the allegorical *A Passion Play*). Its minimal plot, set in 1939, evokes a world on the brink of disaster, centring on a mother and daughter bound together in mutual suffering and hatred by their shared past: an adulterous husband and pander father who procured the rape of his daughter.

Plays include: *Kurzy of the Sea* (MS); *Ann Portuguise* (MS); *She Tells Her Daughter* in *Smart Set*, Nov. 1923; *A Passion Play* in *Others*, Feb. 1918; *Three From the Earth* (1f,3m, 1920) in France; *An Irish Triangle* (2f, 1921) in Ozieblo; *The Dove* (3f, 1926) in Kelly; *The Antiphon* (2f,4m+, 1958) in *Selected Works*, Faber, 1958.

See also: *The Art of Djuna Barnes: Duality and Damnation* by Louis F. Kannenstein, NYUP, 1977; *Djuna* by Andrew Field, NY: Putnams, 1983; App. 2: Schlueter.

Sidney Frances (Cowell) Bateman
American, 1823–81

Bateman was an actress and theatrical manager of theatres in the USA and later in London (including the Lyceum and Sadler's Wells), first with her husband and, after his death, independently. All four of their daughters also became actresses. Many of Bateman's plays (most unpublished) are sentimental melodramas and adaptations of novels. The best-known, *Self*, has similarities to **Mowatt**'s *Fashion* as a satire on New York social-climbing, although it lacks her bite.

Plays include: *Self* (10f,12m), Samuel French, 1856, also in Moses v2; *The Golden Calf or Marriage à la Mode* (5f,7m) St Louis: n.p. 1857, Scholarly Reprint 1976.

Hilary Beaton
Australian, 1955–

English-born Beaton grew up in Australia and since 1973 has divided her career between Australia and New Zealand, where she worked as an actress and drama workshop leader in a women's prison. The hard-hitting play *Outside In* is set in a women's prison, a microcosm of a society, where the inmates re-create a distorted picture of family relationships, emotional abuse, alliance and counter-alliance, while those in the surrogate dominant male roles jockey for position. Verbally and physically violent, it also contains moments of great tenderness. *No Strings Attached* is a comedy thriller about women sky-divers and the desire for revenge.

Plays include: *Sitting on a Fortune* (MS, 1979); *Outside In* (7f) Wellington: Victorian UP, 1984; *Trading Hours* (MS, 1990); *Jumping the Gun* (screen, 1993); *No Strings Attached* (3f) Brisbane: Playlab, 1995.

Aphra Behn
English, 1640–89

Acclaimed by Virginia **Woolf** as the first professional woman writer, who 'earned [women] the right to speak their minds', Behn was probably born Aphra Johnson in Canterbury, Kent. Accounts of her early life differ, but it appears to have been appropriately dramatic: living several years in Surinam and witnessing a slave rebellion, later a spy for Charles II, code-named Astrea, and imprisoned in the Fleet for debt. Seventeen of her nineteen plays have survived. Behn first faced attack for the very audacity of being a woman playwright, but defended herself in witty prefaces. Theatre, she maintained, is a form where men's only advantage over women, a better education, is not relevant. The chief charge against her, before and since, she wrote mockingly, was that her work 'was Bawdy, the least and most Excusable fault in the Men writers . . . but from a Woman it was unnaturall.'

Her plays present women expressing desire, exercising and wittily defending sexual choice (*The Rover*, *The Lucky Chance*), attacking forced marriages and double standards. She compares the financial transaction of marriage to prostitution, while presenting prostitutes sympathetically in plots such as *The Feigned Courtesans* and *The Dutch Lover* where confusions of identity between disguised heroine and courtesan raise questions about the social distinctions made between them. Her sympathetic portrayal extends to other marginal figures and outsiders: women scholars and female Amazons. *The Widow Ranter*, dashing, generous and pipe-smoking, fights alongside her lover. Racial 'others' are also presented with complexity and empathy: American Indians, the rebel slave of her novel *Oroonoko* (1688, dramatized by Thomas Southerne, 1695 and by Biyi Bandele for the RSC, 1999), even Abdelazar, the Moor whose murderous path to power is driven by the desire for revenge on those who have scorned his race.

Plays include: *Abdelazar* (1677); *The Rover* (Part 1, 1 1677) numerous editions including in Pollock and in Spender and Todd; *The False Count* (4f,14m+, 1682); *The Lucky Chance* (7f,12m+, 1686) in Morgan (1981); *The Widow Ranter* (1690) – all in *Five Plays* ed. M. **Duffy**, Methuen, 1990; *The Forc'd Marriage* (6f,11m+, 1671); *The Dutch Lover* (8f,13m+, 1673) in *Selected Writings*, Grove Press, 1950; *The Debauchee* (8f,10m+, 1677); *Sir Patient Fancy* (9f,14m+1678) in Rogers; *The Feigned Courtesans* (5f,10m+, 1679) and in Lyons and Morgan; *The Rover* (Part 2, 8f,14m+, 1681); *The Roundheads* (5f,12m+, 1682); *The City Heiress* (8f,11m, 1682) – all in *The Works of Aphra Behn* vols 5–7 ed. Janet Todd, London: William Pickering, 1996.

See also especially: *The Passionate Shepherdess* (biography) by **Duffy**, Methuen, 1977; *Reconstructing Aphra* (social biography) by Angeline Goreau, Oxford UP, 1980; *Aphra Behn* by Frederick M. Link NY: Twayne, 1968; *Rereading Aphra Behn: History, Theory and Criticism* ed. Heidi Hutner, Charlottesville: Virginia UP, 1993; *Aphra Behn* by Janet Todd, Basingstoke: Macmillan, 1999; App. 2: Pearson; Cotton; Howe; Schofield and Macheski.

Loleh Bellon

French, 1925–

After a successful thirty-year career as an actress, Bellon embarked on writing and, with *Thursday's Ladies* (1976), won international boulevard success for a play informed by feminism. With sharp observation it celebrates the friendship of three women who meet every Thursday for afternoon tea, chat, familiar arguments and jokes, intercutting the action with flashbacks of their earlier lives. Bellon also uses this technique in *Bonds of Affection*, which explores the relationship of mother and daughter, both played by women of about 45, through a series of parallel events and changing roles. The daughter in bed at the opening, scared of being left alone by her mother, is replaced at the end by the mother, frightened that her busy daughter will leave.

Bellon's plays have an elegaic quality, but her language, in Bray's translation, is precise, witty and colloquial. Her plays are notable for the fine roles they offer older actresses.

Untranslated plays include: *Le Coeur sur la Main* (1980); *Une Absence* (1988); *Changement à vue* (1979); *L'Eloignement* (1987).

Translated plays: *Thursday's Ladies* (3f,2m) French, 1988; *Bonds of Affection* (2f,2m, 1984) in Ubu Rep 3. Both tr. Barbara Bray.

See also App. 2: Lamar.

Helen Benbow

Australian, 19th century

The earliest Australian woman playwright to be produced and published, Benbow's melodrama is strong on local colour. *For £60,000!!!* features a defenceless heroine who, despite her protestations of Australian women's independence, is carried off by the villain with the help of ruffianly bushrangers while he encourages the Aborigines to attack her squatter father's station. All are saved by a resourceful maid and the upright hero, Fred.

Plays: *For £60,000!!!: a sensational comedy* (3f,8m+) Castlemaine, Victoria: 1874.
See also: *Australia on the Popular Stage 1829–1929* by Margaret Williams, Melbourne: Oxford UP, 1983.

Simone Benmussa

French, 1932–

Benmussa's upbringing was eclectic: a Tunisian Jew educated in a Catholic convent. A director and playwright who has worked in France, England and the USA, she was formerly literary adviser to the Renaud-Barrault company, where she organized exploratory workshops of plays and in 1958 co-founded the journal *Cahiers Renaud-Barrault*. Her work encompasses translations and adaptations from literary sources which often radically rework and critique the original work and includes Hélène **Cixous**'s *Portrait of Dora*, Agatha **Christie**'s *The Hollow*, Henry James's *The Real Thing*, Nathalie **Sarraute**'s *Enfance*, Edna **O'Brien**'s *Virginia* and *Camera Oscura* from Gertrude **Stein**.

The Singular Life of Albert Nobbs, based on a short story by George Moore, is set in a Dublin hotel where Albert Nobbs, the perfect waiter, is revealed as a woman in disguise. Having begun the pretence for economic reasons she now finds herself trapped in a role in which her identity has been swallowed up. *Appearances*, based on Henry James's short story, 'A Private Life', is set in a Swiss hotel. The play also explores ideas about reality, illusion, performance and ghosts, as James and an actress become fascinated by Lord Mellifont – who disappears when alone.

Untranslated plays include: *La Traversée du Temps Perdu*, Paris: des femmes, 1978.

Translated plays: *The Singular Life of Albert Nobbs* (7f,3m, 1977) tr. Barbara Wright, in Benmussa, *Appearances* (3f,5m, 1980) tr. Barbara Wright, in *Gambit* 35.

See also: Yale/*Theater* 13/1 and *Gambit* 35; App. 2: Diamond in Brater and in Case ed.; Elam Jr in Laughlin and Schuler.

Inez Bensusan

Australian, 1871–1967

Bensusan emigrated from Sydney to England around 1893 to establish a career as an actress. She rapidly became involved in the campaign for women's suffrage, running the Play Department of the Actresses Franchise League and encouraging women like Cicely **Hamilton** and Beatrice Harraden to write plays in support of the cause. In 1913 she set up the Women's Theatre, to establish a permanent company doing plays on women's experience. Her own *The Apple* (1911) is a fierce cry of outrage at the unjust treatment of daughters, as two sisters slave at dismal jobs while the family inheritance all goes to support their brother, Cyril, the apple of their father's eye.

Plays include: *The Apple* (2f,2m) in Hayman & Spender, in Gardner, in Pfisterer; *Nobody's Sweetheart* (MS, 1911).

See also App. 2: Stowell; Holledge; Pfisterer and Pickett.

Kathleen Betsko

English/American, 1939–

Betsko was born in Coventry but married 'a Yank in the hopes of finding Doris Day and maybe living next door to her'. Instead, she found herself living in poverty in an immigrant family in the coal-mining Monongahela Valley, an experience she drew on in her play *Johnny Bull* (later filmed) which explores the culture shock of a lively young Englishwoman confronted by a dour Hungarian community where women's roles are narrowly circumscribed. Escaping with her children to New Hampshire, Betsko worked in factories and eventually graduated from the university, but continues to draw with anger, humour and compassion on her experience as a working-class woman in *Stitchers and Starlight Talkers* (MS), set in a New England textile factory, and *Beggar's Choice* (MS, 1978). Co-editor with Rachel Koenig of *Interviews with Contemporary Women Playwrights*,

Betsko was a key mover in organizing the First International Women Playwrights' Conference at Buffalo, NY in 1988.

Plays include: *Johnny Bull* (3f,2m) DPS, 1985.
  See also App. 2: Betsko and Koenig.

Jean Betts
  New Zealand/Aotearoan, 1955–

At once comic, highly theatrical and provocative, Betts's *Ophelia Thinks Harder* reconstructs *Hamlet* from the point of view of Ophelia, struggling with grief for her dead mother. Suffering brutal treatment by the prince who claims he loves her, suicidal impulses and the demands of father, brother, queen, ghosts *et al.* that she be properly womanly, she receives sympathy from her much-abused maid, is given a rapid introduction to feminism by a cross-dressed Rosencrantz and Guildenstern and ends by making her own choices and joining the theatre.

Plays include: *Bloomsberries* (MS, 1974); *Leaving Home* (MS, 1980); *Ophelia Thinks Harder* (5f,5m) Wellington: Women's Play Press, 1994; *Strange Brew* (MS, 1995); *The Revenge of the Amazons* (in preparation).
  See also: *Playmarket News* 13; *Illusions* (NZ) Winter 1994.

Marie-Claire Blais
  French-Canadian, 1939–

A major Québécois writer best known as a novelist, Blais has also produced stage, TV and radio plays. Blais called *The Execution* 'a drama of destruction and violence', and through a plot centring on the gratuitous murder of a 14-year-old boy by his classmates, the domination of the group by a powerful individual and the indifference of the rest of the student body created a bleak metaphor for America's involvement in Vietnam. The dynamics of a society indifferent or hostile to outsiders is also central to *The Ocean*, in which the focus is on an island community where gay men are marginalized by a tourist community who see them as pariahs. In the six-writer collaboration, *A Clash of Symbols*, women speak of the repressed parts of their daily lives, while in recent work Blais has given voice to lesbian experience.

Translated plays include: *The Execution* (3f,7m+, 1968) tr. D. Lobdell, Talon-books, 1976; *A Clash of Symbols* (1 or 6f, tr. Linda Gaboriau from *La nef des sorcières*), Coach House Press, 1977; *The Ocean* (9f,13m) tr. Ray Chamberlain, Toronto: Exile Editions, 1977; *Murmurs* (1f,1m, radio) tr. Margaret Rose, in *CD*, 5:2, 1979.

Helen Blakeman
English, 1971–

A former actress in the Liverpudlian soap opera *Brookside*, Blakeman's first full-length play, *Caravan*, was noticed by the critics for its assurance, black comedy and sharp and disturbing exploration of working-class tradition and aspirations. In the claustrophobic surroundings of a caravan on the North Wales coast, over several holiday seasons, personal desires for a better life collide with political struggles as two sisters and their mother share and swap partners and babies against a background of the 1990s Liverpool dockers' strike. Less successfully but with similar claustrophobia, *Normal* explores a strained mother– daughter relationship and the effect on a family of hidden secrets and old bereavements, which the daughter enacts on her body through self-mutilation. In a parallel plot other mutilations enacted through cosmetic surgery (cf. **Oglesby**) supposedly offer the fulfilment of female desire.

Plays: *Caravan* (3f,2m, 1997) in Bradwell; *Normal* (3f,3m) Faber, 2000.
    See also App. 2: Sierz.

Martha Boesing
American, 1936–

Prolific author and director of numerous plays (many self-published) for Minneapolis-based At the Foot of the Mountain Theatre, Boesing's feminist commitment is central to her work. In *Antigone Too* the heroine's struggle is juxtaposed with a chorus of women from history – anarchists, Quakers, labour organizers, witches – jailed for their beliefs. Many of her plays are described as ritual dramas and address addiction and recovery (*Junkie!*, MS, 1981), men's conditioning by patriarchal values (*The Gelding*) or, as in the acclaimed *Ashes*, the horrors of nuclear war, in which past disasters that have devastated the earth haunt a dying woman. Others use the form of dreams to explore love between women or motherhood. Archetypes constantly occur, especially images of water and fantasies of swimming.

Plays include: *Love Song for an Amazon* (2f, 1976), *River Journal* (4f,2m, 1975) and *The Gelding* (3m, 1975) in *Journeys Along the Matrix: Three Plays,* Minneapolis: Vanilla Press, 1978; *Pimp* (3f, 1973) in France; *The Story of a Mother* (1978) in Chinoy and Jenkins; *Labia Wings* (5f,1m, 1979), *Song for Joanna* (1f,2m, radio, 1981); *Ashes, Ashes We All Fall Down* (6f, 1982); *Antigone Too: Rites of Love and Defiance* (19f,2+2–4m, 1985); *Trespasso* (3f,3m, 1977) – all Minneapolis: M. Boesing; *The Business at Hand* (1f,1m, 1987) in Jenness.

See also App. 2: Leavitt; Greeley in Laughlin and Schuler.

Bridget Boland
Irish, 1913–88

Boland's plays focus on the moral struggles of individuals and groups under pressure, and *Cockpit* addresses the power of theatre to unite divided peoples. A striking environmental piece, it explores how the political conflicts of war-torn Europe continue to be fought out among its displaced persons, quarantined by British forces in an abandoned German theatre. In *The Return*, Sister Agatha loses her vocation and leaves her closed order after thirty-six years, but finds herself without direction and purpose in a world she no longer recognizes. In *The Prisoner*, a proud imprisoned cardinal undergoes spiritual tortures as his cultured interrogator inflicts systematic moral torments, designed scientifically to extract confession.

Plays include: *Cockpit* (5f,11m+, 1948) in Trewin 1; *The Return* (3f,3m, 1953) in Trewin 9; *The Prisoner* (1f,8m, 1954) in Trewin 10; *Temple Folly* (2f,6m, 1951) London: Evans, 1958; *Gordon* (9m, 1961) in Trewin 25; *Spies of the Air* (screen); *Gaslight* (screen); *Anne of a Thousand Days* (1969, screen).

See also App. 2: Gale.

Carol Bolt
Canadian, 1941–

Winnipeg-born Bolt is a prolific writer, author of many plays for young people (*My Best Friend is Twelve Feet High*, 1972), as well as adults. She started a children's theatre in Montreal in the 1960s and went on to work with Theatre Passe Muraille (cf. **Griffiths**). She has produced much of her best work collectively, especially socially and politically engaged plays such as *Buffalo Jump*, about the trials of farmers and workers struggling for a better life during the Depression in Canada. Most of her plays include songs: the romantic, country and western thriller *One Night Stand*; the rock musical, *Maurice*.

Many of Bolt's plays are based on real people, several addressing native Canadian experience: *Pauline Johnson* (MS, 1970) about the Mohawk poet; *Cyclone Jack*, the story of Tom Longboat, the Indian marathon runner who won the 1907 Boston Marathon. In *Gabe*, a young Metis nation Indian just out of jail is torn between dreams of the wilderness and his spiritual hero, Louis Riel, and a reality of drunken brawls and delusions with his friends, a broken-down rodeo rider and an alcoholic gas-station owner. *Red Emma* explores the early years of the anarcho-feminist Emma Goldman (see also **Owens**) leading up to her assassination attempt on Henry Clay Frick.

Many plays include: *Buffalo Jump* (2f,9m,1d, 1972); *Gabe* (2f,3m, 1973); *Red Emma* (2f,7m, 1974) in *Playwrights in Profile*, Playwrights Co-op, 1976; *Maurice* (1f,4m+, 1974); *One Night Stand,* Playwrights Canada Press, 1977; *Cyclone Jack* (4f,8m, 1974) in *A Collection of Canadian Plays* v4, Simon and Pierre, 1977; *Companeras* (4f,5m+) in Jansen 1993.

See also App. 2: Zimmerman; Wallace and Zimmerman.

Clare Boothe Luce
American, 1903–87

Actress, editor and later member of Congress, Boothe Luce was educated in and married into the wealthy echelons of American society and achieved her major theatrical success in a play that exposes their concerns. Delightfully bitchy in performance, *The Women* is an incisive satire on idle, shallow, upper-class women which was later filmed (script by Anita **Loos** and Jane Murfin). Hollywood provided the context for an equally objectionable group of unscrupulous human beings – actors, agents *et al.* – ready to back-stab and manipulate their way to getting the desired role in *Kiss the Boys Goodbye*. In later plays Boothe turned satire to political and feminist ends: *Margin for Error* ridicules the Nazi mind through a comedy mystery form, while her final play, *Slam the Door*

Softly (1970), is a contemporary updating of Ibsen's *A Doll's House* (cf. **Jelinek**) in which Nora Wald leaves the boorish husband Torvald to find a job.

Plays include: *The Women* (35f, 1937), also in Cerf 1941, Famous 1937, Sullivan and Hatch, Barlow 1994 etc.; *Kiss the Boys Goodbye* (3f,10m, 1938); *Margin for Error* (7m,3f, 1940) also in *Five* – all NY: Random House; *Abide with Me* (MS, 1935); *Child of the Morning* (MS, 1951); *Slam the Door Softly* (1f,1m, NY: DPS, 1971 and in France).

See also: *Clare Boothe Luce* by Wilfred Sheed, NY: Dutton, 1982 (biography); *Clare Boothe Luce: a Research and Production Sourcebook* by Mark Fearnow Westport: Greenwood, 1995. App. 2: Schlueter; Shafer.

Kate Bornstein
American, 1948–

Kate Bornstein began life as Al, a heterosexual male, and worked as a salesman for IBM before her sex change. Now a lesbian woman, she makes performances celebrating queer identities, drawing on her own past lives, the experience of other transsexuals (*The Opposite Sex*), the outer reaches of gender and sexuality such as masochism and bondage, and celebrating otherness and diversity, *Virtually Yours* is a dialogue, with frequent role shifts, between a computer and a transsexual woman whose lesbian lover is becoming a man. Among the texts and characters Bornstein draws on are Valerie Solanas's *SCUM Manifesto* and the writings of French hermaphrodite Herculine Barbin, brought up as a girl and then 'diagnosed' as a man in his late teenage years (see also **Churchill**'s *Mouthful of Birds*). Challenging and provoking, her work questions the male/female dichotomy, an endeavour she continues in her essays in *Gender Outlaw*, addressing queer theatre and life as performance in pieces such as 'Transsexual Lesbian Playwright Tells All'.

Plays include: *Hidden: a Gender: a play* (3f/m,id, 1991) in *Gender Outlaw: On Men, Women and the Rest of Us*, Routledge, 1994; *The Opposite Sex is Neither* and *Virtually Yours: a Game for Solo Performer with Audience* (both 1f/m) extracts in Russell; *Adventures in the Gender Trade* (screen, 1993).

See also App. 2: Barnes in Senelick.

Jane Bowles
American, 1917–73

Self-described as 'Jewish, homosexual, alcoholic, a communist and a cripple', Jane Bowles was born on Long Island and became a Bohemian wanderer with her writer husband, Paul. While producing only a small amount of work: a novel, stories, a play and some fragments, she has been recognized as a remarkable stylist. Tennessee Williams, a great admirer, called *In the Summer-House* the most original play he had ever read, one of 'those rare plays which are not tested by the theatre but by which the theatre is tested'. In form and content an idiosyncratic piece, it focuses on the stifling love, jealousy and dependency of mother–daughter relationships, centrally that of Gertrude Eastman Cuevas and her gauche, prickly daughter, Molly, hiding out in the summer-house of their California coast home, simultaneously clinging to and rejecting her mother. Gertrude escapes into marriage with the Mexican, Mr Solares – and his sister, niece and their extensive entourage – but is drawn back by her need for Molly. But Molly now refuses confinement, appalled by her mother's dependence. *At the Jumping Bean* features a setting from the everyday American surreal of themed restaurants (recalling *In the Summer-House*'s Lobster Bowl), the bizarre environment in which a tragi-comedy of mismatched and misunderstood needs is enacted between a poet, Gabriel, and Beryl Jane, like Molly an awkward child-woman.

Plays include: *In the Summer-House* (10f,5m, 1954) in Barlow 1994 and with *A Quarrelling Pair: a Puppet Play* (2f, 1966) in *Collected Works* NY: Farrar, Strauss & Giroux, 1966; *At the Jumping Bean* (2f,1m, 1955) in *Feminine Wiles*, NY: Black Sparrow Press, 1976.

Muriel Box
English, 1905–95

Box met playwright Sydney Box in 1933 while working as a continuity girl at British Instructional Films. They began a writing partnership and, later, marriage that, separately and together, produced numerous plays and screenplays. With their own production company, Verity Films, Muriel Box became one of the first British women film directors, with over fourteen films to her credit, including work by **Du Maurier** and

Boland, and an adaptation of Elsa Shelley's controversial and outspoken play, *Pick-Up Girl*, filmed as *Too Young To Love* (1960).

A socialist and feminist, her writing centres on women and includes early volumes for the burgeoning amateur market (*Ladies Only, Petticoat Plays*). An incisive and unromanticized analysis of women's experience of auxillary service in the First World War, *Angels of War*, was one of a number of pieces focusing with comedy or realism on the trials of war (evacuation in their joint *Home From Home*, separation in Muriel's *Love in these Days*, 1940–1) and later on disarmament (*Fantastic Flight*). Numerous screenplays included the satirical *The Truth About Women* (1957) and *The Seventh Veil*, (1946, later adapted for stage), focusing on an injured woman pianist's recovery from trauma.

Plays include: *Angels of War* (10f, 1935) in Sykes and in Bourne and in Tylee; *In a Glass Darkly* (3f,1m) in Box. The following with Sydney Box: *Stranger in My Bed* (1f,2m), French, 1965; *Husbands are a Problem* (7f) in Ratcliff; *The Seventh Veil* (4f,8m) London: Rylee, 1951; *Sing a Song of Sixpence* (6f) in Bourne, 1935; *Five Ladies Only* and *Petticoat Plays* – both London: George Harrap, 1934.

See also: *Odd Woman Out* (autobiography) London: Leslie Frewin, 1974; App. 2: Gale.

Neith Boyce
American, 1872–1951

Boyce was one of the key figures of the Provincetown Playhouse (founded 1915) and Greenwich Village literati, along with Susan **Glaspell**, John Reed, George Cram Cook and later Eugene O'Neill. A New Woman and free-thinker, she worked as a journalist as well as writing novels and plays which addressed many of the questions she and her friends were attempting also to resolve in life. Both *Constancy* and *Enemies*, the latter written with her husband, explore the dilemmas and disparities of marriage. In the former, based on Reed's 'open' relationship with Mabel Dodge, Rex is horrified by Moira's cool indifference on his return, as she tells him, 'your idea of constancy is to love a hundred other women and at intervals to come back – to me'. In *Enemies* a couple struggle to resolve his wish for a union of souls and hers for freedom within a relationship. *Winter's Night* and *The Two Sons* also have linked themes, that of two brothers who love the same woman. In *The Two Sons* Paul is rejected by Stella for his manlier brother, Karl. Stella, like other women, is merely sexually desirable while his strongest love and respect is reserved for other men, such as his artist brother.

Plays include: *Winter's Night* (2f,1m, 1916) in France; *Constancy* (1f,1m, 1914) in Ozieblo; *The Two Sons* (2f,2m, 1916) also in Ozieblo; *Enemies* (with Hutchins Hapgood, 1f,1m, 1916). Both in Cook and Shay.

Mary Elizabeth Braddon
English, 1835–1915

Like her near-contemporaries Harriet Beecher **Stowe** and Ellen **Wood**, Braddon is best known for her immensely successful novels, which were equally successful in their numerous, often pirated, theatrical adaptations. Versions of *Lady Audley's Secret* (first performed 1862) and *Aurora Floyd* (1863) toured the world and are still performed today. Melodramas in which mysterious secrets hide behind the closed doors of respectable life, they reflect her own experience of unrespectability – Braddon scandalously lived with her publisher John Maxwell, whose wife was in a mental asylum. Braddon's own plays include both melodramas involving fiendish attacks, avalanches, cliffhanging disasters and heroic self-sacrifice, and comedies with plucky heroines like the circus artist Polly of *Married Beneath Him*.

Plays include: *A Model Husband* (MS, 1868); *For Better For Worse* (MS, 1882); *The Missing Witness* (2f,6m, 1880); *Dross or The Root of Evil* (5f,6m, 1882); *Marjorie Daw* (2f,2m, 1882), *Married Beneath Him* (4f,6m, 1882) – all London: J. & R. Maxwell; *Lady Audley's Secret* (3f,4m, c.1877). *Aurora Floyd* (2f,7m, c.1863) both adapted by C. H. Hazlewood, London: Lacy.
  See also App. 2: Aldrich in Gardner and Rutherford.

Mona Brand
Australian, 1915–

Brand's plays grow out of her commitment to social and political change and have frequently excited controversy. *Here Under Heaven* (1948) was one of the first Australian plays to confront racism towards Asians and Aboriginals. *Strangers in the Land*, an indictment of British colonialism in Malaya, was produced at Unity Theatre Club in London, but deemed likely to cause a breach of the peace and refused further permission by the Lord Chamberlain. It was staged in Moscow, as was *No Strings Attached*, a comedy on US interference in Asia, while *Better a Millstone*, based on the Derek Bentley hanging in Britain, caused new controversy in 1954. *Here Comes Kisch*, produced, like many of her works by the radical New Theatre, Sydney, satirized the authorities' attempts to prevent Czech journalist Egon Kisch from entering Australia for a congress against war and fascism. Brand's own experience also becomes the target for gentle mockery in *Down Under Chelsea* (MS, 1991), exploring the lives of Australian communists, ex-communists and related radicals in both 1940s and 1970s London.

Plays include: *Strangers in the Land* (4f,6m) also in *Two Plays About Malaya* London: Lawrence and Wishart, 1954; *No Strings Attached* (5f,15m); *Better a Millstone* (1954) in *Three Plays*, Moscow: Progress Publishers, 1965; *On Stage Vietnam* (MS, 1967); *Here Under Heaven* (8f,2m) Yackandandah, 1989 and in Pfisterer; *Flying Saucery!* (for young people) Sydney: Alternative Publishing Co-op, 1981. *Here Comes Kisch!* (3f,5m,id), Yackandandah, 1983.

See also App. 2: Tompkins and Holledge; ADS (various); *Enough Blue Sky* (autobiography) Sydney: Tawny Pipit Press, 1995; Tilley in *Australian Drama 1920–1955*; Pfisterer and Pickett.

Vanessa Brooks

English, 1967–

Born in Dulwich, London, Brooks studied at the Central School of Speech and Drama. Many of her witty, realistic comedies were written as writer-in-residence at Alan Ayckbourn's Stephen Joseph Theatre, Scarborough. *Let's Pretend* is set in a run-down Majorca hotel, among 'twilight adventurers', pensioners escaping the British winter who attempt to keep up spirits and appearances. Set in a slimming club, *Love Me Slender* follows 'Achiever of the Year' Siobhan's attempts to inspire, cajole or bully her recruits along the path of discipline and sacrifice towards 'salvation' and 'a new you'.

Plays include: *Penny Blue* (3f,3m, 1994); *Let's Pretend* (4f,3m, 1995); *Love Me Slender* (6f, 1996); *All at Sea* (3f,3m, 1998) – all Warner Chappell; *Poor Mrs Pepys* (MS, 1998).

Riwia Brown

New Zealand/Aotearoan, 1957

Maori playwright Brown lives in Paekakariki and has worked as an actor and director. In 1994 she scripted the acclaimed film *Once Were Warriors* which, like her *Roimata*, is a hard-hitting exploration of Maori identity and urban life. *Roimata* explores the tensions that arise from clashing lifestyles and values when Roimata, a young girl from a coastal village, visits her recently discovered half-sister and discovers a world of bars, sex, drugs and gangs. *Nga Wahine* explores two women's experience of pregnancy.

Plays include: *Roimata* (5f,3m, 1988) in Garrett/Potiki; *Te Hokina* (MS, 1990); *Nga Wahine* (*The Women*, MS, 1992); *Irirangi Bay* (MS, 1996).
See also: *Illusions* (NZ) Winter 1994.

Moira Buffini

British, 1967–

Buffini is actress, writer and director and co-wrote with Anna Reynolds the prize-winning *Jordan* (MS, 1992), based on a true story about a woman who killed her baby. Buffini's plays are fables where narratives of contemporary life are replete with hints at dark doubles, apocalyptic futures and celestial visions. The blind architect of a tower block in *Blavatsky's Tower* lives in top-floor seclusion with his three children. While he experiences angel visitations, life in the block becomes ever more hellish.

The LWT Plays on Stage award winner, *Gabriel* is set on Nazi-occupied Guernsey where a house of women – Estelle, an imaginative ten-year old child, her Jewish sister-in-law and embittered, collaborating mother – hide a naked young man who was saved from the waves, from German officer, Von Pfunz, a man both torturer and tortured by the memory of the camps. Claimed variously as an amnesiac SS man by the Nazis, as a bank clerk suffering from brain tumour by locals, for young Estelle he is a fallen angel and agent of longed-for deliverance. In *Silence* Buffini uses the end of the first millennium in Britain under King Ethelred as an ironic reflection of the preoccupations of the second: cross-dressing, polymorphous sexuality, drug-induced visions. Described by critics as a 'medieval road movie', it is quirky and magical, a comic and moving drama of love, danger and metaphysical yearning peopled with vivid and surprising characters.

Plays include: *Gabriel* (4f,2m) Faber, 1997; *Blavatsky's Tower* (MS, 1998); *Doomsday* (MS 1999); *Silence* (3+f,3+m, 1999) and *Love Play* (14f,14m, 2001) – both Faber.
 See also App. 2: Sierz.

Fanny Burney (Frances D'Arblay)
English, 1752–1840

Even as a child, in King's Lynn, Norfolk, Fanny Burney wrote. She became second keeper of the robes to Queen Charlotte and in 1793 married a French refugee, Alexandre D'Arblay.

 Best known as an epistolary novelist, her most successful works were *Evelina* (1778), *Cecilia* (1782) and *Camilla* (1796). She is also recognized as a diarist, but it remains little known that she also wrote plays. Opposition from her father and problems with managers meant that only one play, the tragedy *Edwy and Elgiva*, was produced on stage in her lifetime. The rest languished for years in manuscript until their recent publication at last made them available. Burney's wonderfully effervescent comedies include a satire of bluestockings, *The Witlings*, whose wittily drawn characters include Mrs Sapient, who utters pronouncements on life of shattering banality, and would-be poetical old Lady Smatter. It has a sequel: *The Woman-Hater*. *A Busy Day* mocks the manners of both high and lower classes. Heiress Eliza Watts returns from the East Indies and the death-bed of her adoptive father to marry Cleveland and finds that her family have meanwhile grown rich on their dealings in the City yet have wholly failed to gain social graces, while Cleveland's family turn out to be impoverished, but terrible snobs.

Plays include: *The Witlings* (7f,6m, 1779) in Rogers; *A Busy Day* (7f,12m,dp, 1801) ed. Tara Ghoshal Wallace, New Brunswick, NJ: Rutgers UP, 1984, also Absolute Classics, 2000 both with *Love and Fashion* (4f,11m, 1798–9); *The Woman-Hater* (8f,9m, 1800–2); *Edwy and Elgiva* (2f,12m, 1794); *The Siege of Pevensey* (1f,12m, 1790) etc. in *The Complete Plays of Frances Burney*, two volumes (*Comedies* and *Tragedies*) ed. Peter Sabor Montreal and Kingston: McGill–Queen's UP, 1995.
 See also: 'Fanny Burney, Playwright' by Joyce Hemlow, *University of Toronto Quarterly* vol. XIX no 2, Jan. 1950; App. 2: Donkin.

Laurie Carlos
American, 1949–

An actress, acclaimed for her performance in **Shange**'s *for colored girls*, Carlos has gone on to make her own startling, strangely shaped works. Her pieces generate their own formal aesthetic through the quirky juxtapositions of association, drawing in recipes, memories, poetry, accounts of black American experience and a theatrical language using gesture, dance, drumming and popular songs. Starting from Carlos's initial texts, the pieces are then scripted from improvisation. They often deal with painful material such as the recollections of childhood abuse (in *White Chocolate For My Father*), racism and, in all her work, stories of slavery. They struggle towards new self-definition and, through shared experience, towards community, as when she distributes her bean salad to the audience at the end of *The Cooking Show*.

Plays include: *Nonsectarian Conversations with the Dead* (MS); *Organdy Falsetto* (MS); *White Chocolate For My Father* (8f, 1992) in Mahone; *The Cooking Show & How the Monkey Dances* (1f) in Russell; *Teenytown* (with **Hagedorn** and **McCauley**, 3f, 1990) in Champagne.
  See also App. 2: Carr.

Marina Carr
Irish, 1965–

Carr, from Co. Offaly, has had a rapid rise to recognition with plays that are at once hauntingly atmospheric, densely poetic and bleakly comic, centring on obsessive passions and absurd desires, combining realism with a mythic undertow. *Low in the Dark* is a surreal exploration of jealousy, suffocation, hunger between men and women, cravings for the other and to be the other. It wields witty visual and spoken vocabularies, based on the ritual interactions of married life: taking baths, knitting, mowing lawns, building walls, offering food and the prolific production of babies. At the heart of *The Mai*, both play and heroine, is her Great Love – or desperate fixation – for a man who continually leaves her, a parallel to her Grandma Fraochlain's obsession for her drowned 'nine-fingered fisherman'.
  The eponymous Portia Coughlan is equally haunted by the dead: her suicidal twin brother, drowned in the Belmont river, where she

eventually follows him after a life of self-destructive affairs, neglected children and marital conflict. The piece is also grimly funny as if, as was said, 'a Greek tragic heroine were comically mislaid in a working-class family that spend its waking hours taking bites out of each other's egos'. *On Raftery's Hill* is a bleak story of incest and wasted lives, in which a family and farm are destroyed by a father for whom livestock and childern are both there to be used, dominated and tampled upon.

Plays include: *Low in the Dark* (3f,2m, 1989) in Grant; *The Mai* (7f,1m) in *PI*, Jan. 1995 and Oldcastle: The Gallery Press, 1995; *Portia Coughlan* (5f,6m) Faber, 1996 and in McGuinness, *By the Bog of Cats . . .* (7f,8m, 1998) – all in *Marina Carr: Plays One*, Faber, 1999; *On Raftery's Hill* (3f,4m) Faber, 2000.

See also App. 2: Stephenson and Langridge, Sierz.

Leonora Carrington
English, 1917–

Lancashire-born Carrington showed an early talent in art, and studied painting in Florence. She met Max Ernst, and they became lovers and key members of the Surrealist movement in Paris. Forced to flee to Spain with the outbreak of war, Carrington experienced a mental breakdown which produced her visionary first-person narrative *Down Below*. She later settled in Mexico. Her work was largely ignored by historians until Whitney Chadwick's ground-breaking *Women Artists in the Surrealist Movement* appeared (1985). Carrington's paintings, writings and little-known theatre pieces employ recurrent mystical and hallucinatory imagery, including rocking horses, giant eggs, child-women with magi-cal powers, vampires, cannibalism, oppressive fathers and defiant daughters. Penelope metamorphoses into a white horse and escapes; Judith ritually beheads the father who encouraged her rape, burns his head and releases her lover, the scorpion Barbaroth, from the ashes.

Untranslated plays include: *Une Chemise de Nuit de Flanelle*, Paris: L'Age d'Or, 1951; *Penelope* (1944), in *Cahiers Renaud–Barrault*, 70, 1969.

Translated plays: *The Invention of Mole* (1f,4m+, c.1970) and *Judith* (1f,4m, 1961) in *The Seventh Horse and Other Tales*, Virago, 1989.

See also: *The Theater of the Marvellous* by Gloria Orenstein, New York UP, 1975.

Jo Carson

American, 1946–

Carson describes herself as 'an eavesdropper in grocery-store lines, beauty parlors, emergency rooms: where life shares itself'. The Appalachians and Eastern Tennessee are the setting for most of her work: finely observed monologues in spare, laconic language, poems she performs that brilliantly capture disjointed conversations, gossip, rambling stories from old-timers, relatives, strangers, curious points of view.

Daytrips is an exploration of old age and Alzheimer's disease, developed, like much of Carson's work, with the Road Company of Johnson City, Tennessee, where she lives and works. Pat struggles to take care of of her mother and 90-year-old grandmother. She must grapple with their delusions that she is her dead aunt or great-aunt, their confusions and obsessions, together with her memories, dreams of killing them, love for them and exhaustion in a play that is densely poetic, moving, funny and frightening.

Plays include: *Daytrips* (4f, 1988) in Filichia; *Little Chicago* (MS); *Stories I Ain't Told Nobody Yet: Selections from the People Pieces* (1 or more f/m) NY: Orchard Books, 1989 and TCG, 1991; *A Preacher with a Horse to Ride* (9f,16m, 1985–90) in De Nobrigo and Anderson.

Angela Carter

English, 1940–93

As a novelist, Carter is famous for her highly imaginative and macabre reworkings of fairy tales and postmodern magic realism. Works such as *Nights at the Circus* or *Wise Children* or *The Passion of New Eve*'s often revolve round worlds of performance, the exploration of shifting sexual identities and the illusions of gender and performance, a theme Carter returned to in adapting Virginia **Woolf**'s *Orlando*.

Several of Carter's novels and stories have been adapted for the theatre by others, and her own fascination with performance led her to re-create stories as radio plays and screenplays, often in turn adapted to stage. *The Company of Wolves* reworked Red Riding Hood, making explicit its subtext of a young girl's sexual awakening, becoming short story, then radio play, then a film, directed by Neil Jordan. Carter's eerie atmospheric creations are especially effective on radio where she relished 'that magical and enigmatic margin, that space of the invisible, which must be filled in by the imagination of the listener'. *Come Unto These Yellow Sands* explored the mind of the Victorian artist Richard Dadd, incarcerated in a mental asylum, who painted such uncanny works as 'The Fairy-Feller's Masterstroke', while *Vampirella* was a chilling feminist reworking of the Dracula myth (cf. Liz **Lochhead**).

Plays include: *Vampirella* (3f,7m, radio, 1976); *Puss in Boots* (5f,8m, radio, 1982); *Come Unto These Yellow Sands* (4f,12m, radio, 1979); *The Company of Wolves* (5f,4m,+1, radio, 1980); *A Self-Made Man* (3f,25m, radio, 1983); *Orlando or the Enigma of the Senses* (10f,15m, 1f/m, libretto, 1979); *The Company of Wolves* (screen, 1984); *The Christchurch Murder* (screen, 1987); *Lulu* (7f,15m, from Wedekind, 1987). All in *The Curious Room*, Chatto and Windus, 1996.

Elizabeth Cary, Viscountess Falkland
English, 1585–1639

While some translations (Mary Sidney, Lady Joanna Lumley) appeared earlier, Cary has attracted critical attention in recent years as the first Englishwoman to publish an original play: *The Tragedy of Mariam the Fair Queen of Jewry*. Brought up strictly, she learned Latin and Hebrew and, forbidden further learning, ran up a large bill paying the servants to smuggle her candles for secret reading. At 15 she was married to Henry Cary, Lord Falkland, and bore eleven children but continued her studies. After long struggles, in 1626 she followed the dictates of her conscience and converted to Catholicism, at which her Protestant husband removed her financial support and her children. *The Tragedy of Mariam*, written about 1604, suggests that the dilemmas of wifely obedience were already very real to her. Set in Palestine, it presents a heroine, torn between wifely love and duty to accept her husband's actions, and her own revulsion and hatred at them. While Herod is away in Egypt, called to give account of the murder of her brother and grandfather and under possible threat of death in reprisal, Mariam realizes the love she felt for him. With his return, her old feelings of repugnance and mistrust revive. It is not difficult for Salome, incensed by Mariam's pride and chastity, to convince Herod that infidelity is the reason for Mariam's coldness and have him condemn her to death. The play presents powerful and complex women characters, including Salome who uses her sexuality to gain her ends and 'be the custom breaker/To show my sex the way to freedom's door'.

Cary also produced the chronicle *History of Edward II* (1627), which includes sections in dramatic form, and presents with sympathy the situation of Queen Isabel, neglected by her husband for his homosexual lover Piers Gaveston.

Plays: *The Tragedy of Mariam the Fair Queen of Jewry* (5f,11m+, 1604, pub. 1613) in Cerasano and Wynne-Davies, 1995, ed. Stephanie Wright, Keele UP, 1996, ed. Margaret Ferguson and Barry Weller with *The Lady Falkland: her Life*, Berkeley: California UP, 1994; *The History of Edward II* (1627, published 1680) extracts in *The Paradise of Women: Writings by Englishwomen of the Renaissance* by Betty Travitsky, NY: Columbia UP, 1989.

See also App. 2: Cotton.

Margaret Cavendish, Duchess of Newcastle
English, 1623–73

Margaret Cavendish was daughter of a wealthy landowner. She married the royalist Duke of Newcastle in 1645 and was exiled with him to the Continent following the Civil War. (His two grown daughters, Elizabeth Cavendish and Jane Brackley, also playwrights, opposed the match.) A highly learned woman who produced works on philosophy, biography and science, Cavendish was the first Englishwoman to leave an extensive body of plays, two volumes of sprawling works. Their length alone has been an obstacle to their being given proper consideration: Virginia **Woolf** called them tedious and unreadable. Recently feminists have brought them new critical attention and productions have been staged.

Cavendish did not envisage the possibility of her plays being performed but saw her 'brain [as] the stage' where her thoughts enacted dramas. While she departs radically from the dramaturgy of her time, many of her stage devices are highly innovative, such as the multiple brief and unsentimental vignettes on the topic of violent and unhappy marriage that she presents within *The Convent of Pleasure*. In the play a group of women vow to live apart from men but, unusually, Cavendish rejects the notion that such a life should be one of self-denial. Featuring 'a Princess in Masculine Shepherd's Clothes' who falls in love with the Lady Happy, the piece has been seen as giving the first dramatic presentation of lesbianism. Many of her plays present powerful images of women, including female orators and women warriors (in *Bell in Campo*). She is also remarkably earthy on occasion, dealing with constipation, pimping and incest among other topics and presenting a penetrating reflection of some of the grimmer realities of Restoration life.

Plays include: *The Several Wits* (9f,10m+); *Youth's Glory and Death's Banquet* (7f,6m+); *Lady Contemplation* (12f,13m+); *The Unatural Tragedy* (11f,9m+); *The Apocryphal Ladies* (5+f,2+m); *Bell in Campo* (7+f,10+m) also extract in *Women Writers of the Seventeenth Century* ed. Katharina M. Wilson and F. J. Warnke, Athens: Georgia UP, 1989; *The Public Wooing* (18f,4m) etc. in *Plays,* London: A. Warren, 1662; *The Sociable Companions or The Female Wits* (5f,15m); *The Convent of Pleasure* also extract in *First Feminists* ed. Moira Ferguson, Bloomington: Indiana UP, 1985; *The Bridals* (5f,10m) etc. in *Plays Never Before Printed,* London: A. Maxwell, 1668.

See also: *A Glorious Fame* (biography) by Kathleen Jones, London: Bloomsbury, 1988; *Women, Texts and Histories 1575–1760* ed. C. Brant and D. Purkiss, Routledge, 1991; App. 2: Cotton; Pearson.

Susannah Centlivre
English, 1667–1723

For centuries the most popular classic woman playwright, Centlivre's finely plotted comedies continued to be staged throughout the nineteenth century, but have since been unaccountably neglected by the twentieth-century theatre establishment. Brilliantly witty, her nineteen plays express an active feminism through prologues challenging continuing male prejudice against women writers – 'To All the Generous Encouragers of Female Ingenuity' – and through their concentration on independent, resourceful heroines. They are highly theatrical, frequently employing the device of convoluted masquerades where characters employ performance to gain their ends: Fainwell in *A Bold Stroke* manages to convince the utterly dissimilar guardians of his beloved Ann (a Quaker, a beau, a stockbroker and a 'virtuoso') of his suitability as husband, while in *The Platonick Wife*, the shape-shifting Isabella transforms herself through multiple disguises to gain her chosen husband. Several pieces focus on gambling: the addicted hero of *The Gamester* loses his estate at the tables and has to be redeemed by the resourceful heroine, while in *The Basset Table*, Lady Reveller, a rich widow, must reform to gain the approval of her suitor Lord Worthy. (*The Basset Table* also features a woman experimental scientist who defends female learning.)

Centlivre's most perennially popular character (who went on to star in his own eponymous sequel, 1710) was Marplot in *The Busy Body*, whose well-intentioned attempts to abet Charles in freeing Isabinda from her oppressive father cause chaos. Many of Centlivre's plots focus on tyrannical fathers who attempt to force compliance from their daughters by shutting them away, a theme consistently repeated in imagery of enclosure. Women steadily resist such circumscription and abet each other in attaining freedom. *The Wonder* revolves round the faithfulness with which Violante clandestinely shelters her friend Isabella, escapee from a forced marriage with an old fool, despite the accusations of sexual disrepute her secrecy brings upon Violante.

Plays include: *The Adventures in Venice* (2f,3m+, 1700) in Kendall; *The Gamester* (6f, 11m, 1705); *The Basset Table* (5f,7m+, 1706); *The Busy Body* (4f,6m, 1709) both in Lyons and Morgan; *The Platonick Lady* (7f,6m, 1707); *Marplot in Lisbon* (5f,7m, 1710); *The Wonder: A Woman Keeps a Secret* (4f,8m+, 1714) in Morgan; *A Wife Well Managed* (2f,3m, 1715); *A Bold Stroke For a Wife* (3f,8m, 1718) London: Edward Arnold/Lincoln: Nebraska UP, 1968 and in Rogers; *The Artifice* (7f,7m, 1723). All in *The Dramatic Works of the Celebrated Mrs Centlivre*, London: John Pearson, 1872.

See also: *The Celebrated Mrs Centlivre* by J. Bowyer, Durham, NC: Duke UP, 1952; App. 2: Butler in Schofield and Macheski; Cotton; Pearson.

Jane Chambers
American, 1937–83

Jane Chambers was one of the first playwrights to write of lesbianism, not as a cause to be organized around or an issue to be championed against heterosexist prejudice, but instead as simply a given. Heterosexuals are the outsiders whose assumptions are challenged. The publisher in *My Blue Heaven* discovers that 'Joe' of Mollie and Joe, 'farm couple of the year', whose doings are celebrated in Mollie's newspaper column, is Josie; Peggy in *A Late Snow* is forced to acknowledge the nature of the college relationship with Ellie she has tried to deny. Chamber's plays are romantic comedies using a realist aesthetic, presenting couples or groups of women, typically in country retreats, dilapidated cottages, lesbian guest houses (*Eye of the Gull*), finding love and struggling to build relationships, but also struggling with disease, alcoholism, developmental disability, racism and the resentments of old lovers. *Last Summer in Bluefish Cove* explores the love that grows between Lil, dying of cancer, and the heterosexual woman she inadvertently invites to her party, against the background of a lesbian holiday community. Elsewhere Chambers is satirical: in *Quintessential Image* a renowned lesbian photographer both 'outs' her closeted television interviewer and reveals that her historically significant shots were taken inadvertently as she pursued the woman with whom she was infatuated.

Chambers died prematurely of a brain tumour and is remembered by the Women in Theatre programme's Playwriting Award, given in her name in recognition of her writing and her extensive involvement in writers' organizations and gay activism.

Plays include: *A Late Snow* (5f, 1974) in Hoffman 1979; *My Blue Heaven* (2f,1m, 1981) and *Last Summer in Bluefish Cove* (8f, 1982) – both NY: J. H. Press Gay Playscript Series, 1981; *Eye of the Gull* (13f, 1971) in Helbing; *The Quintessential Image* (2f, c.1982) in Curb.

See also: interview in *Acting Up!*; App. 2: Curtin; Dolan in Case ed.

Mary Chase

American, 1907–81

Chase's *Harvey* remains one of the most popular American plays. Warm hearted and sentimental, it has been dismissed as escapist and condemned as decadent; Chase's serious point, however, is the importance of fantasy and illusion as humanizing factors in life. Her hero, Elwood P. Dowd, is, by conventional standards, mad, possessed by the belief that he is followed everywhere by Harvey, a faithful six-foot white rabbit. The delusion leads some to condemn him as dangerous for inciting full-scale revolt from the duties and responsibilities of decent America, while others find in Harvey the inspiration to change their lives.

Many of Chase's other plays are equally whimsical and centred on the transformative power of fantasy. *Mickey* mixes actors and puppets as its awkward young heroine stumbles on a fairy kingdom, while in *Mrs McThing* an ageing socialite escapes the constraints of her existence by masquerading as childminder to a lively group of youngsters and discovers a new joy and freedom.

Plays include: *Sorority House*, NY: French, 1939; *Harvey* (6m,6f, 1944); *Midgie Purvis* (8f,8m, 1963); *Mickey* (5f,4m, 1969); *Cocktails with Mimi* (6f,6m, 1974); *The Prize Play* (4f,7m) – all DPS; *Mrs McThing* (10f,9m, 1952) and *Bernardine* (6f, 13m+, 1953) – both: NY: Oxford UP.

See also App. 2: Shafer.

Alice Childress
American, 1920–94

Childress was born in South Carolina, grew up in Harlem and was a member of the American Negro Theatre for twelve years. She received numerous awards during a lengthy career as a writer (17 plays, including many for schools, and several novels for both adults and children). In 1952 *Gold Through the Trees*, the first play by a black woman performed professionally on the American stage, followed her 1949 one-act, *Florence*, one of several plays addressing the power of theatre and the arts in challenging stereotyped black representation. *Florence* tells of the discovery by a black woman travelling north to visit her aspiring actress daughter that the job a 'sympathetic' white actress wants to offer Florence is as a domestic servant. Patronizing white attitudes recur in the Obie-winning *Trouble in Mind* (1955), which explores the pressures on black actors performing in a white liberal's Southern lynching drama to succeed by conforming to convention; the play's heroes, resisting injustice, are white. Wiletta's refusal to acquiesce in this narrative is typical of Childress's politics, emphasizing black people's need to conduct their political struggle on their own terms. *Wine in the Wilderness* addresses a similar challenge in a black context, focusing on a Harlem painter, Bill Jameson, whose triptych of 'black womanhood' purports to represent the actual and the ideal. When friends bring Tommy, refugee of a Harlem riot, to his apartment to pose, presenting her as the 'essence' of black ignorance and vulgarity, her story of struggle and survival challenges their educated middle-class prejudices. *Wedding Band*, set in South Carolina in 1918, tackles the complexities of a 10-year-old – and illegal – interracial relationship between Herman and Julia, the dynamics of their rejection by both black community and his white family and of Julia's consequent isolation from her people and sense of identity.

Plays include: *Mojo* (1f,1m, 1970) also in Richards 1973 with *String* (4f,2m, 1969) DPS, 1971; *Trouble in Mind* (3f,6m, 1955) in Barlow 1994 and in Turner; *Florence* (3f,1m, 1949) in Brown-Guillory; *Wedding Band* (6f,3m, 1966) in Moore and in Wilkerson; *Wine in the Wilderness* (2f,3m, 1969) in Sullivan and Hatch; Hatch and Shine 1987 and in Brown-Guillory.

See also App. 2: Brown-Guillory; Wiley in Schlueter; Bloom; Betsko and Koenig.

Agatha Christie
English, 1890–1976

Christie's plays are country-house murder mysteries, fielding casts of upper-class characters and English eccentrics who nurse private secrets and hidden resentments to be revealed when violence erupts in their midst. Most are adaptations of her novels, many of which have been televised and filmed, sometimes radically departing from original plots to take advantage of new theatrical possibilities in generating suspense. such as the final stage dénouement of *Witness for the Prosecution*. In others, more exotic settings surface: her visits to Egypt with her archaeologist second husband led to both *Murder on the Nile* and her only historical drama, *Akhnaton*, about King Akhnaton and Queen Nefertiti. Christie's interest in psychoanalysis surfaces in plays such as *Appointment with Death*, with its oppressive American matriarch playing sadistic mind-games with her step-children.

The world record for longest-running play is held by Christie's *The Mousetrap*.

Plays include: *Witness for the Prosecution* (5f, 17m+8), in Famous, 1954; *Ten Little Indians* (alt. *Niggers* in UK, 3f,8m, 1944), *Appointment with Death* (7f,9m, 1945); *Verdict* (4f,6m, 1958); *The Hollow* (6f,6m, 1951); *The Mousetrap* (3f,5m, 1952); *Go Back for Murder* (5f,6m, 1960); *Towards Zero* (4f,7m, 1956) – all in *The Mousetrap and Other Plays*, NY: Bantam Books, 1978; *Black Coffee* (3f,10m, 1951); *Murder on the Nile* (5f,8m, 1946); *Spider's Web* (3f,8m, 1954); *The Unexpected Guest* (3f,7m, 1958) – all Samuel French; *Akhnaton* (6f, 16m+, 1937) London: Collins, 1973.

Caryl Churchill
English, 1938–

The most acclaimed post-war British woman playwright, Churchill has won numerous awards. After writing radio plays, Churchill's first stage works came out of the upsurge of alternative theatre companies of the late 1970s. Reflecting the collectivist political discussions of the time, socialist feminism and the influence of Brecht, several were scripted on the basis of group workshops. *Light Shining in Buckinghamshire* draws on the writings of radical groups emerging in the wake of the English Civil War, who began to give voice to social outcasts and question power, language and gender. *Vinegar Tom*, set during Cromwell's Protectorate, explores the orgy of witch-burning as socially deviant women – healers, beggars, rebellious daughters – were sacrificed as scapegoates. *Cloud Nine*, set in Victorian Africa and 1970s London, links colonial patriarchy with the control and colonization of sexuality, at once questioning and celebrating difference in a gloriously theatrical world where women play men and men little girls. The culture and costs, personal and social, of gaining power are addressed in the satirical rhyming musical *Serious Money*, set in the back-stabbing, cynical, greedy world of the 1980s City. *Top Girls*, now recognized as a modern classic, is a moving and complex analysis of women's relationship to power and the costs of sharing in the Thatcherite dream, both for those who participate and for those excluded from it.

Unlike many 1970s contemporaries, Churchill has continued to develop new approaches to theatre, exploring daringly theatrical possibilities by combining densely poetic text with the visual, aural and physical. Risk-taking collaborations with dance company Second Stride have generated disturbing, surreal work: *A Mouthful of Birds*, re-exploring the myth of the Bacchae, ecstasy and possession by hidden forces, *Hotel* and *The Skryker*, whose spellbinding central figure is a part-malignant, part-damaged figure of folklore, haunting a soulless contemporary Britain.

Plays include: *Owners* (5f,3m id 1972), *Traps* (2f,4m, 1977), *Cloud Nine* (3f,4m, 1979) and *Light Shining in Buckinghamshire* (3f,4m,id, 1976) in *Churchill Plays One*, 1985; *Vinegar Tom* (7f,2m, 1976) in Wandor 1; *Objections to Sex and Violence* (4f,4m,1975) in Wandor 4; *Fen* (6f,1m,id 1983), *Top Girls* (7f, 1982), *Serious Money* (3f,5m, 1987) and *Softcops* (12m,id, 1984) All in *Churchill: Plays Two*, 1990 – both Methuen. *Ice Cream* (7m,6f,dp,1989), *A Mouthful of Birds* (with D. Lan, 4f,3m,id, 1986), *The Skryker* (9f,6m, 1994), *Thyestes* (adaption from Greek, 1994), *Mad Forest* (40f/m,dp, 1990); *Lives of the Great Poisoners* (4f,5m, 1990) in *Churchill: Plays Three*, Methuen, 1990. *Lovesick* (4m,2f, 1960), *Abortive* (1m,1f, 1971), *Schreber's Nervous Illness* (1f,6m, 1972) all radio; *Three More Sleepless Nights* (2f,2m, 1980), *Hot Fudge* (5f,5m, 1989) and five more in *Churchill: Shorts* (1990); *Heart's Desire* (4f,2m), *Blue Kettle* (6f,2m, both as *Blue Heart* 1997), *Hotel* (9f,5m, 1997), *This is a Chair* (7f,8m, 1999) and *Far Away* (3f,1m+, 2000) all NHB.

See also especially: *Churchill the Playwright* by Geraldine Cousins (1989) and *File on Churchill* ed. Linda Fitzsimmons (1989) – both Methuen; *The Plays of Caryl Churchill* by Amelia Howe Kritzer, Macmillan, 1991; *Essays on Caryl Churchill: Contemporary Representations* ed. Sheila Rabillard, Winnipeg: Blizzard, 1998; App. 2: Diamond in Hart, Sierz.

Hélène Cixous

French, 1937–

Born in Algeria of French and German Jewish parentage, Cixous is Professor of Literature at the experimental University of Paris VIII and director of the Centre d'Etudes Féminines, founded in 1974. She is the author of over 30 books, including numerous novels and volumes of literary criticism and essays that include several on theatre. Her plays include small-scale psychoanalytical works, which have attracted particular interest in the light of her writings on psychoanalysis, and '*écriture féminine*' such as *The Newly Born Woman* (with Catherine Clément). *Portrait of Dora* dramatizes Freud's case study of a hysteric with whom he used dream analysis, presenting events from Dora's point of view. It makes visible the characters' hidden selves, the desires they do not reveal of their own accord and the oppressive bourgeois society of Freud's day. *The Name of Oedipus*, characteristically linguistically and theatrically experimental, also uses theatre as the space for exploring sexuality. Cixous's later work for theatre includes epic plays for Théâtre du Soleil, collaborations with director Ariane **Mnouchkine** which range from the breadth and sweep of Shakespeare (whom Cixous has translated), to the conflict of East and West , religion and politics in Cambodia under King Sihanouk and the struggle for Indian independence.

Untranslated plays include: *La Pupille*, in *Cahiers Renaud–Barrault* 1972 v8; *L'Arrivante* (1977).

Translated plays: *Portrait of Dora* (2f,3m, 1976) tr. Anita Barrow in Benmussa; *The Conquest of the School at Madhubai* (2f,2m) tr. Deborah Carpenter in W&P 5; *The Terrible but Unfinished Story of Norodom Sihanouk, King of Cambodia* (6f, c.45m+,dp, 1985) tr. J. Flower MacCannell, J. Pike and L. Groth, Lincoln and London: Nebraska UP, 1994 and extract with *Indiada or The India of Their Dreams* (7f,42m+,dp, 1987), extract, both tr. Donald Watson in *The Hélène Cixous Reader* ed Susan Sellers, Routledge, 1994; *The Name of Oedipus: Song of the Forbidden Body* (2f,3m, chorus, 1978) tr. and in Makward and Miller; *Black Sail, White Sail* (MS) tr. Donald Watson.

See also: *Hélène Cixous: a Politics of Writing* by Morag Shiach, Routledge, 1991; 'The Place of Crime, the Place of Forgiveness' (Cixous on theatre) in Sellers; *White Woman Speak with Forked Tongue: Criticism as Autobiography* by Nicole Ward Jouve, Routledge, 1991; Picard in MD 32; Pavlides in *Within the Dramatic Spectrum*, Lanham: University Presses of America, 1986; App. 2: Lamar; Willis in Case ed.; Forte and Sumption in Donkin and Clement; Miller in Keyssar ed.; Bradby and Sparks; Lamont and Savona in Brater.

Doreen Clarke

Australian, 1928–

Clarke left school aged 14 and worked in the Lancashire cotton mills before marrying and emigrating to Australia in 1958. Her work includes community and educational plays. She focuses on the struggles of working-class women to survive against poverty, brutal and drunken husbands and the desperation to which some are driven. Her pieces feature outspoken, bawdy heroines such as cockney May in *Bleedin' Butterflies*, set in a migrant camp in Australia during the Depression, or the two old tarts working the north Queensland towns in *Farewell Brisbane Ladies*. She combines grim realism, pulling no punches in presenting the relentlessness of living with an alcoholic (in *Roses in Due Season*) with sharp comedy and great compassion.

Plays include: *Farewell Brisbane Ladies* (2f) Yackandandah, 1981; *Roses in Due Season* (3f,1m, 1978) and *Bleedin' Butterflies* (3f,3m, 1980) Currency, 1982; *Missus Queen* (MS, 1980); *Salt and Vinegar* (MS, 1982); *My Blood for South Australia* (MS, 1983); *Snakes and Ladders* (2f) extract in *Angry Women: an Anthology of Australian Women's Writing* ed. Brown *et al.*, Petersham, NSW: Hale and Iremonger, 1989.

Pearl Cleage

American, 20th century

Atlanta-based Cleage creates work, powered by her black nationalism and radical feminism, that gives a blisteringly vivid account of contemporary and historical black realities. *Chain* is a monologue by a teenage crack addict chained to the radiator by her parents in desperation to try to break her habit. As she comes down she is torn between her slowly reviving memories of their love and her frenzy to get more drugs. In *Last Bus to Mecca* a prostitute leaving Detroit to make a new start befriends a silent black woman who is at once a suffering individual and 'every physically battered, spirit bruised black woman whose words have been used against her so often they seem beside the point'. Called by Cleage morality plays, she sees them as 'part of a collective redefinition of our sisterhood with an eye towards our survival'. The possibility of making a new start in Kansas in the 1890s also drives the women and men of *Flyin' West*. Escaping from slavery and its aftermath, they set up a black town, Nicodemus, on their own land on the great plains. The dream of a collective future is threatened by the light-skinned husband of one of the women, who sees personal benefit in denying his identity and separating himself from his people. *Bourbon of the Border* is a suspenseful drama confronting the damage done to former civil rights activists, physically and emotionally, and how it left lives permanently scarred.

Plays include: *Blues for the Alabama Sky* (2f,3m, 1995); *Bourbon on the Border* (2f,2m, 1997) *Chain* (1f, 1992) and *Last Bus To Mecca* (2f, 1992) in Miles 1993; *Flyin' West* (4f,2m,1992) in Perkins and Uno and in Turner. All in *Flyin' West and Other Plays*, TCG, 2000. *Hospice* (2f) in King Jr. 1989 and in Madison.

Darrah Cloud
American, 1955–

Cloud studied poetry at Iowa Writers' Workshop before writing her first play and subsequently has also written for film and television. She describes *The Stick Wife*, set in a poor white neighbourhood of 1960s Birmingham, Alabama, as a 'mystery about ignorance'. Its apparently mundane opening scenes in Jessie Bliss's backyard, as she hangs out clothes and is visited by neighbourhood wives, are haunted by 'shadows of light' that seem to dart across, like memories or momentary imaginings. Seemingly banal actions – drinking Coke, answering the phone – are freighted with a sense of dread. The women's fears eventually crystallize in the discovery that a 'coloured' church has been bombed and the realization that their husbands were responsible. In the second act the women are besieged by the Ku Klux Klan in the form of their disguised husbands, figures seemingly recognizable yet wholly alien. The play powerfully evokes their sense of powerlessness, fear and complicity in a world both familiar and insane. *The Sirens* also creates a world of domestic terror and a cycle of violence from which Cloud endeavours to find a sense of dramatic resolution and redemption. The characters are women who killed their abusive husbands and their prison is continually invaded by memories from their previous lives, ghosts who walk through walls, includingthat of Margo, a woman who didn't survive.

Plays include: *The Survivors* (MS, adapation); *Genesis* (MS); *The Mud Angel* (MS); *The Stick Wife* (3f,3m) PiP, 1987; *O Pioneers!* (8f,11m, adapted from Willa Cather, 1989) in Miles, 1993 – both also DPC, 1997; *The Sirens* (6f,5m) in *Theatre Forum* 7 Summer/Fall 1995; *Heartland* (MS, musical, 1997).

Betty Comden

American, 1919–

Betty Comden and Adolph Green were one of the most successful post-war musical partnerships. Comden began her theatrical career as a performer with Green, Judy Holliday and others in a satirical act, *The Revuers*, later playing in many other shows, including their own *On the Town*, written with Leonard Bernstein. It was the first of numerous musicals and, like many of their successful works, is characterized by vibrancy and wit. They often feature sparky heroines like Ella Peterson, operator at Susanswerphone answering service in *Bells Are Ringing*, who saves her clients from sundry disasters and woos drunken playwright Jeff off alcohol and onto love. It is one of several with theatrical themes; others include *Applause*, based on *All About Eve*, and *Fade Out, Fade In*, a gentle spoof of the early days of the talkies in Hollywood. In *A Doll's Life* (cf. **Boothe**, **Jelinek**) they explore Ibsen's Nora's life after *A Doll's House* (1982).

Plays include: (all with Adolph Green) *Billion Dollar Baby* (MS, 1945); *Wonderful Town* (with Jerome Chodorov, Joseph Fields, 5f,24m+, 1953); *Bells are Ringing* (with Jule Styne, 7f,22m+, 1957, also screen); *Fade Out, Fade In* (with Styne, 9f,26m+, 1964); *Applause* (with Charles Strouse *et al.*, 7f,15m+, 1971) – all NY: Random House; *On the Twentieth Century* (with Cy Coleman, 17f/m), French, 1980; *Singin' in the Rain* (screen, 1952); *Aunty Mame* (screen, 1958).

See also: *Offstage* (autobiography) NY: Limelight, 1995.

Jennifer Compton

Australian, 1949–

Born in New Zealand, Compton became an actress and settled in Australia in 1973 where her play *Crossfire* was one of the first plays to come out of the 1970s women's movement. It ignited fierce debate with its investigation of women's conflicts over work, relationships, wanted or unwanted pregnancy. The piece is played over two time frames and the same domestic interior is simultaneously the original 1910s space inhabited by infertile, 'unemployed and unemployable' Jane, a woman in a respectable marriage frustrated with the narrow options open to her, and also the restored 1970s home of Cilla, also married but childless, 'caught in the crossfire' between her friends' radical feminist commitment and her desire for a family. Later plays such as *Julia's Story* return to the conflicts between motherhood and personal creativity.

Plays include: *Crossfire* (4f,2m) Currency, 1976 and in *Plays of the 70s* v3 ed. Katharine Brisbane, Currency, 2001; *They're Playing Our Song* (2f,2m,id) in *Can't You Hear Me Talking to You*, ed. Alrene Sykes, Queensland UP, 1978; *Julia's Story* (1f) in *ADS* Oct. 1992; *Barefoot* (3f,1m, 1994) in Horin; *The Big Picture*, (3f,1m) Currency, 1999.

See also App. 2: Rees v2.

Constance Congdon
American, 1944–

Congdon, born in Iowa and educated in Kansas, is one of the most inventive American playwrights to emerge in the 1980s. She examines the unease and disorientation of suburban life, most tellingly in *Lost Formicans*, which investigates a middle America of shopping malls, TV dinners and marital breakdown through the eyes of alien observers reporting on these strange life forms. The piece is a collage of the emotional landscapes of grandfather's progressive Alzheimer's disease, teenage son's rejection of his divorced mother, conspiracy-theory-obsessed neighbour, kitsch environments and B-movie aliens, presented with sharp dialogue, acid comedy, vivid theatricality and compassion.

Losing Father's Body is a black comedy satirizing middle-class American responses to death, as father's body is stolen en route from the Canadian fishing trip where he died. *No Mercy*, addressing the nuclear issue, brings the same sense of a culture on the edge. Congdon's fluid stage world juxtaposes Los Alamos in 1945, and a 1985 world haunted by the bewildered ghost of J. Robert Oppenheimer and inhabited by apocalyptic preachers, withdrawn children and a dazed veteran blinded by his witnessing of the first atomic test.

Plays include: *Native American* (MS); *Tales of the Lost Formicans* (3f,4m, 1990) also in *Louisville*; *No Mercy* (3f,6m, 1986); *Casanova* (7f,6m, 1991); *Losing Father's Body* (7f,6m, 1994) in *Tales of the Lost Formicans and Other Plays*, TCG, 1994; *Boarders* (6f,3m, 1995) in Frank; *Dog Opera* in Lake and Shergold.

See also: SAD 1989; Wilde in *Theater* Winter 1990–1.

Trish Cooke (a.k.a. Roselia John Baptiste)
British, 1962–

Actress, playwright and children's writer, Cooke was born to Dominican immigrant parents in Bradford, and issues of identity and belonging are central to several of her plays. *Running Dream* moves across three generations and between Dominica and England where Florence and her youngest daughter, Bianca, dream of Ma Effeline's death. Bianca decides to go to Dominica to see the two elder sisters she has never met who were brought up by their grandmother. She discovers both how alien their experiences are and how far they are bound together in a shared resentment of the mother who separated them. Cooke's earlier *Back Street Mammy* (1989) is a complex exploration of adolescent sexual awakening and the dilemmas of unplanned pregnancy. Its use of a chorus commenting on the action reinforces 16-year-old Dynette's ambivalence, torn between the bewildering contradictions of her own changing desires and the opinions of friends, sister, mother, the Catholic church and the man who got her pregnant.

Plays include: *Back Street Mammy* (4f,2m, 1989) in Harwood 2; *No Place Like Home* (3f,3m) in Considine and Slovo; *Running Dream* (7f,2m, 1993) in George; *Gulp Fiction* (MS, 1995); *We Expect Respect* (radio).
    See also App. 2: Croft in Griffiths and Llewellyn-Jones.

Patricia Cornelius
Australian, 1952–

Cornelius has worked with many radical collaborative companies in her native Melbourne. *Lilly and May*, funny and disturbing, presents a pair of Beckett-like women tramps living on the street, their relationship by turns loving, domineering-submissive, protective. In a piece which makes reference to *King Lear*, the three women in *Jack's Daughters* struggle to live up to their father's wartime record of heroism and suffering.

Plays include: *Electric* (MS, 1989); *Lilly and May* (2f), Currency, 1987; Max (MS, 1990); *Taxi* (MS, 1990); *Inside Out* (MS, 1991); *Money* in *Who's Afraid of the Working Class?* (3f,2m, with Andrew Bovell, Melissa Revves, Christos Tsolkas) in *Melbourne Stories: Three Plays*, Currency, 2000.

Sada Cowan

American, 1883–1943

Author of bleak, powerful short plays, often hard hitting and politically committed, Cowan later became a Hollywood screenwriter. *Sintram of Skaggerak* and *Pomp* feature men who reject women and a female-identified religion of physical appeal and sensual beauty for a wild severe nature. *In the Morgue* shows life's inequalities of wealth and position cynically pepetuated after death. *The State Forbids* is a grim, powerful fable condemning a state that forces 'women to have children whether we want them or not . . . and then . . . takes them from us', forbids contraception, abortion and infanticide but orders the conscription of human fodder for the war. *Auf Wiedersehen* warns a complacent audience of the dangers of Nazism: a Jewish seamstress who has brought up the non-Jewish children of her dead business partner finds they are ostracized by the association. She attempts to escape to America but cannot get a visa. Rather than face arrest and bring trouble on them, after she shelters a Jewish neighbour who defied the Nazis, she kills herself.

Plays include: *As I Remember You* (2f,2m+1); *In the Morgue* (4m, 1920); *The Ball and Chain* (3f,4m); *Pomp* (2f,4m); *Sintram of Skagarrak* (1f,1m, 1917) also in Clements; *The Cat* (3f,3m); *Collaboration* (1f,2m); *The State Forbids* (2f,3m) – all in *Pomp and Other Plays*, NY: Brentano's, 1926; *Auf Wiedersehen* (2f,4m, 1937) in France; *East of Suez* (screen, 1925); *Forbidden Heaven* (screen, 1936).

Hannah Cowley

English, 1743–1809

Born in Tiverton, Devon, Cowley settled in London and is supposed to have started playwriting to fulfil a boast that she could produce a better play than the one her husband had just seen. Her attempt, the sparkling *The Runaway* (1776), became a runaway success.

Cowley's best works are satirical, witty comedies with lively heroines, such as *The Belle's Stratagem*, which remained popular through most of the nineteenth century and deserves revival. The belle of the title, Letitia Hardy, is irked by her betrothed husband's failure to appreciate her at their first meeting and, though his honour dictates they marry anyway, she determines only to marry where she is loved. Taking matters into her own hands, she pretends to be, as Letitia, a gauche, awkward girl, while simultaneously disguising herself as a fascinating mystery woman for whom he inevitably falls. In the process she wittily exposes the superficiality with which men judge women. In *A Bold Stroke for a Husband* women also play at being what they're not. Donna Olivia pretends to be a termagant to frighten off the endless string of undesired suitors her father supplies, until she independently finds the man she wants to marry. Meanwhile, her friend Donna Victoria disguises herself as a man to win back her erring husband.

Plays include: *The Runaway* (5f,8m, 1776); *Who's the Dupe* (2f,4m, 1779); *Albina Countess of Raymond* (4f,8m, 1779); *The Belle's Stratagem* (6f,15m, 1781) also in Rogers; *Which Is the Man?* (7f,5m+, 1783); *A Bold Stroke for a Husband* (7f,8m, 1783); *A School for Greybeards* (6f,5m, 1786); *The Town Before You* (7f,12m, 1791). All in *The Plays of Hannah Cowley* ed. Frederick M. Link, 2 vols, NY: Garland, 1979.
See also App. 2: Schofield and Macheski.

Lucinda Coxon
English, 1962–

Coxon began to develop plays with the new writing theatre company, Loose Exchange. In *Waiting at the Water's Edge*, a strange, compelling and highly theatrical fable, she explores the dynamics of master–servant relationships through the story of two young Welsh maids in the 1920s. When the growing attachment between Vi and the mistress's son, Will, ends in his accidental death at her hands, to escape punishment, she takes on his identity. Travelling to Nova Scotia to undertake his new post of strike-breaking company manager she draws on her experience as a miner's daughter to outwit the workers in their struggles, fulfilling her role with devestating ruthlessness. In *Wishbones* Coxon examines desire, shame, childhood and loss in a small-town provincial England setting.

Plays include: *Birdbones* (MS, 1989); *Waiting at the Water's Edge* (3f,2m) seren, 1993; *The Ice Palace* (adapted from Tarjei Vesaas, 9f,4m,9f/m) in *Making* 3; *Wishbones* (3f,2m) Methuen, 1997.

Pearl Maria Theresa Craigie *see* John Oliver Hobbes

Rachel Crothers

American, 1878–1958

The daughter of doctors in Bloomington, Illinois, Crother's initial career was as a teacher of elocution. She moved to New York to study acting before embarking on a playwriting career that, beginning with *Criss Cross* (produced on Broadway in 1899), proved prolific and successful.

Considered radical for her feminism, which is reflected through well-wrought plays focusing realistically on social and ethical problems, she examines painful dilemmas around marriage, sex and careers, especially as they face middle-class urban women. In *A Man's World*, Frank, a woman writer struggles to support her adopted son, the illegitimate child of another woman. She is horrified to discover that the man she loves is the child's father and that he continues to defend a sexual morality that condemns his former mistress and child but sanctions his own behaviour. *Mary the Third* compares three generations of women and their aspirations for marriage: the grandmother who accepted a relationship in which she used feminine wiles to get her way; her daughter whose marriage has become a social façade concealing mutual contempt; and the idealistic granddaughter determined to create something better in her marriage, though the ardent protestations she and her lover make exactly mirror those we have heard from Mary the first and second.

Crothers's later plays often have a caustic tone. *Nice People* satirizes the self-indulgence of the flapper generation, while in *Susan and God* the charming, frivolous heroine is swept up by a new religious faith but forced to confront her failure as a mother and the problems of her marriage.

Plays include: *Criss Cross* (2f,1m, c.1909) in France; *A Man's World* (3f,5m, 1909) Boston: Badger, 1910 and in Barlow 1981; *He and She* (5f,3m, 1911) in Quinn; *As Husbands Go* (5f,7m, 1931); *When Ladies Meet* (3f,4m, 1932) – all Samuel French; *Mary The Third* (5f,5m, 1923) also in Dickinson; *Old Lady 31* (10f,4m, 1916); *A Little Journey* (7f,8m) in *Three Plays*, 1923; *Expressing Willie* (5f,6m, 1924); *39 East* (8f,6m, 1919) and *Nice People* (4f,6m, 1921); in *Three Plays*, NY: Brentano, 1924. *Susan and God* (6f,5m) NY: Random House, 1938.

See also: *Rachel Crothers* by Lois C. Gottlieb, Boston: Twayne, 1979; App. 2: Schlueter; Shafer; Stephens in Case.

Migdalia Cruz
American, 1958–

A Hispanic American born and brought up in the Bronx, Cruz studied playwriting with Maria Irene **Fornes** and served as playwright-in-residence at INTAR Theater in New York. In plays of visceral power, her writing gives bleak and powerful voice to the disenfranchised 'underclass' of urban American society, focusing on the young latinos she grew up with. Getting pregnant in ignorance at 15, Lillian Rivera in *The Have-Little* inhabits a world demarcated by poverty where she seems doomed to repeat her mother's life, dying in her forties 'mostly exhausted by life'. While her friend Michi's intelligence lets her escape to college and other possibilities, Lillian's world and that of the play remain confined to a wretched apartment in the South Bronx and the rituals of Catholicism. In *Miriam's Flowers* a Puerto Rican family undergoes slow motion self-destruction after the death of Miriam's young brother, as the mother drinks herself to death and her daughter inscribes her pain with razor blades, like stigmata, on her body.

Plays include: *Miriam's Flowers* (2f,3m, 1991) in Chavez; *Telling Tales* (3f) in Lane; *Dreams of Home* (2f,2m,2f/m) in Stein and Young 1992; *The Have-Little* (3f,1m, 1991) in Perkins and Uno; *Fur* (MS); *Cigarettes and Moby Dick* (MS, 1995); *Lucy Loves Me* (MS, 1991); *Latins in La-La Land* (MS, 1994); *Frida* (with H. Blecher and R. X. Rodriguez, 1f,1m+, 1992) in Miles 1997.

Gretchen Cryer (and Nancy Ford)
American, 1936–

Long-term collaborators Cryer and Ford created some of the first musicals to deal with the political ferment of the late 1960s. The anti-war rock opera *Now is the Time for All Good Men*, set in a small-town Indiana high school, examines the narrow-minded prejudice and macho image of masculinity celebrated by rural America. Against this she sets a more liberal, dissenting tradition espoused by Thoreau, through the story of schoolteacher Mike Butler, court martialled by the army for refusing to fire in battle, whose past is used by conservative townspeople to pressure the high-school principal to sack him. *I'm Getting My Act Together . . .* was one of the earliest feminist musicals, a witty, pointed examination of the impossibilities of male–female relationships structured as a running argument between entertainer Heather and her manager, Joe, as she, to his horror, rehearses her planned new feminist show, regaling him with her 'Strong Woman Number' and criticizing an industry in which women are 'Put in a Package and Sold'.

Plays include: *Now is the Time for All Good Men* (6f,6f, 1969); *Shelter* (3f,5m, 1973); *I'm Getting My Act Together and Taking it on the Road* (4f,6m, 1980); *The Last Sweet Days of Isaac* (1f,1m, 1970). All NY: French.
    See also App. 2: Betsko and Koenig.

Colleen Curran
Canadian, 1954–

Curran's plays are humane comedies. *Sacred Hearts* is set in a small Alberta community where Bridget, the eminently sane lawyer-turned-sheepfarmer, witnesses an apparent miracle – a statue of the Virgin Mary turning towards her. The event forces her and the community, their radical priest and her career-diplomat brother, to examine their values and beliefs, especially the dangerous possibility that the miracle may be real. In *Cake-Walk* five unlikely contestants clash in a cake-baking competition on Canada Day, while in *Senetta Boynton* the eponymous senator gives an unrestrained account of her recent travels.

Plays include: *Sacred Hearts* (3f,3m, 1990); *Cake-Walk* (5f,2m, 1984) in *Four New Comedies* (1987) – both Playwrights Canada; *El Clavadista* (2f, 1981); *A Sort of Holiday* (1f,1m); *Amelia Earhart was Not a Spy* (1f,2m, 1985) in *Triple Play*, NuAge Editions, 1990; *Senetta Boynton Visits the Orient* (2f,1m, 1991) in Curran; *A Brave Girl* (1f) in Brennan.

Dymphna Cusack
Australian, 1902–81

Cusack, born in Wyalong, New South Wales, was a novelist and friend of Miles **Franklin** with whom she collaborated on several projects. Cusack's socialist commitment is reflected in naturalistic (if sometimes melodramatic) plays that confront racism, war and injustice. In *Comets* a group of mismatched individuals, including an artist, a young girl, an elitist canning factory owner and a young labour organizer, are thrown together by a flood. In the ensuing confrontations Cusack also attacks the artist's dependence on women for self-aggrandizement and the belief that he must be allowed to be emotionally irresponsible for the sake of his work. Tense and highly effective, *Morning Sacrifice* takes place in the oppressive atmosphere of a girls' school staffroom on the eve of the Second World War. Seen as parallelling the workings of fascism, the play portrays a society ruled through manipulation and favours and founded on hypocrisy, betrayal and fear, in which the deputy headmistress hounds a vulnerable young teacher to suicide. *Pacific Paradise* is set in an enlightened island community that refuses evacuation in defiance of the conglomerate Inter-Atom, which would destroy their land through nuclear tests.

Plays include: *Morning Sacrifice* (9f) Sydney: Mulga Publications, 1943 and Currency, 1989 and in Pfisterer and with *Comets Soon Pass* (4f,4m, 1943) and *Shoulder the Sky* (11f,11m, 1945) in *Three Australian Three-Act Plays*, Sydney: Australasian Publishing Co., 1950; *Shallow Cups* (3f,3m) in Eight; *Red Sky at Morning* (3f,3m) Melbourne UP, 1942; *Call Up Your Ghosts* (with Miles **Franklin**, 2f,5m, 1945) in Spender 1988; *Pacific Paradise* (6f, 12m, 1963) St Lucia: ADS, 1991; *Jungfrau* (adapted by Jonathan Hardy, 5f,3m), Currency, 1999.

See also: *Dymphna Cusack* by Norman Freehill, Melbourne: Thomas Nelson, 1975; App 2: Pfisterer and Pickett.

Eliza Lanesford Cushing
Canadian, 1794–1886

Cushing was born in Massachusetts, the daughter of novelist Hannah Foster. She married a physician, Frederick Cushing, and settled in Montreal, becoming the earliest published Canadian woman playwright. As joint editor of and contributor to *The Literary Garland* she published ten plays, including short sketches, dialogues and full-length works, often presenting strong and interesting women characters. Even Estelle in *The Fatal Ring*, seduced and abandoned by the king and then murdered by her vengeful husband, is presented with sympathy and complexity. Cushing's dramatic poems and dialogues mostly deal with questions of love – filial, romantic and spiritual – and their contradictions, or with biblical or historical incidents, including versions of the stories of Ruth and Naomi, Esther and Charles I's youth.

Plays include: *Esther: a sacred drama* (3f, 13m+, with *Judith*: a poem) Boston: J. Dowe, 1840; *The Fatal Ring* (6f,7m), in Wagner, originally in *The Literary Garland* July–Sept. 1840.

Clemence Dane (pseud. of Winifred Ashton)
English, 1888–1965

Actress, artist, novelist, screenwriter and friend of Noël Coward, Dane was the quintessential successful boulevard playwright whose work is, however, often fiercely challenging to stereotypes of acceptable female behaviour. Her 1921 *Bill of Divorcement* caused a sensation with its advocacy of change to the divorce laws. Set in a future where divorce on grounds of lunacy is legal, its heroine continues to insist on her right to happiness with her new fiancé, even when her first husband, confined for 15 years to an asylum, returns to insist that her duty is to stay with him. *Granite* has a fabulaic quality and centres on an angry woman's struggle with the husband and lover, who keep her entrapped on the bleak island of Lundy. *Cousin Muriel* confounds her cousin-employer's and her audience's expectation when she, a nice, respectable woman, is revealed as an embezzler, but her spirited self-defence indicts the frustration of her unchallenging social sphere.

Dane's prolific output included religious and biographical dramas *Will Shakespeare*, *Wild Decembers* (about the Brontës) and *Naboth's Vineyard* (on Jezebel), radio plays and social satire (*Adam's Opera*), while a number experiment with form, incorporating music, poetry and non-naturalistic staging.

Plays include: *Scandal at Coventry* (3f,7m+, 1961); *A Bill of Divorcement* (4f,5m, 1921); *Granite*(2f,4m, 1926); *Wild Decembers* (9f,11m, 1932); *Till Time Shall End* (7f,20m+, 1961) in *The Collected Plays of Clemence Dane vol. 1* (1961); *Will Shakespeare: an Invention* (13f,15m+, 1921) in Morgan, 1994; *The Way Things Happen* (5f,5m, 1924); *Naboth's Vineyard* (9f,29m, 1925); *Adam's Opera* (15f,23m+, 1928); *Mariners* (9+f,5m, 1927); *The Lion and the Unicorn* (12f,17m+, 1943); *Cousin Muriel* (3f,3m, 1940). All London: Heinemann.
   See also App. 2: Cousin; Gale.

Sarah Daniels
British, 1957–

London-born Daniels's career reflects the development and concerns of British feminism through the 1980s and beyond. Her witty, well-wrought, often moving plays map out its issues: the entrapment of women in marriage, the anti-nuclear campaign (*Devil's Gateway*), the rights of lesbian mothers (*Neaptide*), the retrieval of feminist history (*Byrthrite* on sixteenth-century 'witches'; *The Gut Girls*, on the exploitation of workers in a Victorian slaughterhouse).

At their strongest, her plays give passionate voice to feminist outrage – particularly in the acclaimed *Masterpieces* – addressing the sexual objectification of women in pornography. Her earlier plays however occasionally exemplify the weaknesses of 1980s feminism, tending sometimes towards the formulaic, and overemphasizing the presentation of 'positive images' of women. Daniels has spoken of the restrictions imposed by a sense of responsibility to the community and the comparative creative freedom she discovered later of writing a complex and disturbing lesbian character in *The Madness of Esmé and Shaz*.

Themes of women's mental health and their diagnosis as mad when they deviate from socially acceptable norms runs throughout Daniels's work: the bullied wife in *Ripen Our Darkness* is threatened with being committed by her respectable husband, the women in *Head-Rot Holiday* have been incarcerated as psychopaths for petty offences. In *Beside Herself* Daniels departs from her usual naturalism, dramatizing the psychological split of a woman who has been sexually abused by her father, between do-gooding MP's wife Evelyn and her alter ego, Eve, the voice of repressed anger, self-destructiveness and the desire to speak out.

Plays include: *Masterpieces* (3f,3m,id, 1984;): *Ripen Our Darkness* (4f,2m,id, 1981); *The Devil's Gateway* (4f,1m,id, 1983); *Neaptide* (13f,12m,id, 1986); *Byrthrite* (5f,1m, 1986) – all Methuen; *The Gut Girls* (6f,2m+,id, 1988); *Beside Herself* (7m, 11f,dp, 1990); *The Madness of Esmé and Shaz* (6f+,id); *Head-Rot Holiday* (3f+,id, 1992) – all in *Daniels Plays Two*, Methuen, 1994; *Purple Side Coasters* in Goodman, 2000.

See also: Minwalla in *Theater* Summer/Fall 1990; App. 2: Griffiths and Llewellyn-Jones; Stephenson and Langridge; Cousin; Davis in Keyssar ed. Freeman, Sierz.

Frances D'Arblay *see* Fanny Burney

Margaretta D'Arcy
Irish, 1922–

Ardent socialist feminist D'Arcy scripted most of her plays with her husband, fellow political activist the playwright and novelist, John Arden. They use history as the focus for an analysis of the workings of establishment power structures and especially the Irish Republican struggle. Their work has continually brought them into conflict with theatre managements and the institutions of state censorship and funding distribution. Plays include epic political biographies (e.g. of James Connolly), the theatre as microcosm of the social hierarchy (*Royal Pardon*), re-examinations of myth (King Arthur in *The Island of the Mighty*) and of Irish history (*Vandaleur's Folly*), and analyses of the spread of Christianity in the Roman empire and its harnessing to the interests of an authoritarian state (*Whose is the Kingdom?*). D'Arcy has also made films and video (on Greenham Common, Galway rent and rate strike, etc.), while recent work has focused on women's community initiatives, especially pirate radio.

Plays include: *A Pinprick of History* (MS, 1977); *The Island of the Mighty* (9f,24m+, 1974); *The Business of Good Government* (4f, 13m, 1960); *Ars Longa, Vita Brevis* (1f,5m+many, 1964); *The Little Gray Home in the West* (1982, 2f,11m); *Vandaleur's Folly* (8f,22m+,dp, 1981); *Immediate Rough Theatre for Citizens Involvement* (1974–7, various) etc. in *Arden and D'Arcy Plays One*, 1991; *The Non-Stop Connolly Show Parts 1–6* (3m+c.24m/f,dp, 1986); *Whose is the Kingdom?* (1988, radio series). All Methuen.

See also: 'Playing With the Airwaves' in *TDR* 128; *Galway's Pirate Women* compiled D'Arcy, Galway: Pirate's Press, 1996; *Tell Them Everything* London: Pluto, 1981; *Awkward Corners* (with Arden), Methuen, 1988; App. 2: Tompkins and Holledge.

Frances D'Arusmont *see* Frances Wright

Gordon Daviot (a.k.a Josephine Tey)
Scottish, 1896–1952

As Josephine Tey, Elizabeth Mackintosh was the author of detective novels, most famously *The Daughter of Time*, in which her convalescing detective reassesses the evidence against Richard III (later also explored in the play *Dickon*).

Many of her plays as Gordon Daviot are sweeping and historical in theme. Most famous is *Richard of Bordeaux*, an enormous success in its day that confirmed John Gielgud's position as matinée idol in the romantic lead of Richard II, favourite-ridden, manipulated by his uncles and supported by his intelligent young queen. *Queen of Scots* (1934), exploring perennially dramatic material which over the years has attracted women playwrights as different as **Field** and **Lochhead**, focuses on Mary's marriages with Darnley and Bothwell. It presents a queen described as 'too much at the mercy of capriciously feminine nature' and vulnerable to manipulation. The subtext of women's relationship to power and self-fulfilment is more overtly explored in *The Laughing Woman*. Based on the relationship between the sculptor Gaudier and Sophie Brzeska, it addresses the tensions for women arising from the demand that they support men at the cost of subsuming their own creativity. In addition to her West End successes Daviot wrote numerous short plays staged by the burgeoning Little Theatre movement in the inter-war years and religious dramas such as *The Stars Bow Down*, on the life of Joseph.

Plays include: *Richard of Bordeaux* (6f,23m+, 1933) in Browne, 1958, in Famous 1934 and London: Victor Gollancz, 1933; *Dickon* (4f,17m+, 1955) London: Peter Davies, 1953; *The Little Dry Thorn* (4f,7m, 1947); *Valerius* (22m, 1948) all London: Peter Downes, 1953; *The Laughing Woman* (20f,10m) in Famous 1933–4; *Queen of Scots* (6f,20m) in Famous 1934; *The Stars Bow Down* (5f,28m) London: Duckworth, 1939.

See also App. 2: Gale.

April De Angelis

English, 1960–

Daughter of an Italian father and English mother, De Angelis began working as actress and deviser with ReSisters theatre group, for whom she later wrote *Women in Law* (MS), before winning the Second Wave Young Women Playwrights' competition with *Breathless*, a neatly structured Gothic fable exploring women's exclusion from science. De Angelis has developed a reputation for adaptations which are humorous, provocative and theatrical, wittily informing classic texts with feminist perspectives, including *Frankenstein* and *Fanny Hill*. The latter is structured as a dramatic reconstruction of her past life, directed by Fanny herself, as inspiration for the novel she is forced to write by author John Cleland. The theatrical is also central in works such as *Playhouse Creatures*, an examination of the pressures – economic, sexual and cultural – on pioneering Restoration actresses.

De Angelis's original works are poetic, exploratory in form and acute. *Crux* is a feminist history, set in a community celebrating hedonism and pleasure founded by medieval mystic and originator of the Doctrine of the Free Spirit, Marguerite de Porete. *Ironmistress* is a piece loosely based on the experience of Victorian factory owner Charlotte Guest, but also on the highly visible 1980s ironmistress, Margaret Thatcher, and explores the dilemmas and costs of women's power.

In *Hush* and *The Positive Hour* De Angelis broke new ground, passionately examining the climate of increasing political and personal desperation that afflicted liberals, leftists and feminists from the 1980s onwards, witnessing the erosion of values of community and compassion for which they had so long struggled.

Plays include: *Visitants* (radio, 1989); *Black Narcissus* (radio); *Soft Vengeance* (MS, adaptation); *Breathless* (2f) in Gray; *Crux* (4f,2m, 1989) in Robson 1991; *The Life and Times of Fanny Hill* (4f,2m, 1990) in *Frontline 4*. *Ironmistress* (2f,1d, 1988) in Remnant 8; *Hush* (3f,3m, 1992) also in Edwardes 1; *Playhouse Creatures* (5f, 1994); *The Positive Hour* (5f,2m, 1997) in *April De Angelis Plays One*, 1998 and *A Warwickshire Testimony* (6f,3m,1d, 1999) – both Faber.

See also App. 2: Stephenson and Langridge; Cousin; Edgar.

Denise Deegan

British, 1952–

Deegan achieved big West End success with her highly enjoyable, affectionate spoof of Angela Brazil's girls' boarding school novels. *Daisy Pulls It Off* combines breathless direct address to the audience and onstage action as the heroine, a scholarship girl, struggles against the forces of scheming and snobbery to show she is worthy of her place at Grangewood, in the process rescuing her arch-enemies, discovering hidden treasures and her long-lost father, and scoring the winning goal at hockey.

Deegan's other plays include a trilogy: *Harvester's Feast*, *The Hiring Fair* and *Turn the Old Year Go*, exploring Pembrokeshire farming life (all MS).

Plays include: *Daisy Pulls It Off* (18f,2m), French, 1985; *The Project* (MS); *No Birds Sing* (MS).

Teresa Deevy

Irish, 1894–1963

Deevy, from Waterford, wrote her first of more than 25 plays in 1928. Both the one-act *King of Spain's Daughter* and *Katie Roche* centre on stormy, independent young women trapped in narrow circumstances. Annie Kinsella's only escape from a brutal father, who threatens to indenture her as a factory worker, is marriage to a dull but dependable man. Katie Roche marries a sober, reliable older man but is frustrated when he treats her like a child, her trapped vibrancy and romantic desires finding outlet in flirtation. Both take refuge in imagination: Katie in pride at her superior, if illegitimate, origins; Annie in colourful fantasy which transforms the landscape but gets her condemned for lying and tardiness.

Plays include: *Reapers* (MS, 1936); *The King of Spain's Daughter* (2f,3m, 1935) with *Katie Roche* (3f,5m, 1936), in Famous 1935–6 and *The Wild Goose* (3f,5m, 1936) – all in *Three Plays*, Macmillan, 1939; *Light Falling* (MS, 1948); *Temporal Powers* in *Journal of Irish Literature*, May 1985; *Going Beyond Alma's Glory* (4f,2m, 1949, radio) in *Irish Writing* 17, Dec. 1951; *A Disciple* (4f,2m) in *Dublin Magazine* 12, Jan.–Mar. 1937.
See also App. 2: Kearney in *The Theatre Annual*.

Alma DeGroen

Australian, 1941–

DeGroen was born in New Zealand but settled in Australia in 1964, where she has made a major contribution to the development of alternative theatre, her plays addressing the state of marriage, sexual frustration, compulsive housework – reflecting the shifting politics of feminism since 1968. Her pieces are unusual in their focus on the dilemmas of male as well as female roles. In *Chidley* she explores the life of an obsessive nineteenth-century Australian sex reformer, while in *Vocations* men's responses to the challenge of a new balance of domestic and professional roles are as central as women's. In *The Girl Who Saw Everything*, Gareth's meeting with a terrified rape victim, who runs away from his attempts to help her into the path of an oncoming car, precipitates his shocked realization of the violence confronting women. The piece opposes a number of different ways of making sense of a world of continuing violence and desperation, confronting Gareth's confusion and the pessimism of Liz, his feminist historian wife, with 23-year-old Edwina's rejection of 'endism' and despair.

The continuing search for meaning and for identity through creativity is central to DeGroen's most acclaimed play. *The Rivers of China* interweaves the dying Katherine **Mansfield**'s last weeks (cf. **Tomalin**), when she turned to the spiritual leader Gurdjieff for guidance, with scenes from a present-day world where an injured man who believes himself to be Mansfield wakes up to a world where male artistic creativity is outlawed.

Plays include: *The Sweat-Proof Boy* (MS, 1972); *Chidley* (1f,4m,id) in *Theatre Australia* Jan./Feb. 1977; *Going Home* (2f,3m, 1976); *The Joss Adams Show* (3f,4m,dp, 1970); *Perfectly All Right* (1f,2m, 1972) in *Going Home and Other Plays* (1977); *Vocations* (2f,2m,id, 1985) and in Tait and Schafer; *The Rivers Of China* (2f,5m,id, 1988) and in *New Australian Drama* ed. K. Brisbane, NHB, 1990; *The Girl Who Saw Everything* (4f,2m, 1993); *The Woman in the Window* (1999). All Currency.

See also: Wearne in ADS Oct. 1992; Pickett in ADS Apr. 1993; App. 2: Gilbert and Tomkins.

Shelagh Delaney
English, 1939–

Probably the most performed play by a woman in the post-war British repertory, *A Taste of Honey* earned its 18-year-old author immediate acclaim when produced by Joan **Littlewood**'s Theatre Workshop in 1958. Critics recognized the writing of 'a remarkable page of theatre history' while it enjoyed commercial success in London and New York. Delaney's *The Lion in Love*, substantially less well known, focuses on a broader family canvas and the inter-relationships between generations. The setting is less naturalistic and more suggestive than the Salford of *Taste of Honey* (though Littlewood, who substantially revised *Honey*, had resisted naturalism), its landscape of bomb sites, street end and shabby market place where the city surrounds the house 'like a fantastic panorama'.

Women are at the centre of both pieces, although *Lion* presents them in more conventional relationships, the toils of unfulfilling marriages in a poor but cohesive community. The characters in *A Taste of Honey* are socially more marginalized, especially Jo, her black lover, and her homosexual friend Geoffrey, while her mother, Helen, is introduced as a 'semi-whore'. The central relationship between raucous, self-involved mother and dreamy, awkward, neglected daughter is presented with insight and compassion, while Delaney offers a radical alternative to both traditional gender roles and Helen's feckless attempts at family life in the odd ménage of Geoffrey and pregnant Jo.

Plays include: *A Taste of Honey* (2f,3m, 1958); *The Lion in Love* (6f,5m+, 1961) Both Methuen; *The House that Jack Built* (MS, 1979); *Charlie Bubbles* (screen, 1968); *The Raging Moon* (screen, 1970); *Dance with a Stranger* (screen, 1985).
See also App. 2: Griffiths in Griffiths and Llewellyn-Jones, Keyssar, Sierz.

Jean Devanny
Australian, 1894–1962

Devanny was born and brought up in New Zealand, where she married a radical trade unionist and published her first novel *The Butcher Shop* (1923). She later settled in Australia, becoming active in the Communist Party like her friend K. S. **Prichard**. Her only surviving play focuses on the sugar-growing industry in 1930s Australia and the the tensions between Big Mac, the owner/manager, his wife and sons, the small farmers, the foreman and the cane-cutting gangs in a time of political ferment. Government action to keep the sugar industry in the hands of British growers was causing the ruin of Italian and other immigrant farmers, and encouraging recruitment to both fascism and communism which were offering answers to desperate people. The political ferment is paralleled by the personal in the passionate love affair developing between Laurel Macquarie and Toni Muranivich, the Yugoslav farm manager, and in Mac's growing antipathy towards his 'weak', musical younger son.

Play: *Paradise Flow* (4f, 19m) St Lucia: University of Queensland Press/ Brisbane: Hecate Press, 1985.
See also: introduction by C. Ferrier.

Alexis DeVeaux
American, 1948–

DeVeaux, a native New Yorker, is a poet, novelist and performance artist as well as a playwright. Her play *'No'*, adapted by Glenda Dickerson (MS, 1981), is a cycle of poems, scenes and stories which, through a fractured narrative structure (cf. **Shange**), presents the social, political, emotional and sexual experiences of young black lesbians through powerful invective and lush, sensuous language. At the centre of *The Tapestry* is the attempt of a young black woman to succeed with her law studies in spite of the obstacles – the rebuffs of the white institution and its patriarchal language, the pulls of her boyfriend's needs, her girlfriend's distractions, her own desires and the pressures of study – that threaten to drive her mad. Despite the undramatic premise – Jet's attempt to concentrate on her studies – the play is made vivid and imagistic through DeVeaux's disturbing introduction of a chorus who invade the apartment, becoming the throng of those desperate for legal help or choir members from Jet's religious background, surreally enacting a nightmarish church picnic, eating each other's flesh and chewing on the bones.

Plays include: *Circles* (MS, 1972); *A Season to Unravel* (MS, 1979); *Elbow Rooms* (MS, 1987); *The Tapestry* (5f,4m,id, 1976) in Wilkerson.
     See also App. 2: Wilkerson in Hart.

Ghosal Svarnakumari Devi
   Indian, 1855–1932

The sister of poet-playwright Rabindranath Tagore, Devi was, with him, the centre of a distinguished group of writers. Devi's concerns included civic reform, women's issues and theosophy. She published in both English and Bengali, prose and poetry as well as plays, including *Spring Festival* (1879), *Evening Clouds* (1906) and *The Wheel of Fortune*, a biting commentary on the dowry system (1911), all untranslated. *Princess Kalyani* is an allegorical fable whose heroine is plotted against by the wicked stepmother who has infatuated her father. Kalyani represents the embodiment of goodness whose sacrificial death offers spiritual renewal to the kingdom.

Plays include: *Princess Kalyani* (16f,4m) Madras: Ganesh, 1930.

Mahasweta Devi
   Indian, 1926–

Devi brings to her novels and short stories a passionate commitment and a sense of history as she exposes injustice and exploitation. She dramatized versions of the stories to use performance to reach the largely illiterate audience she sought. Her plays draw together folk myths, history and contemporary reality. In *Urvashi and Johnny* a fabled ventriloquist loses his voices to throat cancer, a metaphor for the suppression of democracy. More directly political, *Mother of 1084* presents a woman's attempts, two years after his death, to reconstruct the last hours of her son's life, one of many killed in the Naxalite uprising, by visiting another grieving mother and the woman he loved, who was also tortured for her political beliefs. While her family try to hush up the social embarassment of his memory, the mother becomes politicized and her last speech is a cry of rejection of oppression and suffering. *Water* uses a traditional story of a water diviner's love of the (female) river to present a process of politicization as he rises to a new role, becoming a threat to the local administration as, through him, the people take control of a natural resource.

Plays include: *Mother of 1084* (7f, 15m,dp); *Aajir* (4f,5m+); *Bayen* (2f,5m); *Urvashi and Johnny* (2f,3m+); *Water* (6f, 12m+,dp) tr. from Bengali by Samik Bandyopadhyay in *Five Plays* Calcutta: Seagull Plays, 1986.

Anne Devlin
Irish, 1951–

While she has adapted French playwright Arlette Namiand's *Mainly After Dark* (about unmarried mothers) and, with *Heartlanders*, collaborated with fellow Birmingham-based writers on a large-scale community play celebrating the city's multi-ethnic identity, Devlin remains best known for her powerful plays about her native Northern Ireland. Born into a Belfast Catholic family, her major work, *Ourselves Alone* (the title translates the Irish 'Sinn Fein'), explores the personal and political choices available to the women in a community and a family dominated by the IRA involvement of father, son and son-in-law. Central is the conflict between individual loyalties to lovers or children and the demands of active service in an armed militia. When the pregnant Josie, an active IRA member, is informed that her lover is a British agent she is ordered to have an abortion. Her sister Frieda chooses exile from Ireland as escape from intimidation, disowned by her father for her relationship with a political enemy. Several of Devlin's television plays address similar issues. The personal costs of displacement and political conflict are central to *After Easter,* where the death of her father provokes the heroine's crisis of identity and confrontation with the demons of her Catholic upbringing, a fervid Republican inheritance and the mystical visions or hallucinations that plague her.

Plays include: *Ourselves Alone* (3f, 13m,dp, 1985) in Kilgore and with *A Woman Calling* (9f, 12m, TV, 1984); *The Long March* (6f,6m, TV, 1984) – all in *Ourselves Alone and Other Plays* (1986); *After Easter* (7f,6m, 1994); *Titanic Town* (screen, 1998) – all Faber. *Heartlanders* (with Stephen Bill and David Edgar, 48f,39m+, dp) NHB, 1989.

See also: Greenhalgh in *Terrorism and Modern Drama* ed. John Orr and Dragan Klaic, Edinburgh UP, 1990; App. 2, Edgar.

Fatima Dike
South African, 1948–

A Xhosa born near Cape Town, Dike joined Space Theatre in 1975, creating work which, written in the struggle against apartheid and toured to the townships, was deliberately part scripted, part improvised to elude censorship from the authorities. Her *The First South African* charts the progress through various racial classifications of Zwelinzema, son of a black mother and white father, in a system that offers him social advantage if he denies his family and passes as white. Dike's work vividly evokes life in the townships and increasingly focuses on women such as the three sisters of *So What's New?,* a former singing trio who attempt to make a living, legally or otherwise, in a corrupt system. In *Glasshouse* she examines, through flashbacks, the impact of political events on the relationship between two young women, one black, one white, from the 1976 Soweto riots to the present.

Plays include: *The Sacrifice of Kreli* (4f,11m, 1976) in *Theatre One: South Africa* ed. Stephen Gray Johannesburg: A. D. Donker, 1977; *The First South African* Johannesburg: the Ravan Press, 1979; *So What's New?* (4f, 1991) in CnTR v9 pt3, 1998 and in Perkins, 1998; *Glasshouse* (MS, 1979).

See also: CnTR v9, pts1 and 2; App. 2: Tompkins and Holledge; France and Corso; Gilbert and Tompkins.

Georgia Douglas Johnson
American, 1886–1966

Born in Georgia to an inter-racial couple, Douglas Johnson trained in music and worked as a teacher before marrying a lawyer, Henry Johnson. Their home in Washington, DC became a meeting place for black artists and intellectuals. She wrote poetry and composed music as well as writing nearly 30 plays, many now lost.

Douglas Johnson's most powerful works deal, in spare, concentrated action, with the horrors of lynching in the South. Enjoyment of the only day of rest is violently disrupted in *A Sunday Morning in the South* by the lynch mob baying in the streets at the arrest of Tom Griggs on the evidence of a hysterical white girl. The clamour of the mob and the screams of a young black boy in *Safe* drive a mother to kill her newborn son to make him 'safe' from future lynch mobs (cf. **Grimke**). *Blue-Eyed Black Boy* introduces another key theme in her work, miscegnation, as Jack is saved from lynching by the intervention of his white father, while in *Blue Blood* a young couple's marriage is prevented by their mothers' discovery that both were raped by the same white man.

Plays include: *A Sunday Morning in the South* (4f,4m, 1925) in Hatch & Shine, also in Perkins; *Plumes* (3f,1m, 1927) in Perkins 1989, also in France; *Safe* (3f,2m, c.1929) in Brown-Guillory; *Blue Blood* (3f,1m, 1926) and *Blue-Eyed Black Boy* (3f,1m, c.1930, in Perkins 1989; also Brown-Guillory; *Frederick Douglas* (1f,3m, 1935) and *William and Ellen Craft* (2f,2m, 1935) in Richardson and Miller. Several also in Perkins and Stephens.

See also App. 2: Hull; Brown-Guillory; Bloom; Fletcher in *The Theatre Annual*.

Rita Dove
American, 1952–

Dove, originally from Akron, Ohio, is Commonwealth Professor of English at the University of Virginia and from 1993 to 1995 was US Poet Laureate. An African-American woman, several of her works focus on the struggles of earlier generations of black people, often framing their experience within the context of Greek mythologies. The verse play *The Darker Face of the Earth* powerfully replays the Oedipus story in the setting of an ante-bellum South Carolina plantation where Augustus, an aspiring revolutionary, is picked out to be the lover of his mistress, the

plantation owner, as his father was before him – with devastating consequences.

Plays: *The Darker Face of the Earth* (9f, 12m+) Brownsville, OR: Storyline Press
1994 and NHB, 1999; *The Siberian Village* (1f,2m) in *Callaloo* vol. 14/2, 1991.

Claire Dowie
English, 1956–

Dowie started out as a stand-up comedian in 'alternative' cabaret before
creating her self-described Stand-Up Theatre as author-performer.
Dowie's work is both comic and poignant, drawing on her own experiences to make a sustained onslaught on the prisons of sexual, gender
and behavioural stereotypes. She includes among her targets the stereotypes perpetuated by 1980s lesbianism and feminism, where the butch
and androgynous were rejected as woman-hating in favour of an ethic
celebrating nurturing goddess-worship. Instead Dowie's heroines identify with male heroics, leather jackets and celebrate the Men from
UNCLE rather than the women of Greenham, and her work makes a
hilarious and impassioned plea for freedom from such judgemental
constraints and for space for Otherness.

Enormously moving, the monologue *Adult Child, Dead Child*
recounts with painful lucidity a loveless child's experience of rejection
by her family, as her desperate need for acceptance and attention and its
inept expression drive her further into misunderstanding and mental
illness. *John Lennon* charts the struggle of a young girl growing up in the
Sixties where the roles available to girls appeared limited to screaming,
swooning and standing on the sidelines, continually restricted by the
inevitable obligatory skirt. In *Leaking* . . . Dowie vividly recounts the
experience of a lesbian who gets accidentally pregnant by a gay man.

Plays include: *Cat and Mouse* (MS); *Adult Child, Dead Child* (1987) also in Remnant 7; *Why Is John Lennon Wearing a Skirt?* (1990); *Drag Act* (1993); *Leaking from
Every Orifice* (1993) – all 1f; *Death and Dancing* (with Mark Pinkosh, 1f,1m, 1992)
in *Why Is John Lennon Wearing a Skirt? and Other Stand Up Theatre Plays*, 1996;
All Over Lovely (with Peta Lily, 2f, 1996) and *Easy Access (for the boys)* (1f,4m,
1998) – both Methuen.

See also App. 2: Stephenson and Langridge, Sierz.

Henrietta Drake-Brockman

Australian, 1901–68

Drake-Brockman was born in Perth and lived in Broome in northwest Western Australia, the setting of most of her plays, which explore the hardships and struggle of outback Australian lives and communities. In *Hot Gold,* set in 1940s Kalgoorlie, the temptation to steal from a rich seam he has found at the mine appears to offer Don the chance to get back his girl who has left him for a wealthy Italian. *Men Without Wives* contrasts two women and the commitment to husband, family and the land of tough, no-nonsense against which Mrs Bates convinces Jack Abbot's elegant young wife to stay in the outback.

Plays include: *The Man From the Bush* (2f,6m, 1934) in *Eight Plays by Australians* Melbourne: Dramatists Club, 1934; *The Lion-Tamer* (6f) Sydney: Angus and Robertson, 1948; *The Blister* (1f,8m) also in Martin 1940; *Men Without Wives* (5f, 9m,1938); *Hot Gold* (3f,13m); *Dampier's Ghost* (5m) also in W. Moore. All in *Men Without Wives and Other Plays*, Sydney: Angus and Robertson, 1955.

Sarah Dreher

American, 1937–

Dreher was born in Hanover, Pennsylvania and attended Wellesley College for women in the homophobic 1950s when malicious rumours of 'too close' attachments between students could lead to expulsion. She drew on the experience for *Alumnae News,* set at the home of Stacey Holcomb, a lesbian college professor. Ten years after graduation she is visited by Karen, once her closest friend before the Dean forbade all contact between them as the price of Stacey's getting her degree. Although the women's contemporary meeting and rediscovery of their love is interspersed with flashbacks, as in most of her work Dreher employs a realist aesthetic in work which is 'most[ly] . . . autobiographical, more or less', reflecting contemporary lesbian experience. Exceptionally in *This Brooding Sky* she parodies the lush prose of Gothic romances (cf. **Lavery**'s *Her Aching Heart*), with a nod towards Radclyffe Hall, in the creation of Stephen, 'the moody mistress of Seven Chimneys'. Elsewhere she explores relationships between lesbians in the Women's Army Corps in the Second World War (*Hollandia '45*) and in *8x10 Glossy* the effect of a father's alcoholism and violence on his wife and daughters. One takes refuge in a dull marriage, the other hides behind a tough exterior, unable to express need to her lover.

Plays include: *Ruby Christmas* (7f) and *8x10 Glossy* (5f) in McDermott; *Alumnae News: The Doris Day Years* (3f); *Base Camp* (5f); *Backward, Turn Backward* (4f,1m); *This Brooding Sky* (9f,1m,1m/f); *Hollandia '45* (5f) in *Lesbian Stages*, Norwich, VT: New Victoria Publishers, 1988.

Rosalyn Drexler
American, 1926–

Novelist and established visual artist, Drexler's first plays, like those of **Terry** and **Fornes**, grew out of the ferment of 1960s experiment into the narrative, linguistic and performative possibilities of theatre and its relationship to other arts. From the 1964 Obie-winning musical *Home Movies*, music has played an integral part. The heroine of *Starburn* is lead singer of the punk group Great Mother Goddess Cult; the FBI, on the trail of 'psychiatrist-pimp-pusher' Dr Toloon-Fraak in *Least Existence*, are disguised as a band called the Feds; in *Dear*, a housewife infatuated with Perry Como conjures him out of the television. Grotesque, anarchic, flamboyant, Drexler's plays have been seen as representing a peculiarly American and optimistic absurdism; she acknowledges Ionesco as an influence.

Play is the central element of Drexler's work, generating structure, verbal dazzle, full of punning and oddball juxtapositions, and quirky narrative starting points between figures as diverse as Linda Loman, wife of Arthur Miller's salesman and a giant cockroach, or *Streetcar*'s Southern Belle, Blanche, and Oscar Wilde, in the hotel pieces *Transients Welcome*. Drexler's work expresses an erotic playfulness, reflecting the 1960s origins of her playwriting career, where objects of lust include talking dogs, fellow family members, schoolgirls and cockroaches, together with preoccupations with death, the American family, food, cartoon violence and suburban surrealism.

Plays include: *Hot Buttered Roll* (2f,2m, 1963) in Benedikt; *The Line of Least Existence* (2f,7m); *The Investigation* (1f,4m, 1966); *Softly and Consider the Nearness* (1f,2m); *Home Movies* (4f,5m, 1964) in Poland; *The Bed is Full* (2f,4m) – all in *The Line of Least Existence and Other Plays*, NY: Random House, 1967; *Skywriting* (2f,1m, 1968) in France; *The Writer's Opera* (MS, 1979); *Starburn* (MS, 1983); *Room 17C* (1f,1m); *Lobby* (2f,4m); *Utopia Parkway* (4f,1m) in *Transients*

Welcome, BPP, 1984; *Occupational Hazard* (4f,14m+, 1992) in Lamont; *Dear* (1f,1m), Applause, 1997.

See also: Lamont in *Theater*, Winter 1985; App. 2: Betsko and Koenig; Brown, Olauson.

Maureen Duffy
British, 1933–

Poet, novelist, critic and biographer (of Aphra **Behn** in *The Passionate Shepherdess*, 1977), Duffy's best-known work as a playwright is *Rites* (1969). A highly effective modern version of Euripides' *The Bacchae*, the play is set in a women's public toilet. The play uses the rituals of office chit-chat to create a chorus and to build a female world, at once comic and chilling, apart from and hostile to men, until an attempted suicide causes it to erupt in violence. Her *Pearson/The Lay Off* (MS, 1962) similarly juxtaposes worlds, updating the medieval poem *Piers Plowman* to a London factory setting, while *Washhouse* (MS) enacts a love story between Venus and Diana in a launderette.

Plays include: *The Silk Room* (MS, 1966); *Olde Tyme* (MS, 1970); *Rites* (12f) in Wandor 2 and in Sullivan and Hatch; *A Nightingale in Bloomsbury Square* (2f,1m) in *Factions* ed. Giles and Alex Hamilton, London: Michael Joseph, 1974.

See also App. 2: Wandor 1987, Sierz.

Daphne Du Maurier
English, 1907–89

Daughter of actor-manager Sir Gerald Du Maurier, Daphne Du Maurier is best known for haunting romantic novels, several of them dramatized by herself and many filmed, including *Rebecca*, *Frenchman's Creek*, *Jamaica Inn* and *Don't Look Now*. Her original plays are lush, romantic 1940s melodramas, affirming the virtues of stoic female self-sacrifice. In *The Years Between* Diana remakes her life after her difficult, brilliant husband is shot down over the Mediterranean, takes his place as local MP and falls in love with her neighbour, warm, sympathetic Richard. When, after three years fighting a top secret mission, Michael reappears alive to mock her changes and achievements and demand she once more become his supportive wife, she is forced to choose between her love for

Richard and Michael's apparent need for her. In *September Tide*, middle-aged, devoted mother Stella and her unconventional, whisky-soaked artist son-in-law fall impossibly and movingly in love and agree to part for the sake of his young wife. While apparently asserting the values of obedience and resignation Du Maurier also suggests the need to question them and exposes the painful human cost of such values.

Plays include: *My Cousin Rachel* (adapted by Diana Morgan, 2f,5m) DPS, 1945; *Rebecca* (3f,9m) Gollancz, 1940; *September Tide* (3f,3m, 1949); *The Years Between* (4f,6m, 1945) also in Morgan, 1994, both London: Victor Gollancz.

See also: *Daphne Du Maurier* (biography) by Margaret Forster, London: Chatto, 1993.

Andrea Dunbar
English, 1961–90

Andrea Dunbar was born and grew up on a run-down Bradford council estate and drew powerfully on her own experience for her plays. She died, aged 29, of a brain haemorrhage, leaving three children. The autobiographical *The Arbor*, written with the encouragement of her CSE drama teacher and taken up by the Royal Court Theatre, charts with grimly comic realism the experiences of Andrea, a 15-year-old unmarried mother. In *Rita, Sue and Bob Too*, two schoolgirls plot their seduction by Bob on the way back from babysitting, to get rid of their burdensome virginity. Although the scene mixes the sordid and the horribly comic, Dunbar does not shy away from the consequences for her heroines or Bob as arguments, unwanted pregnancy and marriage break-up follow. In *Shirley*, a tense and brutally funny series of no-holds-barred battles between mother and daughter ends with a temporary truce over a cigarette. Dunbar's characters are pragmatic survivors, women who, with men absent or in prison, cope in conditions of enormous hardship and poverty.

Plays: *The Arbor* (4f,5m+, 1980); *Rita, Sue and Bob Too* (4f,2m, 1982); *Shirley* (4f,9m dp, 1988). All Methuen, 1988.

See also App. 2: Griffiths and Llewellyn Jones, Sierz.

Nell Dunn

British, 1936–

Several of Dunn's novels have been filmed – raw, energetic chronicles of the lives of working-class women, their grim, candid comedy quintessentially 1960s. Her highly successful *Steaming* excited controversy and accusations of encouraging voyeurism with its picture of a group of women who meet regularly at a municipal Turkish baths and then join together to campaign against its closure. The sharing of bawdy jokes, woes, warmth and relaxation creates a space where each woman can make self-discoveries and friendships, where class conflicts can begin to be eroded, risks taken and new steps towards independence embarked upon.

Plays include: *Up the Junction* (TV, 1965); *Every Breath You Take* (TV, 1988); *Poor Cow* (screen, 1967); *Steaming* (6f,1mv) Amber Lane Press, 1981; *I Want* (with Adrian Henri), Jonathan Cape, 1972; *The Little Heroine* (MS, 1988); *Babe XXX* (MS, 1998).
See also App. 2: Wandor 1987, Sierz.

Marguerite Duras

French, 1914–96

Novelist, film-maker, essayist and playwright, Duras was born in Cochin, in southern India, and is celebrated for her subtle evocations of colonial life in French Indo-China. Her childhood experiences, visited and revisited, form the basis of her writing through the various forms through which she tries to capture them, like a haunting and persistent dream. Her later plays often rework material from novels such as *Eden Cinema*, which in turn draws on the earlier *The Sea Wall* and *The Lover*. Her writing has attracted much critical attention from feminists for its exploration of themes of desire, language and gender in a style that is incantatory, experimental and cinematic. Her film *Hiroshima Mon Amour* interwove the memories of passion of a French actress and her Japanese lover with the horrors of the destroyed city.

Many of her early plays stage brief encounters between individuals on the brink of change or changed by encounters with strangers, such as the maid and the travelling salesman who meet in *The Square*, or the lovers who have separated but meet again by chance in *La Musica*. Others compulsively restage past events, such as the elderly couples of *The Viaduct of*

Seine-en-Oise and *L'Amante Anglaise* who have committed murder and endlessly re-examine their motives, awaiting punishment – or punishing themselves. Duras focuses on the inner world of fragments of memory, phrases, glances in moments of suffering before separation and especially the anguish of women. Plays such as *Vera Baxter, Suzanna Andler* and *Savannah Bay* retell significant moments from their protagonists' lives with lyricism and poignancy, evoking memories of love, passion and intrigue.

Plays include: *Hiroshima Mon Amour* (screen, 1960) tr. Richard Seaver; *Une aussi longue absence* (screen, 1961) tr. Barbara Wright, Calder, 1966; *The Square* (1f,2m, 1965), *The Viaduct of Seine-en-Oise* (2f,4m, 1959) both tr. Barbara Bray; *Days in the Trees* (2f,2m, 1965) tr. Sonia Orwell, in *Three Plays*, Calder & Boyars, 1967; *Suzanna Andler* (2f,2m,1968); *L'Amante Anglaise* (1f,1m, 1968); *La Musica* (1f,1m, 1966) tr. Bray, Calder, 1975, also in *Duras: Plays Two*, Oberon, 1997; *Vera Baxter or The Atlantic Beaches* (2f,3m, 1980) tr. Philippa Wehle in Wehle; *La Musica (Deux-ième)* (1f,1m, 1967); *Eden Cinema* (2f,3m, 1977); *Savannah Bay* (2f, 1983); *India Song* (2f,7m, extras: 10f,10m+, 1973) tr. Bray, in *Four Plays*, Oberon, 1992; *Agatha* (1f,1m) and *Savannah Bay* (2f) tr. Howard Limoli, Sausalito: Post-Apollo Press, 1992.

See also: *Duras by Duras* San Francisco: City Lights, 1987; *Marguerite Duras: Writing on the Body* by Sharon Willis Chicago: Illinois UP, 1987; Cody in *Theater* Winter 1983; App. 2: Diamond in Case ed.; Lamar; Miller in Keyssar; Bradby and Sparks; Willis in Brater,

Maria Edgeworth
Irish, 1768–1849

Best known for her comic novels set in her native Ireland, several of which have been dramatized for the stage, Edgeworth also wrote some witty plays and a number of dramatic sketches for children designed to teach proper behaviour. *Love and Law* concerns a feud between two Irish families whom love affairs draw together but legal disputes drive apart. In *The Two Guardians* a wide-eyed West Indian innocent abroad is protected from the machinations of his two custodians by the intelligence of his black servant, Quaco. Both plays contain some richly comic characters.

Plays include: *Love and Law* (4f,6m+); *The Rose, the Thistle and the Shamrock* (5f,5m); *The Two Guardians* (5f,7m) in *Comic Dramas* London: R. Hunter, 1817; *The Absentee* (9f,13m, adaptation of Edgeworth's novel by Marianne Moore), NY: House of Books, 1962.

Helen Edmundson

British, 1964–

Edmundson began writing for women's theatre group Red Stockings with pieces such as *Ladies in the Lift* (MS, 1988), a witty musical celebration of women's friendship. She is best known, however, for her adaptations of nineteenth-century novels, praised for 'sometimes dazzling stylization' and her ability to combine often complex narrative with dramatic drive and compelling theatricality. *The Mill on the Floss* uses three performers to play Maggie Tulliver, expressing the struggles of her conflicting emotions, desires and sense of duty. *Anna Karenina* sets the largely separate stories of Anna and Levin in parallel, with the two calling to each other across the stage 'Where are you now?', both a deft theatrical tool and a device that throws their stories into striking comparison. Her powerful original play, *The Clearing*, is set in Ireland during Cromwell's bloody persecution against both Irish and royalist English settlers, when they were either transported, forcibly transplanted to Connacht or killed. It re-excavates the historical roots of inveterate hatred, as politics prove stronger than love, dividing Irish wife and English husband, though one critic thought he could 'not be alone in feeling we should now be looking forward'.

Plays include: *Coventry Carol* (MS); *The Clearing* (3f,7m,dp, 1994); *The Mill on the Floss* (3f,5m, 1994) and in Frontline 4; *Anna Karenina* (4f,4m, 1992); *War and Peace* (7f,9m,id, 1996). All: NHB.

See also App. 2: Stephenson and Langridge.

Margaret Edson

American, 1961–

Born in Washington, DC, Edson studied History and Literature before working in the cancer unit of a research hospital. Her Pulitzer prize-winning play, *W;t*. draws on all three areas. A tense and moving exploration of illness and the confrontation with approaching death, *W;t* focuses with grim and clinical detail on the pain and indignity undergone by Vivian Bearing – an austere, middle-aged, professor of English Literature and specialist on the metaphysical poet John Donne – as she is treated for ovarian cancer. Bearing utilizes the cool, cerebral rigour she brought to her analyses of Donne's poetry and, as her symptoms are analysed by the doctors, she discovers the limitations of intellectual brilliance, her own loneliness, vulnerability and need for human warmth and, in the final moments of the play, a moment of transcendence.

Play: *W;t* (5f,4m) NY: Faber, 1999, London: NHB, 2000.

Rose English
British, 1950–

English trained at art school and began making site-specific performances such as *Berlin* (1976) and *Death and the Maiden*, often in collaboration with Jacky Lansley and Sally Potter. (Potter, with whom she co-wrote and designed the film *The Gold Digger* (1983), went on to direct *Orlando*, 1993.) Described as a 'Home Counties Ancient Mariner', English's solo shows are eccentric, whimsical, philosophical and magical, performed by herself (*Plato's Chair,* 1982) or with others including a dog, a 5-year-old child (*Moses,* MS, 1987), a horse (*My Mathematics, Venus and Vulcan*, both MS, 1992) and a chorus of philosophers. Her recent work, such as *The Double Wedding* (MS, 1991) and *Walks on Water*, has both interrogated and celebrated the more 'disreputable' traditions of popular performance – show girls, equestrian spectacles, burlesque, drag acts, circus, variety – investigating their forms and juxtaposing metaphysical perusal of ideas of reality and illusion with the performance of trick and spectacle. Her work plays with language and metaphor, celebrating the power of the imagination and theatrical transformation.

Plays include: *The Beloved* (MS, 1985); *Walks On Water* (2+12f, 15m, 1988) in Levy; *Plato's Chair* (1f) extract in *Body, Space Image* by Chris Crickmay and Miranda Tufnell, Virago, 1991; *Tantamount Esperance* (MS, 1993).

See also: MacRitchie in PM, Sept./Oct. 1984, Oct./Nov. 1993; *Staging Feminisms* by Geraldine Harris, Manchester UP, 1999; **Levy** in *A Split Second of Paradise: Live Art, Installation and Performance* ed. N. Childs and J. Walwin, London: Rivers Oram, 1998.

Phoebe Ephron
American, 1916–71

Ephron and her husband often worked in collaboration, using family events as source material for many of their comedies and screenplays.

The father/son-in-law relationship is central to *Howie*, where Walter Simms becomes horribly jealous of and agitated by his daughter's brilliant, flamboyant, unemployed husband. *Take Her She's Mine* comically explores the father's separation difficulties as his eldest daughter goes off to college and experiments with alternative views, lifestyles and men, in the early Sixties.

Drawing on family entanglements has become something of a family tradition: their daughter, Nora, a screenwriter and director (*When Harry Met Sally*, *Sleepless in Seattle*), first achieved fame with the novel and film *Heartburn*, based on her relationship with journalist Carl Bernstein, while her sister Delia has also written plays and novels.

Plays include: *Three's a Family* (8f,8m, 1944); *Take Her She's Mine* (6f, 13m, 1962); *My Daughter, Your Son* (3f,4m, 1969) – all with Henry Ephron, French. *Howie* (6f, 10m) French, 1957; *Bride by Mistake* (screen, 1944); *Wallflower* (screen, 1948); *Belles on Their Toes* (screen, 1950); *Carousel* (screen, 1956).

Marcella Evaristi
Scottish, 1953–

Evaristi is a writer and actress. As a cabaret performer she works with Liz **Lochhead** as well as in her own one-woman pieces, such as *The Works* and *Dorothy and the Bitch* (MS), a bleak unfolding of Dorothy **Parker**'s alcohol-soaked despair at the end of her life. Elsewhere she lays open the emptiness of a culture which offers women only the dream of a wedding dress, and in *Hard to Get* (MS) analysing the failure of communication at the heart of marriage. Many of her plays explore aspects of Scottish identity, its denial by an upwardly mobile middle class, her own Jewish Italian-Scottish background (*Commedia*) or macho posturings (*Terrestrial Extra*, 1986).

Plays include: *Scotia's Darlings* (MS); *Checking Out* (MS); *Wedding Belles and Green Grasses* (MS); *The Hat* (radio, 1988); *Commedia* (3f,3m) Edinburgh: Salamander Press, 1983; *The Works* (1f, radio) in Roberts; *Mouthpieces*, St Andrews: Crawford Centre for the Arts.

See also App. 2: Triesman in Griffiths and Llewellyn-Jones.

M. J. Farrell (a.k.a. Mollie Keane)
Irish, 1904–96

Mary Nesta Skrine, born in Ballyrankin, Co. Kildare, is better known as Mollie Keane, the pseudonym she used for her novels, several of which (*Good Behaviour*, *Time After Time*) have been adapted for television. Her plays, written under the name M. J. Farrell, focus, like her novels, on once-wealthy Irish Protestant families in decaying mansions, obsessed with horses and gambling. Lighter than many of the novels, her witty stage comedies feature vivid comic characters that include devoted butlers who rule the roost and loquacious handymen. Eccentric Aunt Bijou, the lynchpin of the action, appears in both *Spring Meeting* and *Dazzling Prospect*, plagued by indigestion, making secret bets at the racetrack with the housekeeping money and certain of her own opinion on every matter. Money and class are central concerns in *Spring Meeting*, where Sir Richard's meanness and snobbishness – rejecting the working-class Catholic vet as a suitable son-in-law – prevents his daughters from marrying until he is outfoxed at cards by the aptly named Tiny Fox-Collier. In *Treasure Hunt* the members of older generation live in the past, have no idea how to manage money and are horrified by the arrival of paying guests who are 'not quite in the Stud Book'. It was described as 'gracious and grotesque by turns . . . it rockets from wit to horseplay . . . to high comedy'.

Plays include: *Spring Meeting* (4f,5m, 1938); *Treasure Hunt* (7f,6m, 1950); both London: Collins; *Dazzling Prospect* (5f,6m) French, 1961. All with John Perry.

Edna Ferber
American, 1887–1968

Ferber, born in Kalamazoo, Michigan, is best known for her novels and short stories. Several, including the celebrated musical *Show Boat* (1927) and the film *Giant* (1956), were later adapted for stage or screen by herself or others. Many of her key plays were collaborations with George Kaufman and have theatrical themes. *The Royal Family*, a comedy about a stage family, was based on the Barrymores; *Stage Door* is set in a boarding house for aspiring actresses and centring on one, Terry, determined to stick to the stage rather than taking the easier route to success in the movies, while *Bravo!* is about a European refugee playwright pitched into an alien America. Most interesting is *Dinner at Eight*, apparently a society drama about the rich socialites planning to attend the Jordans' dinner party, but which gradually and chillingly reveals the life of each to be on the point of collapse through financial ruin, heart attack, suicide, sexual betrayal, bigamy or career failure, in a society about to go 'over the cliff'.

In 1941 Ferber and Kaufman wrote *The Land is Bright* , a chronicle history of the rise and progress of a wealthy American robber baron and his family across three generations, culminating in their discovery of a new social responsibility united against fascism.

Plays include: *The Eldest* (4f,3m, 1925) in France and in Ozieblo; *Minick* (9f,6m); *Dinner at Eight* (11f, 14m) – both NY: French, 1935; *Bravo!* (7f,9m), DPS, 1949; *The Royal Family* (6f, 11m, 1928); *Stage Door* (21f, 11m, 1936); *The Land is Bright* (12f, 19m, 1941) – all with George S. Kaufman, Garden City, NY: Doubleday; *Dinner*, *Stage Door*, *Royal Family* as *Three Comedies*, Applause, 2001.

See also: *A Peculiar Treasure* and *A Kind of Magic* (autobiographies), Garden City, NY: Doubleday 1939 and 1963; Shafer.

Michael Field (pseud. of Katherine Harris Bradley and Edith Emma Cooper)
English, 1848–1913 and 1862–1913

This aunt and niece jointly and pseudonymously wrote almost thirty poetic plays. Often tragic, the pieces reflect the passionate lesbian relationship between the two women in works such as *Callirrhoe*, where Bacchic possession sweeps like a seductive plague through the city. They feature stormy, defiant female characters, New Women before their time, who challenge the accepted order and assert their moral autonomy and right to love. Well received when 'Field' was believed to be a man, the critical response changed drastically when their gender was discovered.

Plays include: *Callirrhoe* (10f,9m+, 1884), *Fair Rosamond* (5f,6m, 1884); *The Father's Tragedy* (5f,16m, 1885), *William Rufus* (23m+, 1885), *Loyalty or Love?* (7f,9m, 1885); *Canute the Great* (4f,7m+, 1887) – all Clifton: J. Baker & Sons; *A Question Of Memory* (4f,5m) London: Poetry Bookshop, 1918; *The Tragic Mary* (7f, 16m, 1890); *Anna Ruina* (4f,8m+) – both London: G. Bell & Sons, 1899; *Attila My Attila!* (7f,5m+) London: Elkin Mathews, 1896.

See also: Moriarty in *Nineteenth-century Women Writers of the English-Speaking World* ed. Rhoda B. Nathan, Greenwood Press, 1986.

Karen Finley
American, 1956–

Finley, from a bohemian Chicago family, started making performance with *Deathcakes and Autism* at the San Francisco Art Institute following her father's suicide. Shocking, angry, moving, provocative, painful and obscene, Finley's performance texts are relentless, powerful execrations of misogyny, sexual abuse, war, homophobia, greed, state coercion of minds and bodies and a society that no longer cares. They are loaded with fragmented personae and disturbing imagery both verbal and visual as she paints her naked body with glitter and crushed eggs or ritually smears herself with chocolate as if it were excreta.

Always controversial, Finley was one of the performance artists (along with **Hughes** and others) 'de-funded' by the NEA under pressure from the religious right, but she has also been criticized for 'political incorrectness' (for example for the title of one show: *I Like the Dwarf on the Table When I Give Him Head*). *The Constant State of Desire* was banned at the ICA in London by Westminster City Council, reputedly because it contravened a by-law preventing women from taking their clothes off *and* speaking at the same time. Much of Finley's recent work, installations and performances, has been made in response to the devestation of losing friends to Aids, an outcry of rage and grief at loss and governmental indifference to suffering.

Plays include: *The Constant State of Desire*, also in Champagne and in Martin 1996 and in TDR 117; *The Family That Never Was*; *Quotes from a Hysterical Female*; *Modern Prayers*; *We Keep Our Victims Ready* (all 1f) in *Shock Treatment* SF: City Lights, 1990; *The American Chestnut* (MS, 1998)

See also: Schuler in TDR 125; letters in TDR 126; App. 2: Juno and Vale; Carr; Hart in Martin; Schneider; Forte in Case ed.

Hallie Flanagan (Davis)
American, 1890–1969

Flanagan returned to work, teaching college drama and writing, after she was left widowed with children in 1918. *The Curtain*, which explores the dangers of lying and the cost of truth-telling, won the Des Moines Little Theatre contest in 1920 and got her a place on George Pierce Baker's influential Workshop '47 for Playwrights at Harvard. In 1925 she went to

Vassar College to establish a theatre which, under the influence of her research into European theatre (documented in *Shifting Scenes*, 1929) and her experiments with a huge range of performance styles, became one of the most innovative in the USA. In 1935 she was appointed head of the newly formed Federal Theatre Project, under Roosevelt's Works Progress Administration, which she built into a network of national theatres, supporting local work and developing new audiences until its demise under pressure from critics of its left-wing politics.

Flanagan was especially responsible for developing the Living Newspaper form, designed to bring alive and raise awareness of contemporary issues using actors, light, music, movement and tight direction, an elaboration of the formal explorations by Margaret Helen Clifford and herself in *Can You Hear Their Voices?* (1931), which drew on accounts of the desperation of dirt farmers in contemporary Arkansas (cf **Littlewood**). Later, as Dean of the new theatre department of Smith College, she continued such multi-dimensional work in *e=mc²* on atomic power and its constructive and destructive possibilities.

Plays include: *Free* (MS); *Power* (MS); *The Garden of Wishes* (MS); *The Lost Aphrodite* (MS); *No Time for Tears* (MS); *The Sky Will be Lit Up* (with Janet Hartmann, MS); *The Curtain* (2f,2m+2), French, 1920; *Can You Hear Their Voices?* (with Margaret Helen Clifford, 15f,21m) in Barlow 1994 and in France; *e=mc²* (with Sylvia Gassel and Day Tuttle, 2f, 6m+20) French, 1948.

See also: *Arena* by Hallie Flanagan NY: Duell, Sloan and Pierce, 1940. *Hallie Flanagan: a Life in American Theatre* by Joanne Bentley NY: Knopf, 1988.

Marieluise Fleisser

German, 1901–74

Fleisser drew on the claustrophobic atmosphere and stifling petty bourgeoisie of her home town, Ingolstadt in Bavaria, for her best-known plays. The enormous significance of her work, long forgotten, began to be recognized with her rediscovery by Rainer Werner Fassbinder in 1968. Recent criticism (e.g. Fuegi) has concentrated on her relationship with Brecht and his influence on her career. Brecht found Fleisser's first play, *Purgatory*, a perfect example of the *Volkstück* and she became one of a string of women playwrights who enjoyed the dubious status of his protegée/collaborator/lover. While Brecht's direction of *Purgatory* strengthened its critique of respectable values, the risqué action, designed to offend bourgeois sensibilities, earned Fleisser a reputation as a loose woman and she was denounced in her home town, disowned by her parents and pilloried by the press for writing 'the lowest sort of Jewish-Bolshevist gutter trash' (Moray).

Fleisser painted the provincial world in which Hitler would win election victories. *Purgatory* focuses on a group of adolescents in a small Catholic town, a world of warped religious values and pack law in which the two misfits, Olga and the disturbed Roelle, are drawn together only by their non-conformity. His frustration and sexual rejection find expression both in sadistic acts and a desire to become a suffering Christ-figure. *Pioneers in Ingolstadt* charts the encounter between a band of army engineers assigned to build a bridge and the local townsfolk, a catalogue of institutionalized brutality, sexual exploitation and betrayal.

Untranslated plays: *Der Tiefseefisch, Karl Stuart, Der Starke Stamm*.

Translated plays: *Purgatory in Ingolstadt* (4f,9m+, 1924) also tr. Gitta Honegger in Case; *Pioneers in Ingolstadt* (4f,11m+, 1929). Both tr. Tinch Minter & Anthony Vivis in Castledine 9.

See also: *Marieluise Fleisser* by Moray McGowan Munich: Bech, 1987; *The Life and Lies of Bertolt Brecht* by John Fuegi, London: Flamingo, 1994; Ley in MD, Sept. 1988.

Maria Irene Fornes
American, 1930–

Fornes immigrated to the USA from Havana in 1945. A performance of *Waiting for Godot* and a burgeoning 1960s theatre scene where experiment was encouraged, led her to write, producing plays in forms ranging from the vaudeville *Successful Life of 3* to the mock lecture of *Dr Kheal* and the ritual ceremony of *Vietnamese Wedding*. Later plays, such as *Mud*, equally various and formally inventive, describe superficially naturalistic narratives of impoverishment and blighted lives through lean, pared-down speech. *What of the Night?* describes its 45-year progress to a future of economic collapse, the human need for love, fantasy and food that generates a language yearning for escape and transcendence. The acclaimed *The Danube*, its banal exchanges drawn from Hungarian language lessons, presents a social world in which words becomes inadequate to communicate the unspeakable as the characters succumb to physical disintegration, poisoned by nuclear contamination.

Women's self-discovery is central to many of Fornes's plays: in *Fefu and Her Friends*, eight women discuss their lives, terrors and fantasies in an environmental piece that moves from room to room. In *Abingdon Square* the marriage of a young woman to a much older man results in betrayal and death with seemingly tragic inevitability. But Fornes is uneasy with simplistic feminisms: in *Conduct of Life* she presents a brutal analysis of the workings of sexual violence, power and women's collusion in its operation in a police state.

Plays include: *Dr Kheal* (1m, 1968) in France; with *The Successful Life Of 3* (1f,5m, 1965) and *Tango Palace* (2m, 1963) in Ballet 3; *Promenade* (6f,9m, 1965); *Molly's Dream* (3f,3m, 1968) in Poland; *A Vietnamese Wedding* (3f,1m+various, 1967) – all in *Promenade and Other Plays* NY: Winter House, 1971. *Fefu and Her Friends* (8f, 1977) in Marranca and Dasgupta 1 and in PAJ Winter 1978;. *Sarita* (3f,4m, 1984); *Mud* (1f,2m, 1985); *The Conduct of Life* (3f,2m, 1983) also in Osborn, and Lane; *The Danube* (1f,3m,id, 1983) – all in *Maria Irene Fornes Plays*, PAJ, 1986. *Abingdon Square* (3f,5m) in PI Apr. 1990; AT Feb. 1988 and in Miles, 1989; *Springtime* (2f,1m, 1986) in Halpern; in Frank; in Curb and with *Nadine* (4f,2m, 1986); *Lust* (6f,5m, 1989); *Hunger* (2f,3m, 1988) as *What Of the Night?* in Lamont; *Enter THE NIGHT* (2f,1m, 1993) in Marranca; *The Summer in Gossensass* (MS, 1998).

See also: *Fornes: Theater in the Present Tense* by Diane Lynne Moroff, Michigan UP, 1996; *Maria Irene Fornes and her Critics* by Assunta Bartolomucci Kent, Greenwood, 1996; O'Malley in SAD 1989; *Signature Theatre 1999 Presents Maria Irene Fornes* ed. James Houghton, Lyme, NH: Smith and Kraus, 2000; App. 2: Schuler in Schlueter; Geis and Keyssar in Keyssar; Worthen in Brater; Austin in Hart; Savran; Betsko and Koenig; Marranca.

Michelanne Forster
New Zealand/Aotearoan, 1953–

Forster was born in America, but settled in New Zealand in 1973. She draws on her Jewishness and accounts of earlier immigrants in *The Rosenberg Sisters*, about the experience of a trio of singing sisters during the Second World War. *Daughters of Heaven* is based on the same horrific murder case as the 1994 film *Heavenly Creatures* (see also **Carter**). Unlike the film, it follows the story of passionate friends Pauline Parker and Juliet Hulme beyond their murder of Pauline's mother, through trial and imprisonment, and explores the impact on the narrow provincial Christ-church community of accounts of the girls' lesbianism and secret fantasy world, inhabited by heroic film stars and singers and the extravagant denizens of the imaginary kingdom of Borovnia and Volumnia.

Plays include: *Daughters of Heaven* (5f,4m,id) Victoria UP, 1992; *The Rosenberg Sisters* (5f,1m, 1992) in Prentice and Warrington; *Larnach: Castle of Lies* (MS, 1993); *This Other Eden* (MS, 1996); *Dying to Leave* (MS).

See also: Stachurski, MD, Spring 1997.

Rose Franken
American, 1895–1988

A boulevard playwright as well as short-story writer and novelist, Franken also tackles themes of sexual problems and the roles open to women. The immensely successful *Claudia* (1941) is a searching and detailed study of a young married woman whose youth and immaturity lead her to cling to her mother despite her marriage. In *Another Language* (1932) the Hallam family, under the rule of the matriarchal grandmother, perpetuates prejudiced insular values, attempting to cow into submission those who question its authority: an artistic grandson, Jerry, and Stella, wife of the youngest son. Stella's refusal to submit and her support for Jerry force her husband into questioning his own intolerance. (The family appears again in *The Hallams*, 1948.) *Outrageous Fortune* was unusual as one of the first serious and open treatments of homosexuality in a Broadway play. It made a forceful plea for tolerance of difference against the narrow judgementalism of 'proper family values'.

Plays include: *Claudia* (5f,3m) NY: Farrar and Rinehart, 1941; *Another Language* (5f,6m, 1932); *The Hallams* (5f,6m, 1948); *Outrageous Fortune* (7f,4m, 1944); *Soldier's Wife* (2f,3m, 1945) – all NY: French. *Claudia and David* (screen, 1946); *Secret Heart* (screen, 1946); *Beloved Enemy* (screen, 1936).

See also: *When All is Said and Done* (autobiography) NY: Doubleday, 1963; App. 2: Olauson, Shafer, Curtin.

J. E. (Jennie Elizabeth) Franklin
American, 1937–

Franklin made a powerful impact in the New York theatre with the 1970 production of *Black Girl*. Set in a poverty-stricken household in small-town Texas (Franklin's home state), it reworks Cinderella in a realist framework, centring on a young black woman's efforts out of an inheritance of pessimism and failure towards self-discovery and escape, helped by a student teacher as fairy godmother who encourages her to go to college. Billie Jean is an awkward adolescent who aspires to become a dancer, but whose sense of self and possibility, like her room (symbolically a corridor in the middle of the house), are constantly intruded on by the mockery and manipulations of her older sisters (both pregnant as teenagers) who resent her desire for escape. The mother, affectionate to strangers but unable to be so with her own children, is an ambivalent figure, like fathers in others of Franklin's plays. The father in *The Prodigal Sister* disowns his pregnant daugher, while the father in *Christchild*, set during the Depression, superstitiously condemns his son, born with six fingers, as the source of the family's bad luck.

Plays include: *Black Girl* (7f,3m) DPS, 1971 and with 'From Genesis to Revelation' Washington, DC: Howard UP, 1977; *The Prodigal Sister* (20f, 15m,dp) with Micki Grant, NY: French, 1974; *Christchild* (4f,3m) in Smith *Best*, 1993; *Miss Honey's Young'uns* (6f,4m) in Turner 1994.

'Miles' Stella Franklin
Australian, 1879–1954

Best known as a novelist for her ground-breaking *My Brilliant Career* (1901), Franklin wrote numerous plays, the majority unpublished and awaiting research, beginning with work (like *The Waiter Speaks*) in support of women's suffrage, written during extended stays in America and Britain. Only *No Family* appeared during her lifetime. It focuses on the decision of an Australian couple to take into their family a woman with her baby son who, victim of a deception, believes herself married to their son who has died in the war. *Call up Your Ghosts* (1945), written with Dymphna **Cusack**, is a satire on the Australian publishing industry and its neglect of Australian writers, whose unhappy ghosts return to create turmoil in the bookshop where their work is being used merely to prop up table legs.

Plays include: *No Family* (3f,2m, 1946) in W. Moore and in Pfisterer; *Call Up Your Ghosts* (with **Cusack**, 2f,5m) in Spender 1988; *The Waiter Speaks* (MS); *The Survivors* (MS c.1908); *Sophia* (MS1913); *Virtue* (MS, 1917); *The English Jackeroo* (MS c.1917)

See also: *Miles Franklin in America: Her Unknown (Brilliant) Career* by Verna Coleman, London and Sydney: Angus and Robertson, 1981.

Ketti Frings
American, 1915–81

Frings's stage adaptation of Thomas Wolfe's novel *Look Homeward Angel* won the Pulitzer Prize in 1958. It is the moving story of a young boy, Eugene Gant, struggling to break away from a circumscribed existence in his mother's rambling boarding house, where the needs of the patrons have always been placed above those of the family. He becomes trapped between his mother's obsession with making money, his stone mason father's impotent self-consciousness of failure and his consumptive brother's failure to escape. The death of Ben, his brother, at last gives Eugene the impetus to leave to find a larger world outside and within. While Frings wrote a few more plays and with Gary Geld and Peter Udell adapted her Pulitzer success as a musical, *Angel* (1978), she never had a comparable stage success.

Plays include: *Foxfire* (1955), *Beautiful Stranger* (1954), *Mr Sycamore* (1974 – all screen); *Look Homeward Angel* (9f, 10m, 1957) and in Gassner; *Walking Happy* (musical, 1967) – both French.

Sue Frumin
British, 1949–

Many of Frumin's plays draw on family history and her experience as a lesbian and Jew. *The Housetrample*, a one-woman show, evokes the experiences of her mother, a Jewish Czech refugee arriving in wartime Manchester, who worked on the buses and in factories, confronting prejudice and isolation while coping with her fears for her beloved friend Lili, left behind in Prague. Frumin's writing is often funny and fantastic: spoofing soap opera in *Home Sweet Home* (MS) for her own company, Shameful Practice, or foregrounding the lesbian subtext of pantomime (principal 'boy' meets girl) in *Fanny Whittington* (MS). *Raising the Wreck*, produced in **Gay Sweatshop**'s X10 Festival, used song and storytelling in rediscovering the hidden history of women pirates, escapees from social convention and sexual oppression, haunting a sunken galleon.

Plays include: *Bohemian Rhapsody* (MS); *Rabbit in a Trap* (MS); *The Housetrample* (1f, 1984) in Davis 2; *Fine and Dandy,* (MS, 1999).
    See also App. 2: Freeman, Collis in Griffiths and Llewellyn-Jones.

Zona Gale

American, 1874–1938

Gale's writing encompasses short stories, journalism, feminist pieces and radio serials; many of her plays were adapted from or into novels. She was the daughter of a railroad engineer in Portage, Wisconsin, and many of her plays deal with small-town midwestern life. In *The Neighbours* assistance to others reinforces the community when its women rally round to help a widow support her adoptive son. By contrast, *Miss Lulu Bett*, which won the 1921 Pulitzer Prize for drama, and *Mister Pitt*, depict communities that are narrow and judgemental. The downtrodden Lulu, exploited as unpaid cook and housekeeper and belittled as an unmarried woman by her sister and pompous brother-in-law, becomes a social embarrassment when she marries an apparent bigamist. The trivial sameness of small-town life is reinforced by identical repeated scenes of family gossip, creating a context where Lulu's self-assertion, defying the family to demand a chance at happiness, becomes a radical act.

Plays include: *The Neighbours* (6f,2m) in *Wisconsin Plays* ed. Thomas H. Dickinson, NY: Huebsch, 1917; *Miss Lulu Bett* (5f,4m) NY/London: Appleton, 1921 and in Barlow 1981; *Mister Pitt* (13f,5m, 1925); *Faint Perfume* (7f,6m, 1934) – both: NY: Appleton.

See also: *Still Small Voice: the Biography of Zona Gale* by August Derleth, NY and London: Appleton-Century, 1940; *Zona Gale* by Harold P. Simonson, NY: Twayne, 1962; Stephen in *The Theatre Annual* 40, 1985.

Miriam Gallagher

Irish, 1940–

Gallagher comes from Waterford and trained as a speech therapist before beginning to write. She sees her plays as variations on a broad theme of freedom, ranging from work growing out of her experience teaching in men's and women's prisons, to pieces such as *Labels*, an indictment of a callous medical establishment whose answer to psychiatric problems is the constant prescription of drugs. They include musical interludes celebrating Irish composers, dance dramas drawing on legend and a disturbing surreal trilogy on food themes, *Just Dessert* – in *Omelettes*, customers in a restaurant are manipulated by three macabre waiters. *Shyllag* is an atmospheric monologue spoken by an Everywoman and haunted by *Hamlet*. Set in a railway station which is also limbo, it maps a Europe criss-crossed with train lines, travelled by history and its terrors, but also marked by exchanges between people and the search for freedom.

Plays include: *Shyllag* (1f, 1993); *Labels* (4f,4m, 1985); *Omlettes* (6m,2f, 1985); *Lemon Souffle* (3f,3m, 1985); *Easter Eggs* (5f,2m, 1990); *The Sealwoman and the Fisher* (2f,3m+, 1984); *Nocturne* (1f,1m, 1987); *Bohemians* (1f,2m+1, 1987); *Dusty Bluebells* (9f,2m) all in *Fancy Footwork: Selected Plays* Dublin: Society of Irish Playwrights, 1997.

Fatima Gallaire
Algerian, 1944–

Gallaire studied literature and film, first in Algiers then in Paris, where she settled. Her plays focus on outcasts and the socially marginal, the outspoken condemned as crazy, threatened and even killed by the community that rejects them. In *You Have Come Back* a woman returns to her North African village after twenty years, having dared marry a Frenchman, an infidel, in defiance of her father, now dead. His terrible legacy is to condemn her to be clubbed to death by the village elders for her betrayal of Islam, along with those who defend her: her ancient nurse, a cripple, a madwoman and an alcoholic old man. Gallaire's graphic depiction of cruelty is shocking in its brutality. Equally shocking is the language of *Madame Bertin's Testimony*, an old woman's candid account of her sexual experience in marriage, her love and hatred, desire and repulsion for her husband, a double to whom she has become inextricably bound.

Translated plays include: *You Have Come Back* (1988, 13f,3m,dp) tr. Jill MacDougall in *Ubu* 1 and 3 and as *Princesses*, tr. **Oakes**, (MS from agent); *Madame Bertin's Testimony* (5f,1m,dp) tr. MacDougall in *Monologues: Plays from Martinique, France, Algeria, Québec*, NY: Ubu Rep, 1995.

Griselda Gambaro
Argentinian, 1928–

Gambaro is one of the most prolific and significant Latin American authors. Her brilliant and chilling plays reflect and examine the moral and political climate of an Argentina marked by coup and counter-coup, brutal repression and violence: 'this schizophrenic country, dirty yet courteous. Life here is surreal', as Gambaro has described it. Early plays such as *The Walls* (1963) already formed part of 'the theatre of crisis', forecasting the era of the *desaparecidos*, while *The Siamese Twins* (MS, 1967) used an absurdist image to suggest the schizophrenic nature of a psyche divided against itself. A man who is both torturer/hangman and victim was read as a political allegory suggesting the fratricidal persecution of a country torn apart from within. Often described as Gambaro's masterpiece, *Information for Foreigners* is designed as a promenade performance for a series of linked rooms, offering what its author calls, 'a guided tour of the places of repression and indignity'. The text juxtaposes *Othello*, children's games, the deadpan language of censored press articles and grim jokes. *Bad Blood* (1981), set in the 1840s, is a gripping and disturbing play, exploring the barely hidden violence of relationships within a wealthy family that becomes a metaphor for a brutally repressive society where collusion with the powerful becomes the way to escape victimization.

Translations include: *Information For Foreigners* (60+ various, 1970s), also extract in *Literary Review*, Summer 1989; *The Walls* (3m, 1965); *Antigona Furiosa* (1f,2m, 1986) in *Three Plays by Griselda Gambaro* tr. Marguerite Feitlowitz, Evanston, IL: Northwestern UP, 1992; *Loose Ends* (1f,1m) tr. Catherine Boyle, in *Travesia* VI, no. 1; *Putting Two and Two Together* (MS tr. Nick Drake); *Bad Blood* (MS, tr. M. Feitlowitz); *The Camp* (1f,7+m) tr. William Oliver, in Oliver; *Saying Yes* (2m, 1972) in *Latin American Plays* ed. Sebastian Doggart, NHB, 1996.

See also: *Knives and Angels: Women Writers in Latin America* ed. Susan Bassnett, London: Zed Books Ltd, 1990; *Theatre of Crisis: Drama and Politics in Latin America* by Diana Taylor, Lexington, KY: Kentucky UP, 1990; Feitlowitz in *Theater* Summer/Fall 1990; App. 2: Betsko and Koenig.

Lucy Gannon
English, 1948–

Gannon began as a writer for theatre following 20 years as nurse, military policewoman and residential social worker, experiences she has drawn upon in much of her work. She has become best known in recent years for her television work, which includes the highly successful series *Peak Practice*, *Soldier, Soldier* and *Bramwell* (about the career and personal struggles of a Victorian woman doctor).

Both the acclaimed *Keeping Tom Nice* and *Dancing Attendance* deal with the effect of taking care of someone with a disability. Tom is a severely disabled 24-year-old whose parents have devoted their lives to his care in a mixture of love, rage, frustration and denial of their own needs and emotions. *Dancing Attendance* becomes a power struggle between Jack Slaney, owner of a printing firm who is confined to a wheelchair following a stroke, his daughter and the unemployed man whom he takes on as carer.

Gannon is concerned with what the desperation of long-term unemployment does to an individual or a town. In *Raping the Gold*, she concentrates with her usual humour and gritty realism on a Midlands community where joblessness has become the norm. Gabby, former boss of the closed-down chainworks, now focuses all his energy and inspiration on archery and the dream of piercing the golden centre of the target; Stuart attempts ineptly to instil the values of caring, and Leon has no target for his rage and frustration at recognising that the only way to escape a hopeless future is 'to stand on [someone] else to do it'.

Plays include: *Wicked Old Nellie* (MS); *Janet and John* (MS); *Trip-Trap* (TV); *Tender Loving Care* (MS); *Testimony of a Child* (MS); *Raping the Gold* (1f,6m, 1988); *Keeping Tom Nice* (2f,3m, 1990) also in Kilgore; *Dancing Attendance* (1f,2m, 1990). All Warner Chappell.

Margareta Garpe
Swedish, 1944–

Feminist playwright and director whose productions include Ibsen's *Ghosts* for Swedish TV and a documentary, *Calcutta One Day*, Garpe has also written screenplays. *For Julia*, like *Child in Our Time*, confronts the effects of adult actions on children who have to deal with their consequences. Its compassionate examination of the relationship between a mother and her daughter takes place as Julia, preparing to leave home, confronts her self-involved actress mother with the effect of her kicking out the live-in lover of eight years' standing and her suicide attempt on the child who loved him like a father and who found her body. Other plays include the influential *Good God Girls* (1975) which traces the development of the Swedish feminist movement from 1924 to 1974, one of a series of plays co-written with director Suzanne Osten, and *All Days, All Nights* (1992), about the problems of old age.

Untranslated plays include: *The Witches, Let them Burn; Sally and Freedom*.

Unpublished translations include: *Child in Our Time* (tr. V. Lindfors, 1978).

Published translations: *For Julia* (2f,1m, 1985) tr. Harry G. Carlson, in Brask.

Barbara Garson
American, 1941–

Journalist and activist, Garson was a veteran of the Free Speech Movement in Berkeley and her best-known play began life as a brief skit against the Vietnam War. *MacBird!* achieved enormous notoriety in the late 1960s for its brilliant topical satire which used Shakespeare's *Macbeth* (along with snatches of *Hamlet* and *Julius Caesar*) as the framework for a biting political satire on Lyndon B. Johnson's presidency and the country's bloody involvement in Vietnam, events which fit almost uncannily well into the outline of Shakespeare's narrative. JFK becomes the murdered and deposed Duncan or 'Ken O'Dunc'. The three witches are recast as a beatnik woman, a black activist and an old leftist, demonstrators against the war,. There is no redemptive force in this world and MacBird's opponents are united only in opposition, while their leader, Robert Ken O'Dunc, explaining his fulfilment of the prophecy that none with human heart can depose MacBird, declares that his father had each son's heart cut out at birth and 'in their place, precision apparatus/Of steel and plastic tubing was inserted'. Garson went on to write further skits and puppet shows for the anti-war movement.

Plays include: *The Department* (MS); *Going Co-op* (MS); *MacBird!* (5f, 14m) NY: Grove Press, 1967.

Gay Sweatshop (Women's Group)
Founded Britain, 1976–

The alternative theatre movement of the late 1970s and early 1980s placed great emphasis on authenticity of experience as the root of work, and collaborative process as the way of generating material. *Care and Control*, commissioned to address the legal and societal pressures facing lesbian mothers in custody battles, was scripted by **Wandor** out of company workshops. It was the second Gay Sweatshop women's play following the key coming-out play, Jill Posener's *Any Woman Can* (1976 in Davis 1).

Other writers began to find individual voices through the creative process: Kate Phelps, Angela Stewart-Parks who scripted Sweatshop's *I Like Me Like This* (MS, 1979) with Sharon Nassauer, and Tash Fairbanks who went on to write with the Siren theatre company. Later the company hosted the Gay Sweatshop x10 and x12 seasons, in part aimed at redressing the company's male-dominated balance by finding plays by and about lesbians. Jackie **Kay**'s first play was read in x10 (followed by the commissioning of *Twice Over*) as were Sue **Frumin**'s *Raising the Wreck* and plays by Cath Kilcoyne (*Julie*, 1985 in Davis 2), Maro Green and Caroline Griffin (*More*, 1989 in Remnant 6) and Adele Saleem, the later work reflecting a diversity of lesbian experience including black, disabled and Jewish voices.

Plays include: *Care and Control* (5f,2m, 1977) in Wandor/Strike. See App. 1 for Davis and Remnant anthologies).

See also App. 2: Freeman, introduction to Osment anthology; Collis in Griffiths and Llewellyn-Jones, Sierz.

Shirley Gee
English, 1932–

After working as an actress, Gee began writing for radio, achieving success with *Stones* in 1974, followed by many other radio plays or adaptations (including Galsworthy's *The Forsyte Saga*), several of which were later adapted for stage. *Typhoid Mary*, a thriller in form, like many of Gee's plays based on historical fact, charts the increasingly bewildered passage through New York of Irish immigrant Mary Mallon, desperate to work and spreading disease, death and terror in her wake (cf. **Schenkar**). *Ask For the Moon* parallels historical and contemporary exploitation, juxtaposing on stage sweated garment workers in Thatcherite Britain with Victorian lace workers, beset by poverty, illness and blindness, but maintaining a pride in their work denied to their modern counterparts. Both *Never in My Lifetime*, a love story between a Catholic girl and a Protestant British soldier in Northern Ireland (winner of the Susan Smith Blackburn Award), and *Warrior* explore the desperate divisions of war. Hannah Snell in *Warrior* disguises herself as a boy to follow her husband to the wars and discovers its catastrophe first hand and through the calamitous visions of future destruction that begin to haunt her both at sea and later on stage when she and her comrades turn to theatre to broadcast their anti-war message.

Plays include: *Typhoid Mary* (3f,3m,id) in BBC Radio, 1979; *Never in My Lifetime* (5f,4m) in BBC Radio, 1983, also French; *Flights* (TV, 1986); *Against the Wind* (MS, radio); *Ask For the Moon* (6f,1m) Faber, 1986; *Warrior* (3f,8m) French, 1991.

Pam Gems
English, 1925–

Born in Hampshire, Gems grew up in poverty with a single-parent mother before joining the WRNS and attending Manchester University as an ex-servicewoman. She began writing as a response to the isolation of bringing up children and in the 1970s moved to London where she encountered the new wave of feminism. Female characters, historical, contemporary, literary or semi-mythical are central in her work from her first major success onwards. *Dusa, Fish, Stas and Vi* focuses on four women sharing a flat: Dusa, desperate to find her kids taken by her ex-husband; anorexic Vi; Stas, earning her PhD tuition fees as a call-girl; Fish trying to reconcile her political commitment and feminist independence with her devestation at her boyfriend's leaving.

Several of Gems's plays deal with gender confusion and cross-dressing: the dilemmas of Queen Christina of Sweden, raised as a boy but told as an adult that her duty is to marry and bear a successor to the throne, or *Aunt Mary* which, through the marriage of two transvestite writers, explores a high camp underworld – and its vulnerability to hostile outsiders. The enormous success of Gems's *Piaf*, a biographical play interspersed with Edith Piaf's songs, features a gutsily drawn central character who provided the model for the more recent *Marlene* (1996), about Dietrich. *Camille* also featured an unusually tough central female role in a desentimentalized reworking of Dumas's story, exploring issues of consumption, commodity and female objectification. *La Pasionaria* also reappraised a mythologized heroine, the peasant woman who became an impassioned member of the Communist Party at the approach to the Spanish Civil War. In *Stanley,* British artist Stanley Spencer is the subject of this more recent biographical play that wittily and insightfully juxtaposes the power of his tormented imaginative passion and the adolescent mess of his emotional relationships with women. Highly prolific, Gems's work encompasses translations and adaptations, including **Przybyzsewska** (*The Danton Affair, The Snow Palace*) and Chekhov.

Plays include: *My Warren and After Birthday* (MS, 1973); *The Amiable Courtship of Miz Venus and Wild Bill* (MS, 1973); *Go West Young Woman* (MS, 1974); *Dusa, Fish, Stas and Vi* (4f, 1976) in Wandor 1 and French, 1977; *Queen Christina* (11f, 19m) Amber Lane Press, 1977 and in Remnant 5; *Aunt Mary* (2f,2m, 1982) in Wandor 3; *The Treat* (MS, 1982); *Camille* (7f,21m,dp, 1984); *Loving Women* (2f,1m, 1984) and *Piaf* (5f,9m, 1979) in *Three Plays*, Penguin, 1985; *La Pasionaria* (MS, 1985); *Deborah's Daughter* (3f,4m, 1994) and *Stanley* (6f,6m+, 1996) – both NHB; *Marlene* (2f,1m,id, 1999) and *The Snow Palace*, (3f,3m, 1998) – both Oberon.

See also App. 2: Carlson in Hart; Griffiths and Llewellyn-Jones; Stephenson and Langridge; Betsko and Koenig.

Alice Gerstenberg
American, 1885–1972

Born in Chicago and educated at Bryn Mawr college, Gerstenberg began writing plays for students in about 1908 before having her first major hit with a dramatization of Lewis Carroll's *Alice in Wonderland* in New York in 1915. She later helped establish the Playwrights Theatre of Chicago.

Many of her plays deal with social rituals and surfaces and the more savage emotions they repress. In *He Said and She Said* – doubts are sown in an old friendship by a gossip-monger: the repeated variations of 'who said what to whom' take on an incantatory pattern, an early example of Gerstenberg's formal experiment. In *Overtones*, the polite surface of two women's afternoon tea is interrupted by the savageries of their primitive selves, raging to fulfil their desires for money or love. Several pieces have theatrical settings satirizing contemporary drama, from playwriting-by-numbers commercial melodrama in *The Pot Boiler* which ends with the cast crying 'Shoot the author', to the mock-futurist *Illuminati* and the Little Theatre movement (in which Gerstenberg was herself active) of *Upstage*, where a pretentious European director is ousted in favour of a theatre that will begin 'to express the soil, seed and harvest of our own Americans'.

Plays include: *He Said and She Said*– (3f,1m); *Overtones* (4f, 1915) also in Sullivan and Hatch; *The Unseen* (2f,1m); *The Buffer* (4f,2m); *Attuned* (1f); *The Pot Boiler* (2f,5m, 1917); *Hearts* (4f); *Beyond* (1f); *Fourteen* (3f); *The Illuminati in Drama Libre* (1m,1f) – all in *Ten One-Act Plays*, NY: Longmans, Green & Co., 1921; *The Setback* (3f,1m); *Mere Man* (5f); *The Menu* (2m,1f); *Facing Fact* (2f,1m); *Upstage* (9f,3m); *Rhythm* (2m,1f); *The Opera Matinee* (14f); *At the Club* (5m); *The Puppeteer* (1f,1m); *Latchkeys* (5f,6m) in *Comedies*; *Alice in Wonderland* (1929) – all NY: Longmans, Green & Co., 1930. See also: Shafer.

Rebecca Gilman

American, 1964–

Winner of many awards in the USA and the UK, *The Glory of Living* is a visceral and desolate piece exploring lives of deprivation, lovelessness and casual brutality in the backroads of the American South. Lisa leaves her whoring mother to take off with Clint on a rape and killing tour. She lures young girls back to cheap motels; he rapes them and, on his orders, she kills them. In the second act she unnerves her defence lawyer with her deadened moral sense and fatalistic acceptance of a sentence to Death Row. She incriminates herself and the society she lives in when she says of victims, 'if I hadn't called the police . . . wouldn't anybody even know they were gone?'. Her next play, *Spinning into Butter*, is set in a comfortable, white, middle-class, liberal arts college in Vermont. It's a hard-hitting and provocative exploration of white middle-class guilt around racism, in a society which responds with complacency, evasion, silence and cynical tokenism. Gilman explores the horrified embarrassment which confronts Sarah, the Dean of Students, when she admits to her own racism, fear and hatred of black people and the self-loathing and desire for exoneration which it conceals.

Plays include: *Speech Therapy* (MS, 1999); *The Land of Little Horses* (MS); *The Glory of Living* (4f,5m, 1999); *Spinning into Butter* (2f,5m, 2001); *Boy Gets Girl* (3f,4m, 2001). All Faber.
　　See also App. 2: Sierz.

Zinaida Nikolaevna Gippius

Russian, 1869–1945

Renowned as a symbolist poet, Gippius also wrote stories, diaries, literary criticism and plays that expressed her radical sexual attitudes advocating bisexuality, androgyny and female equality. With her husband, poet and philosopher Dmitry Merezhkovskii, she was a member of the Russian 'Silver Age', which believed in attaining a synthesis of spirituality and art. She became central to a major intellectual circle in late nineteenth-century St Petersburg that encouraged the translation into Russian of the French Decadents and Symbolists. Her *Sacred Blood* is a haunting Christian symbolist fable about a *rusalka* or mermaid's desire for an immortal soul. *The Green Ring*, published with an afterword giving its theatrical history, explores the gradual liberation of Finotchka from the turbulent emotional manipulations of her mother and disillusioned discovery of her idealized father's ongoing affair, as she finds support and strength in the ferment of philosophical and spiritual ideas espoused by a group of ruthlessly idealistic young people on the threshold of the new century.

Untranslated plays: *Yes and No*; *Poppy Blossoms*.

Translated plays: *Sacred Blood* (3f,2m, 1901, tr. M. F. Zirin and C. Schuler) in K. Kelly; *The Green Ring* (10f,10m, 1914, tr. S. S. Koteliansky) London: C. W. Daniel, 1920.

See also: Arkin and Shollar, *Selected Works*, Illinois UP, 1972; App. 2: Schuler in Laughlin and Schuler.

Susan Glaspell
American, 1876?–1948

Born in Davenport, Iowa, Glaspell worked as a journalist before marrying George Cram Cook and moving to Greenwich Village where they became key members of the bohemian artistic community there that included **Boyce** and **Millay**. In 1916 they founded the highly influential Provincetown Players that produced many of Eugene O'Neill's early plays and most of Glaspell's work.

Light early pieces, such as *Suppressed Desires*, satirize psychoanalysis and contemporary marriage, but her most acclaimed and powerful work deals with outsiders, the marginal and otherness, especially in relation to the feminine. The two women of the classic *Trifles*, are, from the point of view of the male authority figures, minor characters, assigned to collect clothes for the arrested Mrs Wright, while the men search for clues to the murder of her husband. However it is the women who piece together from trifles a story of isolation, sterile marriage to an insensitive man and a motive for murder – and who choose to suppress the evidence to protect a woman with whom they can too easily identify. Claire, in the remarkable *The Verge*, rejects social convention, morality and family in passionate pursuit of creativity and the alien, desperately striving to produce a new species of plant, which becomes a complex metaphor suggesting spiritual revelation, female passion and madness. The Pulitzer prizewinning *Alison's House*, inspired by the life of Emily Dickinson, explores the Stanhope family's conflict over the discovery of love poems to a married man by the celebrated Alison Stanhope, eighteen years dead. There are those who would destroy the poems to preserve the sanctity of her memory and those who assert that her expression of the struggle between love and self-denial must be allowed speech.

Plays include: *Trifles* (2f,3m, 1916) in numerous anthologies inc. Kriegel, Barlow; *Close the Book* (5f,3m, 1920); *The People* (2f,10m,dp, 1917); *Woman's Honour* (6f,3m, 1918); *Suppressed Desires* (2f,1m, 1915) also in Cook, Ozieblo; *Tickless Time* (with George Cram Cook, 4f,2m, 1918) – all in *Trifles and Six Other Short Plays*, London: Benn, 1926; *Trifles, Inheritors* (5f,11m,dp, 1921); *The Verge* (4f,5m, 1921); *The Outside* (2f,3m, 1917–18), also in France and in Clements – all in *Plays by Susan Glaspell* ed. C. W. Bigsby, Cambridge: CUP, 1987; *Bernice* (3f,2m) London: Benn, 1924; *Alison's House* (6f,5m) French, 1930 and in *Six Plays*, London: Victor Gollancz, 1930.

See also: *Susan Glaspell* by Arthur Waterman, NY: Twayne, 1966; *Susan Glaspell: Essays on her Theater and Fiction* ed. Linda Ben-Zvi, Ann Arbor: UMI, 1995; App. 2: Ozieblo and Larabee in Schlueter.

Joanna McLelland Glass

Canadian, 1936–

Glass, originally from Saskatoon, trained as an actress before marrying and settling in the USA. Her tightly constructed plays deal poignantly with loss and with struggles between generations. While *Grandmother's House* suggests a conventional family drama – where the extended family, returning for Thanksgiving, will be eventually reunited despite differences – it works against such easy resolutions. After the death of the matriarchal grandmother, her daughter refuses to assume her role, asserting her own right to peace, privacy and creativity when her divorced children propose a mass return to the family home (cf. **Stern**). In *If We Are Women* two grandmothers are forced to confront their granddaughter's independence and refusal to live out their frustrated dreams of college education. *Artichoke* frames the action within a narration of events from the point of view of two eccentric bachelor farmers, reinforcing their folkloric quality and a sense of community that is both supportive and stifling in which Margaret, estranged from her husband, aches for romantic fulfilment. *Play Memory* similarly frames the action within the heroine's memories of her childhood and teenage years, presenting a bruising chronicle of a proud man's descent into alcoholism, violence and willed self-destruction following his betrayal and public humiliation, and the emotional damage he inflicts on his daughter.

Plays include: *Canadian Gothic* (2f,2m) in *Best Short* 1978 and with *American Modern* (1f,1m), DPS, 1977; *Artichoke* (2f,5m), DPS, 1979; *To Grandmother's House We Go* (6f,2m), French, 1981; *Play Memory* (3f,6m, 1983) in Bessai & Kerr, also French, 1984; *If We Are Women* (4f) Playwrights Canada and French, 1994. Both also with *Yesteryear* in Sherman.

See also: *The Joanna Glass Papers* compiled Jean M. Moore & Jean F. Tener, Calgary: Calgary UP, 1989.

Sue Glover
Scottish, 1943–

Glover's work reclaims Scottish history and especially women's experience within it, focusing on the isolated and outcast, whether Alexander Selkirk, the original for Defoe's Robinson Crusoe, in *Largo* or Rachel, the nobleman's wife in *The Straw Chair*. Dismissed as mad and forcibly exiled to the island of Hirta (St Kilda) for threatening to reveal her husband's political duplicity, Rachel's situation is parallel to and yet different from that of the young minister's wife, Isabel, whose exile to the island enables her to discover both friendship with the Gaelic-speaking local women and love for her husband. In the acclaimed *Bondagers* Glover traces the lives of six women farmworkers in the Borders of 1860 over the course of a year from one hiring fair to the next, exploring the economic, political and sexual pressures that impact on their lives, the insecurity of their existence, the tensions between the married tenants' wives and the single women workers. Permeated by the rhythms of work and the lyric cadences of the local language and song, the piece creates a haunting and vivid evocation of another era.

Plays include: *The Seal Wife* (5f,1m, MS, 1980); *Sacred Hearts* (MS, 1994); *An Island in Largo* (1981); *The Bubble Boys* (4f/m, 1981) in *You Don't Know You're Born* ed. Rony Robinson, Hodder & Stoughton, 1992; *Bondagers* (6f, 1991) in *Made in Scotland: an Anthology of New Scottish Plays* ed. Ian Brown and Mark Fisher, Methuen, 1995 and with *The Straw Chair* (3f,1m, 1988) Methuen, 1997.

See also: Horvat and Bell in Christianson and Lumsden; App. 2: Stevenson and Wallace; Triesman in Griffiths and Llewellyn-Jones.

Rose Leiman Goldemberg
American, 1928–

A native New Yorker born on Staten Island, Goldemberg has taught playwriting and written non-fiction. In *Marching As To War* a soldier leaves his bride to fight in the American revolutionary war, but gradually this fades into the Civil War, the First and Second World Wars and finally Vietnam in a nightmarish vision of ceaseless war, while his bride endlessly waits. *Letters Home* is based on Aurelia Schober Plath's edition of her daughter's letters (see **Plath**). An affecting and powerful piece, it explores the question of each one's responsibility towards the other and the intense struggle between artist daughter and loving mother as she fights to keep her child from suicide. Goldemberg also wrote an acclaimed special about immigrant life in America, *Land of Hope*, and a CBS five-hour mini-series, *A Celebration of Woman*.

Plays include: *Letters Home* (2f, 1979), in Miles 1980 and Wandor vol. 2; *Marching As To War* (2f,4m+) DPS, 1971; *Doubles for Time-Life* (screen); *The Rabinowitz Gamble* (MS); *Gandhiji* (MS, 1970); *The Crossroad* (MS, 1975).
    See also App. 2: Helle in Hart.

Ruth Gordon
American, 1896–1985

Best known as a highly successful actress, Gordon was married to writer-director Garson Kanin, with whom she developed much of her stage work, he directing, she performing or writing. Their own relationship contributed to screenplays such as *Adam's Rib* (1949) and *Pat and Mike* (1952) that wittily dissect contemporary marriage, memorably brought to life by Katharine Hepburn and Spencer Tracy. Ahead of her time, her plays are also notable for presenting couples in which the woman works, wisecracks and initiates action equally with the man. *Over Twenty One* drew on her Second World War experiences as an army wife, as the heroine takes over her husband's job as newspaper reporter when he starts officer training.
    Further plays and screenplays have backstage themes. *A Double Life* is about an actor playing Othello and the autobiographical play *Years Ago* is an affectionate portrayal of her adolescent stage-struck aspirations and her eccentric family's reaction (later filmed as *The Actress*, 1953). In

The Leading Lady, Gordon dissects a less than successful marriage, marred by the husband's jealousy and bullying. After he dies, the play charts actress Gay Marriott's progression from being one half of a stage couple to eventual independence and an individual career.

Plays: *Over Twenty One* (5f,6m) NY: Random House, 1944; *Years Ago* (5f,4m) NY: Viking, 1947; *The Leading Lady* (9f,11m) DPS, 1949; *A Very Rich Woman* (8f,7m) French, 1964.

See also: *Myself Among Others*, NY: Atheneum, 1971, *My Side*, NY: Harper and Row, 1976 (autobiographies); App. 2: Shafer.

Elsie Park Gowan
Canadian, 1906–99

Gowan moved from Scotland to Edmonton, Alberta in 1912, where she worked as a teacher and attended the university, becoming involved in the Little Theatre movement alongside her friend and fellow playwright, Gwen Pharis **Ringwood**. A prolific dramatist, especially for radio, her work reflects her interest in the past (in plays on aspects of Canadian history) and her socialist, feminist and pacifist beliefs.

In *The Hungry Spirit* Marian resists moral pressure from her mother and brother to give up her hard-won savings and college plans to support her brother and enable him to marry the young woman he has got pregnant. In the comedy, *Back to the Kitchen*, the author of a book proposing that women's only place is in supporting men is forced to rethink when the city's women refuse to serve or work for him. He is beaten up as a fascist and only saved by the ministrations of a woman doctor. Strong women figures appear throughout Gowan's work from geologist Miranda in *Caveman*, who persuades writer John Duncan away from his position of fence-sitting to take an active part in resolving a violent land dispute, to the feisty, rejected mail-order bride in *Breeches*.

Plays include: *God Made the Country* (MS, 1933); *Breeches From Bond Street* (2f,4m, 1949); *The Last Caveman* (3f,8m, 1938); *Homestead* (1f,2m, 1933); *The Hungry Spirit* (3f,2m, 1935); *High Green Gate* (5f,4m, 1952); *Back to the Kitchen, Woman!* (9f,2m, 1941) in *The Hungry Spirit: Selected Plays and Prose* ed. Moira Day, Edmonton: NeWest Press, 1992.

See also: Wagner in THC, 8, 1987

Oriel Gray
Australian, 1920–

While most of Gray's published plays are for children, her adult plays, like many of those of her generation, grew out of her political activity and were often produced by the left-wing New Theatre League (cf. **Brand**, K. S. **Prichard**). She also wrote work for radio and adaptations such as the poignant, highly effective *Lawson*, based on Henry Lawson's campfire tales of outback life. Gray addressed contemporary Australian social issues in works such as *Western Limits* (MS, 1946), with its Land Girl heroine and focus on land erosion and racial problems in the outback. This was an issue also central to *Had We But World Enough* (MS, 1948), in which local prejudice erupts when a young woman teacher casts an Aboriginal as Mary in a Nativity play. *The Torrents* shared the major Playwrights Advisory Board prize in 1955 with Ray Lawlor's *Summer of the Seventeenth Doll*, but remained unpublished until recently. Its independent New Woman heroine arrives to work on a newspaper in a goldmining town, shocking her colleagues, but eventually winning support for her courage in supporting change. Notably, though she encourages the proprietor's playboy son to become a serious journalist, she rejects his marriage proposals because of his immaturity.

Plays include: *Sky Without Birds* (MS, 1950); *Burst of Summer* (3f,7m, 1960) in *Plays of the 60s* v1, Currency, 2000; *The King Who Wouldn't* (MS, 1952); *Drive a Hard Bargain* in Duncan 1955; *Lawson* (8f,18m+,dp, 1943) Yackandandah (revised) 1989; *The Torrents* (2f,11m) in Spender.

See also: *Exit Left: Memoirs of a Scarlet Woman* (autobiography), Sydney: Penguin, 1985; Hillel in *Australian*; App. 2: Rees.

Bonnie Greer
American, 1948–

An African-American born in Chicago, Greer was instrumental in setting up the Public Theater's Playwriting in Schools programme in New York City under Joseph Papp. She then settled in London where she recreated the programme with ReSisters theatre company. She works as broadcaster, director, critic and is author of the novel *Hanging by Her Teeth* (1993) which, like several of her plays, addresses black people's experience of and influence on Europe.

Vigil Part II grew out of the desire to explore women's silence as protest, means of oppression or 'mute testimony to life as lived'. It focuses on a black woman in her ghetto apartment, leafing through fashion magazines, watching television, ironing her maid's uniform, fantasizing – a constant bombardment of images of white glamour.

Silence is no longer the response in *Munda Negra*, whose heroine speaks her rage with eloquent bitterness in a powerful piece which explores the confrontation between a black American culture experienced by Anna as one of self-assertion and resistance and a black British tradition of compromise. Her conflicts are also internal as she struggles with Little Anna, the white self-image she painted as a child, with Catholicism and, as a critic, with a Western art tradition that erases or distorts black people. Central is the question of who can best bring up the black daughter of Neville, Anna's dead ex-lover, she or his white wife. Relationships of daughters with, often absent, mothers is also central to both *Dancing on Black Water* (MS, 1994) and the mystery, *Saudade* (MS, 1994).

Plays include: *Zebra Days* (MS); *A Few White Boys Talking* (MS); *In the Country of the Young* (MS, 1993); *Vigil Part II* (1f) in *Acting Up!*, *Heresies*, vol. 5, no. 1, issue 17; *Munda Negra* (3f,3m) in Brewster 3; *Striding the Blast* (MS, 1997); *The Other Europe – Omar* (MS, 1998).

Lady Augusta Gregory
Irish, 1852–1932

A chance meeting between Gregory and W. B. Yeats in 1898 drew her deeply into the Celtic Literary Renaissance movement and led to the founding of the Abbey Theatre. Over the next thirty years she served as its fundraiser, manager and producer and as playwright, with Yeats and Synge, formed the triumvirate of major Irish nationalist poetic playwrights, drawing inspiration from the legends and life of Ireland, especially the Western Isles.

Gregory's plays, nearly fifty of them, include translations from Irish and of Molière into the western Irish idiom. Many are set in Cloon, a mythologized version of her own village of Gort on the borders of County Clare and County Galway, and include marvellously funny comedies and poetic, atmospheric tragedies. Gossip, community judgement and the mythologizing tendency in Irish culture are central concerns, analysed in tragi-comic mode in *The Image* or celebrated in comic mode in *Spreading the News* (in which a minor incident is distorted out of all proportion into adultery and murder) or in *Hyacinth Halvey*, whose hero desperately tries to rid himself of an unearned reputation for virtue. Tragedy emerges where loyalty to or betrayal of the nationalist struggle forms a stark backdrop to events. In *The Gaol Gate* Cahel's wife and mother undertake to spread word of his heroism in dying for refusing to betray the cause, while *The Deliverer* uses the story of the rejection of Moses by the Israelites in Egypt to condemn Ireland's rejection of Parnell. The piling of distortion on misinterpretation on prejudice on fear is taken to a bitter conclusion. Other plays (*Devorgilla, Kincora*) draw on the myths of Ireland, while yet others are moral and magical fables.

Plays include: much anthologized are *Spreading the News* (3f,7m, 1904); *The Rising of the Moon* (4m, 1907); *The Workhouse Ward* (1f,2m, 1908); *Dave* (2f,3m, 1927); *Twenty Five* (3f,3m, 1903); *Hyacinth Halvey* (2f,4m, 1906); *The Gaol Gate* (2f,1m) *The Image* (2f,5m, 1909) e.g. see Martin, Pollock, Hogan & Kilroy, Arkins and Shollar, Thomas, Wilde. All plays are in Ann Saddlmyer's 1970–1 edition of *Collected Works*: v1: *Comedies*, v2; *Tragedies and Tragi-Comedies*. v3; *Wonder and the Supernatural*. v4: *Translations, Adaptations, Collaborations*. Also *Selected Plays* ed. Mary Fitzgerald. All Gerrards Cross: Colin Smythe.

See also: *Lady Gregory: Fifty Years After* ed. Ann Saddlemyer and Colin Smythe, Gerrards Cross: Colin Smythe, 1987; *Lady Gregory: the Woman Behind the Irish Literary Renaissance* by Mary Lou Kohfeldt London: André Deutsch, 1985.

Susan Griffin
American, 1943–

Griffin is a poet and writer on ecology and feminism whose best-known books are *Women and Nature* and *Pornography and Silence*. *Voices*, much produced in the late 1970s by women's groups, has no action but consists of the interwoven poetic monologues of five women of different ages describing their stories: Maya, writing a thesis on the death of the American family after the break-up of her own; Erin, trying to escape desperation; Grace reinventing herself on her own at seventy . . . In *Thanksgiving* Martha and her sister Sarah are haunted by memories of those family members no longer at the feast and of their forced separation as children.

Plays include: *Voices* (5f) French, 1979 and extract, with *Thanksgiving* (5f,2m, 1982, extract) in *Made From This Earth*, London: The Women's Press, 1985; *The Everlasting Reich* (MS); *The Little Deaths* (MS).

Linda Griffiths

Canadian, 1953–

Actress and director, Griffiths began writing as a contributor to the collaborative work of Théâtre Passe Muraille. She went on to work with colleagues such as director Paul Thompson in scripting work from her improvisations. *Maggie and Pierre*, enormously popular across Canada, was described as 'a fantasy of love, politics and the media', in which she played both the Trudeaus and the journalist who pursues them in an investigation of the process of contemporary mythologization. *O. D. in Paradise* charts the transformations wrought on several Canadian couples by a Jamaican holiday.

Griffiths's technique of devising work from documentary material is most powerfully fulfilled and was most radically challenged in *Jessica*, the result of an immensely rigorous and painful exploration undertaken by Griffiths and 'halfbreed' Native Canadian Metis activist and writer Maria Campbell on whose life it is based. The published book documents their experience of working together and Griffiths's forced confrontation with her identity as a white woman, whose attempt to embody Campbell's experience would, necessarily at some level, be an appropriation, and Campbell's inseparable sense both of theft and misinterpretation and of magical discovery in the translation of her experience to theatre.

Plays include: *The Darling Family* (1f,1m) Blizzard, 1991; *Maggie and Pierre* (with Paul Thompson, 1f who plays 1f,2m), Talonbooks, 1980, also Coach House Press, 1995; *The Book of Jessica: a theatrical transformation* (with Maria Campbell, 2f,3m), Coach House Press, 1989; *The Duchess: Pieces of Wallis Simpson* (8f, 10m+) in Jansen 1993; *O. D. in Paradise* (with Patrick Brymer, 4f,4m, 1983) in Rudakoff; *A Game of Inches* (1f, 1991) in Sherman.

See also: Tompkins in CTR no 74; CTR 38, 1983; Grant in Brask.

Angeline Weld Grimke

American, 1880–1958

Grimke was the mixed-race daughter of a black civil liberties lawyer and a white woman, brought up in Boston. She published many poems, including lesbian works. *Rachel* (staged 1916) is a moving and powerful indictment of a racist society and one of the first plays by a black woman to be published. Its heroine is a bright, vivacious young woman whose hopes of a better life for herself, her family and her race are shattered by her encounter with the social ostracism and rejection that confronts her brother and lover trying to find work despite their qualifications, and by the disclosure that her father and another brother were lynched in the South. Her discovery of the cruelty inflicted on her black children in school from an early age because of their race leads her to reject her lover and swear never to have children herself.

Play: *Rachel* (10f,3m) Boston: Cornhill, 1921 and in Hatch and Shine, and in Perkins and Stephens.
    See also: Abramson in *SAGE: a Scholarly Journal on Black Women*, 1985; App. 2: Hull, Keyssar in Brater, Brown-Guillory.

Tanika Gupta
British, 1963–

Of Bengali descent, Gupta writes for stage, radio and television, exploring the encounter of British and Asian cultures, the collision of identities and in particular the need of young British Asians to confront their parents' experience as emigrés with their own Asian inheritance. Lyrical pieces, they have the quality of fables and draw on ritual, the theatrical magic of flashbacks and dual scenes to suggest a spiritual dimension to experience, colliding this with everyday reality. *The Waiting Room* is structured around the Hindu belief in a three-day waiting period following a death, in which the soul, before leaving the earth, faces its past life, stripped of evasions and subterfuge, and through dreams, memories and even haunting, confronts those it is leaving behind. When she is met by Immortal Soul in the guise of an adored Bollywood star, Priya is shocked to discover she has died of a stroke. She must grapple to accept death and to come to terms with the son she has left behind, his under-achievement and hurt, while he too struggles to acknowledge his sense of guilt over the death of his baby sister and his love for the mother who rejected him. Other plays like *Skeleton* (based on a story by Rabindranath Tagore), rework Asian myths like the tale of a man seduced by dreams of the beautiful woman whose skeleton he has bought for his medical research.

Plays include: *Skeleton* (3f,4m,id, 1997); *The Waiting Room* (2f.4m. 2000) – both Faber; *A River Sutra* (from Gita Mehta, MS, 1997); *Voices on the Wind* (MS, 1995); *Ananda Sanada* (MS); *On the Couch with Enoch* (MS, 1998); *Flesh and Blood* (MS, 2000); adaptation of Brecht's *The Good Woman of Szechuan* (MS, 2000).
    See also: Stephenson and Langridge.

Jessica Hagedon

American, c.1950–

Hagedorn grew up in Manila in the Philippines, moving to the USA with her family in 1960s. In San Francisco she wrote poetry, studied at the American Conservatory Theater and became involved with a group of women artists of colour, including Thulani Davis and Ntozake **Shange**, experimenting with form and interdisciplinary performance. She formed a band, the Gangster Choir, and began to devise performance interludes between songs, from one of which *Tenement Lover* evolved. In a fragmented fashion it explores aspects of immigrant experience as scenes circle round recurrent figures: a guerrilla fighter, Bong-Bong, slowly going crazy in the strange new land; a white sunbather protected by barbed wire on a perfect beach; and Ludivinda, terrified that her prized television may break down. Songs, dream narratives, musical interludes from the onstage band, projected slides and voice-overs about politics in the Philippines mix a disturbing cocktail.

On *Teenytown* she collaborated with **Carlos** and **McCauley** in a performance incorporating and reworking minstrel show gags, poetry, tap dance, multiple characters to explore projections of otherness, exoticism, ideas of exile and identity in a racist society. Hagedorn's other work includes the novel *Dogeaters* and a collection of poems, *Dangerous Music*.

Plays include: *Mango Tango* (MS); *Petfood* (MS); *A Nun's Story* (MS); *Holy Food* (radio); *Waste Land* (video, 1993); *Crayon Bondage* (2f) ext. in *Acting Up!*; *Tenement Lover: No Palm Trees in New York City* (3f,3m, 1988) in Berson; *Teenytown* (with **Carlos** and **McCauley**, 3f, 1990) in Champagne.

See also App. 2: Carr.

Cicely Hamilton

English, 1872–1952

Hamilton was one of the most active and successful members of the Women Writers Suffrage League whose campaigning plays, performed by the Actresses Franchise League, have gained new critical attention in recent years. (Other members included the composer Ethel Smyth, writers Beatrice Harraden, Bessie Hatton, Chris St John and her lover, the director and founder of the experimental Pioneer Players, Edy Craig, daughter of Ellen Terry. See also **Bensusan**, Elizabeth **Robins**.)

In *How the Vote was Won* (written with St John), clerk Horace Cole is rapidly converted to a champion of votes for women after all his female relatives descend on him and demand that he provide for them. Hamilton had an earlier success in the striking 'new woman play', *Diana of Dobson's* (1908). Combining realism and comedy it is an enjoyable and insightful analysis of the marriage market. Diana Massingberd, trapped as a low-paid shop girl, 'living in', fined for infringements of the company rules, decides to use an unexpected inheritance to live for one month as a wealthy woman. Among the idle rich in a Swiss hotel, the widow Massingberd is courted as a great catch for impecunious upper-class men like Victor, prepared to be kept, but not to keep a wife, who is nonplussed when she reveals her true situation. The final act reunites the two on the Thames Embankment where Victor is sleeping rough, having taken seriously her taunt that he would be unable to live by his own earnings for three months. Hamilton's romantic ending does not obscure the stern economic realities she exposes. Hamilton wrote several other one-acts on aspects of gender relations and later plays dealt with the devastation of war.

Plays include: *Diana of Dobson's* (9f,4m, 1908) in Fitzsimmons & Gardner and in Morgan 1994; *How the Vote was Won* (with Chris St John, 8f,2m, 1909) in Hayman & Spender and in France; *A Pageant of Great Women* (46f,1m, 1909) in Gardner; *Jack and Jill and a Friend* (1f,3m, 1911) French, 1911; *The Child in Flanders* (1f, 16m, 1925) in Martin.

See also: *The Life and Rebellious Times of Cicely Hamilton* by Lis Whitelaw Women's Press, 1990; App. 2: Gardner and Rutherford; Holledge; Stowell.

Eunice Hanger

Australian, 1911–72

Born in Rockhampton, Queensland, Hanger's commitment to developing Australian drama led to her building a major collection of unpublished playscripts, now at the University of Queensland where she taught. She also edited several anthologies, such as *Khaki Bush and Bigotry* (1968), and was the author of essays such as 'Place in Australian Plays' (1962). Her verse drama *Flood*, highly commended in the 1955 Playwrights Advisory Board competition (see **Gray**), explores the impact of a threatened flood on the relationships of a group of country people, employing commentary by a Greek-style chorus. *Upstage* spoofs Shakespeare, re-uniting his women to discuss their problems with men and other matters. *2D* (1958) explores the interplay of staff, visitors and patients in hospital ward 2D through interaction and interior monologue.

Plays include: *Foundations* (MS); *Upstage* (14f) French, 1952; *2D* (7f,4m,id, 1958); *Flood* (7f,5m, 1955) also in Pfisterer; and *The Frogs* (3f) in *2D and Other Plays* ed. Alrene Sykes, Queensland UP, 1978.
  See also: Pfisterer and Pickett.

Lorraine Hansberry
  American, 1930–65

Chicago-born Hansberry became, at the age of 29, the first woman, the youngest American and first black playwright to win the New York Drama Critics Circle Award Best Play of the Year for *A Raisin in the Sun*, now recognized as a seminal work in the emergence of black American drama. In the realist stage tradition, it explores black aspirations and choices through the hopes, failures, struggles and conflicting ambitions of the Younger family over the acquisition of grandfather's insurance money and their determination to buy a house, despite the opposition of white neighbours. It has been filmed, adapted as a musical, affectionately lampooned and continues to be widely performed.

  Hansberry's other works are less well known but equally engaged in political and personal struggles. Several published posthumously, but others, detailed in Carter (see below), are still unpublished. *The Sign in Sidney Brustein's Window*, set in the early 1960s in Greenwich Village's bohemian intellectual community, focuses on a relationship torn apart by misunderstanding; on issues of integrity, creativity, racial politics, political commitment and choices of cynicism or idealism. It was produced shortly before her early death from cancer. *Les Blancs* is in part a response to and a re-framing of *Hamlet* in the context of African independence struggles, where the demand made upon the hero by a spirit is the overthrow of the colonial government. The most visually rich of her plays, it analyses the workings of power under colonialism, its poisoning of human relationships and the legitimization of European domination by its gift of 'culture'. *What Use Are Flowers?* also responds to an earlier text, Beckett's *Waiting for Godot*. It confronts the absurdism of a desperate world – a post-nuclear landscape – with the human search for love and purpose that invests the world with meaning.

Plays include: *A Raisin in the Sun* (3f,7m, 1959) NY: Signet, 1966 and in Busby; in Hatch and Shine; in Remnant 1986; *The Sign in Sidney Brustein's Window* (3f,6/7m) NY: Signet, 1966 and in *Three Negro Plays* ed. C. E. Bigsby, Harmondsworth: Penguin, 1966; *Les Blancs* (3f,8m+), *The Drinking Gourd* (4f, 13m+), *What Use Are Flowers?* (1m +childre, c.1961) in *The Collected Last Plays* NY: Plume, 1983; *Toussaint* (2f,1m, 1961, ext.) in Wilkerson; *To Be Young Gifted and Black: Lorraine Hansberry* (4f,2m to 15–20 f/m, adapted by Robert Nemiroff from Hansberry's writings) NY: Signet, 1969.

See also especially: *Hansberry's Drama* by Steven A. Carter, NY: Meridian, 1993; *Lorraine Hansberry* by Anne Cheyney, Boston: Twayne/G. K. Hall, 1984; App. 2: Bloom; Wilkerson in Case; Ashley in Schlueter; Parks in Laughlin and Schuler; Brown-Guillory.

Zinnie Harris

British, 1973–

Harris worked as writing tutor at an AIDS hospice before developing her first commissioned plays. Her two published plays concern people thrown into extreme situations and the failure of language to articulate their experience. *By Many Wounds* movingly explores the impact of a daughter's disappearance on a mother, step-father and teenage sister and the subsequent discovery of her murder, while on holiday in France. Harris creates a powerful tension as unspeakable emotions, terror and blame are barely contained beneath a surface of attempted continued normality. *Further than the Furthest Thing* is loosely based on the story of Tristan da Cunha: a centuries-old community is ejected by volcanic eruption, displaced to an alien 'H' England' and kept there because their home offers possibilities as a nuclear test-site. Harris invents a dialect for the group as sparse and bleakly poetic as the remote wind-swept island, through which both their yearning to return and their sinister history struggle to find speech.

Plays include: *Some Kind of Dawn* (MS); *Biohazard* (MS); *Silver Whale Fish* (MS, 2000, radio); *Gravity* (MS, 2000); *By Many Wounds* (2f,1m, 1998); 1998; *Further than the Furthest Thing* (2f,3m, 2000).

See also App. 2: Sierz.

Catherine Hayes

British, 1949–

The desperate emotions of family relationships, bitingly yet compassion-ately depicted, are central to Hayes's work. She came to prominence with the success of *Skirmishes*, a bleak visceral exploration of sibling rivalries, pent-up anxieties, resentments, expectations and dreads, exposed as two sisters await the death of their mother who lies centre-stage in bed. Jean has spent much of her life caring for mother while Rita ran away to make her own life with the married lover her mother disapproved of. In later plays Hayes's themes recur in show-business contexts such as *Long Time Gone* (MS), a fictional account of the Everly Brothers' partnership, rivalry and estrangement. In *Not Waving* a middle-aged woman comedian's attempts to deny the breakdown of her career, the onset of menopause, the suicide of her former lover and manager and the anger of her children are undermined as her hidden anxieties seep into her act.

Plays include: *Skirmishes* (3f, 1982); *Not Waving* (2f,1m, 1984) – both Faber; *Dear Sandra* (MS).
    See also App. 2: Griffiths in Griffiths and Llewellyn Jones; Todd.

Eliza Haywood

English, 1693–1756

A feminist, prolific novelist, editor of *The Female Spectator* (the first periodical written by a woman) and briefly a publisher, several of Hay-wood's plays open with prologues attacking prejudice against female writers. Although Isabella, heroine of the tragedy *The Fair Captive* is vic-timized, Mrs Graspall of *A Wife To Be Let* resists her husband's scheme to sell her favours to Sir Harry Beaumont, a situation given moral com-plexity by her own attraction to Harry, while her fellow heroines are witty, independent women who take charge of their fates.

Plays: *The Fair Captive* (3f,6m, 1721); *A Wife To Be Let* (6f,9m, 1724); *Frederick, Duke of Brunswick* (3f,7m+, 1729); *The Opera of Operas or Tom Thumb the Great* (5f,11m+, 1733). All in *The Plays of Eliza Haywood* ed. Valerie C Rudolph, NY: Garland, 1983
    See also: *Eliza Haywood* by Mary Anne Schofield, Boston: Twayne, 1985.

Anne Hébert

Canadian, 1916–

Hébert was born in St Catherine and brought up in Quebec City, but has lived for many years in Paris. A novelist and established poet, as well as theatre and film writer, she has received many awards. Her plays are fables set in distinctive landscapes that take on a timeless, fairy-tale quality. *The Murdered Shopkeeper* takes place in a small French town haunted by hidden secrets and long-nursed grievances. A French Canadian journalist discovers that the dead haberdasher, Adelaide Menthe, over the years murdered the instigators of her humiliation when, a mock Cinderella, she was stripped of her finery at a long-ago ball. *The Guests on Trial* recounts a densely allegorical fairy tale of a hidden murder, pacts made with the devil, ugliness and beauty transformed into their opposites, drownings and prophetic dreams. The play centres on the two daughters of an innkeeper who gains sudden success as people swarm to experience the strange attractions of the sinister landscape that springs up around the inn, at its heart a black flower with a heart of blood growing out of a dark pond.

Untranslated plays include: *La Cage*; *L'Île de la Demoiselle* (c.1990).

Translated plays include: *The Guests on Trial* (6f,9m, radio, 1952) in CD 9, 1983; *The Murdered Shopkeeper* (4f,7m, TV, 1967) in CD 10:2, 1984; *The Unquiet State* in CD 14:2, 1988. All tr. Eugene Benson and Renate Benson.
 See also: THC, 8, 1987; Benson in CD 6:1, 1980, *Anne Hébert* by Delbert W. Russell, Boston: Twayne, 1983.

Lillian Hellman

American, 1905–84

Probably the most performed (barring **Christie**) and widely recognized twentieth-century woman playwright, Hellman employs skilful realism and her best work is brilliantly crafted, powerfully characterized and both passionate and highly perceptive in its analysis of the workings of power and corruption.
 Set in Alabama, *Another Part of the Forest* and *The Little Foxes* incisively delineate the machinations of the Hubbard family. A Civil War profiteer is defeated by the outmanoeuvrings of his son, Ben, whose

oedipal conflict adds another layer of complexity, and by the conse-quences of his former treachery. Years later, he sees the triumph of his daughter, Regina, prepared to let her husband die in ruthless pursuit of wealth and a scheme which 'will pound the bones of this town'. Hell-man's forceful moral analysis does not spare the weak: bystanders, col-laborators and victims who allow themselves to be manipulated, though they are sometimes allowed to become agents of moral redemption.

The despoilers of *The Children's Hour*, which ignited controversy for its naming of lesbian desire, are a cruel child and gullible grandmother whose deadly rumour-mongering destroys the school and the lives of two young women. Revived in 1952, the piece spoke potently to the destructive climate of blacklisting, detailed in her memoir, *Scoundrel Time* – Hellman, like others, was called before the House of UnAmerican Activities Committee. Hellman's political commitment is evident in the analysis of social struggle of *Days to Come* and the damning commen-tary on the futility of appeasement in Europe of *The Searching Wind*. *Watch on the Rhine* brings the fascist danger home, focusing on the struggle between a German socialist activist and a Nazi agent/informer, both refugees in Washington, DC, and their host's consequent discovery of her own political commitment. Hellman also published several trans-lations/adaptations.

Plays include: *The Little Foxes* (4f,6m, 1939) in Cerf, 1941 and Barlow, 1994; *Another Part of the Forest* (5f,8m, 1946); *The Children's Hour* (12f,2m, 1934) in Sullivan and Hatch; *Days to Come* (1936); *Watch on the Rhine* (5f,8m, 1941); *Toys in the Attic* (4f,4m+, 1960) – all in *Six Plays*, NY: Vintage, 1979 and all with *The Autumn Garden* (7f,5m, 1951); *The Searching Wind* (3f,11m, 1944), *Candide* (with Leonard Bernstein's music, 1957) in *Collected Plays* (CP) Boston: Little, Brown, 1972; *North Star* (1943), *Dead End* (1957) – both screen.

See also: many including *Lillian Hellman: Her Legend and her Legacy* by Carl Rollyson, NY: St Martin's Press, 1988; *Conversations with Lillian Hellman* ed. Jackson Bryer, Jackson: Mississippi UP, 1986; App. 2: Schlueter; Shafer; Curtin.

Beth Henley
American, 1952–

Henley's plays have been called Southern Gothics and are characterized by quirky charm, eccentric characters and touches of grotesquerie, in a landscape where violent and absurd deaths are never far away and events are simultaneously shocking and absurd. Henley's most popular works, *The Miss Firecracker Contest* and the immensely successful *Crimes of the Heart* (1981), are dramas of family life that veer, via daffy humour and tragic events, between absurdity and warm sentimentalism. Pulitzer Prizewinner *Crimes of the Heart*, in which Babe has shot her bullying politico husband in the stomach because she 'didn't like his looks', has been called a Mississippi *Three Sisters* (cf. **Wasserstein**). Marshael's dead husband in *The Wake of Jamey Foster* was kicked in the head by a cow and his funeral ignites a welter of family arguments, revelations of infidelities, childhood cruelties and arson, in a chaotic household, the whole laced with wild humour. *Abundance* tackles the experience of pioneer women in the 1860s, setting out as 'mail-order brides' to homesteads in Wyoming territory, over twenty-five years of shared hardships and mismatched marriages. Henley's heroines include pregnant 15-year-olds, ageing dancers and card sharps, waifs, strays, belles and beauty queens, brawling, dreaming of escapes or struggling to find compromises with the demands of Southern womanhood.

Plays include: *The Wake of Jamey Foster* (4f,3m); *The Miss Firecracker Contest* (4f,2m); *The Lucky Spot* (3f,4m, 1987); *Abundance** (2f,3m) in *Four Plays* Portsmouth NH: Heinemann, 1992; *Crimes of the Heart* (4f,2m) NY: Viking Press, 1982 and in *Louisville*; *Am I Blue* (4f,3m) in Halpern and in Delgado 1983; *The Debutante Ball* (MS, exts. published) All but * in *Beth Henley Collected Plays vol. 1* Lyme, NH: Smith and Kraus, 2000; *Signature* (3f,3m, 1990); *Control Freaks* (2f,2m, 1992); *Revelers* (3f,4m, 1994); *L-Play* (3f,3m, 1995); *Impossible Marriage* (3f,4m, 1998) All with * in *Beth Henley Collected Plays vol. 2* Lyme, NH: Smith and Kraus, 2000; *Hymn in the Attic* (2f,1m, 1982) in WCP 17/18; *No Mercy* (screen, 1986); *True Stories* (screen, 1986); and screen adaptations of her own plays.
    See also: Shepard in MD 39, 1993; Gagen in SAD 1989; App. 2: Karpinski in Schlueter; Guerra in Hart; Betsko and Koenig.

Judith Herzberg
Dutch, 1934–

As a Jew born in Amsterdam, Herzberg spent the war in hiding with Dutch families, an experience she draws on in a number of her plays, including *The Wedding Party*, where the paper-thin veneer of the now is constantly broken by memories, fears and questions from an all-too-present past. The fractured narrative is composed of fragments of overlapping conversations at a wedding party, punctuated by recitals of frighteningly prosaic lists and instructions: what to take with you to the camps, how to hide a child by erasing its history and memories to ensure its survival. Contemporary relationships are fractured by loss, most pointedly expressed through the wedding couple's four mothers: bride Lea's real mother, an Auschwitz survivor; Riet the wartime mother who took her in; bridegroom Nico's stepmother; and the absent figure of his real mother, dead in the camps. The piece addresses the anger and guilt of survivors and of children left behind, saved (cf. **Samuels**). *The Caracal* is a sharp, comic monologue made up of a series of fragmentary phone conversations, as the woman speaker, head of a school for special needs who is expecting a year-long-awaited call from her lover, attempts to deal with colleagues, wrong numbers, obscene callers, her sister and the father of a missing pupil.

Translated plays: *Scratch* tr. Gert-Jan Kramer (6f,4m, 1988) Amsterdam: Uitgeverij International Theatre and Film Books, 1995; *And/Or* tr. Herzberg and Rhea Gaisner (MS); *The Wedding Party* (7f,7m, 1982) tr. author with Vergano and Gaisner in *Dutch Plays* ed. Della Couling, NHB, 1997; *The Caracal* (1f, 1988) tr. Rina Vergano, in Robson, 1997.

Dorothy Hewett
Australian, 1923–

Hewett, from Perth, Western Australia, is author of more than 18 plays, as well as novels and poetry. She has been awarded the Order of Australia for her service to literature and is one of the most acclaimed playwrights of her generation. She shared the communist sympathies of numerous contemporary Australian playwrights (cf. **Gray**, **Brand**, Katherine **Prichard**) and expressed them in *This Old Man . . .* (1966), a rollicking, affectionate portrayal of the Dockerty family in 1950s Redfern, a working-class Sydney suburb. Despite the realism of its portrayal of alcoholism, unemployment, teenage pregnancy and poverty, it already contains elements of vivid expressionism, snatches of song, children's skipping rhymes, a chorus, both Greek and music-hall in resonance, of three tipsy ladies on a park bench, and an old man who is Father Time himself.

Hewett's best-known play, *The Chapel Perilous*, remains startling for its audacious, sexually ardent, outspoken heroine, who terrified onstage the puritans of the Communist Party, and off-stage the critics with her forthright individualism. It remains woefully unusual as a play with a female heroine in quest of meaning (cf. perhaps only **Wertenbaker**'s Mary Traverse). Hewett's plays field a rich range of theatrical device and imagery, drawing on popular entertainment in the Crystal Palace of *Bon-Bons* (1972) that incarnates Dolly's Hollywood dreams, using puppet-like effigies in *Golden Oldies* and *Tatty Hollow*, employing tightrope-walking, melodrama and touring Shakespeare in *Makinupin*. This evocation of 1912–20 small-town Western Australia does not, despite its celebratory qualities, shy away from the horrors of genocide and Aboriginal degradation, in which actors each double as twinned characters, the socially acceptable and the marginal, the storekeeper and the star-gazer brother, romantic heroine and her 'half-caste' sister 'Touch of the Tar'. Densely allusive, Hewett's plays exude dynamism, drawing on a rich palette of ritual, folk mythology, poetry, song, using hybrids of English, Aboriginal and white Australian cultures.

Plays include*: *This Old Man Comes Rolling Home* (9f,7m, 1976); *Mrs Porter and the Angel* (6f,7m, 1969); *The Chapel Perilous* (5f,6m+, 1972) also in Tait and Schafer; *The Tatty Hollow Story* (2f,6m, 1976) in *Collected Plays* vol.1, 1992; *Bon-Bons and Roses For Dolly* (4f,5m, 1976); *The Golden Oldies* (2f,1d,2mv, 1976) with *Susannah's Dreaming* (2f,6m, radio, 1985); *The Man From Makinupin* (7f,7m,1d, 1979); *Nowhere* (2000) – all Currency; *The Beautiful Mrs Portland* (4f,4m) Nov./Dec. 1976; *Pandora's Cross* (4f,5m) Sept.–Oct. 1978 – both in *Theatre Australia*.

See also: *Dorothy Hewett: the Feminine as Subversion* by Margaret Williams, Sydney: Currency, 1992; *Hecate* v5, no.2, 1979 and v3 no.1, Feb. 1977; *Wild Card* (autobiography) Virago, 1990.

Dorothy Heyward
American, 1890–1961

Dorothy Hartzell Kuhns attended George Pierce Baker's influential Workshop '47 and began her writing career with light comedies like *Nancy Ann*, featuring ingenous charming young heroines and based on the frivolous social world she knew. Later she collaborated with her husband DuBose Heyward, son of an impoverished aristocratic Southern family, their most famous work being the play, *Porgy*, the basis of the

---

* Where dates in the main text differ from those in the bibliography, the former refer to production, the latter to publication.

musical *Porgy and Bess* by DuBose with George and Ira Gershwin. In it Porgy's love transforms a fallen woman, when her lover flees after killing a man. The Heywards' work was unusual in its time in creating serious roles for black performers in mainstream theatre. In *Set My People Free* (MS), Dorothy wrote about Denmark Vesey, a Charleston slave who bought his own freedom and then plotted a slave uprising. In the musical *South Pacific* (Rodgers and Hammerstein borrowed the title) a black man on a Pacific island during the war finds for the first time a society without racial prejudice. *Mamba's Daughter*, set in the South Carolina islands, is a powerful tragedy of three generations of black women, ending with Hagar's murder of the man whose attempted blackmail of her daughter threatens her singing career.

Plays include: *Love in a Cupboard* (2f,2m 1926); *Nancy Ann* (1927); *Little Girl Blue* (with Dorothy De Jagers, 3f,5m, 1931) – all NY: Samuel French; *Porgy* (with Dubose Heyward, 5f,18m+) London: Ernest Benn, 1929; *Mamba's Daughter* (with Dubose, 13f,13m+) NY: Farrar and Rinehart, 1939.

John Oliver Hobbes (pseud. of Pearl Maria Theresa Craigie)
American/English, 1867–1906

Successful boulevard dramatist and novelist, Hobbes/Craigie (she wrote under both names) was the daughter of an American businessman who had settled in London. She married (and later separated from) banker Reginald Craigie and drew on the familiar high society background she came from for her plays, which led to some criticisms of her narrowness of view. They focus on the love problems of witty society people – who should marry whom and why – and were largely very well received. Praise was heaped on *The Ambassador* in which idealistic young Juliet throws off stuffy, socially respectable Beavedere in favour of a more dubious match with St Orbyn, the world-weary ambassador, for whom her love provides renewal. In *The Wisdom of the Wise* a young girl is overwhelmed with contradictory advice on how to behave towards and how to manage her husband until she discovers that he loves her for herself and that the would-be advisers have ulterior motives.

Plays include: *The School for Saints* (7f,10m, 1896); *The Ambassador* (11m,16f, 1898) also in Scullion; *The Wisdom of the Wise* (8f,8m, 1901). All London: T. Fisher Unwin.

Joan Holden

American, 1939–

Holden describes her work as 'political cartoons'; she is 'only inspired when being funny'. All made in collaboration with the socialist San Francisco Mime Troupe, her plays draw on a variety of popular theatre forms: vaudeville and melodrama, Westerns and comic strips. Figures from popular culture, from super-heroes to mysterious 'inscrutable orientals', subvert their stereotypes as they come to people incisive agit-prop plays, drawing on broad Commedia dell'Arte performance styles and Brechtian aesthetics to confront racism, sexism, capitalist exploitation, the military industrial machine and American imperialism. Her earliest work, an adaptation of Goldoni's *L'Amant Militaire*, grew out of the company's need for anti-Vietnam War material. *The Independent Female*, a mock melodrama, features a 'beautiful, innocent but impressionable' heroine led down the road to ruin by the devilish plotting of the unspeakable feminist villain. The 1980–2 Factwino series emphasizes the need for political education, featuring a wino endowed by a magical bag lady with the power to produce facts, challenge media lies and get his audience to ask questions.

Plays include: *Steeltown* (MS); *Spain/36* (MS); *The Independent Female* (3f,3m, 1970) in France; with *False Promises/Nos Enganaron* (6f, 18m+12,dp, 1976); *San Fran Scandals* (4f,2m, 1973); *The Dragon Lady's Revenge* (3f,9m+2, 1971); *Frijoles* (2f,7m+, 1975); *Frozen Wages* (4f,4m, 1972) in *By Popular Demand: the San Francisco Mime Troupe* (with collaborators on some scripts inc. Steve Friedman, Patricia Silver, Andrea Snow *et al.*) SF: San Francisco Mime Troupe, 1980; *Factperson* (1980), *Factwino Meets the Moral Majority* (1970), *Factwino vs. Armageddonman* (1981) (all 5f,5m+,id) in WCP 15–16; *The Mozamgola Caper* (with Robert Alexander, John O'Neal 23+f/m in *Theater* Winter 1983
See also: Interview in *Theater*, Spring 1987; TDR 86.

Margaret Hollingsworth

Canadian, 1940–

British-born Hollingsworth became a Canadian citizen in 1968 and has worked full time as a writer or in theatre (as director, dramaturge and teacher) since 1974. Much of her best work deals with the experience of exile and isolation, both the alienation of an unfamiliar environment and loneliness within marriage and within individual consciousness.

The Apple in the Eye and *Diving* are largely interior monologues affirming enjoyment and self-discovery through language. The attempt to remake one's self through the encounter with the strange also becomes a political metaphor for the need for Canada to achieve separate identity from the (indifferent) mother country. Hollingsworth's best-known play, *Ever Loving*, examines the experience of three war brides from the time of their arrival in Canada, from England, Scotland and Italy to a chance reunion 32 years later. She uses a fragmented, episodic structure that shifts between time, place and character. Where middle-class Diana has found some freedom through her battle with the land (farming in Alberta) and her shared involvement with her husband in politics, Ruth, a working-class Scot, has remained trapped by poverty, child-bearing and a brutish man, while Luce has freed herself through divorce and gained a measure of independence. In *Islands* Muriel can only discover autonomy through a retreat from relationship, rejecting both her domineering mother and her lesbian lover. The theatrical space allows ultimately an affirmation of both connection and division. In *In Confidence* two middle-aged women share the stage, in their Toronto and Vancouver kitchens, close friends now divided by a continent. Gradually, movingly, they confess in monologue what they could not reveal in person, the secrets of their marriages, testifying to the importance of their friendship in discovering their own sexuality in middle age.

Plays include: *Ever Loving* (3f,3m, 1980); *Islands* (3f, 1983); *The Apple in the Eye* (1f,1m, 1983); *War Babies* (2f,3m,1d, 1984), *Diving* (1f,1mv, 1983), in *Willful Acts: Five Plays* Toronto: The Coach House Press, 1985; *The House that Jack Built* (1f,1m), *It's Only Hot for Two Months in Kapuskasing* (2f,1m, 1986); *Poppycock* (3f,1m); *Prim and Duck, Mama and Frank* (2f,2m), in *Endangered Species*, Toronto: Act One Press, 1988; *Alli Alli Oh* (2f, 1977); *Mother Country* (5f,2m, 1980); *Operators* (3f, 1981) and *Bushed* (4f,2m, 1981) – all Toronto: Playwrights Canada; *In Confidence* (2f) Victoria, BC: Scirocco Drama, 1994.

See also: CD 11:1, 1985; McCaughey in CD 14:2, 1988; App. 2: Zimmerman; Hodkinson; Wallace and Zimmerman.

Karen Hope
British, 1962–

Hope's plays appear to be fuelled by a fascination with the extremes of human behaviour and obsession: driven child prodigies in *Ripped*, a woman murderer in the acclaimed and chilling *Foreign Lands*. Loosely based on the Mary Bell case, *Foreign Lands* is a psychological study of enormous intensity, taking as its premise the possibility of a character motivated by pure evil, in the form of a woman released into the community after serving twenty years for the murder of five little boys. Hope handles the tension of gradual revelation of her character's past, and her growing relationship with the landlady's idiot-savant daughter, with skill and enormous menace.

Plays include: *Ripped* (MS, 1991); *Foreign Lands* (4f, 1993) in Edwardes 2 (App. 1). See also App. 2: Sierz.

Debbie Horsfield
English, 1955–

Born in Manchester and educated at Eccles Grammar School and Newcastle University, Horsfield won the Thames TV Writers Award in 1983 and was appointed Writer in Residence at the Liverpool Playhouse in the same year. She has written radio drama for the BBC, work for touring companies such as Black Theatre Co-op and for Croydon Warehouse and Chichester Festival Theatre.

The plays that make up *The Red Devils Trilogy* explore the lives of four young working-class women, all devoted Manchester United fans: violent, angry, unemployed Beth; ambitious Nita; Phil, who is afraid to pursue the academic opportunities open to her; and Alice, only interested in having a good time, getting married and having babies. We follow them through the years from late adolescence, desperate to get tickets to the Wembley Cup final, through their early twenties – their relationships, ambitions and the possibilities – or lack of them – open to them.

Horsfield's sardonic northern humour, vivid dialogue and pointed observation have transferred well to her television work in recent years in the popular series *Making Out*, about the lives of a group of women working in a Manchester plastics factory, and *Born to Run*, centring on a family of second-hand car dealers. In *The Riff-Raff Element* the upper-class Southern Tundishes are forced to live cheek-by-jowl with the vulgar Northern Belchers, an encounter which Horsfield treated with great wit and inventiveness, avoiding obvious stereotypes.

Plays include: *Red Devils* (4f) in Wandor 3 and with *True Dare Kiss* and ... *Command or Promise* ... (both 5f,3m,id, all 1983) in *The Red Devils Trilogy*, Methuen, 1986; *Out on the Floor* (MS); *In Touch* (MS); *All You Deserve* (MS).

Velina Hasu Houston
American, 1957–

Daughter of a Japanese mother and a half African-American, half Native American serviceman father, Houston draws on her family biography in her plays, exploring issues of Amerasian identity, in particular the conflicting pressures on women.

Asa Ga Kimashita is set in Japan during the post-war American occupation in the 1940s. Traditionalist father Kiheida Shimada struggles against accepting his country's defeat and the changes forced upon his family, both land reforms which will divide his orchards between his neighbours and the love of his younger daughter, Setsuko, for a black American soldier, while his wife, Fusae, encourages her daughter's self-fulfilment. Setsuko reappears in *Tea*, probably the most widely performed play by an Asian-American woman. It brings together four women whose husbands have been assigned to the isolation of Fort Riley, Kansas, because of their marriages to Japanese brides. The women gather at the home of a fifth, Himiko, to mark her death, sharing tea and talk as they failed to when she was alive. While Himiko lingers, an uneasy and unseen presence on the edge of the gathering, the women enact the roles of their husbands, daughters and themselves in flashback, sharing memories of meeting their husbands, encounters with racism, adjusting to a new life. In gaining understanding across their differences they can acknowledge the pressures and marital violence that drove Himiko to suicide.

Plays include: *Asa Ga Kimashita (Morning Has Broken)* (5f,5m, 1981) in Houston, 1993; *Tea* (5f, 1987) in Uno; *Albatross* (MS, 1988); *Necessities* (MS, 1990); *Broken English* (MS, 1991); *Kokoru (True Heart)* (5f,1m) in Houston, 1997; *As Sometimes in a Dead Man's Face* (2f,1m, 1994) in Nelson.

Tina Howe
American, 1937–

Art is central to all Tina Howe's strange, individual plays, whether in the physical settings which provide her starting points, such as the house deluged with monstrous vegetation in *One Shoe Off*, the roles of the characters themselves or situations bordering on the surreal, as in *Approaching Zanzibar*. In *Zanzibar* the Blossom family drive through a countrywide road movie of American discovery and self-discovery to a dying aunt, Olivia, who makes installations designed to be destroyed by nature and time. A more conventional piece, the award-winning *Painting Churches*, concerns an eccentric Boston family of painters in which the daughter's portrait of her parents becomes a means to resolve their troubled relationship. *Museum* is itself part installation, an art show devised to be explored by the audience before the play begins. Then, through a series of visitors, artists and curators, satire and farce mix with performance art and revelation with charlatanism.

Satire on contemporary pretensions is a key element in *The Art of Dining* alongside a celebration of food as art. The mix reflects Howe's inter-disciplinary beginnings at Sarah Lawrence College and the influence of Dadaism and Ionesco-inspired absurdism which animates *Birth and After Birth*'s grotesquely comic cartoon of parenthood and childhood, centring on Nicky's (played by an adult) fourth birthday party.

Plays include: *Museum* (9f,9m,id, 1978); *The Art of Dining* (6f,3m, 1979); *Painting Churches* (2f,1m, 1983) and in Kilgore and *Coastal Disturbances* (5f,4m) in *Coastal Disturbances: Four Plays*, TCG, 1989; *Birth and After Birth* (2f,3m, 1974) in Moore, Lamont and with *Approaching Zanzibar* (5f,6m, 1989) and *One Shoe Off* (2f,3m, 1993) in *Approaching Zanzibar and Other Plays*, TCG, 1995; *Teeth* (1f,1m) in Halpern; *Pride's Crossing* (3f,4m, TCG) 1998.

See also: SAD 1989; Lamont in MD 36, 1993; App. 2: Backes in Hart; Betsko and Koenig; Barlow in Brater

Hrotsvitha of Gandersheim
German, c.935–1005

Hrotsvitha is the earliest known woman playwright, a writer of Latin drama whose six plays, influenced by the Senecan classical dramatist Terence, stand alone between the Roman drama and medieval miracle plays.

Hrotsvitha, like later nun playwrights such as Hildegard of Bingen, Katherine of Sutton or, in the seventeenth century, **Sor Juana**, was born into a noble family and educated in the convent, the major source of learning for women in the medieval world. Women play central roles in her dramas of conversion, such as *Dulcitius* and *Sapienta*, centring on the 'laudable chastity of Christian virgins' despite rape and brutal torture. In her dramas of redemption they reject lives of prostitution, like Thais in *Paphnutius*, or *Abraham*, in which Abraham's niece Mary is rescued by her hermit uncle and returns to the life of religious contemplation and penance she left in shame. Episodic, they include lively dialogue and comic scenes, such as Dulcitius's making love to the soot-blackened kitchen pots and pans, under the delusion that they are women.

The plays have recently attracted much attention from feminist critics addressing Hrotsvitha's scholarly learning, her equation of femininity with Christianity and her women characters' rejection of sexual objectification.

Many translations of her plays include: *Abraham* (1f,4m) also in Hill and in Pollock; *Dulcitius* (4+f,3+m); *Paphnutius* (2f,3m+); *Sapienta* (4+f,2m); *Callimachus* (1f,4+m), *Gallicanus* (4+f,8+m) all tr. Christopher St John in *The Plays of Roswitha*, NY: Benjamin Blom, 1923, reissue 1966; also tr. by L. Bonfante in *The Plays of Hrotswitha of Gandesheim*, New York UP, 1979.

See also especially: *Women Writers of the Middle Ages* by Peter Dronke, Cambridge UP, 1984; *Hrotsvitha: the Theatricality of her Plays* by Marguerite Butler, NY: Philosophical Library, 1976; Case in TJ, Dec. 1983; Schroeder in TiD 11; *Medieval Women Writers* ed. K. M. Wilson, Manchester UP, 1984.

Holly Hughes
American, 1955–

The reigning queen of 'dyke noir', Hughes trained in the visual arts but rejected painting for performance art and installation. Her early works, many of them written for the WOW (Women's One World) café in New York's East Village, are glorious lesbian spoofs of popular genres: the hardboiled tough-guy detective story of *Lady Dick*, the anguished history of perversity of *Well of Horniness*. In the Obie-award-winning *Dress Suits to Hire*, written for **Split Britches**, she retains the game-playing delight of her first pieces while exploring the menacing and erotic territory of an obsessive butch–femme relationship, though this too is laced with comedy and parody.

Hughes's recent self-performed monologues, lyrical, surreal and tangential, trace the playful adventures of metaphor, combining real memory with incidents and stories. The speaking voice is never singular but always fissured with conflict, fictions, other selves, references to popular culture and a continual rewriting and restoring of family history brought into a wider political context. Celebration of her mother's sexuality, meat or her girlfriend's body collide, alongside pain at continuing violence against women, anger and grief. Ironically, this multiplicity of contradictory voices in her work has led to her being rejected by certain feminist critics as both inauthentically lesbian due to the heterosexual 'tropes' evident in the work, while also being attacked from the right wing. She was, with Karen **Finley**, one of the artists 'de-funded' by the NEA because of her work's outspokenly lesbian content.

Plays include: *The Well of Horniness* (11f , 1988) in Shewey; *Lady Dick* (9f, 1985) in TDR 131; *Dress Suits to Hire* (2f) in TDR Spring 85 and Martin; *World Without End* (1f, 1989) in Champagne – all with *Clit Notes* (1f) in *Clit Notes: a Sapphic Sampler*, Grove Press, 1996; *Salon de la mer: Meat* (1f) in Russell.

See also: Epstein in TDR 152; App. 2: Davy in Hart and Phelan; Carr; Davy and Schneider in Martin; Juno and Vale.

Zora Neale Hurston
American, 1891–1960

Hurston's work for theatre has been forgotten beside her achievements as a novelist and short-story writer. She aspired, however, to theatrical success, and wrote or devised almost twenty plays, musicals and revues over her career, performing in several of them. *Fast and Furious* (MS, 1931) and *Jungle Scandals* (MS) brought minimal success, but *The Great Day* (MS, 1932), set in a railroad camp and drawing on a range of black musical traditions, was better received. *Color Struck* addresses the bitterness of self-hatred generated by a society that privileges whiteness, through the narrative of Emma, a black woman whose obsessive jealousy of her lover's apparent attraction for light-skinned women and self-hatred of her own skin drives him away. *The First One* (1927) satirically retells the biblical story of Noah's drunkenly cursing Ham and his children with blackness.

Recent productions of Hurston's work include writer-director George C. Wolfe's critical and popular success with *Spunk*, a stage adaptation of three Hurston stories, and the production in 1991 of *Mule Bone*, a vibrant folk comedy based in a black community in Florida. Co-written with Langston Hughes, its original failure was a painful experience which destroyed their friendship (see Bass and Gates's introduction).

Plays include: *The First One* (5f,4m+, 1927) in Hatch and Hamalian and in Perkins; *Color Struck* (3f,2m, 1925) in Perkins; *Mule Bone* (with Langston Hughes, 22f,19m, 1931) NY: Harper Perennial, 1991; *Polk Country* (MS, 1944); *Spunk* (adapted by George C. Wolfe, 2f,4m) TCG, 1991; *The Fiery Chariot* in *Zora Neale Hurston Forum* 11, 1989.

See also App. 2: Shafer; Hill in Hart and Phelan.

Elizabeth Inchbald
English, 1754–1821

Inchbald ran away to London from Suffolk, aged 18, to become first an actress, then the most successful woman playwright of her generation, as well as critic and editor of several major series of plays.

From 1787 to 1811 she wrote eleven original plays and ten adaptations, including *Lovers' Vows* from the controversial German dramatist Kotzebue. It is Inchbald's adaptation that causes consternation when enacted in Jane **Austen**'s *Mansfield Park*. *A Mogul Tale* was the first of many popular farces she wrote with an astute eye to audience taste, capitalizing on contemporary crazes for ballooning, mesmerism and the exotic East. Inchbald's political liberalism and establishment critique are already evident in her presentation of a mogul who challenges conventional stereotype and criticizes tyranny. In *Such Things Are* she based her hero on the prison reformer John Howard, and her picture of prison life on contemporary British jails, combining this with satirical comedy, mocking the absurdities of the cowardly governor and his vulgar wife.

Inchbald's plays depart from the contemporary romantic conventions of comedy in her use of wittily contrived plots frequently based on small incidents – the passage of a shawl from one owner to another in *Appearance is Against Them*, for instance – to teach lessons of self-knowledge and responsibility, though she is sometimes over-eager to point a moral at the expense of more complex questions.

Plays include: *I'll Tell You What* (4f,8m, 1786); *Such Things Are* (3f,13m, 1788), also in Pollock and in Rogers; *Everyone has His Fault* (4f,9m, 1792) in Nicoll; *The*

Wedding Day (4f,4m+, 1794); *Wives as they Were and Maids as they Are* (3f,7m+, 1797) – all in *Selected Comedies* ed. R. Manvell London: University Presses of America, 1988; *A Mogul Tale* (4f,5m, 1788); *Appearance is Against Them* (6f,6m, 1785); *Animal Magnetism* (2f,6m); *The Midnight Hour* (3f,6m, 1787); *Lovers' Vows* (4f,9m, 1798) – all in *The Plays of Elizabeth Inchbald* ed. Paula Backscheider, NY: Garland, 1980.

See also: *Elizabeth Inchbald: England's Principal Woman Dramatist and Woman of Letter in 18th Century London* by Roger Manvell, London: University Presses of America, 1988; App. 2: Macheski and Rogers in Schofield and Macheski.

Debbie Isitt
British, 1966–

Trained as an actor at Coventry Centre for Performing Arts, Isitt was joint founder of the acclaimed company Snarling Beasties. Beasties productions match striking visual and physical theatre with vivid texts, most of them written and directed by Isitt herself, who also acts in many of them.

Grim fables of heterosexual life behind the respectable net curtains of suburbia, they feature transvestism, agoraphobia, domestic violence, sexual betrayal, with deliberately stereotyped characters whose monstrousness is unleashed by marital and societal pressures that erupt in confrontations of stylized violence. Mr Peach in *Nasty Neighbours*, commissioned for the British Little Theatre movement, promises his wife the consumer home of her dreams from their semi-detached Englishman's castle, hiding from her the mounting bills and his own failure as a double-glazing salesman, while his desperation finds a ready target for blame in the anti-social Chapmans who have moved next door. It has since been filmed, directed by Isitt (2000). A similar fairy-tale quality is central to *Matilda Liar!* a chilling contemporary gothic with its starting point in Hilaire Belloc's cautionary tale of the come-uppance of a compulsive liar, which inspires the play's intermittent use of rhyme. Matilda's truth-drug-induced reform proves more threatening, however, ripping up the fictions on which family equilibrium rests and revealing everyone's hidden secrets.

Plays include: *Punch and Judy: the Real Story*; *Femme Fatale*; *Out of the Ordinary* (1993, all MS); *The Lodger* (screen, 1992) *The Woman who Cooked Her Husband* (2f,1m, 1993); *Matilda Liar!* (3f,2m, 1994); *Nasty Neighbours* (3f,3m, 1995) – all Warner Chappell; *Squealin' Like a Pig* (MS, 1998).

See also App. 2: Stephenson and Langridge, Sierz.

Corinne Jacker

American, 1933–

Born in Chicago into a working-class Jewish family, Jacker was a precocious child, writing plays from the age of nine and adapting Chekhov. She abandoned work as a director after encountering sexism and class prejudice but continued writing producing work for stage, screen and radio. Many of her plays deal with radical life changes, from divorce in the Las Vegas-based *In Place* to breakdown in the Obie-winning *Harry Outside*, when an architect finds he can no longer be confined by interior spaces but sets up his studio in the woods, rejecting an alienating, banalized society. Death and dying are central to many of Jacker's plays. In *Later*, a mother and two daughters try to make sense of their memories of their husband/father and their attempts to measure up to the son he never had, and to imagine a new life without him. In *Bits and Pieces* Iris's efforts to make sense of her loss by tracking down the people around the world who received her dead husband's donated organs, interspersed with scenes of his dying, becomes a metaphor for her attempt to remake herself and accept mortality.

Plays include: *Harry Outside* (4f,3m, 1975); *The Chinese Restaurant Syndrome* (2f,1m); *Later* (3f, 1979); *My Life* (4f,5m, 1977); *Night Thoughts* (2f) and *Terminal* (2m, 1977); *Domestic Issues* (3f,3m) – all DPS; *In Place* (2f,1m) in Delgado 1984; *Bits and Pieces* (3f,2m,id, 1975) in Moore and with *Breakfast Lunch Dinner* (2f,1m) in *Two Plays*, DPS, 1975.

See also: TQ 1978; App. 2: Betsko and Koenig.

Elfriede Jelinek

Austrian, 1946–

One of the most controversial contemporary feminist dramatists, Jelinek's work is fierce, funny and frequently bleak. Her plays present an uncompromising analysis of women's subjection and complicity within a capitalist system where their subjectivity will always be denied. Experimental in form, the dense linguistic patterning of her plays eludes translation.

The *Nora* play (cf. **Boothe**) deconstructs Ibsen's *A Doll's House*, presenting a future in which Nora escapes drudgery in a factory when her value as a sexual commodity is appreciated by businessman-politician Weygang, to be exploited and traded for profit in a transaction which eventually returns her to her husband, Torvald. *Krankheit . . . (Illness or Modern Woman)* is a wild black comedy in which Emily Brontë is transformed into the lesbian vampire assistant to a gynaecologist. It explores male projections of female evil, but works with their inherent power to express and explore female anger and aggression. *Services* satirizes the sexual hungers and consumerism of the Austrian bourgeoisie in a reworking of Mozart's *Cosi Fan Tutte* set in a sordid motorway service station where Claudia and Isolde have arranged to meet a 'Bear' and 'Moose' for some animal sex. Increasingly informed by a poststructuralist analysis, later work such as *Totenauberg*, a dissection of the ideas of Heidegger, rejects character and dialogue in favour of 'planes of conflict', collided discourses, scattered with puns and wordplay.

Untranslated plays include: *Krankheit oder Moderne Frauen, Clara S.*

Translated plays include*: *What Happened After Nora Left Her Husband* (5f,8m+) tr. Tinch Minter in Castledine 10; *Totenauberg (Death/Valley/Summit)* (4f,6m+ various) tr. Gitta Honnegger, in Weber; *Services* (4f,7m,id) tr. Nick Grindell, Methuen, 1996; *President Evening Breeze* (2f,4m+) tr. Helga Schreckenberger and Jacqueline Vansant in *Contemporary Austrian Folk Plays* ed. Richard H. Lawson, Riverside, CA: Ariadne Press, 1996.

See also: Sieg; *Yale/Theater*, Spring/Summer 1994.

Ann Jellicoe
English, 1927–

Jellicoe was one of the few women playwrights to emerge from the Royal Court Theatre's first great period. Her best-known play, *The Knack*, became a classic Swinging Sixties film and remains a regular feature of college repertoires, especially in America. It concerns a gawky young woman's encounters with three men who share a flat: artless Colin, nervously discovering sex; eccentric Tom; and Tolen, who boast of his knack with women.

The success of *The Knack* has sadly overshadowed Jellicoe's other plays. *The Sport of My Mad Mother* is a particularly interesting piece, a ritualistic and disturbing dissection of youth culture, which the author described as 'concerned with fear and rage at being rejected from the womb or tribe'. *The Giveaway* is or a surreal comedy in which a family win a lifetime's supply of cornflakes.

---

* Individual dates given are of original plays, not translations.

In the 1980s Jellicoe established the Colway Theatre Trust to put on plays in and with the community. Professional writers including herself, Sheila **Yeger**, Howard Barker and David Edgar would be commissioned to create a play for a town such as Bridport or Sherborne or her own Lyme Regis, providing a role for anyone who wanted one, on-stage or off. Jellicoe's own community works such as *The Reckoning* (MS, 1978) drew on historical events. *The Tide* (MS, 1980) follows the careers in the nineteenth century of a smuggler and the founder of a carpet factory in the Axe Valley; *The Western Women* (MS, 1984, based on a story by Fay **Weldon**) tells of the women's struggle to maintain the town's defences in the siege of Lyme Regis during the Civil War.

Plays include: *The Sport of My Mad Mother* (3f,4m, 1958) and in *The Observer Plays*, 1968; *The Knack* (1f,3m, 1962); *Shelley or The Idealist* (5f,6m); *The Giveaway* (3f,3m, 1970) – all Faber. *The Rising Generation* (many f/m) in Durband 2.

See also: TRI 1988; *Community Plays and How to Put Them On* by Jellicoe, Methuen, 1987, Snyder in MD 37 (1994); *Theatre Research International*, 1988; App. 2: Wandor 1987; Todd; Taylor in Griffiths and Llewellyn-Jones; Sierz.

Gertrude Jennings
British, 1877–1958

Jennings worked as an actress before becoming one of the most prolific women playwrights of the inter-war period, turning out numerous one-acts, many of them with largely female casts, often produced both professionally and by the flourishing Little Theatre market. She is best known today for her pro-suffrage comedy *A Woman's Influence* written for the AFL. Herbert Lawrence, realizing how he has been manipulated by the feminine wiles of his wife's flirtatious friend Mrs Perry, is persuaded to support the struggle for votes to give women a legitimate way of exercising influence.

Jennings's plays are marked by sharp social observation, often of working-class characters, such as the canny nurse of *The Rest Cure*, an aspiring writer who scares an effete poet into running away and leaving her his typewriter. Her three-act comedies include the highly successful *Young Person in Pink* and *Family Affairs*, which presents an unsentimental picture of the shabby facade of middle-class respectability as the Madehursts struggle to survive and maintain appearances through a barrage of crises: affairs, incipient divorce, bankruptcy and the return of the black sheep older son.

Plays include: *Acid Drops* (6f,1m), *Between the Soup and the Savoury* (3f, 1910, also in Marriott 3), *Pros and Cons*, *The Rest Cure* (4f,1m) in *Four One Act Plays*, 1914; *Allotments* (2f, 1918); *Cat's Claws* (3f, 1923); *Elegant Edward* (with E. Boulton, 1f,4m, 1919); *Five Birds in a Cage* (3m,2f, 1915) in Marriott 4; *Love Among the Paint Pots* (4f,6m, 1922); '*Me and My Diary*' (5f,1m, 1922); *The New Poor* (4f,1m, 1920); *Oh These Authors!* (8f,3m, 1925); *Poached Eggs and Pearls* (6f,3m, 1916); *Waiting for the Bus* (10f,2m, 1919); *A Woman's Influence* (4f,1m, 1913) in Spender & Hayman and in Gardner; *The Bathroom Door* (3f,3m, 1916); *Family Affairs* (8f,4m) in Famous 1934; *The Bride* (5f) in Marriott 1931; *The Young Person in Pink* (12f,2m, 1921); *The Olympian* (7f,4m, 1955). All French.

See also App. 2: Gale.

Catherine Johnson
British, 1957–

Bristol-based Johnson writes realistic, sharply comic plays focusing on marginalized or troubled members of a disintegrating British society, especially rootless young men, those who lose or opt out and those who try to exploit social breakdown for gain. Brothers Will and Gary are former members of a punk band, marooned in the Thatcherite 1980s in *Boys Mean Business*. While Gary adapts to the enterprise society with half-baked dreams of making money from a drug deal, Will maintains a semi-coherent rebellion in which self-destruction, nostalgia and social revolt are mixed. In *Renegades*, the plans of a Wild West fan and his violent brother for their private security firm to benefit from the rising crime rate in a leafy Bristol suburb erupt in a confrontation with New Age squatters. In *Dead Sheep* (as in *Rag Doll*, about child sexual abuse or *Shang-a-Lang* about three former glam-rock fans hitting 40), Johnson's focus is on women. Three drying-out addicts on an outward bound weekend with a macho guide and their evangelical Christian carer confront recovery or despair halfway up a mountain. Most recently Johnson has had huge popular success with the book of the Abba musical *Mamma Mia!* (1999).

Plays include: *Rag Doll* (MS, 1987); *Boys Mean Business* (2f,3m) in PI v5, no. 4, Nov. 1989 and in Dromgoole; *Dead Sheep* (3f,2m) in PI v7, no.1, Aug. 1991; *Too Much Too Young* (MS, musical, 1992); *Renegades* (MS, 1995); *Shang-a-Lang* (3f,3m) Faber, 1998.

Eva Johnson
Australian, 1946–

Born in Daly River, Northern Territory, Johnson was brought up at a Methodist mission. A writer, teacher, actress and director, she is actively involved in Aboriginal land rights, the black women's movements and community development. Johnson's plays highlight the pain and injustice suffered by Aboriginal people and issues such as forced sterilization and contraceptive dumping, the destruction of the land by Western farming methods and mining, and the Australian government policy of the 1940s–60s of separating mixed-race children from their Aboriginal families. Johnson was herself snatched from her mother at the age of two and was 42 before she next saw her family. *Murras* traces the history of a family over three decades, from forcible removal from the land to eventual involvement in the struggle to regain it. The image of *murras* or hands, preparing food, making art, handcuffed, is central to a piece that powerfully incorporates chants, music, dance and ritual. *What Do They Call Me?* consists of monologues by three Aboriginal women: one sister brought up in a white family has been denied all knowledge of her Aboriginal identity and is shocked by discovery of her real family, the other sister is a radical lesbian feminist and activist for black rights, while their mother, in a prison cell, struggles against police harassment, memories of abuse and the loss of her daughters.

Plays include: *Djinderella* (MS); *Mimini's Voices* (MS); *Onward to Glory* (MS); *What Do They Call Me?* (3f, 2000) in Spender 1991 and in Parr; *Murras* (3f,3m) in *Plays from Black Australia*, Currency, 1989 and in Tait and Schafer.

Judith Johnson
English, 1962–

Johnson was born in Birkenhead and trained as a teacher before starting to write and has worked extensively for radio (including *Swiftlines and Sweetdreams*, MS), television, community groups, TIE and young people's theatre companies including Y-Touring and Red Ladder.

Her first play, *The Edge* (MS, 1988), is a powerful exploration of a working-class single mother struggling to survive on the edge of breakdown, while *Working Away* (MS, 1987), which won the Second Wave

Young Women Playwrights competition, is a sharp comedy based on Johnson's experience of working as a Butlin's catering assistant against the background of Liverpool's Toxteth riots in 1981. Her plays are marked by a gritty humour and powerful realism and reflect the experience of the generation that grew up under Thatcherism in a world of inner-city decay and unemployment. *Somewhere* draws on the experience of herself and her friends who left school at 16, celebrating freedom, drowning futures in the dole queue, dreaming big dreams, on their parents' booze – and revisits the group ten years on. *Uganda* won the 1994 Thames Best Play Award. What she describes as 'the most difficult thing I have ever written' is a moving exploration of the effects of bereavement on a family trapped in a numbed ritual of grief, circling their widowed father's misery, unable to change or move on.

Plays include: *Somewhere* (4f,6m, 1993) in Edwardes 1; *Uganda* (4f,3m, 1995) in Edwardes 3; *Stone Moon* (6f,1m,+10, 1995) in *Making Scenes* 1; *Shellfish* (MS, 1998). See also App. 2: Stephenson and Langridge.

Jennifer Johnston

Irish, 1930–

Born in Dublin and educated at Trinity College, Johnston is the daughter of writer and director Denis Johnston and actress Sheila Richards; she is married with four children and lives in Derry. While in many novels she addresses the Troubles, and in *Andante in Poco Mosso* the timeless tranquility of a chamber music rehearsal is shattered by the violence of Belfast, in most of her other plays they tend to enter only obliquely. They are treated as a strand of the memories, continually replayed by an individual in pieces that are often, as she called *The Porch*, 'almost a monologue'. In *The Nightingale . . .* the present is less real than Maimie's drunken running quarrel with her long-dead actor husband, called up by her imagination. Actor Tony's childhood recollections (in *The Invisible Man*), as he dresses to play King Lear, are of his distant reserved father, now a dying old man. His relationship with his dresser sustains him, as does Flora's in *The Desert Lullaby*, with Nellie, for years her attendant and protector. Pregnant by her brother, Flora was incarcerated with her mother's connivance and declared 'harmlessly insane' in a piece that hauntingly explores suffocating family tensions, love and loss.

Plays include: *The Nightingale and Not the Lark* (2f,1m, 1980) also in Delgado, 1981; *The Porch* (2f,1m, 1986); *The Invisible Man* (2m, 1987) Dublin: Raven Arts Press, 1988; *Andante in Poco Mosso* (2f,3m) in Delgado, 1983; *Three Monologues*: *Twinkletoes*; *Mustn't Forget High Noon*; *Christine* (1f) and *The Desert Lullaby* (4f,1m, 1996) – both Belfast: Lagan Press.

Charlotte Jones
British, 1968–

A populist comedy writer, Jones however delves deeper exploring her subjects with warmth, compassion and irony. Her first play, *Airswimming*, involves two young women incarcerated in a mental institution since the early 1920s and moves backwards and forwards through the decades to show the effects of imprisonment and the drudgery of their repetitive tasks levened only by their 'airswimming' to music. Imaginative and slightly surreal, it retains its edge as a social-historical commentary. *In Flame* uses a dual time scheme between two sets of women – one in 1908 in Yorkshire and the other in present-day London – to point up how little has changed within individuals even when external circumstances appear quite different. Again madness is a theme, one which recurs in *Martha, Josie and the Chinese Elvis*, a less structurally ambitious work which does however allow Jones to explore a broader range of quirky, oddball but continually believable characters. Four people assemble in Bolton for Josie Botting's sixtieth birthday party. Josie is a dominatrix who has lost the will to dominate, Martha is her obsessive/ compulsive cleaner, Lionel is a former client of Josie's but now just wants a full head of hair, while her daughter wants to be a champion figure-skater. Into this menage comes the surprise guest, the Chinese Elvis, an Elvis impersonator who can't 'do' Elvis and doesn't know the songs. Jones explores the encounter of this disparate group with sympathy and much laughter, avoiding the potential for sentimentality through the sharpness of her writing.

Plays include: *Airswimming* (2f) MS, *In Flame* (4f,2m, 2000), *Martha, Josie and the Chinese Elvis* (4f,2m, 1999). Both Faber.

Marie Jones

Irish, 1951–

One of the founder members of Belfast-based Charabanc Theatre Company for whom she wrote her early plays, Jones is one of the most vibrant contemporary Irish women playwrights. Her language vividly reflects the speech rhythms of 'ordinary' people in Northern Ireland, full of ribald humour, often drawing on interviews and conversations with members of the community. *Lay Up Your Ends* (MS) and *Oul Delf and False Teeth* (MS) had historical themes in the 1911 strike of women workers at a Belfast linen mill and women's hopes for a better life after the Second World War. The effect of lorry-driver Kenny Duncan's severe stroke on the women in his life is explored in *The Hamster Wheel*, which, like all Jones's work, is moving, painful and funny, a piece that questions the costs both of the traditional female virtue of self-sacrificing devotion and of its withdrawal. *Somewhere over the Balcony* (MS) addresses the Troubles through the lives of the women in Belfast's notorious Divis flats, analysing the adjustments people make when living in an unlivable situation of continuing long-term violence: denial, drugs, escapism, emigration, profiteering and pain.

Her more recent plays are for men. The acclaimed *A Night in November* (1996) centres on a major adjustment of vision as Kenneth McCallister, a Protestant dole clerk attending the World Cup qualifying match, is hit by the sectarian hatred that pours from his fellow Ulstermen against the Irish team. He is shocked into radically questioning the values of his tribe, making a trip to New York in support of the Republic of Ireland team and to a joyous discovery of himself as Irish. In the popular *Stones in His Pockets* two men play all the parts as a Hollywood film crew descend on an isolated Irish town, and Jones explores the impact of their invasion and imposition of a idealized fiction of rural life on a real community.

Plays include: *Gold in the Streets* (MS); *The Girls in the Big Picture* (MS); *The Hamster Wheel* (3f,3m, 1990, in Grant); *Women on the Verge of HRT* (MS, 1996); *Stones in His Pockets* (2m) and *A Night in November* (1m, 1994), NHB, 2000.

See also: Maria Dicenzo in TJ 45, no.2; App. 2: Banks and Swift.

Stephanie Jones

New Zealand/Aotearoan, 20th century

Jones's *The Tree* was acclaimed in its day as a bridge between the work of amateur companies and New Zealand's growing professional theatre. It is an understated drama, partly in flashback, of a family after the death of the frustrated, domineering mother, left to circle the ineffectual father, caught in a lethargy symbolized by the over-large tree in the yard which he continually promises to cut down, but never does. The play ends as Hilda, driven away by her mother's harshness, realizes that it is she, not her petted sisters, who has inherited her strength of will.

Plays include: *Dust on the Table* (MS); *Julia's Day* (MS); *The Tree* (4f,2m) Christchurch: Whitcombe and Tombs, 1960.

Patricia Joudry

Canadian, 1921–

Joudry was born in Spirit River, Alberta and grew up in Montreal. She first established herself as an actress, then went on to support her family as a radio dramatist, producing regular episodes of the Canadian sitcom *Penny's Diary* and the American *The Aldrich Family*, as well as numerous individual radio plays before beginning to write for the stage in 1954.

During several years in London from 1962, she produced plays such as *Semi-Detached*, exploring prejudice between French-Canadian and English-Canadian neighbours and *Will You Walk a Little Faster?*, a comedy on progressive education. Joudry's prolonged flirtation with spiritualism and New Age ideas generated both a belief that she was channelling plays from dead dramatists and, later, some gentle satire on the 1960s in works such as *A Very Modest Orgy* (1981), a farce on the impact of the sexual revolution on an upright middle-class couple and their children's several obsessions with horses, urban danger and whole-food lifestyles. *Teach Me How to Cry*, praised for its insight and ironic wit, is a Romeo and Juliet story of high-school students, both social outsiders, drawn together in small-town Canada. *The Song of Louise . . .*, a chilling short play, centres on Stanley's desperate, smothering need for the wife he has supported through a series of dreadful accidents and her eventual realization that they were not accidental.

Plays include: *Galatea* (MS); *The Obsessors* (MS); *Wind in the Wasteland* (MS); *Three Way Destiny* (MS, 1944); *Teach Me How to Cry* (7f,3m) DPS, 1955 and in Wagner; *The Sand Castle* (2f,3m), Playwrights Canada, 1981; *Think Again* (3f,7m) in CTR 23; *Three Rings For Michelle* (3f,2m, 1960) and *The Song of Louise in the Morning* (2f,1m, 1955) – both DPS.

See also: *The Dramatic World of Patricia Joudry* by Aviva **Ravel**, Ottawa: National Library of Canada, 1985.

Miriam Kainy

Israeli, 1942–

Kainy began working in the theatre in 1966, seeing her first play, *The Return*, produced at Tel Aviv's Cameri Theatre in 1973. This was her first of three plays addressing the Israeli–Palestinian conflict. In the powerful 90-minute monologue *Like a Bullet in the Head*, a young Israeli scholar defends himself against accusations of attacking his wife and his young Arab assistant, Hassan. Standing as metaphor for the paranoia of nationalism, the scholar's increasingly desperate attempts to prove that the poet he is researching died in Israel not Egypt, as Hassan believes, have become bound up in his growing suspicion about the relationship between his wife and Hassan.

In Kainy's later plays feminism is central: re-examinations of Hypatia or Antigone and Ismene, or, *Bavta*, a historical musical about women in the second century AD. *The End of the Dream Season* uses comedy to explore a struggle over possessions and values, confronting a matriarchal lineage, through which her grandmother leaves her house to Yosefa and her descendants, with a patriarchal one for which Yosefa's decision to have an illegitimate child threatens family social standing and the family business, Amsalem and Sons. Its protagonist was one of the first economically, emotionally and sexually independent heroines in Israeli theatre.

Translated plays: *The End of the Dream Season* (3f,3m) tr. Helen Kaye and Kainy, in Baraitser; *Like a Bullet in the Head* (MS,1m).

See also: *Theatre in Israel* ed. Linda Ben-Zvi, Ann Arbor: Michigan UP, 1996.

Sarah Kane

British, 1971–99

Kane burst onto the scene in 1995 with an explosion of controversy over *Blasted*. Critics were divided between those who announced a worthy successor to Edward Bond's *Saved*, the last play to excite such vitriol (and banned by the censor in 1965) and those who condemned its 'feast of filth' and 'catalogue of lurid on-stage depravity', horrified by its graphic presentation of cruelty. Supporters, Bond included, praised Kane's moral vision and fierce humanity. Set in a classy Leeds hotel room, the action opens with Ian, a dying journalist, and Cate, a sickly young woman, in an encounter marked by racist abuse, rape, masturbation and violence. The scene is shattered by a mortar explosion and invaded by a soldier who recounts further horrors and, between sobs, rapes the man and blinds him. The play closes with him seen by flashes of light, defecating, cannibalizing the corpse of a baby, dying. Variously read as a comment on nationalism, on a Britain descended into horror and moral despair, on the desperation of a lost generation, it was compared in style to Quentin Tarantino, to Artaud and, in moral and physical content, to the Greek classics.

Greek tragedy was the ground of Kane's equally powerful second play, *Phaedra's Love*, which revisits Phaedra's incestuous passion for her stepson. Hippolytus, blankly chewing junk food as Phaedra gives him a blow job, becomes a wholly unworthy figure, redeemed only by his candid and unapologetic admission of his vileness.

Kane's tragic suicide ended a career which, with *Crave*, had discovered a new Beckettian spareness and poetic vision, presenting a bleak, devastating world redeemed by the desperation of love. Her last play, *4:48 Psychosis*, produced posthumously, gave voice to an intolerable vision of despair, its last words 'please open the curtains' pointing to a world outside the inevitability of suicide, which the writer herself could not reach.

Plays include: *Blasted* (1f,2m, 1996) in Edwardes 2; *Skin* (screen, 1995); *Phaedra's Love* (4f,5m+, 1996); *Cleansed* (2f,5m, 1998); *Crave* (2f,2m, 1998); *4:48 Psychosis* (2f,1m). All in *Complete Plays*, Methuen, 2000.

See also App. 2: Stephenson and Langridge, Sierz.

Manjitpal Kaur

Indian, 1948–

Pal, born in Faridkot, is a published poet and Reader in the School of Punjabi Studies at the University of Amritsar. Her poetic dramas rework Punjabi legends to address contemporary women's dilemmas: *Sahiban* juxtaposes an ancient love story with the struggle for fulfilment of a middle-aged woman, and *Sundran,* in its exploration of female desire, critiques earlier reworkings of the legend of Sundran. *Bandhan* (*Shackles*) focuses on the struggle of a woman writer to get critical attention in a system more interested in her body than her literary abilities.

Untranslated plays include: *Sahiban* (1986); *Bandhan* (1988); *Sarup* (1988).

Translated plays: *Sundran* (6f,8m+, 1991, tr. Dr Tejwant Singh Gill); bilingual edition: Amritsar: Ravi Sahit Parkashan, 1994.

See also: Panjit K. Singh in *Women and Theatre: Occasional Papers* 1, Warwick University, 1992.

Jackie Kay

Scottish, 1961–

Kay grew up in Scotland, the adopted Afro-Caribbean daughter of a white family. She has worked as Literature Officer at the Arts Council of Great Britain, and as poet she has published *A Dangerous Knowing* (1985) and *The Adoption Papers* (1991) about her own adoption and that of her own child. Her novel, *Trumpet,* appeared in 1998.

Chiaroscuro was commissioned by Theatre of Black Women. The play explores the lives of four young black women through dance, music and dialogue, revealing their awakening sexual, political and racial identities. Central are the themes of communication and silence and of naming and selfhood. In her second play, *Twice Over,* first produced by **Gay Sweatshop**, Evaki, reading her grandmother Cora's diaries after her death discovers that Cora was a lesbian. The play presents a variety of responses to the revelation, from Evaki's own progression from incredulous horror to understanding, through Cora's lover's fear of exposure which conflicts with her need to express her grief publicly, to their friend Jean's total incomprehension. The action is overlooked by Cora herself, dead but returned to approve her granddaughter's discovery, to reminisce, enact earlier moments from the relationship in flashback and belatedly to encourage her own and Maeve's coming out.

Plays include: *Every Bit of It* (MS); *Twice Through the Heart* (1996, MS, libretto); *Chiaroscuro* (4f, 1986) in Davis 1; *Twice Over* (6f, 1988) in *Gay Sweatshop: Four Plays & a Company* ed. Philip Osment, Methuen, 1989; *Generations* (1f) in Goodman 2000; *Twilight Shift* (MS) .
See also App.2: Croft in Griffiths and Llewellyn Jones; Goodman; Freeman.

Mollie Keane *see* M. J. Farrell

Charlotte Keatley
English, 1960–

Keatley's major accomplishment rests so far on the huge success of one play, *My Mother Said. . .*, produced internationally. The quintessential mother–daughter drama, set in Manchester over four generations, it explores the frustrations, joys, expectations, desires, fears and resentments of their relationships and the changing ambitions and possibilities open to each woman, shifting back and forth between time frames. Keatley has written of her wish to 'acknowledge the debt . . . to the efforts of women in the past who made progress for us bit by bit through small changes in their daily lives'. It was called 'a warm poignant elegy about growing up, growing old and growing or not growing wise'. Keatley's other work, mostly set in the north-west, includes visual performance pieces and children's work.

Plays include: *Underneath the Arndale* (MS, 1982); *Dressing for Dinner* (MS, 1983); *My Mother Said I Never Should* (4f), Methuen, 1988.
See also: NTQ 22, May 1990; App.2: Stephenson and Langridge.

Frances Anne (Fanny) Kemble
English, 1809–1903

A member of the celebrated Kemble theatrical family, by the age of 20 Fanny Kemble had written her first play and made a glowing stage début as Juliet. She gave up acting for marriage with a Georgia plantation owner, but the marriage failed, in large part due to her fierce opposition to slave-holding. Best of her six plays (including translations) are the verse tragedies, strongly Shakespeare influenced. Most powerful is *An English Tragedy*, which charts its blackmailed heroine's fall into sexual obsession, adultery and then into guilt, madness and eventual death. (See also play by **Luckham** on Kemble's life.)

Plays include: *Francis the First* (4f, 15m+) London: John Murray, 1832 and in Scullion; *Star Of Seville* (4f, 16m) London: Saunders & Otley, 1837; *An English Tragedy* (2f,7m+, 1838) in *Plays*, London: Longman, etc., 1863.

See also: Kemble's *Journals* (on slavery) and writings on Shakespeare (extracts in Malpede, see App. 2); *Fanny Kemble and the Lovely Land* by Constance Wright, London: Robert Hale, 1972.

Jenny Kemp
Australian, 1949–

Highly visual in her approach, writer and director Kemp teaches at the Victorian College of the Arts in Melbourne. Her multi-media pieces reject linear narrative in favour of repeated sequences of action, movement and video, influenced by surrealism and the work of archetypal psychologist James Hillman. *The Black Sequin Dress* excavates the cultural meanings of falling – its terror, danger and humiliation, falling in love and its vulnerability and pleasure, the Fall into knowledge and death. Repeated images of a woman slipping over on a dance floor are juxtaposed with references to the journey to the Underworld across the River Styx and with monologues that, playing with the etymology of words, evoke memories and desires, in a piece which attempts to find a theatrical language to explore the psyche. In *Remember* a fractured interior landscape of remembered terror constantly intrudes upon the hospital room reality of a woman who has been raped.

Plays include: *The Black Sequin Dress*, (4f+1fv,2m) Currency, 1996; *Call of the Wild* (4f,1m, 1989) in Allen and Pearlman; *Sheila Alone* (MS); *Remember* (3f,2m, id, 1993) in Tait and Schafer.

See also: Minchinton in *Performance Research*, v3, 2.

Adrienne Kennedy

American, 1931–

One of the most visionary American playwrights, Kennedy's disturbing and highly evocative poetic plays broke new ground for black American theatre in the 1960s. Work such as *Funnyhouse of a Negro* is haunted by historical or semi-mythical figures – Bette Davis, Patrice Lumumba, Queen Victoria – and by images of baronial castles and Roman ruins, the detritus of the European imagination as Kennedy mines the cultural inheritance of evil, madness and self-loathing attached to blackness, to kinky hair, to mixed blood. Set in nightmarish spaces characters obsessively relive snatches of memory and imagination, aspects of fragmented black identities. Catholic religious imagery runs through many of the plays. In *A Rat's Mass*, while the white girl Rosemary walks in procession and stands 'exalted' on a great slide, 'Brother and Sister Rat', two black children, recite relentless images of Nazis, blood, the threat of lynching and exclusion. The class of black schoolgirls in *A Lesson* ... are taught by a great White Dog under the gaze of religious statues.

In recent work Kennedy has created an alter ego, Suzanne Alexander, a prominent writer who reflects on her working process, weaving stories, memory, descriptions of horror, re-creating and reflecting on past events such as the brutal beating of a young middle-class black man in the autobiographical *Sleep Deprivation Chamber* (written with her son Adam Kennedy).

Plays include: *Funnyhouse of a Negro* (5f,3m, 1964) also in Hatch and Shine; *A Rat's Mass* (3f,6m, 1966) also in Poland; *A Lesson In Dead Language* (8f, 1970); *A Movie Star has to Star in Black and White* (5f,5m, 1976) in Marranca and Dasgupta 3; *Sun* (1m, 1968) – all in *Adrienne Kennedy in One Act*, Minnesota UP, 1988; *The Lennon Play: In His Own Write*, NY: Simon and Schuster, 1972; *She Talks to Beethoven* (1f,1m, 1989) in Halpern and with *The Ohio State Murders* (4f,4m, 1992); *The Film Club* (1f) 'a monologue by Suzanne Alexander'; *The Dramatic Circle* (2f,3m, radio) also in Mahone, in *The Alexander Plays*, Minnesota UP, 1992; *Sleep Deprivation Chamber* (2f,5m+5) TCG, 1997; *Motherhood 2000* (1f,4m, 1994) in Marranca.

See also: Wilkerson in TA 40, 1985; *People who Led to My Plays* by Kennedy, TCG, 1987; App. 2: Meigs in Schlueter; Betsko and Koenig.

Margaret Kennedy

British, 1896–1967

Known first as a novelist, Kennedy had enormous commercial success when Basil Dean persuaded her to join him in adapting her *The Constant Nymph* for the stage in 1926. It focuses on some of the many illegitimate offspring of the brilliant but impecunious composer Sanger. Kennedy celebrates the bohemian lives of artists, rejecting acclaim, financial gain and bourgeois sexual convention in favour of pursuing inspiration. Lewis Dodd makes a foolish marriage with Florence, devoted to building a successful career for him, failing to realize that he should have waited until Tessa, Sanger's daughter and Dodd's kindred spirit, was old enough to marry. Rejecting his recently won critical acclaim, they run away together, but she dies of a heart attack in their sordid 'romantic' lodgings, escaping a world of compromise and squalor (a dénouement that allows her to remain conventionally virginal). Kennedy's emerging critique of bohemian irresponsibility, suggested in the ending, is central to the sequel, *Escape Me Never* (1933). Here, the conflicts of responsibility and artistic freedom are more evenly addressed in the choice facing Fenella, between two Sanger brothers: dependable Caryl and brilliant womanizing composer Sebastian, who is prepared to abandon his wife and dying baby to pursue art and the woman who inspires him.

Plays include: *The Constant Nymph* (11f, 12m, 1926) and in Morgan 1994; *Come With Me* (9f, 16m), Heinemann, 1927 – both with Basil Dean; *Escape Me Never* (3f,4m+), Heinemann, 1934; *Autumn* (with Gregory Ratoff, 7f,6m, tr. from Ilya Surguchev) in *Five Plays Of Our Time* ed. Sydney Box, London: Thomas Nelson & Sons, 1939.
  See also: *The Constant Novelist* by Violet Powell, Heinemann, 1983.

Jean Kerr

American, 1924–

Humourist and popular boulevard playwright, Kerr has attributed her comic perspective on life as a means of compensating for her great height (5ft 11in or 1.8m). Much of her work has been produced in collaboration, especially with her husband, essayist and drama critic Walter Kerr, with whom she also produced a large family, the topic of much of her comedy. Plays, humorous articles and films like *Please Don't Eat the Daisies* (1960, featuring Doris Day as Kerr) explore the ironies and absurdities of family life and companionable, shared marriage. In *Lunch Hour*, two rejected spouses, one a marriage guidance counsellor, whose partners are having an affair, concoct a fictional liaison of their own to win them back. In *Mary, Mary*, an ex-wife intrigues to win back her former husband. In more serious vein, *Poor Richard* presents a Dylan Thomas-style poet, forced to conquer fear and confront his ambivalent emotions for his dead wife, which he has formerly evaded and drowned in a bottle.

Plays include: *Our Hearts were Young and Gay* (9f,8m, from Cornelia Otis Skinner and Emily Kimbrough), Chicago: DPS, 1946; *The Songs of Bernadette* (11f,7m, with W. Kerr, 1958); *Jennie Kissed Me* (10f,4m) DPS, 1949; *Poor Richard* (2f,3m) NY: Doubleday, 1965; *Mary, Mary* (2f,3m, 1961) and in Gassner; *Goldilocks* (with W. Kerr, 3f,7m, 1958); *King of Hearts* (2f,9m, 1954) in *Mary Mary and Other Plays* Greenwich, CN: Fawcett, 1964; *Finishing Touches* (3f,5m), DPS, 1973; *Lunch Hour* (2f,3m) Garden City: Doubleday, 1981.

Wendy Kesselman
American, 1940–

Kesselman's powerful *My Sister in This House* returns to the source material that inspired Jean Genet's *The Maids*, the real-life murder in Le Mans of a mother and daughter by their maids, Christine and Lea Papin. Kesselman's play, adapted for the cinema as *Sister My Sister* (1996), disturbingly re-creates the oppressive atmosphere of claustrophobic middle-class existence where, while the Papins retreat into a self-contained, attic world in which they are at once sisters, mother and daughter and lovers, the mistresses are domineering and impatient to find fault with their flawless work and, in frustration with their respectable idleness, become increasingly obsessed with their servants' taciturn independence. The mounting tension builds towards explosive violence.

The majority of Kesselman's other plays are written for children. The bilingual *Maggie Magalita* centres on a young Hispanic girl's frustration with her immigrant grandmother's inability to speak English, which reinforces her sense of being an outsider. *I Love You . . .*, also focusing on the experience of outsiders and on language and identity, movingly explores the relationship between shy, bookish, adolescent Daisy and her grandmother, Polish-speaking Jewish survivor, Nana. *Olympe and the Executioner* focuses on the life of the French Revolutionary playwright and pamphleteer, Olympe de Gouges.

Plays include: *My Sister in this House* (4f,3mv, 1981) in Hanna and in Kilgore; *Maggie Magalita* (3f,1m, 1987); *I Love You, I Love You Not* (2f, 1988), French; *Olympe and the Executioner* (5f,7m, 1989) in Munk; *The Juniper Tree: a Tragic Household Tale* (2f,1m) DPS, 1985; *Becca!* (musical) New Orleans: Anchorage Press, 1988.

See also App. 2: Mandl in Schlueter; Hart in Hart; Schroeder in Keyssar ed.

Stella Kon

Singaporean, 1944–

Kon, born in Edinburgh, Scotland, is a novelist and playwright whose monodrama *Emily of Emerald Hill* has been hugely successful in Asia, acclaimed as showing 'the most fully realized, complex human character in the history of Singapore drama in English'. Based on Kon's own grandmother, a Singaporean matriarch from the Nonya Chinese community, Emily conducts her gentle domination of the lives of her family and friends, presiding over affairs by phone or conducting elaborate parties as élite hostess, in a play which moves between time frames across Emily's and her society's lives. Like *The Bridge* and *Trial* it was a first prizewinner in Singapore's National Playwriting Competition. Other educational plays in the *Emporium* collection address mother–son conflicts and use myth and history to explore young people's need to challenge hypocrisy, intolerance and hatred.

Plays include: *The Naga in the Swamp* (1f,8m, 1f/m+); *Asoka* (3f, 10m+); *Kumba Kumba* (5f,7m); *Emporium* (7m); *In the Repair Shop* (1f,4m) in *Emporium and Other Plays*, Singapore: Heinemann Educational Books, 1977; *Emily of Emerald Hill* (1f, 1984) London: Macmillan, 1989; *The Scholar's Mother* (2f,3m) in *Prize-Winning Plays 1* ed. Robert Yeo Singapore: Ministry of Culture, 1980; *Trial* (MS, 1986); *The Bridge* (1f, 17m, 1992); *Dragon's Teeth Gate* (4f,9m, 1990); *Silent Song* (2f,3m, 1992). All Singapore: Constellation Books.

See also: Pakir in *Perceiving Other Worlds* Singapore: Times Academic Books, 1991; Jit in *Tenggara* 23, 1989; App. 2: Tompkins and Holledge.

Clare Beecher Kummer

American, 1886–1958

Kummer has been seen as a precursor to playwrights such as Philip Barry and S. N. Behrman, her witty, satiric, slightly risqué comedies often compared to European work by contemporaries. She began life professionally as a songwriter before producing the highly successful 'Good Gracious Annabelle', based on her discovery of servants in the splendid Long Island mansions living in luxury while their masters are away. Her unconventional heroine, finding herself homeless, penniless and cited as a co-respondent in a divorce case, enlists as cook and recruits her impecunious artist friends to other positions before redis-covering her long-lost, now wealthy, husband. Other plays capitalized on the popularity of her quirky, comic characters. Rollo of *Rollo's Wild Oat* is determined, before settling down, to play Hamlet and embarks on mounting a production to riotous effect.

Plays include: 'Good Gracious Annabelle' (4f, 10m, 1916); *The Rescuing Angel* (4f,7m, 1923); 'Be Calm, Camilla!' (3f,6m, 1918); *Rollo's Wild Oat* (5f,7m, 1920); *A Successful Calamity* (4f,8m, 1922); *Pomeroy's Past* (5f,5m, 1926); *Her Master's Voice* (4f,3m, 1934) – all NY: French; *The Robbery* (2f,3m, 1921) in *One Acts Plays vol. 1* (Thomas).

See also App. 2: Shafer.

Marie Laberge
French-Canadian, 1950–

Laberge, who also directs, is author of more than 18 plays, whose self-declared themes are '. . . oh! so light (death, love, madness, solitude . . .)'. Alienation, suicide, alcoholism and addiction also haunt her stages, but so do love and passion, whether between a married couple (*Deux Tangos. . .*) or a mother and her adoptive daughter (*Sisters*). In *Anse à Gilles* Laberge explores the forces that drive a young widow to escape village life and else-where those that destroy the village itself when its social and economic centre collapses. Most powerfully her plays address the breakdown or per-version of human communication between husbands and wives or others. *Night*, set in a shabby motel room, is a shocking and powerful monologue. The relentless barrage of words as a father attempts to communicate with his silent, anorexic daughter reveal, even while he continues to hide from the realization himself, his possessiveness and incestuous desire for her, and her retreat into increasingly self-destructive behaviour.

Untranslated plays include: *Ils étaient venus pour . . .* (1976); *Eva et Evelyne* (1981); *Deux tangos pour toute une vie* (1982); *Pierre ou Consolation* (dramatic poem, 1992); *Le banc* (1981).

Translated plays include: *Before the War, Down at Anse à Gilles* (3f,1m) tr. Alan Brown, 1981; *Night* (1f,1m, 1984) in Remnant 7, *Take Care* (4f,1m), *Sisters* (2f) – all three tr. Rina Fraticelli. MSs from CEAD.

See also: THC, 8, 1987.

Myrna Lamb
American, 1935–

Lamb, from New Jersey, was one of the first American playwrights to give dramatic expression to the growing women's movement in the 1970s. Like **Arden** in Britain, she draws on the collage of theatrical techniques that characterized contemporary experiment, including symbolism, grotesque parody, Brechtian song, dance, slide and film projections. *The Mod Donna*, the first feminist musical, is published with an essay on marriage, while scenes from a soap opera, in which a wealthy couple adopt a young woman as sexual plaything to spice up their marriage, are juxtaposed with songs by a chorus of women.

While Lamb's plot reads as time-bound and tend to ramble, her lyrics remain witty, incisive and passionate, and her shorter polemical pieces, such as *But What have You Done . . .*, a forceful argument for abortion rights, retain their force in a climate where, in the USA, they are again under threat. In pieces such as *Apple Pie* (described by Patraka as 'agony set to music'), in which a woman is systematically humiliated and victimized by a tyrannical court, Lamb has sometimes been criticized for the hyperbolic use of Holocaust imagery to describe the oppression of women.

Plays include: *The Mod Donna* (10f,3m); *But What have You Done for Me Lately?* (2f,2m); *The Butcher Shop* (2m); *The Serving Girl and the Lady* (2f); *In the Shadow of the Crematoria* (1f,1m); *Monologia* (1f or m), *Pas de Deux* (1f or m) – all 1969 as *The Mod Donna and Skyklon Z*, NY: Pathfinder Press, 1971; *Apple Pie* (3f,7m, libretto) in W&P 2; *I Lost a Pair of Gloves Yesterday* (1f) in Moore.

See also: Patraka in W&P2.

Else Lasker-Schüler
German, 1869–1945

Lasker-Schuler, born in Elberfeld to a middle-class Jewish family, became part of a bohemian circle, reinventing herself and her world, dressing in costume to live out the roles of 'Princess Tino of Baghdad' and 'Joseph, Prince of Thebes' in the streets and cafés. Central to her work are her conflicts as a marginalized figure within both German and Jewish traditions, while her intense, lyrical poetry also reflects the personal tragedies of her life: divorces, poverty, the death of her son. Her books banned by the Nazis, she fled to Switzerland in 1933 and then to Palestine, where she died.

Her first play, *Die Wupper* (1909, produced 1919), is set in the industrial city of Wuppertal. Written in regional dialect, it is an epic exploration of the lives of the people and their struggle for better conditions, but also addresses the spiritual and sexual impact of social and economic realities through the marginal figures of three tramps. The sweeping, visionary *IandI*, produced by Judith **Malina** in 1990, confronts aspects of Jewish identity and the horrors of the Nazi regime. Framed within a theatrical metaphor, as a woman poet prepares to see Max Reinhardt stage her latest work, it reworks Goethe's *Faust* (cf. **Mnouchkine**), drawing on a mass of classical and popular cultural referents. It is set in Hell where Mephisto, marvelling at their murderous vigour, entertains Goebbels and Goering, both eager 'to learn a little more about the business' but appalled by the lava mass that engulfs their soldiers, sucking them into the underworld.

Untranslated play: *Arthur Aronymus und seine Väter* (1932).

Translated plays: *Dark River* (9f, 11m+, 1909) tr. from *Die Wupper* by Jane E. Curtis, Dissertation: Catholic University of America, 1982; *IandI* (3f,23m+,dp, n.d.) tr. Beate Hein-Bennett in Case.

See also App. 2: Sieg.

Marghanita Laski
British, 1915–88

Novelist and journalist and for several years Chair of the Arts Council, Laski's play was a contribution to the anti-nuclear movement in the 1950s and shocked audiences when broadcast on television. It addresses the effects on Britain of nuclear war, the existence faced by a handful of survivors and both the horrors and moral dilemmas confronting them in attempting to re-create a society.

Play: *The Offshore Island* (2f,9m) London: Mayfair, 1959.

Bryony Lavery
British, 1947–

Lavery's work developed out of the alternative theatre movement that emerged in the 1970s. She has worked with numerous feminist, youth and community groups, including her own Les Oeufs Malades (later called Female Trouble), Women's Theatre Group, Theatre Centre, often producing plays that use a Brechtian presentational approach, mixing songs, cabaret, jokes, multiple quick changes of role and theatrical devices. *Wicked*, developed with the women ex-offenders' company, Clean Break, features a magic show. The characters are wicked women shut up in boxes, the prisoners of travelling showman, Bailey; a ventriloquist's dummy who parrots the right lines; homeless people; freaks; a knife act who mutilates herself; and a banshee who howls in anger and speaks in limericks. The popular *Her Aching Heart* parodies the romances of Georgette Heyer and Daphne **Du Maurier** in a lesbian love story between the hell-raising Lady Harriet Helstone and buxom young wench Molly Penhallow. Rewriting male versions of history is central to both *Origins of the Species* and *A Wedding Story*. Archaeologist Molly's unearthing of a 4-million-year-old woman in *Origins* is the impetus for an exploration of human evolution and women's often ignored role within it, as well as a questioning of her own past, while *Witchcraze* draws parallels between seventeenth-century witch-hunts (cf. **Churchill**) and media and establishment scapegoating of Greenham Common women.

Plays include: *Bag* (MS, 1979); *For Mary, Betty and Ida* (MS, 1982); *Kitchen Matters* (MS), *Origins Of the Species* (2f) in Remnant 6; *Witchcraze* (3f) in Griffin & Aston; *Ophelia* (extracts) in Goodman 1999; *Numerical Man* (14f/m) and *Uniform and Uniformed* (3f,8m) in *Masks and Faces*, London: Macmillan Education, 1984; *Calamity Jane* (MS, 1984); *Her Aching Heart** (2f), *Two Marias* (4f), *Wicked* (3f) – all Methuen, 1991; *Goliath* (from Beatrix Campbell's novel, 1f) in Castledine 11,* and *Nothing Compares To You* (6f,1m,id) in *Plays One*, Methuen, 1998; *Frozen* (MS, 1998); *More Light* (17f,2m) in *New Connections*; *Behind the Scenes at the Museum* (from Kate Atkinson's novel, 6f,3m) and *A Wedding Story* (3f, 2m) – both Faber, 2000.

See also App.2: Todd; Stephenson and Langridge; Reinelt in Hart and Phelan; Freeman.

Maureen Lawrence

British, 1937–

Lawrence, who began playwriting after raising a family, has also written novels and worked as a teacher, an experience reflected in many pieces for TIE. Her most revived play, *Tokens of Affection*, is set in a unit for maladjusted young girls who have been excluded from school, rejected or abused by parents and are caught in a system that prioritizes minimizing costs and behavioural manipulation through rewards and punishments over emotional understanding and genuine help. Lawrence writes with fine observation and enormous emotional honesty, reflecting the turmoil of teenagers whose behaviour jolts between adult knowingness, violent bravado and child-like neediness. In *Father's Day* she focuses with equal compassion and fierce realism on the effect on a family of the father's slow-motion collapse into Alzheimer's disease (cf. **Carson**). More recent plays are historical-biographical in focus: *Real Writing* (MS, 1995) examines the relationship between Russian poets Anna Akhmatova and Lydia Chukovskaya. The award-winning *Resurrection* concerns the relationship between Dr Johnson, the philologist, and his black servant, Francis Barber, questioning the limits and effectiveness of liberal paternalism in a racist society. Despite being left Johnson's property, Barber was cheated out of it by the burghers of Johnson's native Lichfield and died in the poorhouse. In the second half of Lawrence's play Barber's deathbed is attended by the ghost of Johnson as he attended Johnson's in the first half, while their memories are played out in flashback.

Plays include: *Tokens of Affection* (7f, 1986) in Castledine 9; *Black Ice* (MS, 1986); *Father's Day* (MS, 1993); *Resurrection* (2m, MS, 1996); *Real Writing* (MS, 1997); *Twins* (2f) Faber, 1998.

Tobsha Learner

Australian, 1959–

Learner's plays are concerned with the haunting of the present by myth, memory and history, drawing on naturalistic and expressionistic performance vocabularies: a table that bleeds, a mermaid's cry. In *Wolf* she explores male sexual compulsion, interweaving artist Daniel's reworked narrative of the Red Riding Hood story (cf. **Carter**), an attempt to make sense of what drives his obsession, with his sexual exploits over several decades, and their effect on his wife and friends. *Witchplay* is a blackly humorous monologue as a 70-year-old Jewish medium in Australia becomes animated by the tortured and persecuted of history, from a seventeenth-century witch to her own family, dead in Auschwitz. In *The Glass Mermaid* the haunted are a Bosnian refugee and the friends and family of Karl who has committed suicide by drowning, as they try to make sense of devestation and loss and remake their lives.

Plays include: *Wolf* (3f,2m,id, 1992); *The Glass Mermaid* (3f,2m, 1994); *Witchplay* (1f, 1995); *Miracles* (6f,6m,dp) – all Currency; *The Gun in History* (2f+,2m,id, 1994) in Horin; *S.N.A.G. (Sensitive New Age Guy)* (MS, 1992).
    See also App. 2: Tompkins and Holledge.

Doris Lessing
   South African/British, 1919–

Lessing's plays, like her novels, draw on the experience of left-wing intellectuals, especially women like herself, in the 1950s. In a theatrical context, where for the radical new male dramatists the woman's place was, typically, behind the ironing-board, Lessing's writing was ground-breaking in showing professional women, sexual but refusing marriage, passionately engaged in questions of political commitment and personal morality: how best to live. *Each His Own Wilderness* centres on the tense relationship between a middle-aged woman and her son, where her rebellion against her socialist non-conformity expresses itself as a desire for normalcy and domesticity. Despite attempts to move towards a symbolic staging, when the walls dissolve so the room becomes part of the city outside to suggest a universality in the confrontation of the sexes between Kerouac-style drifter Dave and his lover Anna, *Play with a Tiger* remains primarily naturalistic, weighted with stage directions describing the characters' states of mind. In *The Singing Door* Lessing creates an allegorical piece, suggesting a post-nuclear landscape where humanity survives in a multi-levelled underground bunker, strictly hierarchic and bureaucratic. In this environment, genuine belief in the enduring official prophecy of the 'opening of the door' becomes an act of faith and of rebellion.

Plays include: *Each His Own Wilderness* (3f,4m) in Browne, 1959; *Play with a Tiger* (3f,3m, 1962) in Sullivan & Hatch; *The Singing Door* (19+f/m) in Durband – all in *Play with a Tiger and Other Plays*, London: Flamingo, 1996; *Care and*

Protection (TV); *Do Not Disturb* (TV); *Between Men* (TV); *The Making of the Representative for Planet 8* (MS, libretto, music by Philip Glass).

See also: Krouse in *World Literature Written in English* 15, 1976; App.2: Wandor 1987.

Kathy Lette
Australian, 1958–

Now British-based and best known in recent years for her comic novels (*Mad Cows, Foetal Attraction, Altar Egos*), Lette had an earlier incarnation as a playwright, especially for youth theatre. Her acute ear for contemporary slang was displayed in the successful *Grommitts* (cf. fellow Australian Debra Oswald's *Dags*), which explores the teenage sub-cultures of Australia and the pressure to fit in and be a Waxhead (surfer), Vegiehead, Bongbrain, Headbanger and the like, with an acute ear for contemporary slang. Jodie, an obsessive footballer, finds herself increasingly an outsider from her gang and in terrible danger of becoming a grommitt ... the ones who don't fit in.

Plays include: *Wet Dreams* (MS); *Perfect Mismatch* (1f,1m) in *Shorts at the Wharf* v1 1985 and *Grommitts* (3f,2m, 1988) – both Currency.

Deborah Levy
British, 1959–

Levy was born to Jewish, anti-apartheid activist parents in South Africa. During her childhood her father underwent imprisonment and the family later moved to Britain. Trained at Dartington College of Arts, she has published poetry, stories and novels including *Swallowing Geography* and *The Unloved*. Her poetic plays and performance texts experiment across genres – *Pax* was described as, 'a dense hallucinatory journey through a future steeped in a European past'. Like many of Levy's plays, *Pax* used an innovative combination of music, dialogue, movement and visual imagery in its exploration of cultural landscapes haunted by the memory of war, represented by the image of an empty house presided over by the 'Keeper' and visited by the 'Mourner', a modern woman haunted by fears of nuclear threat. *Clam* is equally haunted by the possibility of nuclear war. Its man and woman characters are at once

Vladimir Lenin and Nadia Krupskaya, Alice and Harry, doctor and patient, as they enact a poetic and theatrical exploration of European history. *Heresies* was commissioned by the RSC women's group, a number of actresses frustrared by the quantity and and quality of roles on offer to women, and produced through a series of workshops. An exploration of power and female creativity, its emblematic characters include a refugee, a futuristic architect, a courteson and a housekeeper. In creating *The B File*, Levy worked with an international cast and a translator at the Magdalena Project in Cardiff. She incorporated the translator into the cast of a piece featuring five versions of the same character, Beatrice, who is, in her many guises, interpreted and interrogated in an investigation of dislocation, borders, imaginary geographies, homesickness and desire. Later works have continued to investigate hybrid and fragmented identites, and to explore the possibilites of theatrical form including the interaction of film and the live event. Shakespeare (mis)remembered, distorted, re-invented is a constant point of reference, whether Ophelia's perpetual unhappiness and marginality, or contemporary 'millennial numbness', beyond God and politics, *Macbeth – False Memories*.

Plays include: *Dream Mamma* (MS, 1985); *Our Lady* (MS, 1986); *Blood Wedding* (MS, 1994, libretto, from Lorca); *Ophelia and the Great Idea* (MS, 1985); *Call Blue Jane* (MS, 1993); *Shiny Nylon* (MS, 1994), *Heresies* (7f,2m) and *Eva and Moses* (1f,1m) Methuen, 1987; *The B File* (5f, 1993) also in Levy, *Pax* (4f, 1984) also in Remnant 6; *Clam* (1f,1m, 1985) also in Lowe 1; *Honey, Baby* (2f,3m, 1995); *Pushing the Prince into Denmark* (2f, 1991); *Macbeth – False Memories* (2f,3m, 2000) in *Levy: Plays One*, Methuen, 2000.

Wendy Lill

Canadian, 1950–

Originally from Vancouver, Lill now lives in (and serves in parliament for) Nova Scotia. This is the location of her prize-winning *The Glace Bay Miners' Museum* (an adaptation of Sheldon Currie's short story) set in the industrial landscape of Cape Breton in 1947, where Margaret MacNeil guides the visitor through the museum she has established in her home to memories and lives destroyed by the mine-owners' neglect and greed. Lungs preserved in formaldehyde serve as grim memorial to her grandfather's life strangled by coal dust, and to her husband's bagpipe-playing before he was crushed with her brother in a rock-fall. Earlier plays cover subjects such as the suffrage activism of Francis Beynon and Nellie McClung, and the treatment of native Canadians and their cultural legacy (*Sisters, Heather Rose*). Lill's *All Fall Down*, inspired by Arthur Miller's *The Crucible*, provides a compelling dissection of the effect on a community of allegations of sexual abuse at a day-care centre, as doubt and rumour ignite an atmosphere of hysteria.

Plays include: *The Occupation of Heather Rose* (1f, 1986) in Bessai & Kerr; *Memories of You* (4f,1m) Toronto: the Summerhill Press, 1989; *All Fall Down* (2f, 1fv,2m,2mv, 1985); *The Fighting Days* (3f,1m, 1985) and in CTR 42, Spring 1985 and in Tylee; *Sisters* (4f,2m, 1991) – all Vancouver: Talonbooks; *The Glace Bay Miners' Museum* (2f,3m, 1996, based on Sheldon Currie's novel); *Corker* (2f,4m, 1998) – both: Burnaby BC: Talonbooks.

Sonia Linden* (alt. Lyndon)
British, 20th century

Linden's *Present Continuous* addresses issues of cultural difference and relativism, criticizing both English arrogance and traditional Japanese female subservience through the experience of a young English teacher posted to a rural community and the effect of her friendship and example of feminist independence on the Japanese woman she lodges with. Setsuko is first encouraged to defy her family but then left increasingly isolated and desperate when Jane moves away to the greater excitements of Tokyo and greater intellectual rewards of a friendship with an educated Japanese woman. Linden's *The Strange Passenger*, set in the Terezin concentration camp, restages the time-honoured conflict of the material world and the artistic impulse, focusing on the Czech composer Viktor Ullman and the terrible irony of the new creative liberation he discovered in captivity and its effect on those around him.

Plays include: *Present Continuous* (3f) Tokyo: Sanyusha Publishing Co., 1986; *Now and at the Hour of Our Death* (MS, 1988); *The Strange Passenger* (3f,2m, 1995) in Linden 1998; *The Jewish Wife* (MS, 1997).

---

*Linden changed her name in 1997, rejecting her ex-husband's name in favour of one reflecting her German-Jewish origins and, in a letter to the author, gives her year of (re)birth as 1997.

Joan Lipkin
American, 1954–

Lipkin comes from Chicago and is artistic director of the St Louis-based That Uppity Theatre Company. Her best-known play, the pro-Choice musical *He's Having Her Baby*, wittily uses the stock feminist convention of role reversal to expose the absurdities and inequities of sex role conventions and lack of access to contraception. Joey is forced to go all the way on his first date with Liz and ends up pregnant at fifteen confronting the problems of single-parenthood in a world of predatory females, sexual harassment and restricted abortion rights.

The interrogation of gender behaviours and their social acceptability is also central to *Small Domestic Acts*, which plays on lesbian identities through the experience of two couples, one straight: Frank and Sheila; the other butch–femme lesbians: Frankie and Sheila. As the friendship between workmates Frank and Frankie grows over their mutual enjoyment of beer and cards, the growing attraction between the two Sheilas destabilizes both relationships. The piece draws on Pirandellian techniques foregrounding the characters' re-enactment of their story, each questioning the relative sympathy given his or her position, and on Brecht, encouraging the audience to examine the social and political choices enacted before them.

Plays include: *Small Domestic Acts* (3f,1m, 1995) in Curb; *The Girl Who Lost Her Voice* (1f) in Goodman 2000; *He's Having Her Baby* (with Tom Clear, 3f,3m,id) in Lipkin and Gainor (planned for 2001).
See also: Lipkin in Donkin and Clement (App. 2) and in *Australian Feminist Studies* 21, Autumn, 1995; NTQ 9,36, 1993; App. 1: Wolf in Curb.

Joan Littlewood
English, 1914–

A working-class Londoner, Littlewood won a scholarship to RADA but rejected its narrow bourgeois conception of theatre. She ran away to Manchester, meeting Jimmie Miller (aka Ewen MacColl) and joined his Theatre of Action company, the Red Megaphones. There she produced socialist agit-prop in depressed 1930s Salford while making a living as an actress at Rusholme Rep.

While most critical attention has focused on Littlewood's career as director, it is inseparable from her work as writer. She collaborated on scripts such as *War*, which exposes the political motives behind the slaughter of the First World War, a theme she returned to in 1963 with *Last Edition*, a Living Newspaper (cf. **Flanagan**), dealing with unemployment, mining disasters and the Spanish Civil War, and *John Bullion*, a constructivist 'ballet' exposing the military-industrial complex. To survive she also wrote numerous other scripts, from a soap opera called *Front Line Family* (with Marjorie Banks, MS) and other plays for BBC radio, to a nativity play for the Rep. She achieved major recognition in the 1950s and 1960s with the establishment of the Theatre Workshop in Stratford, east London. Littlewood also worked with writers such as Shelagh **Delaney** and Brendan Behan to develop raw scripts, adapted Balzac, Lewis Carroll, Wolf Mankowitz and most famously scripted *Oh, What a Lovely War!* (1963), the ground-breaking anti-war musical.

Plays include: *War* (1932 with PJP, 8f/m,dp) in *Theatres of the Left 1880–1935* by Raphael Samuels, Ewen MacColl and Stuart Cosgrove, Routledge and Kegan Paul, 1985; *The Voyage of the Chelyuskin* (MS, c.1935); *John Bullion* (10f,13m,dp, c.1935); *Last Edition* (c.10+m/f,dp, 1940) both with MacColl in *Agit-Prop to Theatre Workshop* ed. Goorney and MacColl, Manchester UP, 1986; *The Long Shift* (with Gerry Raffles, MS, 1951); *Oh, What a Lovely War!* (with Theatre Workshop and Charles Chiltern, 5f,14m,id) Methuen, 1965.

See also: *Joan's Book* (autobiography) 1994; *The Theatre Workshop Story* by Howard Goorney (1981), both Methuen; App. 2: Tompkins and Holledge; Callaghan in Laughlin and Schuler.

Liz Lochhead
Scottish, 1947–

Lochhead, from Motherwell, is a poet and performer besides being the most important contemporary Scots woman playwright. *Blood and Ice* stands alongside her poetry collection *Dreaming Frankenstein* (1984), outcomes of a continuing engagement with issues of female creativity and the myths surrounding Mary Shelley. The play takes place within Mary's consciousness, mixing memory and imagination in an exploration of the monstrous female, repressed rage, sexuality and maleness: the psyche of the woman writer. Lochhead returned to Gothic horror in *Dracula*, a brilliant re-creation of the familiar story, linguistically rich, theatrically powerful and chilling. She reinstates the centrality of both Lucy, focusing on her anorexia and sexual hysteria, and the madman-savant Renfield.

Lochhead's work includes political satire combined with black comedy, in the form of a Scots translation of Molière's *Tartuffe*, tart performance poems and monologues, and *Mary Queen of Scots . . .* (part of a continuing collaboration with the Communicado Theatre Company that includes *Jock Tamsin's Bairns*, an alternative Burns-night festivity). A re-examination of Scottish history, the myth of nationhood, the inheritance of Calvinism and John Knox's hatred of the 'monstrous regiment of women', it juxtaposes the careers of Queens Mary and Elizabeth, each differently frustrated in the attempt both to wield power in a male world and find love. Each actress transforms instantly to play the maid of the other (cf. **Maraini**), the 'wee hoors' condemned by Knox, and ultimately the twentieth-century children chanting the skipping songs, sectarian refrains and bastardized history of the title.

Plays include: *Disgusting Objects* (MS, 1982); *Sweet Nothings* (MS, 1984); *Shanghaied* (MS, 1984); *Same Difference* (MS); *Blood and Ice* (3f,3m, 1982) in Wandor 4; *Country and Western in Kyle, Encore for the Arts* (both 1f,2m), *Hillhead Election Song* (2f,1m), *Six Men Monologues, Sharon: Incest* (1f); and others in *True Confessions* (1985); *Tartuffe* (1986) – both Edinburgh: Polygon Books; *Mary Queen of Scots got Her Head Chopped Off* (4f,4m,id, 1987) and *Dracula* (5+f,6m,id, 1985), Penguin, 1989; *Britannia Rules* (MS, 1998); *Cuba* (14f,5m, 1997) in *NEW* and Faber Connections, 2001; *Quelques Fleurs* (1f,1m, 1991) in *Scotland Plays* ed. Philip Howard, NHB, 1998; *Perfect Days* (3f,3m, 1999); *Medea* (after Euripides, 9f,6m, 2000) – all NHB.

See also: *Liz Lochhead's Voices* ed. Robert Crawford and Anne Varty, Edinburgh UP, 1993; Koren-Deutsch in MD 3, Sept. 1992; App. 2, Christianson in Christianson and Lumsden; McDonald in Reynolds; Sierz.

Christine, Countess Longford

Irish, 1902–80

In 1930, Countess Longford and her husband, the wealthy landowner Edward Pakenham, Earl of Longford, became joint shareholders in the Gate Theatre, Dublin in 1930, joining Hilton Edwards and Micheal MacLiammoir in saving the theatre from bankruptcy.

Already a novelist and dramatist (including adaptor of **Austen** and **Edgeworth**), Countess Longford went on to write many more plays, most of them comedies about Irish and Anglo-Irish interaction and their efforts or failures of adjustment in the new Free State and changed economic circumstances. In *Mr Jiggins* the English and the Irish cousins of a crusty old Irish landowner, desperate to escape their sunken social fortunes, eagerly compete to be made his heir. In *Tankardstown* a hotelier profits on the black market from government inefficiency and the flood of English tourists, eager to escape the hardships of rationing. *Patrick Sarsfield* is a historical play set in 1690 about the defeat of James II and his Irish supporters. An obituary described Longford as a 'reluctant genius' for her influential management of the Gate.

Plays include: *Queen and Emperors* (MS, 1932); *Mr Jiggins of Jigginstown* (2f,8m, 1933) in Canfield; *The United Brothers* (5f,5m, 1942); *Lord Edward* (5f,11m, 1941); *Patrick Sarsfield* (4f,8m, 1943); *The Earl of Straw* (3f,10m, 1945) – all Dublin: Hodges Figgis; *The Hill of Quirke* (1958); *Tankardstown* (4f,8m, 1948) – all Dublin: P. J. Bourke.

See also: *No Profit but the Name* by John Cowell, Dublin: O'Brien Press, 1988.

Anita Loos
American, 1893?–1981

Best known for the novel *Gentleman Prefer Blondes* (1925), which she dramatized the following year, Loos was a prolific screenwriter, turning out more than two hundred screenplays between 1912 and 1958, the majority of them produced, as well as ten plays and four musicals. Her screen adaptations from other women playwrights include **Boothe Luce**'s *The Women* and **Crothers**'s *Susan and God*. Films such as the sexually outspoken *Redheaded Woman* (1932) prompted calls for tighter censorship. Her work often features caustic, witty, go-getting heroines – her heroine in *The Whole Town's Talking* refuses marriage with the unsophisticated Chester until he can boast at least one affair. Loos's stage adaptations included J. Canelle's *King's Mare* (1967) and her long-running version of *Gigi*, by French novelist/playwright Colette. Gigi, intended for a courtesan, following in the family tradition, instead wins her intended lover as husband, to her mother's and grandmother's horror.

Plays include: *The Fall of Eve* (MS, 1925); *Gentlemen Prefer Blondes* (10f,7m) DPS, 1926; *The Whole Town's Talking* (with John Emerson, 7f,5m) NY: Longman Green, 1928; *Happy Birthday* (10f,11m) French, 1947; *Gigi* (5f,2m) NY: Random House, 1952; *Cheri* (MS, 1959) – both from Colette; *The Amazing Adele* (MS, 1955).

Screenplays include: *When Ladies Meet* (1941); *I Married an Angel* (1942); *Saratoga* (1937); *Mama Steps Out* (1937); *Biography of a Bachelor Girl* (1935); *The Matrimoniac* (1916); *The Women* (from **Boothe Luce**, 1939).

See also App. 2: Shafer.

Cecilie Loveid
Norwegian, 1951–

Author of poetry and prose as well as plays for theatre, performance art, radio and television, Loveid writes in a lyrical, fragmentary style, experimenting with the relationship of language to the female body and its erotic experience. The rival desires between mother, father and daughter for time and affection are central in *The Ice Goes Out*, the title an image of awakening spring when the ice starts to breaks up. Set in 1939 the radio play *Seagull Eaters*, which won the Prix Italia, focuses on Kristine's dream of becoming an actress. Set against a background of the advance of fascism in Norway and the internment of the Jews, it centres round an image drawn from Henriette Schonberg-Erken's cookbook, the last book left in Kristine's poverty-stricken home. The exotic dish of seagulls comes to represent simultaneously aspirations beyond the mundane and those who consume the rich things of the earth and destroy others in the process, such as Kristine herself, who is seduced by the owner of the local delicatessen and persuaded to give up her acceptably Aryan baby to the Give-the-Führer-a-Child campaign. Densely patterned imageries brilliantly interweave references to Ibsen and Chekhov, fairy tales, recipes, the screeching of gulls and the cries of children.

Untranslated plays include: *Tiden Mellom Tidene*.

Translated plays include: *Seagull Eaters* (6+f,9m+, 1983) tr. Garton, in Garton & Sehmsdorf; *Sensible Animals* (MS) tr. Garton; *The Ice Goes Out* tr. Nadia Christensen (1f,2m, MS); *Maria Q* (MS) tr. William Mishler.

Teresa Lubkiewicz
Polish, 20th century

Lubkiewicz's strange haunting piece *Werewolves* was acclaimed by *Plays and Players* on its first production in 1978 as having 'a possessed and frightening intensity' and has since been revived by Kaut-Howson at

156

Theatr Clwyd in Wales. Set in a peasant community, it stands in the great surreal tradition of Polish plays (Mickiewicz's *Forefather's Eve*, Wyspianski's *The Wedding*) where dead and living and unborn characters inhabit the same space, as a wake for Farmer Thrush's mother is invaded by wolf-men, a young girl flies and a corpse comes back to life.

Translated play: *Werewolves* (6f,8m) tr. Helena Kaut Howson in *P&P*, Nov. & Dec. 1978.

Claire Luckham
British, 1944–

Born in Nairobi, Kenya, Luckham began her playwriting career collaborating with her then husband, director Chris Bond, on *Scum: Death, Destruction and Dirty Washing* for the socialist feminist theatre company Monstrous Regiment. The piece explores the process of political change as, during the Paris Commune of 1871, a group of laundresses take over when their employer flees the city and begin to shape and defend a new society. Informed by the heady political energy of 1976 and collaborative working processes, it draws on Brechtian models and, like most of Luckham's plays, is interspersed with songs. Brechtian aesthetics inform many of Luckham's plays, drawing attention to their status as theatre (*Dramatic Attitudes*) and, even where the material is historical, their relation to the present.

Luckham's best-known and internationally successful play, *Trafford Tanzi*, is a consciousness-raising fable set in a wrestling ring. Tanzi battles against female stereotyping with her mum, her teachers and the feminine wiles of Platinum Sue, before finally engaging her husband, Dean, in equal fight, loser to do the housework. Its ideological force and entertainment value grow from the spectacle of woman's strength in physical activity, though the politics of celebrating physical force have been questioned. *The Choice*, described as 'emotionally wrenching', draws on Luckham's own memories of her Down's syndrome brother, interspersed as monologues within the story of a couple confronted with the decision whether to terminate a pregnancy where the foetus has Down's.

Plays include: *Scum* (with Chris Bond, 5f,2m, 1976) in Hanna; *Fish Riding Bikes* (MS, 1979); *Trafford Tanzi* (3f,3m, 1980) in Wandor 2 and with *The Dramatic*

Attitudes of Miss Fanny Kemble (7f, 10m,dp, 1990) and *The Seduction of Anne Boleyn* (4/5f,4m, 1998) in *Claire Luckham: Plays One*, Oberon, 1999; *The Choice* (3f,2m, 1992) in Castledine 10; *Moll Flanders* (musical, with George Stiles and Paul Leigh, 4f,5m) French, 1994.

See also App. 2: Itzin, Wandor, 1986, Reinelt in Case ed.

Alison Lyssa

Australian, 1947–

Playwright, dramaturg and former director of the Australian ITI, Lyssa's plays reflect her strong feminist commitment. She has developed work with Sydney's Women and Theatre project and with women from Telopea and Sydney's Cantonese-speaking communities. Her works layer contemporary reality with myth and history, such as in *The Boiling Frog*, whose protagonists journey from seventeenth-century London to a contemporary Britain threatened by nuclear technology, seeking to understand the relationship between science and power. Most effectively in *Pinball*, she layers the action of a lesbian mother's struggle for custody of her son with the judgement of Solomon, drawing witty and incisive parallels and juxtaposing biblical and contemporary language, as well as rewriting *King Lear* in which Cordelia refuses to be sacrificed for her father's madness. The piece becomes a complex, linguistically rich and highly effective play which also explores attitudes to children, within the women's movement and outside it.

Plays include: *The Year of the Migrant* (MS, 1980); *Pinball* (4f,2m,id, 1982) in Wandor 4 and in Parr; *The Boiling Frog* (MS, 3f,3m); *The Hospital Half Hour* (2f,1m) in *Australian Health Review*, Dec. 1983; *Who'd've Thought?* (MS, 1990).

See also App. 2: Tompkins and Holledge.

Dame Edith Sophy Lyttelton

English, 1865–1948

Married to MP Alfred Lyttelton, Edith was active in the Conservative and Unionist Women's Franchise Association and wrote a number of short plays, mostly religious in theme. Most interesting is *Warp and Woof*, set in the backroom of a fashionable dressmakers where the fitters and seamstresses are sweated late into the night to complete orders, sleeping on the job to begin again at dawn. The constant pressure and insecurity of their lives are contrasted with those of their pampered customers in a piece which, though melodramatic, is hard-hitting in its criticisms. It was a great success on its first production (1904), in which Mrs Patrick Campbell starred as the resolute heroine Theodosia Heming.

Plays include: *Warp and Woof* (12f, 5m) London: T. Fisher Unwin, 1908; *Peter's Chance* (4f,8m) London: Duckworth & Co, 1912; *The Thumbscrew* (4f,2m) NY: Longman's, 1912.
See also App. 2: Stowell.

Rachel McAlpine
New Zealand/Aotearoan, 1940–

McAlpine is a poet , novelist and teacher from Fairlie, South Canterbury. Her plays are written for young people and feature songs ranging from numbers improvised during rehearsals to raps, and dances from bop to breakdancing and disco. They explore youth cultures and teenage conflicts with parents, teachers, each other, over schoolwork, surfing, smoking, pregnancy. *Peace Offering* is set at a camp where children, learning by correspondence, begin to communicate despite their differences and fears of the Other, a fear compared to the nuclear stand-off of the Cold War. In *Power Play*, a group of teenagers, pakeha and Maori, learn to take responsibility for their own decisions, including saying 'No' to cigarettes.

Plays include: *Driftwood* (10f,7m, 1985) Victoria UP, 1986; *Power Play* (11f,6m, 1990); *The Stationary Sixth-Form Poetry Trip* (7f,5m, 1980) – both Playmarket; *Peace Offering* (7f,6m+,id) Auckland: Heinemann, 1988; *Farewell Speech* (adaptation with Cathy Downes, MS); *Paper Towers* (MS).

Robbie McCauley
American, 1942–

Writer and performance artist McCauley addresses the history of African-American experience through pieces parodying stereotyped racist images, such as the minstrel show in *Teenytown*, made with fellow cast members of **Shange**'s *for colored girls* . . . (**Hagedorn** and **Carlos**), and elsewhere through family memory and story, to address 'the survival of black people in the United States'. 'Bearing witness about racism informs everything I do', she has said, and the need to open dialogue about the unspoken and unspeakable is central to her work. In *Mother Worked* she creates a first-person monologue describing her mother's working life, her struggles against prejudice and for promotion. The deeply disturbing *Sally's Rape*, performed by McCauley herself and white actress Jeannie Hutchins, confronts black/white relationships and how they are informed by the history of racism, evoking in white audience members, and addressing, issues of white complicity and guilt. The piece draws directly on her mother's accounts of her great-great-grandmother's experience under slavery, culminating in a devastatingly immediate re-creation of a slave market as McCauley is displayed for examination on an auction block as the audience are told to chant 'Bid 'em in'.

Plays include: *Sally's Rape* (2f, 1989) in Mahone and in Hatch and Shine 1987; *Teenytown* (with **Carlos** and **Hagedorn**, 3f) in Champagne; *My Father and the Wars* (MS, 1985); *Indian Blood* (MS, 1987); *Mother Worked* (1f) in Russell.

See also: Thompson in TJ 48,2, 1996; App. 2: Carr; interview in Martin; Whyte in Hart and Phelan.

Esther McCracken

English, 1902–71

McCracken, from Newcastle upon Tyne, worked as an actress before beginning playwriting, hitting long-running success with *Quiet Wedding*. Seen by critics as especially appealing to women (cf. D. **Smith**), this is the anatomy of the havoc caused in the nice middle-class Royd family by wedding plans: barrages of useless presents, dress fittings *et al.* McCracken returned to the Royds in *Quiet Weekend*, set pre-war at a weekend cottage and staged in 1940, supplying the contemporary audience's need for reassurance during the Second World War by emphasizing the old 'ordinary' ways of living. Both have been described as 'pleasant, formless and innocuous comedies'.

Rather more grit is evident in *No Medals*, focusing on the difficulties of maintaining a household in wartime as widow Martha Dacre provides emotional sustenance and practical support to family and billeted lodgers against a background of rationing, bombing and queues. Though critics felt its focus remained, to quote one: 'discomfort in chintz . . . the trivial round but the genteel task', more recent feminist readings have highlighted the frustration expressed by Martha at her circumscribed role.

Plays include: *The Willing Spirit* (2f,3m, MS, 1936); *White Elephants* (MS, 1940); *Quiet Wedding* (9f,5m, 1938); *Quiet Weekend* (8f,5m, 1942); *No Medals* (7f,9m, 1944) – all French; *Cry Liberty* (MS, 1950).

See also App. 2: Gale.

Carson McCullers
American, 1917–67

In 1946, McCullers, already famous as a novelist, was encouraged by Tennessee Williams to dramatize her book, *The Member of the Wedding*. Onstage it became a huge Broadway success and an American classic, going on to be filmed. Set in McCullers' native Georgia, it centres on Frankie, a young, restless, over-imaginative girl growing up with her black 'Mammy' and a neighbourhood boy. Feeling she is not part of anything, neither child nor adult and desperate to belong, she fantasizes she is a 'member' of her brother's wedding and will go with the couple when they leave town . . . and meets predictable disappointment.

The Square Root of Wonderful focuses on a young woman, twice married to, twice divorced from, the same troubled writer who drinks and beats her, while his mother, a former Southern belle, thinks her unworthy of him. Her choice to change her life, and reject his latest proposal in favour of a new life for herself and her son with a new lover, precipitates his suicide but also her renewed understanding of wonder.

McCullers', recurrent themes of isolation and the strangeness of love are repeated in her novels, most of which have been filmed, including *Reflections in a Golden Eye* with Elizabeth Taylor (1967) and *The Ballad of the Sad Café* with Vanessa Redgrave (1991).

Plays include: *The Member of the Wedding* (7f,6m) NY: New Directions, 1951; *The Square Root of Wonderful* (4f,3m) Boston: Houghton Mifflin, 1958; *The Ballad of the Sad Cafe* (6f, 14m, adapted by Edward Albee) Boston: Houghton Mifflin, 1963.

See also App. 2: Shafer; McBride in Schlueter; Carr in Barranger.

Ann-Marie MacDonald
Canadian, 20th century

An actress who has worked primarily in collaborative contexts, MacDonald began *Good-Night Desdemona* while touring with **The Anna**

Project and developed it with director **Rubess**. Its heroine, academic Constance Ledbelly, dissents from traditional interpretation of Shakespeare's tragedies and is transported into the world of the play, intervening to disrupt and deconstruct their tragic endings in favour of wild comedy, sexual anarchy and theatrical invention, becoming simultaneously author, fool and heroine.

The Arab's Mouth is a playfully plotted Gothic thriller-farce set in a *fin-de-siècle* Scottish baronial castle haunted by strange freakish creatures, mysterious nuns, scheming doctors and the dog god, Anubis. Its scientific heroine, Pearl, is intent on discovering the key to the mysteries, while her decadent, hysteric brother languishes, neurotically eating shortbread. The piece wittily draws on Freud, Frankenstein, genetic engineering, Egyptian mythology, Darwinism and lots of tartan. MacDonald's first novel, *Fall on Your Knees* (1996) achieved critical and popular acclaim.

Plays include: *Clue in the Fast Lane* (MS, with Beverley Cooper); *Good-Night Desdemona, (Good Morning Juliet)*, Coach House Press, 1990 (3f,2m); *The Arab's Mouth* (3f,3m,id), Blizzard, 1995; *Nigredo Hotel* (MS, libretto).
See also App. 2: Wilson in Much.

Claire MacDonald
British, 1954–

A founder of the influential 1980s physical and visual theatre company Impact Theatre Co-op, MacDonald has gone on to work as joint artistic director of Insomniac as well as writing and teaching extensively around contemporary live art and performance. Her evocative texts convey a world of urban decay with post-nuclear resonances, inhabited by isolated and fractured individuals and fraught with erotic tension. In both *Imitation of Life* and *Storm from Paradise* a man and a woman occupy a room, conjuring up the external world and an imaginary theatrical reality, a joint fantasy of a city or a garden inhabited by their alter egos, through shared story-telling, evading, colluding with, contradicting or resisting each other's version in what becomes a gendered struggle for dominance. The man and woman in *Storm* develop a joint narrative. As the man relates an account of Bishop's efforts to extend the garden and subdue the desert landscape with pumping engines and machinery, the woman counters with a narrative of its destruction, by storms and dereliction.

Plays include: *An Imitation of Life* (MS); *Beulah Land* (MS); *The Other Side* (MS); *Heartless* (MS); *Storm from Paradise* (1f,1m, 1988) in Levy.

Sharman MacDonald
Scottish, 1951–

Glaswegian MacDonald worked as an actress before the success of her first play, *When I was a Girl I used to Scream and Shout*, a candid exploration of adolescent rites of passage and mother–daughter relationships set on a Scottish beach. Like several of her plays it focuses on an older, deserted, woman, in this case a proper, slightly eccentric Scottish matron, bringing up her child with fierce respectability, folk wisdom, stifling love and in sexual naïvety, and on the bewildered response of that child. Set in the 1950s, *Shades* subtly explores the relationship between a 10-year-old boy and his young widowed mother as she prepares for a date and he resists her leaving, possessive and hostile to the man who threatens their relationship.

MacDonald creates detailed and perceptive character studies in plays marked by brisk salty dialogue that yet have an elegaic quality. They are haunted, in vivid evocations of childhood, by memory, by death that is the *Winter Guest* of the title of her 1995 play (and 1997 film) and by loss, especially of children, aborted or given up for adoption to safeguard reputations in *When I Was a Girl* and *When We Were Women*. Elsewhere self-definition is central: for adolescents, discovering sexuality and identity (*Borders. . .*) while *The Brave*, set in post-revolutionary Algeria, confronts a group of Scots with issues of personal responsibility towards another culture, following an accidental killing that forces them to question their attitudes to feminism and nationalism.

Plays include: *When I was a Girl I used to Scream and Shout* (3f,1m, 1984), *When We were Women* (3f,2m, 1989), *The Winter Guest* (5f,3m, 1995) in *PI*, Mar. 1995; *The Brave* (2f,4m+,1d, 1988) – all in *Sharman MacDonald Plays One*, 1995; *Borders of Paradise* (2f,5m) in *PI*, July 1995; *All Things Nice* (4f,2m, 1991); *Shades* (2f,2m, 1992); *Sea Urchins* (5f,5m, 1998) – all Faber; *Hey Persephone!* (MS, Opera, 1998).

See also App. 2: Stephenson and Langridge; Stevenson and Wallace; Triesman in Christianson and Lumsden.

Claire McIntyre
British, 1953–

McIntyre worked as an actress in rep and for groups like WTG, co-scripting *Better a Live Pompey than a Dead Cyril* (a dramatic adaptation of the work of Stevie Smith) with Stephanie Nunn (MS, 1980), before embarking on a solo writing career with the award-winning *Low Level Panic*. Her work explores the nightmares of late twentieth-century existence, a world constantly invaded by news of murders, attacks, bomb blasts, terrors, and intermittently by their realities – prowlers, heavy breathers, a man on a train brandishing a gun – that continue to haunt and imprison women in fear. In McIntyre's stage world these terrors continue to be part of the characters' emotional baggage, walking through the walls like Chris's embodied anxieties, Pest and Luggage, in *My Heart's a Suitcase*; internalizing a continual male watcher within the women's fantasies and self-image in *Panic*.

The attempt to insulate the world against the intrusions of human dereliction, ugliness and poverty is equally central to McIntyre's work. In the comfortable world of businessman Michael in *The Thickness of Skin* the schizophrenic next-door neighbour is an embarrassment, the homeless unemployed man, taken in by his sister Laura, a mistake; even the dry rot in his house is somebody else's problem. For Laura, he answers her loneliness and assuages her middle-class guilt. *My Heart's a Suitcase* centres on the power of money to protect consciousness against the needs of others and the hatred it can ignite in those without, a theme examined provocatively and with complexity. While her friend Hannah rejects materialistic desires, Chris, gnawed by envy and frustration, is as much enslaved by money as wealthy Tunis whom she despises and resents.

Plays include: *Low Level Panic* (3f,2mv, 1988) in Harwood 1; *My Heart's a Suitcase* (4f,2m, 1990); *The Thickness of Skin* (4f,3m, 1996) – all NHB; *I've Been Running* (MS, 1986, also radio).
See also App. 2: Stephenson and Langridge, Edgar, Sierz.

Jenny McLeod
English, 1963–

A black British writer from Nottingham, McLeod began writing in her teens with the success of *Cricket at Camp David* (MS, 1987). Focusing on family relationships and tensions prior to a wedding, it explores the conflict between the black and white communities, where the local cricket match becomes the battleground, a focus to express a desperate need for communication. *Island Life*, set in an old people's home, gently explores the relationship of three old ladies, one black, two white, and their self-protective world of dotty imaginings, fantasized escapes and memory. Jamaican Emmy stands out as an especially finely drawn character with her stories of her brutal husband and the daughter who, she constantly declares, will one day visit her.

A review said of McLeod's prize-winning *Raising Fires*: 'it's rare to find a new play that so convincingly reconstructs the past.' Set in 1603, its topic of persecution of witches (cf. **Lavery, Churchill, Rubess**) is re-examined and linked to contemporary witch-hunts through the central character of Tilda, adopted West Indian daughter of the local minister, the focus of local prejudice and blame for the outbreak of fires that are destroying the village.

Plays include: *Island Life* (4f, 1988) in Hanna; *The Wake* (TV, 1990) in *Debut on Two* ed. V. Licorish and Philippa Giles, BBC Books, 1990 ; *The Wild at Heart Club* (5f, 10m, 1994) in *Making Scenes* 2; *The Mango Tree* (MS, 1990); *Just Like a Genie* (MS); *It's You* (MS); *Raising Fires* (4f,4m) Bush Theatre, 1994; *Victor and the Ladies* (MS, 1995); *Poison* (with David Kramer, Taliep Petersen, MS, musical, 2000).

See also App. 2: Stephenson and Langridge; Croft in Griffiths and Llewellyn-Jones; Reinelt in Hart and Phelan.

Antonine Maillet
Canadian, 1929–

Born in Bouctouche, New Brunswick, Maillet has been called 'the eulogist of Acadia' for her work (over 30 novels and plays including translations of Shakespeare), inspired by the traditions and history of her Acadian people. She has been awarded the French Prix Goncourt and in 1982 was made a Companion of the Order of Canada. Her one-woman play *La Sagouine* has gained the status of a contemporary Canadian classic. Its heroine is an Acadian washerwoman, a shrewd and irreverent observer of her fellows, who speaks her experience of poverty with pride.

Class struggle in rural Canada is a central theme of Maillet's work. In *The Rabble* the snobbish inhabitants of uptown engage in every possible machination in their attempt to get the vulgar 'folks from across the tracks' moved off their land. In *Gapi and Sullivan* Gapi the lighthouse keeper, philosopher husband of La Sagouine, is reunited with his globe-trotting friend Sullivan as they reminisce about the women whose love they once shared but find old jealousies inevitably reviving. *Evangeline the Second* is an old Acadian trapped in Montreal, living with her son and his wife. Her meetings with three other elderly exiles in the park allow them to share their reminiscences and their sense of dispossession.

Translated plays include: *La Sagouine* (1f, 1985); *Gapi and Sullivan* (2m, 1989); *Evangeline the Second* (1f,3m, 1987) – all tr. Luis de Cespedes, Simon and Pierre; *The Rabble* (6f, 13m) tr. Makward and Miller, in Makward and Miller.

See also: CTR Summer 1986; Gobin in CTR 25, 1982; Collet in CD 13:1, 1987; App. 2: Hodkinson.

Judith Malina
American, 1926–

An actress and director, Malina was joint founder with Julian Beck in 1951 of the Living Theatre in New York. Living Theatre, one of the key post-war American avant garde theatre companies, did the first US performances of Gertrude **Stein**, Jean Cocteau, Pirandello and numerous others. Later Malina helped script group-devised pieces such as the influential *Paradise Now*, an anarchic and highly physical series of rituals, a spiritual and political 'voyage [which] is a descent toward Permanent Revolution'. She has led women's groups in the USA and Italy in devising work. More recently she has directed **Malpede**'s *Kassandra* and *Us* and translated and directed **Lasker-Schuler**'s *IandI*.

Plays include: *Mysteries and Smaller Pieces* (with Julian Beck, cast various) in *The Great American Life Show* ed. John Lahr and Jonathan Price, NY: Bantam, 1974; *Paradise Now* (c.16m/f) NY: Random House, 1971; *From the Legacy of Cain* (cast various, Favela Project No 1) in *Scripts* vi, 1, Nov. 1971.

See also: *The Diaries of Judith Malina* 1947–1957, Grove, 1984; *The Enormous Despair* by Malina, NY: Random House, 1972.

Karen Malpede
American, 1945–

Part Jewish, part Italian-American, Malpede's work reveals a forceful commitment to a theatre of social change and a radical feminism allied to pacifism and anarchism, expressed both through playwriting and critical work. She is editor of *People's Theatre In Amerika* (1972) and *Women in Theatre: Compassion and Hope,* which re-claims the work of women such as Augusta **Gregory** as the paradigm of a theatre where poetic and theatrical vision was allied to political struggle. *Lament for Three Women* addresses both grief at the death of her father and women's ambivalent confrontation with patriarchy. Like most of her early work it uses poetic language, mythologizing experience, creating a sense of ritual enactment. This technique works most effectively in dealing with conflict, as in *The End of War,* which interrogates the dilemmas facing women in wartime, in the context of the 1916 political struggle of Ukrainian anarchists, where atrocities like rapes are committed on all sides and friends seem tactically indistinguishable from enemies. Elsewhere, as in *Sappho and Aphrodite,* despite its notes of sexual jealousy and mother–daughter antagonisms but without the tension of real conflict, Malpede's dense poetic lyricism can tend to cloy with sweetness. *Us* enters the heart of conflict with a blistering and intensely erotic examination of sexual passion over two generations and across racial divides, confronting incest, sexual violence and desire in a highly experimental piece, using multiple transformations and cross-gender role-playing, originally directed for Living Theatre by **Malina**.

Plays include: *A Monster has Stolen the Sun* (9f,5m+, 1981); *Sappho and Aphrodite* (5f, 1984); *The End of War* (3f,4m+, 1977) in *A Monster has Stolen the Sun and Other Plays,* Marlboro, VT: The Marlboro Press, 1987; *A Lament for Three Women* (3f, 1974) in France; *Going to Iraq* (MS, 1992); *Us* (1f,1m,id, 1992) in Lamont; *Kassandra* (MS, 1993 from Christa Wolf).
See also App. 2: Malpede; Betsko and Koenig.

Delarivier Manley
British, 1663–1724

Manley received a vitriolic press from contemporaries for her scandalous *romans à clef* and sexually outspoken plays. Her work is unapologetically feminist and where others prefaced their published plays with requests that they not be judged too fiercely for daring to write though mere women, Manley did not do so. She published *The Royal Mistress* with dedicatory poems from friends such as Catherine **Trotter** and *The Lost Lover* with an ironic apology thanking 'the Well-natur'd Town' for its negative reception: '. . . I am satisfied the bare Name of being a Woman's Play damn'd it beyond its own want of Merit.' In what is otherwise a fairly conventional romantic comedy Manley gives powerful voice to the position of the rejected woman, Belira, whom her lover Wilmore wants to cast off in favour of a more advantageous match. Belira speaks out passionately in defence of her own sexual desire, protesting (unsuccessfully) at being simply disposed of.

Manley's plays abound in bold women, most strikingly in *The Royal Mischief* (1696) whose terrifyingly assertive heroine is killed off at the end, but not before she has drugged her husband with the help of her lover, effortlessly seduced her husband's nephew despite his recent marriage and renown for virtue, engineered murder and given a powerfully outspoken defence of female sexual passion:

> *What to conceal desire, when every*
> *Atom of me trembles with it, I'll strip*
> *My Passion naked of such Guile, lay it*
> *Undressed, and panting at his feet, then try*
> *If all his Temper can resist it.*

Plays include: *The Lost Lover* (7f,9m) London: R. Bentley, 1696; *The Royal Mischief* (3f,5m+, 1696) and in Morgan; *Almyna* or *The Arabian Vow* London: William Turner & Egbert Sander, 1707; *Lucius*, London: John Barber, 1717.

See also: *A Woman of No Character* by Fidelis Morgan London: Faber, 1986; *Three Augustan Women Playwrights* by Constance Clark, NY: Peter Lang, 1986; App. 2: Cotton; Pearson.

Emily Mann
American, 1952–

Mann's major plays draw on interviews, statements of witnesses and friends, court reports and TV footage in powerful, moving and complex dramatizations of political events that have rocked America, re-examining their effect on lives, communities and the national psyche.

In *Annulla* (1988), Mann used the encounter between a Jewish survivor living in London and her interviewer as a means to address her own identity and family history. Annulla's account, imbued with her prickly, sardonic personality and acute memories, becomes a harrowing account of the impact of history on the individual.

Execution of Justice re-creates the trial of Dan White for the murder of San Francisco gay supervisor Harvey Milk and liberal mayor George Moscone, bringing out the complex of social, political, sexual and personal motives which contributed to White's act and the infamous 'Twinkie' defence (his psychological state was claimed to be the result of excessive junk food). *Greensboro'* addresses the notorious gunning-down of protestors by the Ku Klux Klan in 1979, exposing the legal machinations and establishment complicity which allowed assassinations to go unpunished. The impact of violence on individuals, victims and perpetrators is also central to *Still Life*, a brilliant investigation of the effect of the Vietnam War on a veteran, his wife and his lover as he obsessively relives the atrocity.

Plays include: *Execution of Justice* (9f,26m) in Shewey and *AT*, Nov. 1985, in Leverett and Osborn; *Still Life* (2f,1m) in Leverett and DPS, 1982; *Annulla, an Autobiography* (2f, 1985) in Schiff 1996 – all with *Greensboro'*: *A Requiem* (5f,6m, id, 1996) in *Testimonies – Four Plays*, TCG, 1997; *Betsey Brown* (with Ntozake **Shange**, 4f,4m) extract in *SAD*.

See also: Interview in *Theater* Winter 1990–1; bibliography in *SAD*; App. 2: Isser; Savran; Betsko and Koenig.

Mary Manning
Irish, 1907–99

An influential figure in Dublin theatre in the 1930s, Manning was principal drama critic of the *Irish Independent* and a key force in the development of the Gate Theatre, going on to edit its house magazine, *Motley*. She later emigrated to the USA, co-founding the Poets Theatre in Boston with Denis Johnston.

Youth's the Season...? (1933) is a lively and pointed satire on the Bright Young Things of 1920s Dublin, on wasted talent and self-deceptive complacency, where the homosexual would-be artist Desmond is afraid to rebel against his father while his academic sister deludes herself that she is too rational to love. Manning paints a world of 'imitation Bloomsbury' and 'unoriginal sin' where the most incisive character, bitter self-destructive Terence, astutely analyses his own and others' failings but remains wedded to self-destruction.

Manning was acclaimed for adaptations of *The Voices of Shem* from James Joyce's *Finnegans Wake* and Frank O'Connor's novel *The Saint and Mary Kate* (MS, 1968). Her monologue *Go Lovely Rose* re-creates the frustration of vibrant young Rose Fitzgerald Kennedy when her college plans are blocked by her father's opposition to women's education, and her subsequent determination to redirect her energies through marriage.

Plays include: *Youth's the Season . . .?* (7f,7m) in Canfield; *Storm Over Wicklow* (MS, 1933); *Happy Family* (MS, 1934); *The Voices of Shem* (1f,3m,8f/m) Faber, 1957; *Outlook Unsettled* (MS, 1970); *Go Lovely Rose* (1f) in *Massachusetts Review*, Winter 1988.

Katherine Mansfield (pseud. of Kathleen Beauchamp)
New Zealand/Aotearoan, 1888–1923

A strikingly dramatic figure who dressed in different guises, lied and spun fictional versions of her past and on one occasion compèred a cabaret at the reputedly lesbian Cave of the Golden Calf, Mansfield also enjoyed performing her celebrated short stories at readings. She also published brief plays and dialogue sketches that remain little known and hard to find, only touched upon by biographers such as **Tomalin** (whose own play is based on Mansfield's life).

Many of her plays were originally written between 1911 and 1917 for A. R. Orage, editor of the radical magazine *The New Age*. Others have only been published from manuscripts since Mansfield's death. They include an early dramatic poem (*The Laurels*), a Chekhovian portrait of her own family (*Toots*), satires performed in Bloomsbury, monologues, but most are brief, acerbic sketches finely observed from life: women at the coronation or gossiping on the bus, making and avoiding assignations, discussing friendships or shivering in rented rooms.

Plays include: *Toots* (3f,2m); *The Laurels* (3f,3m); *Stay-Laces* (6f,1m); *The Festival of the Coronation* (2f,4m); *Late at Night* (1f); *The Black Cap* (1f,1m) and five more in *Katherine Mansfield Dramatic Sketches* Palmerston North, NZ: Nagare Press, 1988.
See also: *Katherine Mansfield: A Secret Life* by Claire **Tomalin**, NY: Viking, 1987.

Dacia Maraini
Italian, 1936–

Prize-winning novelist, journalist and feminist Maraini became involved in theatre in the late 1960s, establishing a series of theatre companies under the auspices of the Italian Communist Party. In 1973 she founded the women's Compagnia della Maddalena, initially developing and producing women's plays, later running seminars on women's theatre, especially playwriting (on which Maraini has published extensive essays and criticism).

Linguistically rich and complex, Maraini's plays address issues of women's sexuality and power, violence and resistance, remaking myth and history. In *Dreams of Clytemnestra* she reframes the mythical story within the context of a contemporary Italian city where Clytemnestra is both the Greek heroine and a mother and former garment worker, diagnosed as mad, confronting her brutal husband. Both *Dialogue* and *Veronica Franco* examine attitudes to prostitution, something she does literally in the Brechtian *Dialogue*, where the actress interrupts the action to debate questions with the audience. Her sixteenth-century counterpart, courtesan and poet Veronica Franco, also insists on seeking sexual pleasure and exercising her own choice of partners, rather than being a commodity, while both present marriage and wage drudgery as parallel and less rewarding forms of prostitution. *Mary Stuart*, like **Lochhead**'s version, uses two actresses to each play both a queen and her attendant and explores the isolation, political pressures and social and sexual entrapment of their roles.

Translated plays include*: *Dialogue between a Prostitute and her Client* (1f,1m, 1980); *Crime at the Tennis Club* (1f,4m) both tr. Tony Mitchell; *Mary Stuart* (2f, 1984) tr. Christopher Pearcy with Nicolette Kay; *Dreams of Clytemnestra* (5f,4m+, 1989) tr. Tim Vode; in *Only Prostitutes Marry In May* ed. Rhoda Helfman Kaufman, Toronto: Guernica Editions, 1994; *Veronica Franco* (3f,7m) tr. Sian Williams and Marion Baraitser, in Baraitser; *Mussomeli – Dusseldorf* (2f,1m, radio, 1991) tr. **Hollingsworth**, in Jansen; *Mela* (MS) tr. Christine Furnival.

See also: Mitchell in TJ, Oct. 1990.

Una Marson

Jamaican, 1905–65

Marson was a political activist who worked for the League of Coloured Peoples (LCP) in Britain in 1932 and later became a peace campaigner and a BBC broadcaster with the World Service, producing *Caribbean Voices*. While her significance as a ground-breaking poet has begun to be recognized, her theatre work has remained a footnote until Jarret-

* Dates given are dates of translation.

Macauley's rescue work in 1997. With Horace Vaz, Marson wrote the first play to be produced by a black company in Britain (LCP), while Jamaica saw productions of *At What a Price* (MS, 1932), *London Calling* (MS, 1937) on student life in London, as well as the successful *Pocomania* (1938) which deals with a young woman's growing fascination with Revivalist religion. Highly atmospheric, the piece, written partly in patois, presents the charismatic Revivalist meetings with their compelling drumming as a religion associated with women and the poor while their wildness and eroticism threaten male church and medical authority and their representatives.

Plays include: *Pocomania* (7f,7m+) Kingston: n.p., 1938.

See also: *The Life of Una Marson 1905–1965* by Delia Jarret-Macaulay, Manchester UP, 1997.

Jane Martin
American, 20th century

Speculation runs rife as to the identity of 'Jane Martin': a man, a consortium of writers? The plays are copyrighted to 'Alexander Speer, as Trustee' and biographical information stops at identifying 'her' as a Kentuckian.

'She' is prolific, first brought to prominence by numerous monologues which, typically, are vivid dialect accounts of unusual oddball lives: a female rodeo-rider's complaint at the increasingly commercial circuit which values glamour over skill; an old lady's recital of her love affair with McDonald's; a twirler's description of her art that becomes an account of spiritual revelation – 'blue-collar Zen'. *Vital Signs* used the same format of multiple monologues from wildly diverse characters, building a picture of the outer margins of American experience. *Keely and Du* addresses the conflict over abortion rights through the kidnapping of Keely, a young woman pregnant after rape, by members of the Religious Right intent on keeping her prisoner until she has the baby or forcing her back into a proper family relationship with her repentant, born-again ex-husband. The piece focuses on the growing dependence between her and Du, her middle-aged captor and comforter. In *Cementville*, set in the sports arena locker-room of a one-horse town, Martin presents a world of violence and tawdry glamour as a group of female wrestlers strut their stuff. *Jack and Jill* explores the relationship between a 1990s couple, relentlessly analysing, assessing and re-assessing their commitment, conflicts and desire.

Plays include: *Clear Glass Marbles* (1f) and *Rodeo* (1f, both 1981) in Marranca and Dasgupta 3; *Twirler*, also in Delgado, 1983 – all with *Lamps, Dragons, French Fries, Marks, Handler, Fifteen Minutes, Scraps, Audition* (all 1f) in *Talking With*, French, 1983; *Vital Signs* (6f,2m) French, 1990; *Keely and Du* (3f,4m, 1993) in Smith 1995; *The Boy Who Ate the Moon* (1f,1m, 1981); *Cul de Sac* (1f, 1981); *Shasta Rue* (1f, 1983); *Summer* (4f,4m, 1984); *Travelin' Show* (1m, 1987); *Cementville* (9f,5m, 1991); *Criminal Hearts* (3f,2m, 1992); *Middle-Aged White Guys* (3f,4m, 1994); *Pomp and Circumstance* (2m, 1995) All in *Jane Martin Collected Plays 1980–1995* Lyme, NH: Smith and Kraus; *Coup/Clucks* (4f,4m and 1f,7m, 1985) in *Louisville; Jack and Jill* (MS).

See also: Powers in *Theater* 13:3.

Louisa H. Medina

American, c.1813–38

During a short, crowded career Louisa Medina wrote as many as 34 plays for the Bowery Theatre (run by her husband, actor-manager Thomas Hamblin) and other New York stages before dying of apoplexy aged 25. Many of her plays were dramatizations of novels, large scale, sensational and melodramatic, such as Edward Bulwer-Lytton's *The Last Days of Pompeii* (1834). Several have American Indian themes. *Nick of the Woods* (1838) is set in a pioneer community, its log huts and woods inhabited by wolves, grisly bears, panthers, a treacherous British wicked uncle, comic cowboys, a chorus of settlers, barbarous natives and a noble self-sacrificing Indian maiden who saves the hero. *Ernest Maltravers* boasts a wildly convoluted plot full of family secrets, mad scenes, long-lost heirs, alpine brigands and a mysterious casket with a secret revelation.

Plays include: *Nick of the Woods* (5f,13m) Boston: W. V. Spencer, 1856 and in *Victorian Melodramas* ed. James L. Smith London: Dent, 1976; *Ernest Maltravers* (3f, 10m+, 1837) and in Kritzer; *The Last Days of Pompeii* (4+f, 12m, c.1856) – both, NY: Samuel French.

Cassandra Medley

American, 20th century

An African-American, Medley's work was supported by the New York-based Women's Project, directed by Julia Miles (see App. 1 for several WP collections). Much of Medley's work gives voice to older black women, as in *Mildred*, and in the monologues for Ms Mae, as she has her hair done, included in Joan Micklin Silver and Marianne Boyd's WP-produced musical revue *A . . . My Name is Alice* (1985). Edie, in *Waking Women*, confides in her neighbour her fears for her 15-year-old niece, Pinkie, brought up in sexual ignorance by her fundamentalist mother and now in the throes of a difficult labour. WP also commissioned *Ma Rose*, which interweaves flashbacks in a moving exploration of the impact on a Midwest black family of the grandmother's growing senility. Her illness inflames conflict between the family, descending on Ma Rose's house to divide up the spoils of her long life. Old antagonisms are rekindled between her granddaughter and namesake Rosa, an educated and self-assured successful lawyer, and the rest of the family, their stay-at-home satisfaction igniting her insecurities, sense of pressure and responsibility to succeed.

Plays include: *Ma Rose* (4f,1m, 1988) in Miles 1989; *Waking Women* (1f) in Halpern; *Mildred* (1f) in *13th Moon* v10, Nos 1 & 2; *Dearborn Heights* (2f) in Stein and Young 95/96 and in Smith EST 1995; *Terrain* (MS).

Eve Merriam

American, 1916–92

Poet, screenwriter, director and playwright, several of Merriam's plays are based on works in other forms. The musical *Inner City*, from her poem cycle *Inner City Mother Goose*, focuses on lives of children in ghetto neighbourhoods. *Out of My Father's House*, based on her collection of women's letters and journals, *Growing Up Female in America*, has been described as a 'hypothetical conversation' or 'timeless interaction' between women including Mother Jones, Elizabeth Cady Stanton and astronomer Maria Mitchell. In *The Club*, the denizens of a male club in 1903 sing songs of the period, toast and joke about 'the ladies' from a position of effortlessly assumed superiority, their familiar attitudes thrown into critical perspective by their roles being performed by women. *And I ain't Finished Yet* celebrates the struggles and endurance of black women in America. Other plays address women's experience of ageing and society's attitudes towards them.

Plays include: *Out of My Father's House* (with Paula Wagner and Jack Hofsiss, 6f, 1975) in Moore; *The Club*, (7f, 1976); *Inner City* (5f,4m, c. 1969); *And I ain't Finished Yet* (2f,2m). All French.
    See also App. 2: Betsko and Koenig.

Jyoti Mhapsekar
Indian, 1949–

Mhapsekar, a librarian by profession, was born in Maharashtra, the daughter of social activist parents. She is president of Stree Muki Sanghatna, a women's liberation organization in Bombay, for which she has written all five of her plays. They address social problems affecting women in Indian society, including the sale of young women into prostitution, illiteracy, contraception and dowry murders. *A Girl is Born* has been performed throughout India and abroad more than 1000 times over 14 years, and has been translated into seven languages. Vigorous and effective, it uses songs and multiple role changes to address the problems of women in a society where the birth of a girl is still too often the cause of anger and lamenting, where a daughter is seen as a drain on resources for the family who complain at having to provide her with a dowry but refuse to provide her with an education.

Tranlated plays: *A Girl is Born* (7f) tr. from Marathi by Shubha Khandekar, Bombay: Shramik and Indian Education Society, 1994; *No Dowry Please* (MS, 1986); *Oh My Goodness Bapre Bap* (MS 1994).

Gcina Mhlope
South African, 1958–

Mhlope became an actress at the Market Theatre of Johannesburg, contributing to collectively devised shows before becoming the theatre's first black resident director in 1989. Mhlope lived for her first eight years with her devoted grandmother in Durban, until she was kidnapped and taken to live with her mother in the harsh, rural Transkei, an experience she re-creates in *Have You Seen Zandile?* Prevented from communicating with her grandmother Zandile writes letters in the sand in hope the birds will take them to Gogo. She comes to have a deeper understanding of her mother, although she continues to rebel against a future of an arranged marriage and to struggle for education and escape. Performed in Xhosa and English, the piece presents a funny, enormously poignant and sensitive image of childhood.

Plays include: *The Snake with Seven Heads* (MS); *Somdaka* (MS, 1989); *Love Child* (MS); *Have You Seen Zandile?* (with Maralin Vanrenen, Thembi Mtshali, 3f,) NY: Heinemann, 1988 and in Perkins, 1998; *Born in the RSA*. (4f,3m, contributing writer) in *Woza Africa!: an Anthology of South African Plays* ed. Duma Ndlovu, NY: George Braziller, 1986; *The Good Woman of Sharksville* (from Brecht, with Janet Suzman, MS, 1995).

See also: Kagan-Moore in TDR 125; Strausbaugh in AT, Apr. 1989; CnTR v9, pts 1 and 2.

Edna St Vincent Millay
American, 1892–1950

Originally from Rockland, Maine, Millay graduated from Vassar in 1917 and moved to Greenwich Village, New York, where she became a central figure in bohemian circles and worked as actress and writer. A prize-winning poet, most of her plays are written in verse, with fabulaic qualities and romantic historical or fairy-tale settings. *The Lamp and the Bell* (1921), commissioned by Vassar's alumnae association and set in medieval times, celebrates female friendship. In *Two Slatterns and a King* a king plans to marry 'that maid whose kitchen's neatest' but marries a 'slut', due to the workings of Chance. Millay wrote the innovative *Aria da Capo* for Provincetown Players, an anti-war piece in which Columbine and Pierrot, forced offstage by the Masque of Tragedy, are replaced by the shepherds Thyrsis and Corydon. whose game of creating a wall between them escalates, through envy and suspicion, to mutual destruction. The lovers return to continue their scene, ignoring the bodies behind them. Millay's dramatic poem *The Murder of Lidice* (1942) addresses the specific atrocities of contemporary war, the Nazi destruction of the Czech village of Lidice. *Conversation at Midnight* presents a contemporary symposium as nine men discuss religion, culture and politics.

Plays include: *Here Comes the Bride* (7f,2m); *Implacable Aprhrodite et al.* in *Distressing Dialogues* (most 1f,1m, 1924, as Nancy Boyd); *Aria Da Capo* (1f,4m, 1919) also in Cook and Shay, in Martin 1940, in Ozieblo; *Two Slatterns and a King* (2f,2m); *The Lamp and the Bell* (29f, 19m+, 1921) – all in *Three Plays* (1926); *The King's Henchman* (8f, 13m, libretto, 1927); *Conversation at Midnight* (9m, 1937) – all NY: Harper and Bros; *The Murder of Lidice* (4f,2m, adaptation, 1942) DPS.

See also: *Edna St Vincent Millay* by Norman A. Brittin, NY: Twayne, 1967.

May Miller

American, 1899–?*

As a teacher of speech and drama at Frederick Douglass High School in Baltimore, Miller began writing plays to provide her students with material about black heroes and heroines. Many were collected in a volume she edited with Willis Richardson, together with work by her friend Georgia **Douglas-Johnson**.

Miller produced a total of more than twenty short plays before turning to poetry, ranging from the biblical *Graven Images*, based on verse 12:1 in *Numbers* ('And Miriam and Aaron spake against Moses because of the Ethiopian woman he had married') to biographical vignettes about historical figures such as Sojourner Truth and plays exploring community life, like *Riding the Goat*.

Unlike many fellow playwrights such as Zora Neale **Hurston** (another friend), Miller includes white characters in many of her works. She exposes the moral horror of lynching in *Nails and Thorns* through a white woman's desperation at what lynching does to 'every soul in that town. They crucified everything that was worthwhile – justice and pride and self-respect'. *Stragglers in the Dust* is a chilling piece about racism, set at the Tomb of the Unknown Soldier in Washington, DC, through white horror at the suspicion that the dead soldier was black.

Plays include: *Harriet Tubman* (3f,4m+) also in Perkins; *Christophe's Daughters* (4f,3m) also in Perkins; *Samory* (6m+); *Sojourner Truth* (1f,6m+) – all 1935, in Richardson & Miller; *Stragglers in the Dust* (1f,4m, 1930) in Perkins; *Riding the Goat* (2f,2m, 1929) in Perkins and in Brown-Guillory; *Graven Images* (2f,5m+) in Hatch & Shine; *Nails and Thorns* (2f,3m, 1933) in Hatch and Hamalian, 1991 and in Perkins and Stephens.

See also App. 2: Brown-Guillory; Shafer.

* Extensive enquiries have failed to establish whether Miller has died, and if so, when.

Susan Miller
American, 1944–

Linguistically and formally inventive, Miller's plays deal with women in quest of identity in a society that seeks to impose limited definitions on them creatively and sexually. Her central characters are single women, usually lesbian or bisexual, struggling with the convolutions of experience towards greater understanding and self-acceptance. Ronnie in *Confessions* is at last able, years later, to confront her love for her androgynous college friend Coop; Perry in *Cross Country* remakes her life and self in Los Angeles; the life of Raleigh in *Nasty Rumour* is shown in flashbacks while she undergoes an operation for a cerebral haemorrhage and her friends await news of her condition. *My Left Breast* and *Repairs* movingly address the experience of breast cancer.

Plays include: *Flux* (MS, 1976); *Nasty Rumours and Final Remarks* (4f,3m, 1979) in Curb; *Confessions of a Female Disorder* (8f,7m+, 1975) in Hoffman 1979; *My Left Breast* (1f, 1993) in Smith 1994; *Cross Country* (3f,1m, 1976) in WCP 1; *Repairs* (2f,1m, 1995) in Frank.

Paula Milne
British, 1947–

Best known as a screenwriter, Milne's award-winning *The Politician's Wife* was praised for its incisive portrayal of the scandal following the discovery of a Tory minister's adulterous affair, the Party's attempted cover-up and his wife's subtly plotted revenge. *Earwig* is a satire on television drama, a self-reflective piece, piling fictional layer upon layer. The heroine is a 'quality' novelist under financial pressure to write for popular television soaps who, to save her credibility, hires an actor to be her 'front' and writes his scripts. But 'she' is herself revealed to be the creation of a team of television writers in increasing disagreement over her story, depending on their perception of audience demand, politics and network pressures.

Play: *Earwig* (9f, 16m) in *PI* v6, no 3 & 4, Oct. & Nov. 1990.

Mary Russell Mitford

English, 1786–1855

Author of highly wrought poetic dramas, Mitford supported her mother and spendthrift father by her writing. Her works include classical and historical, often Renaissance, tragedies, frequently with extra female characters added or developed, and shorter dramatic sketches. Her *Charles the First* presents Cromwell heroically and ran foul of the Lord Chamberlain's blanket ban on plays about Charles's reign because of their possible encouragement of regicide. *Inez de Castro* focuses on a heroine highly popular with the Victorians, the epitome of the long-suffering wife whose devotion endures when her princely husband is pressured to cast her off in favour of a better marriage.

Plays include: *Rienzi* (5f, 10m+, 1828); *Foscari* (2f,7m, 1826); *Charles the First* (3f,20m+, 1834); *Sadak and Kasalrade* (3f,7m, 1835); *Inez de Castro* (2f,8m+, 1842) in *The Dramatic Works of Mary Russell Mitford*, London: Hurst and Blackett, 1854, 2 vols.

Ariane Mnouchkine

French, 1939–

Artistic director of the celebrated Théâtre du Soleil, Mnouchkine is creator of spectacular epic performances interrogating myth and history, drawing on influences and styles ranging from Eastern kabuki and kathakali to European fairground performances, clowning and Jacques Lecoq's mime work. Most famously in *1789* and *1792* the group explored the political dynamics of the French Revolution, drawing on their own experience of May '68.

Mnouchkine went on to lead further collective creations in *L'Age d'Or* (1975), *Molière* (from Bulgakov, 1978) and to direct Shakespeare's history plays, Aeschylus's *Atrides* cycle and, as director, to collaborate with writer Hélène **Cixous** on *Le Roi Sihanouk* and *L'Indiade*. *Mephisto* is adapted from Klaus Mann's novel which explores the gradual capitulation and cooperation of former radical actor Henrik Höfgens. Höfgens was based on Gustaf Gründgens, who became Hitler's favourite performer and apologist for the Nazi regime, celebrated for his role as Mephisto in Goethe's *Faust*. Where Istvan Szabo's 1981 film adaptation focuses primarily on Höfgens, Mnouchkine theatricalizes the novel and broadens the focus to look at several characters, including Erika Mann, and their rejection, collaboration or compromise with a brutal regime.

Translated plays include: *1789* (director, script by Sophie Lemasson, Jean-Claude Penchenat, 11f, 16m,) tr. Alexander Trocchi in *Gambit*, v5, no.20; *Mephisto* (8f, 17m,dp,1979) tr. **Wertenbaker** in Munk and in Baraitser.
See also App. 2: Cohn in Brater.

Monique Mojica
Canadian, 1954

Feminist, actress and director, Mojica is a Native Canadian (Kuna-Rappahanock) who founded Native Earth Performing Arts, and has also written for television. Her plays reclaim native heroines from sentimental storybook accounts, both the traditional Pocahontas as self-sacrificing Indian maiden risking all for love to save Captain John Smith, and white suffragettes' romanticization of Sacajawea as loyal and devoted guide to Lewis and Clark. Her plays offer multiple alternative histories presenting native women, past and contemporary, who are sold into slavery, brutally treated, free, warriors, mothers, angry, homesick, irreverent, spiritual, hardworking, funny, resistant.

Plays include: *Princess Pocahantas and the Blue Spots* (2f, 1990) in CTR 64 and with *Birdwoman and the Suffragettes* (5f,6m, radio, 1991) Toronto: Women's Press, 1991; *This is for Aborelia Dominguez* (1f) in Nolan, Quan, etc.; *Sea Cows* (with Makka Kleist, MS); *A Fast Growing Mold Bitter as Shame* in *Gatherings: the En'owkin Journal of First North American People* v3, 1992.
See also: CTR Fall 1991 (Native Theatre issue edited by Mojica); App. 2: Grant in Brask; Gilbert and Tompkins.

Lady Mary Wortley Montagu
English, 1689–1762

Essayist, poet and letter-writer as well as a playwright, Lady Mary eloped to marry the man of her choice and went to Turkey with him when he was appointed ambassador, where she studied smallpox inoculation and attempted to get it introduced in England. Her only play, *Simplicity*, based on Marivaux, is an enjoyable comedy of swapped identities, in which a betrothed couple change roles with their servants to test each other's feelings and fall in love. A modern production (Exeter, 1988) interspersed the text with Wortley Montagu's real letters.

Play: *Simplicity* (2f,5m) in *Essays & Poems* ed. Robert Halsbrand & Isobel Grundy Oxford: Clarendon Press, 1977.

Eleanor Elizabeth Montgomery
New Zealand, 19th century

Writing in Wanganui in the late nineteenth century, Montgomery is the earliest identified New Zealand woman playwright. Little is known of her life but she wrote poems and three melodramas, which may have been produced locally. The central character of the one-act *Madame Béranger* is secretly a writer whose husband is horrified when he discovers an ardent love letter in her handwriting, until it is revealed that she is the inspirational French novelist Madame Béranger and the letter a fiction. *The Snow Vision!* features conventional secret marriages, a guilt-wracked hero and sinister dream-like tableaux alongside contemporary political references and an independent heroine.

Plays: *Madame Béranger* (1f,2m, 1887); *The Snow Vision!* (6m,3f, 1891) – both: Wanganui: Wanganui Herald Newspaper Co.; *At Bay* (4f,7m) London: bound MS, 1905.
    See also: entry by Fiona Farrell Poole in *The Book of New Zealand Women* by C. MacDonald, M. Penfold and B. Williams. Wellington: B. Williams Books, 1991.

Cherrie Moraga
American, 1952–

Born to an Anglo father and a Chicana mother in California, Moraga says that she first came to appreciate language through listening to the stories told by the women of the family. She joined Maria Irene **Fornes**'s writing group at INTAR, New York's Hispanic-American Arts Centre, before she returned to the West Coast where most of her plays are set.
    Moraga's earlier plays explore identity, especially sexuality, confronting both the sexism and homophobia in the Chicano community and the racism and classism of the lesbian and feminist community. *Giving Up the Ghost* presents the struggles of three Chicana women towards self-definition: Amalia in her forties, Marisa in her twenties and Corky, Marisa's

younger self, a tomboy, tough and unable to express her attraction for women which she displaces into aggressive behaviour. Like all Moraga's plays it mixes Spanish and English, using spare, lyrical and powerful language to expose the ways in which women are damaged by traditional definitions of masculinity and femininity, activity and passivity. Of her play *Shadow of a Man* (1990), Moraga has written that 'the family is this private place, so anything is allowed to happen there, any kind of power exchange, any kind of control; it's the first place you learn to suffer, also the first place you learn to love.' The play concerns the effect of Catholicism on a girl's sense of self and the development of her sexuality in the context of a Chicana family. *Heroes and Saints* (1992) is set in the San Joaquin valley of California, centre of pesticide poisoning where, in this surreal play, Cerezita Valle is born without a body – a result of poisoning and a symbol both of her cultural invisibility as a Mexican woman and of a great wisdom and power, a character compared to the pre-Columbian Olmecas heads as imagery of Catholic martyrdom is mixed with political struggle.

Plays include: *Giving Up the Ghost* (3f) LA: West End Press, 1986 and in Lake and Shergold; *Shadow of a Man* (4f,2m) in Chavez; *Heroes and Saints* (6f,4m+), in Perkins and Uno.

See also: Y. Bajarano Interview in *Third Woman*, 3 i–ii, 1986; App.2: Yarbro-Bejaro in Hart and Phelan, and in Case ed.

Hannah More
English, 1745–1833

More's first and last plays were designed 'to promote a regard to Religion and Virtue in the minds of Young Persons'. *A Search after Happiness*, written for the Bristol school that More ran with her sisters, gives young women advice on the proper way to conduct their lives (such as practising female graces, not apeing those of men). Her own ambitions were higher. In 1774 she made the first of many visits to London, becoming friends with the Bluestocking group and actor-manager David Garrick, and began writing for the professional stage. Of her three tragedies, the most powerful is *Percy* which deals with an anti-war theme and conflicts between love and duty. It features Gothic motifs and a heroine who, though obedient in action to her father, asserts the impossibility of bending her feelings to his will and is driven mad by a forced marriage and the death of her beloved. More later repudiated the public stage and wrote moral and biblical dramas.

Plays include: *A Search after Happiness* (8f, 1763); *The Inflexible Captive* (2f,5m+, 1774); *Percy* (2f,6m, 1778) Bristol: J. W. Arrowsmith, 1911; *The Fatal Falsehood* (2f,3m, 1779); *Moses in the Bulrushes* (4f+); *Daniel* (5m); *Belshazzar* (1f,2m+); *David and Goliath* (7m+) and in *Sacred Dramas* (1782) reprint, Bern: Herbert Lang, 1973 and all in Kohut. All the above in *The Complete Works of Hannah More* (1836) NY: Zenger Reprint, 1976.

See also: *Hannah More* by M. G. Jones, NY: Greenwood, 1968; App. 2: Donkin.

Lillian Mortimer
American, ?–1946

Highly successful as an actress, author and producer in popular melodrama (and briefly vaudeville), Mortimer's first play appeared in 1895 but real success came with *No Mother to Guide Her* which toured and continued to be revived until at least 1913. The rip-roaring drama features a deep-dyed villain, numerous attempted murders (generally thwarted by the culprit's careless failure to check the victim is dead!), druggings, a ruined and abandoned maiden, a much put-upon hero and heroine and a comic 'Noo Yawk' soubrette, Bunco, who repeatedly saves the day and proved so popular she reappeared in several sequels and a novelization. Later plays (at least 42 published, many unpublished) follow equally popular formulae, feature 'fillum shooters' and vaudeville performers, with women's parts including reformatory girls, 'ultra-modern' women and country baseball fans.

Plays include: *The Shadow of the Gallows* (MS); *The Girl of the Streets* (MS); *Bunco in Arizona* (MS); *A Man's Broken Promise* (MS); *No Mother to Guide Her* (5f,7m+, 1905), in *America's Lost Plays* v 8 ed. Garrett H. Leverton, Princeton UP, 1940; *Ruling the Roost* (5f,5m, 1926); *Headstrong Joan* (5f,5m, c.1927); *No Account David* (4f,6m, 1929); *Six Wives on a Rampage* (7f,4m, c.1934) – all Chicago: T. S. Denison.

Anna Cora Mowatt (Ritchie)
American, 1819–70

Mowatt made a runaway marriage from France to a spendthrift husband and wrote the splendidly funny *Fashion* to earn money, and later became an actress. *Fashion* remains the most anthologized play by an early American woman playwright. Its satirical target is the American *nouveau riche*, frantically importing the latest European trends and effortlessly deceived by every con-man who sets himself up as an arbiteur of French fashions.

Mrs Tiffany has run her family to the brink of bankruptcy to support her high living; her daughter Seraphina is torn between marriage to the wealthy Snobson and the charms of the self-styled French Count Joli-maître, a valet in disguise. Their superficial values are set against those of truth, industry and independence, represented by virtuous heroine, Gertrude, and a bluff upstate farmer, Trueman. True American values are also central to *Armand*, despite its French setting, in which the heroine chooses the merits of poor but honest love over the seductions of wealth.

Plays include: *Fashion or Life in New York* (5f,8m+) in Barlow, in Scullion, etc. and with *Armand or the Peer and the Peasant* (3f,8m+) in *Plays*, Boston: Ticknor & Fields, 1855.

Gina Moxley
Irish, 1957–

Actress and writer/performer for radio, Moxley wrote her first stage play for Dublin-based company Rough Magic. Set in Cork – critics have praised her 'fighting filthy Cork dialogue' – her fiercely unsentimental plays centre on young people growing up, struggling to make sense of a brutal and bewildering adult world. In *Dog House*, the everyday arguments and fights of the other Lime Lawn families are counterpointed by the real dangers of the Martins' home where the father enforces a regime of arbitrary rules and brutal discipline (cf. **Stephenson**). In *Danti-Dan*, set in 1970, it is the young people themselves who manipulate or are victimized as they explore the perilous new ground of sexual experimentation. At its centre is 13-year-old Cactus, a remorseless force, discovering her sexuality and intelligence and the power they give her over others.

Plays include: *Danti-Dan* (3f,2m, 1995) in McGuinness; *Dog House* (8f,4m, 1997) in *New Connections* and *Connections* series, Faber 2001.

Lavonne Mueller
American, 1945–

Director of playwriting at the University of Iowa, Mueller is one of several playwrights consistently championed by Julia Miles's The Women's Project. Her drama, prolific and various, ranges across subject matters, vividly evoking various linguistic contexts and forms that encompass musicals and children's plays. She draws on biographical material in *Letters to a Daughter from Prison: Indira and Nehru* (MS, 1989) and *Colette in Love*, exploring the mingled conflict and interdependence of Colette's desires to write, to perform and to love. In *Little Victories* biographies are transformed by juxtaposition as American suffragist Susan B. Anthony, travelling in the American West, encounters Joan of Arc, struggling to gain military knowledge and acceptance, as both attempt to survive in male-dominated environments. Mueller's own experience, growing up on army posts, fuels a fierce opposition to war, which is centrally or peripherally the topic of much of her work. In the brutally satirical *Five in the Killing Zone* the efforts of a team of soldiers in the Vietnam War to find a body to take the place of the Unknown Soldier are stymied by the brilliance of pathologists at identifying individuals from the most damaged body parts. In *Killings on the Last Line* in 1979, the Year of the Child, working women in a Chicago reactor parts factory struggle to survive in a climate of decaying machines, insecure work, inadequate childcare and chemical contamination.

Plays include: *Warriors From a Long Childhood* (MS); *Killings on the Last Line* (9f,1m, 1979) in Miles 1980; *Little Victories* (2f,4m,id, 1983) in Miles 1984; *Colette in Love* (2f,2m, 1986) in Miles 1987; *Five in the Killing Zone* (5m, 1985) in Miles 1989; *The Only Woman General* (1f,1m,id, 1984) in *13th Moon* v10, nos 1 & 2; *Violent Peace* (1f,1m, 1990) in Miles 1993; *Jim's Commuter Airlines* (1f,1m, 1990) in Frank; *Breaking the Prairie Wolf Code* (4f,2m) DPS, 1986.

See also: interview in JDTC Fall 1994.

Rona Munro
Scottish, 1959–

Many of Munro's plays are marked by a vivid evocation of the landscapes and folk traditions of her native north-east Scotland. Her first play, *Fugue*, used a ghost story as the means to explore the mental breakdown of a young woman caught in a dead-end job and sense of directionlessness and, less effectively, the relationship between her and her inexperienced psychiatrist. Similarly, *Piper's Cave* employed the folk story of a piper wandering forever inside a hollow hill as metaphor for lives in crisis, in a piece about a woman's encounters with male desperation and violence. Munro's attempt, in *Piper's Cave*, to create, in Helen, a figure who incarnates the landscape itself, are fulfilled in the *Maiden Stone*, which won the Peggy Ramsay award. In it, the fecund wet-nurse and storyteller, Bidie, with her 'brood' of half-animal children, is inseparable from her harsh and fantastic environment. The piece centres on the encounter between her and Harriet, an actress, driven and tenacious, dragging her family on despite hardship and continual pregnancy to the next, often illusory engagement. Both women, one allied to, the other defiant of, the land, are identified with nature, both nurturing and destructive. Defiance and refusal to submit are central to *Bold Girls*, joint winner of the Susan Smith Blackburn award. Set in a Belfast Catholic extended family, three women, their men dead or 'lifted' by the British Army, survive on illusion, bravado and humour.

Plays include: *Piper's Cave* (2f,1m, 1985) in Remnant 5; *The Way to Go Home* (MS); *The Dirt Under the Carpet* (2f,1m,id) in BBC Radio, 1988; *Bold Girls* (4f, 1991) French and in Harwood 3: *Saturday Night at the Commodore* (1f, 1989) in Cameron; *Your Turn to Clean the Stair* (3f,2m, 1992) and *Fugue* (4f, 1983) – both 1995; *The Maiden Stone* (4f,3m+, 1995) – all London: NHB; *Men of the Month* (TV, 1994); *Ladybird, Ladybird* (screen, 1994); *Snake* (MS, 1999); *Haunted* (MS, 1999).

See also App. 2: Stevenson and Wallace; Horvat and Bell in Christianson and Lumsden.

Iris Murdoch
Irish, 1919–99

Celebrated novelist and philosopher until the distressing onset of Alzheimer's disease, Murdoch, remained a devotee of Plato despite his banning of artists from his model Republic, rejecting their art as an imitation of an imitation, a distraction from the ideal. Her work constantly circled round Platonic concepts such as love as entrance to knowledge (*The Black Prince*) and the nature of freedom (*The Three Arrows*, set in imperial Japan). In *Acastos* she employed the Platonic dialogue form to explore the purpose of theatre and religion. 'Everything I write,' said Murdoch of her other great influence, 'probably is *Hamlet* in disguise, the god of love and art, the Black Eros'. The play is reworked as contemporary tragical comedy in *The Black Prince* and as political tragedy in *The Servants and the Snow* (later rewritten as a libretto for William Mathias). *The Servants* explores issues of authority and obedience as a young heir to a country estate in nineteenth-century Europe finds his liberal reforms colliding with the nightmarish rituals and trappings of an ancient and ingrained system.

Plays include: *The Italian Girl* (with James Saunders, 4f,3m) in P&P Feb. 1968 as *An Italian Straw Hat*, French, 1968; *A Severed Head* (with J. B. Priestley, 4f,3m) in *Plays of the Sixties* vol. 2 ed. J. M. Charlton London: Pan, 1967; *The Three Arrows* (4f,9m); *The Servants and the Snow* (2f, 10m, both 1985), *The Black Prince* (4f,3m) all in *Three Plays*, London: Chatto & Windus, 1989; *Art and Eros* (6m) and *Above the Gods* (7m) in *Acastos* Penguin, 1986; *Joanna, Joanna* (4f,7m, c.1994), *The One Alone* (1995) – both London: Colophon Press with Old Town Books.

Peta Murray
Australian, 1958–

Wallflowering uses the metaphor of ballroom dancing for the central couple, Peg and Cliff, both to explore her tentative steps towards change and his gradual acceptance that he will never realize the great ambitions of his youth. Temporarily out of step first with the world, then with each other, they eventually discover their readiness 'to learn a new dance'. Meanwhile, a parallel couple, Peg and Cliff's romantic vision of themselves, enact their fantasy of being ballroom champions. Theatre-in-education is the context for much of Murray's work, and in *Spitting Chips* tomboyish Sybil, known as Spud, finds a way to express her anger at, and ultimately accept, her mother's death through her friendship with an old lady and through her passion for drumming.

Plays include: *This Dying Business* (MS, 2f,1m, 1990); *Wallflowering* (2f,2m, 1992); *One Woman's Song* (MS, 1993); *Spitting Chips* (2f,2m, 1995) – both Currency.
   See also App. 2: Tompkins and Holledge.

Phyllis Nagy
American, 1962–

Nagy was born in New York and is now based in London. Her plays, vividly written and structured like Chinese boxes, draw on popular mythology, the colliding discourses and lifestyles of postmodern cities and sundry weirdnesses of landscapes, American or British, haunted by Hollywood movies, desires sparked by game shows, *National Enquirer* stories and urban myths. They are inhabited by unexpected characters whose identities shift, disguises and sexualities, erotic and highly theatrical, fraught with coincidence and written in quirky, comic dialogue notable for one-liners like the much-quoted: 'Female impersonation is a rather curious career choice for a woman, Miss Coo', that opens *The Strip*. Nagy's plots shift across continents, trailing a fabulaic wake. Set in the meat-packing district of New York in a blazing heatwave, *Weldon Rising* is a searching exploration of loyalties in the gay community in the wake of the murder of Natty Weldon's lover by a homophobe. Refusing easy answers, Nagy's work suggests multiple and complex motivations for events and reactions: Sarah Casey's vanishing in *Disappeared*: killing or escape?; the sexual encounter of *Trip's Cinch*: rape or seduction?; Lily's matricide in *Butterfly Kiss*: attention-seeking from her lepidopterist father or lesbian lover, or a mercy killing in response to her mother's growing insanity?

Plays include: *Entering Queens* (MS, 1993); *Weldon Rising* (2f,4m, 1992) in Castledine 1994 and with *Disappeared* (3f,5m, 1995) Methuen, 1996; *Butterfly Kiss* (2f,3m,1994); *The Strip* (5f,5m,1995) all in *Plays One*, Methuen, 1998; *Trip's Cinch* (2f,1m) in Smith, 1994; *The Scarlet Letter* (adapted from Nathaniel Hawthorne, 3f,4m) French, 1995; *Neverland* (3f,4m) Methuen, 1998.

See also: Stephenson and Langridge; Freeman, Edgar, Sierz.

Sally Nemeth

American, 1959–

Chicago-born Nemeth explores the impact of public calamity and economic devestation on individuals in her plays. The explosion that kills her husband in *Mill Fire* devastates Marlene's life, leaving her torn by frustrated physical longing for her dead husband and unwilling to forgo her anger, accept and join the ranks of widows taking the company's monthly payout as compensation for not enquiring too far into the circumstances of the accident. Realistic scenes chart the progress towards the disaster in flashbacks, interwoven with fantasies in which Marlene revives her dead husband and ritualized recitals of memories by a chorus of fellow widows. *Holy Days* takes place in the dried-up earth of the 1930s Kansas dust bowl as Nemeth traces the struggles for survival of two families, in a piece described in Britain as having 'the effect of a body blow to the solar plexus'. The stage space of *Water Play* is physically invaded by water dripping through the roof, soaking the characters and obsessing their dreams, fantasies, fears and desires.

Plays include: *Holy Days* (2f,2m) BPP, 1991; *Spinning into the Blue* (MS); *Mill Fire* (5f,4m, 1988) in Miles 1989; *Water Play* (1f,2m, 1995) in Frank.

Anne Nichols

American, 1891–1966

Nichols, born in Georgia and raised in Philadelphia, wrote more than 20 plays. Athough *Just Married* and *Linger Longer Letty* (musical, MS) were successes, she is known for one, *Abie's Irish Rose*, that proved immensely popular on Broadway (a record 2327 consecutive perform-ances), on subsequent tours, revivals and as a movie, making its author a millionaire. Irish Catholic Rose Mary Murphy and Jew Abie Samuels attempt to hide their marriage, which is anathema to both Yiddisher papa and Irish daddy, despite their eventually being married three times – by a Methodist minister, a rabbi and a priest. Reconciliation is finally brought about by the birth of twin babies. While exploiting colourful stereotypes to the utmost, Nichols presents the experience of service abroad in the First World War as one where differences were overcome and individuals like Abie and Rose met across divides.

Plays include: *Springtime in Mayo* (MS, 1919); *The Gilded Cage* (MS, 1920); *Abie's Irish Rose* (2f,6m, 1922) French, 1937 and in Cerf and Cartmell; *Just Married* (with Adelaide Matthews, 5f,9m) French, 1929.
     See also: Shafer.

Heather Nimmo

Australian, 1952–

The Kalgoorlie gold fields are the setting of both Nimmo's *Touch of Midas*, one of several of her plays for young people, and *The Hope*, a keen observation of the effect on a young couple's relationship of life in a hard-drinking, macho town under a sweltering sun, where sex is a transaction and dreams are of making enough money to escape. Her *Murray's Reward* (MS) deals with a mining family in Tasmania.

Plays include: *The Hope* (2f,4m) Currency, 1987; *Boots* (MS, 1991); *Fossils* (MS, 1993); *Whispering Demons* (MS, 1994); *One Small Step* (1f) Currency, 1995.

Marsha Norman

American, 1947–

Kentucky-born Norman is one of the most successful post-war American women playwrights, acclaimed for her depictions of life on the social margins stalked by poverty, exploitation, disease.

Arlene, recently released from prison in *Getting Out*, is haunted by her former violent self, Arlie, imprisoned for second-degree murder, the culmination of a spiral of forgery, prostitution and robbery. Her attempts to start again, to get out, are belied by continued entrapment by her mother's non-understanding, a history of family neglect and abuse, the demands of her former boyfriend and pimp, and the paternalistic exploitation of retired prison guard, Bennie, whose 'taking care' of her is payable in sex.

The acclaimed Pulitzer Prizewinning *'Night, Mother* revolves round a mother's attempts to thwart her daughter's decision, justified with bleak rationality, to commit suicide, travelling a labyrinth of emotional dead-ends, sickness and failed family ties in a piece critics called 'devestating', a 'benign explosion'.

Norman's *Third and Oak* plays are subtle evocations of chance meetings between individuals such as the short encounter at the laundromat between a recent widow struggling to let go of her husband and a young woman, two years married, awaiting the return of her philandering husband. Norman has also written a Tony-winning musical version of *The Secret Garden*.

Plays include: *Getting Out* (5f,7m) NY: Avon, 1979 and in Kilgore; and in *Louisville*; with *The Hold Up* (1f,3m, 1980); *The Traveller in the Dark* (1f,3m, 1984); *Third and Oak: The Laundromat* (2f) and *The Pool Hall* (1f,2m, 1978) in *Four Plays*, TCG, 1988 and with *Loving Daniel Boone*; *Sarah and Abraham*; *Circus Valentine, Three Speeches* in *Marsha Norman: Collected Works vol. 1* Lyme, NH: Smith and Kraus, 1997; *'Night, Mother* (2f) NY: Hill and Wang, 1983; *Trudy Blue* (6f,5m) in Humana 1995; *The Secret Garden* (11f,12m), TCG, 1992.

See also: *Marsha Norman: a Casebook* by Linda Ginter Brown, Garland, 1996; Scharine in TiD 11; App. 2: Burkman in Schlueter; Kane in Brater; Spencer and Dolan in Hart; Savran; Schroeder in Keyssar 1996, Betsko and Koenig; Brown and Stevenson in Laughlin and Schuler.

Meredith Oakes

Australian, 1946–

Although born in Sydney, Oakes has lived in London since 1970. She began her career as a music critic, journalist and translator from German: her work includes Lenz, Bernhard and Horvath.

Her own plays explore the workings of power, especially clashes between men as they negotiate their position in the pecking order. This is refracted through a comic lens in *The Editing Process*, a delicious satire on a publishing world of moribund and mendacious old-timers hit by the new world of buy-outs, image consultancy, arbitrary promotions and sackings. Publications like *Footnotes in History* are edited into history almost before the ink is dry on the contract for their take-over and the fittest manoeuvre wildly for advantage, hoping to survive.

In *Faith* Oakes examines the tensions between soldiers and the demands of duty, patriotism and humanity when a group of soldiers in the Falklands War are ordered to kill a mercenary. The powerful *The Neighbour*s, like *Faith*, is a realistic drama, a brutal narrative of a war between two young men on a London council estate that escalates out of control, in a climate of economic hardship where those nearest become targets for scapegoating. Oakes has also written several opera libretti, including *The Triumph of Beauty and Deceit* (TV), *Jump into my Sack* (MS, 1996) and *Solid Assets*.

Plays include: *The Neighbour*s (4f,4m, 1993); *The Editing Process* (3f,5m, 1994); *Faith* (1f,5m, 1997) – all Oberon; *Mind the Gap* (MS, 1995).

Joyce Carol Oates

American, 1938–

Born in rural New York state, Oates is a prolific writer producing numerous acclaimed novels and stories together with plays, often adapted from her short stories. Many focus on stifling relationships between parents and children or explore aggression and social disaffection, the nightmares of contemporary America. Alienated adolescents are central both to *Ontological Proof* where Shelley, rejecting family and her past, attempts to erase her identity through anorexia, drugs, submission to rape, colluding in becoming an object of possession, passed between men; and most extremely to *Spider Monkey*, its protagonist a young psychotic murderer.

Not always successfully, Oates experiments with theatrical form. *Miracle Play* takes a plot of drug-related murders and torturings, a cycle of revenge and counter-revenge, with a racial aspect as a white pimp and dealer attacks a black hooker and her brothers and a cop encourages her to testify against him. The deliberately stereotyped plot and characters are designed to move, as described in Oates's preface, between three dimensions: natural, farcical self-parody and mystical.

Plays include: *Ontological Proof of My Existence* (1f,3m, 1972); *Miracle Play* (2f,8m, 1974), *The Triumph of the Spider Monkey* (2f,4m, 1979) in *Three Plays*, Los Angeles: Black Sparrow Press, 1980; *Tone Clusters* (1f,1m) in Halpern, in Stein and Young 1992–3 and with *The Eclipse* (2f,1m) as *In Darkest America*, French, 1991; *The Call* (1m), *The Anatomy Lesson* (2f), *'I've Got Something For You'* (2m); *The Secret Mirror* (1m) all in *From the Secret Mirror* in *The Kenyon Review*, Fall 1992; *The Adoption* (1f,1m,3f/m) in Guare; *The Interview* (1f,2m); *Gulf War* (2f,2m); *Negative* (2f); *Here She Is* (6f,3m); *Black* (1f,2m, 1994, also in Miles 1997); *The Perfectionist* (3f,3m); *Homesick* (1f,1m) and others in *The Perfectionist and Other Plays*, Hopewell, NJ: The Ecco Press, 1995.

Tamsin Oglesby
British, 1965–

Oglesby, a former director, writes plays addressing envy and competition between women. In *Two Lips Indifferent Red*, a society which judges and drives women to judge themselves by appearances forces division between Angela, her cosmetic-surgeon husband – who urges facelifts and tummy-tucks – and her supermodel daughter, Jo, beside whom, physically, she will always be found wanting. Oglesby's chorus of beauticians reinforce the constant refrain of anxiety about size and shape, self-loathing and fear of ageing. In *My Best Friend*, the reunion of two old schoolfriends in France is invaded by a third and with her by echoes of old rivalries and insecurities. Oglesby deals with the anguish of exclusion from the group, the cruelty of young girls and the tricks of memory which protect us from former pain.

Plays include: *Two Lips Indifferent Red* (5f,2m, 1995) in Dromgoole, *My Best Friend* (3f) Faber, 2000.

Edna O'Brien
Irish, 1932–

O'Brien is best known for her novels, many autobiographical, some then dramatized. *A Pagan Place* is a delicate observation of family and place from the point of view of a young girl growing up in the west of Ireland, which critics described as Chekhovian, full of ironies, finely drawn characters and a sense of community at once stifling and sustaining. Sexuality, its threats, awakening and costs, is central to the experience of both the heroine, Creena, abused by the priest, and her sister. The sister returns pregnant from the glamour of Dublin to the judgementalism of home, running away again to escape the fate of childbirth as a fallen woman under the stern eyes of the nuns at the Magdalen laundry. Paradoxically for Creena, discovering a vocation, nuns represent freedom

Family conflict is central to *Our Father*, focusing on a family reunion, and *A Cheap Bunch of Nice Flowers*, in which daughter Ria attempts to assert her individuality beside her vibrant mother, eccentric radical journalist Winnie. Seducing her mother's lover, she imagines herself pregnant and protects herself with fantasies of weddings from the reality of her mother's dying.

O'Brien's most acclaimed play, *Virginia*, uses a fluid and elliptical style, drawing together passages from **Woolf**'s novels and diaries, exploring the struggle between desire and its 'proper' expression, the claims of her art and those of an upper-class social context, her 'madness' and the demands of reason that she repress it.

Plays include: *The Wedding Dress* (5f,1m) in *Mademoiselle*, Nov. 1963; *A Cheap Bunch of Nice Flowers* (4f,3m+, 1962) in Trewin 26; *Zee & Co* (alt. *X, Y & Zee*, film, 1970) Penguin, 1970; *A Pagan Place* (11f,9m), Faber, 1973; *Virginia* (2f,2m) London: Hogarth Press, 1973; *Flesh and Blood* (MS, 1985); *Our Father* (MS, 1999); *Stag* (MS); *Blood Memory* (MS); *Madame Bovary* (MS, 1987).

See also App. 2: Helle in Hart.

Mary O'Malley
Irish, 1941–

Writer and former actress/dancer of London Irish descent, O'Malley's hilarious evocation of a west London convent school in the late 1950s, *Once a Catholic*, was great box office success at the Royal Court and in the West End. It charts the course of three Marys through the fifth form and their awkward attempts to gain a sexual education: hapless Mary Mooney, whose guileless innocence is interpreted by the nuns as deceitful wickedness and taken advantage of by boys; and her friends, clever, sophisticated Mary Gallagher and guilty rebel Mary McGinty. *Look Out Here Comes Trouble* presents a wry, compassionate picture of a residential psychiatric hospital and its patients, a world of the 'abnormal' that varies only slightly from that of the normal, while *Oy Vay Maria* wittily explored family reactions to a Catholic–Jewish marriage (cf. **Nichols**).

Plays include: *Oy Vay Maria* (TV); *Percy and Kenneth* (TV); *If Ever a Man Suffered* (MS); *A Needle's Eye* (MS); *Talk of the Devil* (MS); *Once a Catholic* (10f,5m) in *P&P*, Oct. & Nov. 1977 and in Trewin 47; *Look Out Here Comes Trouble* (6f,8m, 1979) – both also Ashover: Amber Lane Press.

See also App. 2: Wandor 1987.

Tess Onwueme
Nigerian, 1955–

Born at Ogwashi-Uku, Onwueme now teaches in the USA. Her work addresses issues of world politics and the impact of hunger and exploitation on Africa's poor, particularly women. In *The Desert Encroaches* she employs animals symbolically, as the ferocious creatures of the North prey on the placid Southern ruminants. Formally her work draws on dance, ritual, song, chanting and other aspects of traditional African performance. Like **Aidoo**'s, Onwueme's plays address women's role as leaders (*Parables for a Season*) and the impact of education in challenging traditional values. The dilemma of women, no longer prepared to accept cultural oppression but thereby often isolated, is often central. It divides Honor, in *The Broken Calabash*, from her mother's generation, although Wazobia in *Reign* is supported by other women in refusing to give up power at the end of her regency. The narrow class base of much feminism is criticized in the epic *Tell it to Women*, where arrogant Western-educated Ruth and Daisy seem incapable of understanding the struggles of the rural women they aim to represent, an ignorance which leads to tragedy but also, as the tribal women reject intimidation and patronage, to their discovery of a renewed confidence and freedom.

Plays include: *Legacies* (2f,4m,id, 1989); *The Desert Encroaches* (1f,5m, 11+,id, 1988); *The Broken Calabash** (4f,6m+, 1984) and *The Reign of Wazobia** (7f,7m+) in *The Reign of Wazobia and Other Plays* (1992) – both Ibadan: Heinemann Educational Books; also *Parables for a Season** (8f,4m+5) in Ntiri – all* in *Three Plays* (1993); *Tell it to Women* (9f,4m+, 1997) – both: Detroit: Wayne State UP.

See also: *Artrage* Autumn 1989; App. 2: Amuta in Otokunefor and Obiageli; Dunton.

Rena Owen
New Zealand/Aotearoan, 1960–

Daughter of a Maori father and pakeha mother, Owen is best known as an actress, acclaimed for her role in the film *Once Were Warriors* (see **Brown**). She developed her autobiographical first play with the British company of women ex-prisoners, Clean Break. *Te Awa I Tahuti* is structured as a series of encounters between a young Maori woman, in London's Holloway Prison for drug offences, and her British psychotherapist. It powerfully explores issues of cultural identity as Toni confronts the pain of her brother's suicide, her Maori father's violent alcoholism, her own self-destructive behaviour and the frustration of a colonized people while her Maori chants and songs express and assert her claim to her own cultural space.

Plays include: *Te Awa I Tahuti* (2f, 1987) in Garrett/Potiki; *Daddy's Girl* (MS).
See also App. 2: Gilbert and Tompkins.

Rochelle Owens
American, 1936–

Brooklyn-born Owens came to prominence in the 1960s with plays that, like **Terry**'s, **Fornes**'s and **Drexler**'s, employed daring new theatrical vocabularies. Where Drexler's tone is free-floating playful optimism, Owens, influenced by Artaud, presents a grimmer view of a society animated by grotesque and primitive drives, the desire for sex, power, food.

The Obie-award-winning *Futz* centres on the sexual passion of a farmer for a pig and his destruction by the repressive inhabitants of an inbred Puritan community. Written in a language incorporating groans, cries and distorted words, the piece reveals Owens's fascination with language, reflected in her poetry, including experiments in performance and with shamanic verse. Set in alien locales – imaginary Greenlands, Africas, Constantinople – her plays use allegorical spaces to explore collective projections of the exotic other. In *Istanboul* the natives are objects of erotic fantasy for Christian women, while their Crusader husbands plan to establish a shrine and enlist a saint to exploit their commercial potential.

Many of Owens's works feature powerful roles for women, creatures of magnetism (such as *Istanboul*'s St Mary of Egypt) or appetite, like Beclch in *Beclch*: ruthless, bloodthirsty, highly sexed, exploiting and manipulating both African natives and her white husband in fulfilling her lusts. Elsewhere Owens deals with the desire to define and control in creative struggle between author and historical character – in *Emma Instigated Me* about Emma Goldman (see **Bolt**) or the obsessive unanswered letters of Chucky to his ex-wife in *Chucky's Hunch*.

Plays include: *Futz* (5f,9m+,dp, 1965) in Hoffman 2, Poland; *Beclch* (5f,10m, 1966); *Homo* (2f,6m, 1966); *Istanboul* (5f,4m, 1965); *The String Game* (2f,7m, 1963) in *Futz and What Came After*, NY: Random House, 1968; *OK Certaldo* (2f, 10m,dp, 1973); *He Wants Shih* (2f,11m+, 1970); *Farmer's Almanac* (1f,3m+3, 1968); *Kontraption* (2f,9m,+3f/m, 1972); *Coconut Folk Singer* (2f,1m, radio, 1973) in *The Karl Marx Play* (7f,4m, 1973) *and Others*, NY: P. Dillon & Co., 1974; *Emma Instigated Me* (7f,2m,4f/m, 1975) in PAJ Spring 1976; *Chucky's Hunch* (1m) in Marranca and Dasgupta 2; *The Widow and the Colonel* (3f,2m) DPS, 1977.

See also App. 2: Murray in Brater, Betsko and Koenig.

Louise Page

English, 1955–

Page grew up in Sheffield, becoming a writer in the late 1970s, a period of committed feminist theatre companies and issue-based plays aimed at raising awareness. This was reflected in her early work on themes such as deafness (*Hearing*, MS, 1979), chemical adulteration of food (*Flaws*, MS, 1980) and the then taboo subject of breast cancer (*Tissue*, 1978), which addressed multiple aspects of the experience in an episodic structure: body image, self-examination, prosthetics, though Page moves beyond didacticism in a sensitive, poetic treatment of bodily trauma. It has been written that she 'writes intimate unforced dramas that catch us up in other people's crises, opening up vast territories of feeling beneath the surface of ordinary lives'.

Her best-received plays examine aspects of mother–daughter relationships. *Real Estate* explores the conflicts sown in a family when long-estranged career woman Jenny, now 38, returns pregnant to her mother and stepfather with the expectation that Gwen should give up her real estate career to care for her grandchild. She is faced with Gwen's insistence on her late-won independence and her stepfather's desire for fatherhood. *Salonika*, in which a sprightly elderly mother and prudish spinster daughter visit the seashore where the father fell in the First World War, crosses from Page's characteristic naturalism, where tea is drunk, knitting patterns discussed, into a dream-like, surreal world where the dead father rises from the sand. It is both a subtle character study and a moving anti-war piece. Other plays address women's relationship to power and the conflict between ambition and loyalty: *Golden Girls*, about a women's Olympic relay team; *Diplomatic Wives*, about support for a husband's career and Christine's own diplomatic ambitions.

Plays include: *Goat* (MS); *Tissue* (2f,1m,id, 1978) in Wandor 1; *Falkland Sound/ Voces de Malvinas* (MS, 1983); *Salonika* (2f,3m, 1983); *Real Estate* (2f,2m, 1985); *Golden Girls* (8f,5m, 1984); *Beauty and the Beast* (6f,6m+,id, 1986); *Diplomatic Wives* (2f,1m, 1989) – all Methuen; *Agnus Dei* (3f,4m) in Roberts; *Hawks and Doves* (1992); *Another Nine Months* (MS).

See also: NTQ 22, May 1990; App. 2: Betsko and Koenig, Cousin, Sierz.

Dorothy Parker

American, 1893–1967

Poet, reviewer, short-story writer, wit, Parker was a key member, with Edna **Ferber** and others, of the influential Algonquin Round Table group of authors. She worked as drama critic for *Vanity Fair* and reviewer for other magazines, later writing for Hollywood. After the death of her second husband she took to drink, dying alone in a hotel bedroom in Manhattan. It is a fate perhaps foreseen in *Ladies of the Corridor*, a poignant examination, delineated with compassion and Parker's characteristic acerbic wit, of the lives of women, widowed or divorced, living in a hotel, struggling to stay financially and emotionally afloat, leading lives of isolation, desperation or defiance. *The Coast of Illyria* also charts a struggle against despair, focusing on powerful dramatic territory in the lives of sister and brother writers Mary and Charles Lamb and their circle, she succumbing to terrifying bouts of madness in one of which she had murdered her mother; he, devoted to her, taking refuge in drink from the realization of what his devotion will cost him: his lover and happiness. Parker also wrote lyrics for three revues, one, *After Such Pleasures*, adapted from her own writings.

Plays include: *Mr Skeffington* (1944); *Saboteur* (1942); *Trade Winds* (1938); *A Star is Born* (1937) (all screen); *The Ice Age* (MS, n.d.); *Close Harmony or The Lady Next Door* (with Elmer Rice, 5f,4m, 1924); *The Ladies Of the Corridor* (with Arnaud d'Usseau, 9f,7m, 1953) – both: NY: French; *Here We Are* (1f,1m, 1931) in *24 Favourite One Act Plays*, ed. Bennett Cerf, NY: Doubleday/Dolphin, 1958; *The Coast of Illyria* (with Ross Evans, 6f,7m, 1949) Iowa City: Iowa UP, 1990.

See also: *Dorothy Parker* by Arthur F. Kenney, Boston: Twayne, 1978.

Suzan-Lori Parks
American, c.1964–

Most often compared to Gertrude **Stein**, Adrienne **Kennedy** or the Absurdists, Parks's work focuses on language, its distortions, shifts and transformations, orality and subtle variations, rejecting conventional narrative but employing jazz aesthetics: repetition and revision. While she resists reductive interpretation and categorization of her work as 'only about being black', rewriting the 'unrecorded, dismembered, washed out' histories of African-American experience is central to many of her plays – densely metaphorical, playful, often farcical explorations of voyeurism, performance and fakery.

The parts of *Imperceptible Mutabilities* are linked by the repeated section, *Third Kingdom*, a retelling of the passage from Africa to America, its characters Kin-seer, Shark-seer and Over-seer focusing a history of alienation and loss. *Venus* recounts the history of an African woman imported to a London freak show in 1810. The Foundling Father of *The America Play* builds 'an exact replica of the Great Hole of History' and trades on his uncanny resemblance to Abraham Lincoln to offer theme-park customers the chance to play John Wilkes Booth and shoot him. In *Snails*, Molly/Mona is alienated from white language, she and her friends being presented as objects of a naturalist's objectifying anthropological analysis. Peopled by 'characters' called 'Black Woman With Fried Drumstick' and 'Old Man River Jordan', *Death of the Last Black Man*'s circular sequences recount a history of near-deaths by lynching, fire and electrocution, while Ham (cf. **Hurston**) rewrites the biblical lineage of slavery as 'That thuh mother and Yuh Father, thuh son brought forth uh odd lot called: Yes Massuh, Yes Missy, Yes Maam n Yes Suh Mistuh Suh'.

Plays include: *The Death of the Last Black Man in the Whole Entire World* (5f,6m, 1989–92) in Lamont, in *Theater* Summer/Fall 1990, in Mahone and with *Betting on The Dust Commander* (1f,1m, 1987); *Pickling* (1f, 1988); *Devotees in the Garden of Love* (3f, 1991); *The America Play* (2f,3m, 1990–3); *Imperceptible Mutabilities in the Third Kingdom* (includes *Snails*, etc., 3f,2m+,id, 1986–9) also in Elam and Alexander, in *The America Play and Other Works*, TCG, 1995; *Venus* (4f,8m, 1996) in *Theatre Forum* 9, Summer/Fall 1996 and TCG, 1997.

See also: Solomon in *Theater* Summer/Fall 1990; TDR 147.

Lorae Parry
New Zealand/Aotearoan, 1955–

Parry is an actress and director whose work deals with aspects of gender identity and sexuality. *Frontwomen* is a classic lesbian self-discovery romance as Stephanie, a suburban wife and mother, meets high-flying workaholic newscaster Frederika and falls in love. Set in a working-class suburb of Sydney, *Cracks* is a lively, effective and witty piece. Its title character is an unruly 25-year-old 'no-hoper' in love with her junkie best friend, working in a factory making television knobs and singing in a karaoke bar by night, whose dreams of escape are inspired by her fascination with the figure of Charlotte Badger, who found her way to New Zealand by dressing as a man and inciting a mutiny. *Eugenia* was an Italian immigrant woman in 1916 who lived as a man, seduced women, fought with men and was tried for murder, whose story, performed by a group of modern-day high-school students, ignites hidden tensions between pupils, school board and staff. Parry is also co-deviser/performer with Susie McGlone of the hilarious Digger and Nudger comedy duo (scripted with **Betts**), would-be politically correct Kiwi men trying to get in touch with their femininity.

Plays include: *Strip* (with Celia West, Lynne Brandon, MS); *Frontwomen* (4f,3m, 1993); *Cracks* (4f,1m, 1994) – both Wellington: the Women's Play Press; *Eugenia* (4f,2m) Victoria UP, 1996.

Julia Pascal

British, 1949–

Writer and director, and founder of Pascal Theatre Company, Pascal's work has typically explored the fragmented European Jewish heritage in the wake of the Holocaust. The myth of the *Dybbuk* is replayed by prisoners awaiting transport to Auschwitz from their memories of Anski's classic Yiddish drama, fragmented and juxtaposed with fragments of their former lives. In *Theresa*, the life of Viennese Jew Theresa Steiner, betrayed to the Nazis by the British authorities on Guernsey, is explored in a dance drama addressing the hidden history of collaboration. Collaboration is also the topic of *Year Zero/L'Année Zéro* (MS), a satirical investigation of the Vichy regime which, like many of Pascal's pieces, is bilingual in French/English.

Plays include: *Men Seldom Make Passes* (based on **Parker**, MS, 1978); *Far Above Rubies* (MS, 1984); *St Joan* (MS, 1997); *Theresa* (3f,2m,id, 1990) also in Goodman, 2000; *A Dead Woman on Holiday* (3f,2m,id, 1991); *The Dybbuk* (3f,2m,id, 1992) as *Holocaust Trilogy*, Oberon, 1998.

Lyudmila Petruschevskaya

Russian, 1938–

Born in Moscow, Petruschevskaya began to receive recognition for her stories and plays with the onset of *glasnost* and a climate where the disquieting realism of her bleak representations of contemporary life could gain acceptance. Her plays, described as Chekhovian, paint with vivid comedy, precise detail and colloquial language following the inconsequential rhythms of actual conversation, the mundane preoccupations of Muscovites with money, accommodation, food and drink, revealing the fascinations of the commonplace. In *Cinzano* three men escape the familial and financial complexities of their lives by getting progressively dead-drunk, sharing semi-coherent ramblings and fantasies. The *Three Girls in Blue*, each obsessed with their own problems and preoccupations, argue over how to split the cost of their rented dacha, the leaking roof, their children, the misdeeds of their lovers, while in one of them, Ira's love affair, attempts at romance compete with her anxieties over her sick child, need for baby-sitting help and the cost of taxi fares. The parents in *Music Lessons* attempt to win their son from ill-mannered Nadia and engineer his marriage with their approved daughter-in-law, Nina, in a piece reflecting the inter-generational pressures of living in cramped, over-crowded apartments.

Plays include: *Three Girls in Blue* (8f,6m) tr. Liane Aukin, in *Stars in the Morning Sky: New Soviet Plays* ed Michael Glenny, NHB, 1989; and with *Cinzano* (3m), also tr. Elise Thorun in *Theater* 20:3; *Smirnova's Birthday* (3f,1m); *Love* (2f,1m); *Music Lessons* (7f,6m); *The Stairwell* (2f,2m); *Nets and Snares* (1f); *The Execution* (5m,dp); *The Meeting* (1f,1m+1); *Isolation Box* (2f); *A Glass of Water* (1f,1m) all in *Cinzano: Eleven Plays* ed. and tr. Stephen Mulrine, NHB, 1991; *I'm for Sweden* (2f,1m) and *Columbine's Flat* (1f,2m) tr. T. Crane and M. Latsinova in *Soviet Literature* 1989–90 no 3; *A Girl Like That* (1f, MS) tr. Mulrine, MS from Michael Imison Playwrights.

See also: Vainer in *Theater* 20:3.

Winsome Pinnock
British, 1961–

The daughter of Jamaican parents, Pinnock's plays often mine the rich seam of the earlier generation's experiences of immigration. Pinnock studied drama at Goldsmith's College, London and joined the Royal Court Young Writers Group. She began writing for young people's and community groups with *A Rock in Water*, a biographical piece about 1950s black activist Claudia Jones, and *The Wind of Change* (MS), which focused on the experiences of an idealistic young nurse, her eager arrival in the 'mother country' and her growing disillusionment when faced with racial prejudice.

In later works such as *A Hero's Welcome*, runner-up for the Susan Smith Blackburn Award, she explores the pressures that forced people into choosing to emigrate from the West Indies and the pain of leaving. Set in 1947 it focuses on conflicting desires of those, like Minda, ready to do anything to escape the desperate poverty of island life, and Len, returned home a wounded hero after the war, who is resolved to stay on the island and 'build a better world'. The reality of his wartime heroism, eventually revealed, is of a war zone in a Liverpool munitions factory where black workers were paid less than the whites who refused to work with them.

Leave Taking, Pinnock's most produced play, is a painful and funny exploration of the conflict of mother and daughters, centring on Enid Matthews, whose determination to make a better life for her children has led her to reject her history and culture to try to fit in. *Talking in Tongues* addresses the thorny politics of sexual relationships between blacks and whites, the anger and jealousy ignited when a black woman finds her boyfriend with a white woman. The most consistently acclaimed of the black British women playwrights whose work emerged in the 1980s, Pinnock's plays are realistic, subtle, moving and provocative.

Plays include: *Bitter Harvest* (screen, 1992); *Picture Palace* (MS, 1988); *Leave Taking* (4f,1m, 1988) in Harwood 1; *A Rock in Water* (10f,6m, 1987) in Brewster 2; *A Hero's Welcome* (5f,3m, 1990) in PI and in George; *Talking in Tongues* (8f,4m, 1991) in Brewster 3; *Mules* (3–12f, 1996) Faber; *Water* (MS, 2000).

See also App. 2: Croft in Griffiths and Llewellyn Jones; Stephenson and Langridge; Edgar; Sierz.

Mary Pix

English, 1666–1720?

Satirized, with her friends **Trotter** and **Centlivre**, as the 'female wits' in an anonymous 1697 play, Pix was daughter of an Oxfordshire clergyman and married a London merchant. She produced one novel, a poem and, between 1696 and 1709, 13 plays – with the exception of three (less successful) tragedies, enormously witty comedies distinguished by marvellously complex plots, adroitly resolved. Foolish old men abound: the ageing husband of *The Spanish Wives* who keeps his wife locked up with his other property and drives her to run away with her former lover (though his wiser friend wins true affection by his gentle treatment of his wife); Senator Bondi of *The Deceiver Deceived*, who fakes blindness to avoid unwanted state duties and has to pretend ignorance as his wife and daughter conduct their amorous affairs before his 'sightless' eyes.

Comic love intrigues are juxtaposed with more serious emotional affairs in *The Innocent Mistress* as the witty debaucher Sir Francis Wildlove confronts his growing temptation to reform and marry the charming Mrs Beauclair, while Sir Charles Beauclair endures a passionate 'platonic' love for Bellinda, and remorse for the marriage made for money which now traps him. Pix's comic gallery includes deftly drawn adolescents: a hefty wine-tippling teenager and a scornful daughter of a foolish mother; sharpers; servants worn out with managing their masters' intrigues; exquisite French fops and would-be playwrights. *The Beau Defeated* confronts the transactions between Country, Quality and

Pix's familiar City as absurd Mrs Rich, a wealthy widow, desperately tries to disown her origins. Though Pix's work remains some of the most accessible, funny and perceptive of its time, she continues to be sadly neglected by major companies.

Plays include: *The Spanish Wives* (4f,7m, 1696) also in Kendall and in Rogers; *The Innocent Mistress* (10f,9m, 1697) also in Morgan; *The Deceiver Deceived* (7f,9m, 1697); *Queen Catherine or the Ruins of Love* (3f,8m, 1698); *The False Friend or The Fate of Disobedience* (6f,6m, 1699); *The Beau Defeated or The Lucky Younger Brother* (9f,8m, 1700) also in Lyons and Morgan; *The Double Distress* (3f,6m, 1701); *The Different Widows or Intrigue à la Mode* (9f,9m, 1703); *The Conquest of Spain* (2f, 10m, 1705); *The Adventures in Madrid* (6f,7m, 1706) all in *The Plays of Mary Pix and Catherine Trotter* ed. Edna Steeves, Garland, 1982.

See also: *Three Augustan Women Playwrights* by Constance Clark, NY: Peter Lang, 1986; App. 2: Cotton; Pearson; Steeves in Schofield and Macheski.

Sylvia Plath
American, 1932–63

Plath's tragic life and harshly brilliant work has inspired a number of dramatic pieces (e.g. **Goldemberg**). *Three Women*, written for BBC radio in 1962, is a moving exploration of the wonder, anguish and ambivalence of pregnancy and childbirth, set in a maternity ward where one woman gives birth to a son, another to an unwanted daughter who she leaves at the hospital, while a third miscarries. In Plath's little-known *Dialogue Over a Ouija Board* a husband and wife argue over whether the spirit that appears to speak to them, spelling out strange words and phrases, is a revelation from beyond or an unconscious expression of their united poetic voices, but realize it will remain uncertain, an 'equivocal thicket of words'.

Play: *Three Women* (3f) in *Winter Trees*, (1971) and with *Dialogue Over a Ouija Board* (1f,1m) in *Collected Poems* (1981). Both Faber.
See also App. 2: Devlin in Chinoy and Jenkins.

Vivienne Plumb

New Zealand/Aotearoan, 1955–

Wellington-based Plumb has published short fiction as well as the award-winning *Love Knots*. The piece playfully and poignantly explores loss, memory and sibling rivalry as Blossom and her sisters meet to divide up the household spoils after their mother's death.

Prosaic arguments about tablecloths and tea sets are broken by visions of Mumma as an unlikely angel, magic tricks, dreams of white cockatoos and Blossom's excavation of the garden in search of a lost doll and her past.

Plays include: *Fruct* (MS); *Love Knots* (6f,2m) Wellington: the Women's Play Press, 1994; *Fact or Fiction: Meditations on Mary Finger* (1f, MS, 2000).

Sharon Pollock

Canadian, 1936–

One of the major contemporary playwrights from Canada, many of Pollock's plays take historical and biographical themes as their starting points to explore other issues: national identity, racism (through the denial of East Indian immigrants' right to disembark in Canada in *Komagatu Maru*), profiteering (bootlegging across the US border in *Whiskey Six Cadenza*), suffrage activism (*The Making of Warriors*), native rights and land ownership (tensions between white settlers and indigenous claims in *Generations*). *Walsh* is a study of the 'White Sioux' Superintendent, responsible for Sitting Bull during his exile in Canada, his developing relationship with the Indian and growing disillusion with his own government's capitulation to American pressure for Sitting Bull's return and imprisonment. Set at a reunion of soldiers and civilians to commemorate the battle of Yorktown, *Fair Liberty's Call* examines with fierce moral complexity the aftermath of the American War of Independence from the point of view of English loyalist founders of Canada as they interrogate what they have fought for, what rejected: 'Where do you put your eye to find the heartbeat of a country comin' into being?'

Other Pollock central characters include Jack the Ripper, Sarah Bernhardt and, to particular acclaim, Lizzie Borden, of the infamous axe murder, re-enacted in *Blood Relations*. Shifting perspectives on her possible guilt and motivation enable Pollock to explore the complexities of sexual repression, power, desire and the family.

Plays include: *Generations* (2f,5m, 1981) and in Perkyns; *Blood Relations* (4f,3m, 1980) also in Wandor 3, CTR 29, and Talonbooks, 1984; *One Tiger to a Hill* (2f,8m, 1980) in *Blood Relations and Other Plays*, Edmonton: NeWest Press, 1981; *Heroines* in *Three Plays* Studio City, CA: Players Press, 1992; *Walsh* (1f,11m,id) Talonbooks, 1973 and in Wasserman vi; *Whiskey Six Cadenza* (5f,7m+, 1993) in Bessai and Kerr; *Doc* (3f,2m) Playwrights Canada, 1986 and in Wasserman v2; *Saucy Jack* (1f,3m, 1993), Blizzard, 1994; *Fair Liberty's Call* (3f,5m) Coach House Press, 1995; *The Komagatu Maru Incident* (3f,3m) in *Six Canadian* 1978; *The Making of Warriors* (6f,4m) in Jansen, 1991.

See also: *The Sharon Pollock Papers: the First Accession* ed. S. Mortensen and S. A. Owen Calgary: Calgary UP, 1989; McCaughey in CD 14:2, 1988; Stone-Blackburn in CD 15:2, 1989; Johnson in CD 10:2, 1984; Nothof in MD Winter 1995; App. 2: Zimmerman; Conolly; Sullivan in Donkin and Clement; Gilbert and Tompkins; Pollock in Much.

Katherine Susannah Prichard
Australian, 1883–1969

Probably best known as a novelist, Prichard also wrote 17 plays, several of them lost, ranging from suffrage dramas (cf. **Bensusan**, Miles **Franklin**) for the AFL in London to campaigning socialist plays to *Brumby Innes* which has been described as 'The Great Australian Play'.

In *Pioneers* divisions are revealed in the relationship between a husband and wife, settlers in the outback, when she helps two escaped convicts, identifying their position outside the law with her own sense of a dubious past and social marginality, while he is driven by a desire to be accepted as a law-abiding, upstanding member of the community. Written in 1927, the frank sexuality of *Brumby Innes* left it unperformed until 1972. It is remarkable exploration of a traditional Australian ethic of masculinity and the desire for dominance over both Aborigines and women. Brumby is consistently identified, as his name implies, with the animal: the boss horse for whom women are brood mares, whether the unwilling 13-year-old Wybia whom he snatches from her mate, igniting a conflict with the Aborigines, or May, who succumbs to his raw sexuality despite his rejection of her civilized values and of love as 'the smoke you women put up to do men out of being plain, ordinary, decent male animals'. A respecter only of the laws of possession and strength, he is prepared to subdue both the land and its inhabitants and demands a harem of 'gins', black or white, as his right. *Bid Me To Love*, a comedy about the snares of open marriages, is often seen as a companion piece.

Plays include: *The Burglar* (MS, c.1909); *Forward One* (8f, 1935) in Pfisterer; *The Great Man* (MS, 1923); *Pioneers* (1f,5m, c.1937) in W. Moore; *Persephone's Baby* (MS, 1955); *Brumby Innes* (6f,9m, 1927) also in Spender and with *Bid Me To Love* (4f,4m, c.1927) Currency, 1974.

See also: Throssell in *Australian Drama 1920–1955*; Pfisterer and Pickett.

Rebecca Prichard
English, 1971–

Prichard has rapidly won acclaim for her sharply observed pictures of inner-city teenage life, at once harsh and funny, and her finely honed ear for street language. Girls growing up in London's Essex suburbs bitch, 'bunk off' school, form temporary alliances, compete for boyfriends in the award-winning *Yard Gal*, thieving, grafting, getting spliffed and hanging out in gangs in Hackney's mean streets. The riotously comic trio of the first half of *Essex Girls*, set in a graffiti-scrawled school toilets, are counterpointed by the grim second-half image of their possible futures: single mother Kim, struggling to cope with a howling baby while the violent father rants outside her council flat and her friend's account of her exploits underline Kim's lost freedom. *Fair Game* adapts Israeli playwright Edna Mazya's *Games in the Backyard* into grittily contemporary English, with mounting tension as 13-year-old Debbie's desperation to be accepted by the older boys gives vent to pent-up shame, frustrations, rage and sexual violence.

Plays include: *Essex Girls* (5f,1mv, 1994) in *Coming on Strong: New Writing from the Royal Court* (1995); *Fair Game* (1f,4m, 1997); *Yard Gal* (2f, 1998) – all Faber; *Slow Drift*, (MS, 1998).

See also App. 2: Edgar, Sierz.

Stanislawa Przbyszweska

Polish, 1901–35

The illegitimate daughter of symbolist playwright Stanislaw Przbyszweski (1868–1927), Przbyszweska lived an isolated life marked by drug addiction and tragedy and wrote three powerful linked plays exploring events of the French Revolution. Rediscovered thirty years after her death, they have since become a vital part of the Polish repertoire and the basis of the 1983 film *Danton* and an RSC adaptation, *The Danton Case*. A biographical play about Przbyszewska, *The Snow Palace* by Pam **Gems**, first performed in London in 1986, interweaves characters from her plays into her drug and starvation-induced fantasies. Pessimism and idealism contend in plays that, in jaunty colloquial language, trace the development of events from the death of Marat through the career of the towering, complex figure of Robespierre, using historical events as a means to investigate the dynamics of revolutionary change and political possibility.

Plays: *Ninety Three* (1f,5m) tr. Edward Rothert in *Gambit* 33/34; *The Danton Affair* (3f,22m,20x, 1924) and *Thermidor* (9m, 1929) tr. Boleslaw Taborski, Evanston, IL: Northwestern UP, 1989.

See also: *A Life of Solitude* (biography and letters) by Jadwiga Kosicka and Daniel Gerould, London: Quartet, 1986.

Therese Radic

Australian, 1935–

A novelist and music historian as well as playwright, Radic has published several biographies, including a life of Nellie Melba and works on music, especially Australian music, including *Whitening the Songlines* (1991). *Some of My Best Friends . . .* is a collage of writings by and about early Australian women convicts, servants, free settlers and gold diggers among others. Most of Radic's later plays are dramatized biographies, packed, sometimes over-packed, with incident and densely theatrical. In *Madame Mao* a troop of Red Guards transform themselves and the stage to fill all necessary roles and present the great sweep of events from Jiang Qing's early life as an actress through the Cultural Revolution to Mao's death and her eventual imprisonment. *A Whip Round for Percy Grainger* dramatizes the eventful life of the neglected Australian composer: 'a

flagellant with an incestuous obsession about his syphilitic mother . . .
sexual deviant, fitness fanatic . . . eccentric, vagrant', concert pianist,
anti-semite . . . Like Radic's *Peach Melba*, replete with Melba's famous
arias, it features extensive extracts from the composer's work.

Plays include: *Some of My Best Friends are* Women (with Leonard Radic, 3/4f,2m,
1983); *A Whip Round for Percy Grainger* (2f,3m, 1984) – both, Yackandandah
Playscripts. *Madame Mao* (1f,1m+, 1986); *Peach Melba/Melba's Last Farewell*
(2f,1m+1, 1990); *The Emperor Regrets* (5m,id, 1992) – all Currency.
   See also App. 2: Tompkins and Holledge.

Aishah Rahman
   American, c.1936–

Where much black theatre of the 1960s and early 1970s reinforced
stereotyped portrayals of black women as, at best, mere helpmates in
the struggle for Black Power, Rahman challenged such images, exploring
relationships between black men and women. In *The Lady and the
Tramp* each is forced to see beyond surface judgements, and *Transcendental Blues* takes place in Wilma's mind as she confronts memories of
her rejecting foster mother and shadowy father, and grotesque images of
her aborted children. Later work addresses sexuality, reproductivity and
identity using experimental forms, drawing on elements of ritual or
mixing the spoken word with the wail of the saxophone, musical numbers with extended monologues, like Wilma's riffs of pain, desire and
longing for Charlie 'Bird' Parker's music in *Unfinished Women*. Set in the
Hide-A-Wee Home for Unwed Mothers, it juxtaposes episodes from a
group of young women's last days before giving birth with scenes in the
boudoir where Parker coughs out his last days. The award-winning
Mojo. . ., written in response to the notorious shooting of 10-year-old
Clifford Glover by police, looks movingly at a family's struggle to deal
with their anger and grief at a similar killing.

Plays include: *Transcendental Blues* (3f,6m); *The Lady and the Tramp*
(1f,1m+,1mv), both in Baraka; *Unfinished Women Cry in No Man's Land While a
Bird Dies in a Gilded Cage* (7f,2m, 1977) in Wilkerson; *The Mojo and the Sayso*
(2f,3m), BPP, 1991 and in Mahone and in Hatch and Shine 1989.
   See also App. 2: Wilkerson in Hart.

Ayshe Raif

British, 1952–

Daughter of Turkish-Cypriot immigrants, Raif works in radio and television as well as theatre. Her naturalistic plays draw from her experience of deprived London neighbourhoods and their characters: three old ladies who meet each morning to share reminiscences and new developments, or the emotional manipulations and compulsions of a possessive mother–daughter relationship *(Fail/Safe)*. In *Caving In* Maggie's desperate need to have a baby though her husband is serving a long sentence, takes on the force of obsession.

Plays include: *Victims* (MS); *A Party for Bonzo* (MS); *Café Society* (4f) French, 1983; *Caving In* (2f,2m, 1989) in Remnant 8; *Fail/Safe* (4f, 1986) in Robson 1991.

Franca Rame

Italian, 1929–

Rame is an actress and was co-founder in 1970 with her husband (1996 Nobel Prize winner Dario Fo) of La Commune. This theatre collective presents plays which use political satire of Italian authorities – the law, state, church, even the communist establishment – and improvise drawing on the Italian traditions of Commedia dell'Arte, to work for radical political change. Her plays, most of them self-performed monologues, range from farcical comedy to harrowing and gritty realism in addressing feminist issues.

A Woman Alone, locked in her flat by her jealous husband, copes with the demands of howling baby, importunate lover, ringing phone and groping brother-in-law, a figure bandaged from head to foot but still feeling her up . . . In *Waking Up* a working mother dashes through her morning preparations and domestic responsibilities, trying to avoid waking her husband, cope with the needs of her baby and find her house key. Other monologues are based on actual accounts of women's resistance against fascism: a mother confined to a mental asylum for protesting at her son's killing by the Mafia, Rame's own chilling experience of rape. '*Questions of Terrorism and Repression*' take the point of view of Ulrike Meinhoff, who died in suspicious circumstances, and Irmgard Moeller who 'attempted suicide', both in German jails. *The Odd Couple*, co-written with Fo, is a wry satire about a husband's and wife's attempts at adultery, laced with left-wing psychobabble analysis of relationships.

Published translations include: *The Same Old Story*; *Medea* (also in Goodman, 2000); *A Woman Alone*; *Waking Up* (alt. *Rise and Shine*) in *Female Parts* adapted **Wymark**, London: Pluto, 1981, and with *Bless Me Father for I have Sinned*; *Michele Du Lanzone*; *The Rape*; *Alice in Wonderless Land*; *The Whore in the Madhouse*; *Nada Pasini, The Eel-Woman*; *Mạmma Togni*; *Fascism 1922*; *An Arab Woman Speaks*; *The Bawd*; *I'm Ulrike – Screaming*; *It Happened Tomorrow*; *A Mother, et al.* (with Fo, all 1f), tr. Gillian Hanna, Ed Emery, Christopher Cairns in *A Woman Alone and Other Plays*, Methuen, 1991; *An Open Couple – Very Open* (1f,1m) in *Theater* 16:1. Many adapted by Estelle Parsons in US as *Orgasmo Adulto Escapes from the Zoo* NY: BPP, 1985.

See also: Interview, *Theater* 17:1, Spring 1985; Serena Anderlini in *Theater*, 16:1.

Aviva Ravel
Canadian, 1928–

Ravel's plays explore the convolutions and contradictions of identity as a Canadian (she was born in Montreal), a Jew and a woman. In *The Twisted Loaf* Bessie, a dying Russian Jewish immigrant, faces her younger self, a woman in flight from the remembered horrors of pogroms, struggling to build a life of security for her family and to maintain a Jewish heritage, threatened by the alien traditions of the new country. As her consciousness fragments, however, she is forced to realize how far she has stifled her daughters' growth and ambitions with her limited image of a life fulfilled only through marriage. Elsewhere, as in *Second Chance*, women address the possibilities of making new life choices. *Vengeance* uses a thriller structure to highlight issues of denial and responsibility as elderly, comfortable Stephania is confronted with her act of betrayal, which delivered her Jewish friend into Nazi hands. *Dispossessed* has been both vilified for its negativity and acclaimed for its innovative form and its confrontation with despair as the characters struggle against the ties of emotion, family and culture which both support and suppress them.

Plays include: *Moon People* (2f) in *Six Canadian* 1978; *Dispossessed* (1f,2m, 1977) in Perkyns; *The Twisted Loaf* (3m,6f) Playwrights Co-op, 1970 and with *Soft Voices* (2f, 1966) in *A Collection of Canadian Plays v3*, Toronto: Bastet Books, 1973; *Vengeance* (2f, 1989) also in Curran; *Mother Variations* (1989); *The Courting of Sally Schwartz* (1990) – all Playwrights Canada. *Dance Like a Butterfly* (1f, 1993) in *Canadian Mosaic*, Simon and Pierre, 1995.

See also: Conolly in CD 11:1, 1985; App. 2: Hodkinson.

Sylvia Rayman

British, 1923–86

Rayman worked as a waitress in a snack bar while writing her first play. She focused on the abuse of unmarried mothers and their children in baby farms in a society which made them social outcasts, a contemporary evil which excited controversy when exposed on stage in her 1951 *Women of Twilight* (filmed 1952). It is a forceful piece presenting a group of women living in the squalid surroundings of a London house, exploited by the sadistic proprietress who abuses and neglects the children or sells them into adoption. Critics praised its strong individual characterization though suggesting it sometimes verged on melodrama.

Plays include: *Women of Twilight* (11f) London: Evans, 1952; *Time to Speak* (MS, 1957); *Justice in Heaven* (MS, 1958).
    See also App. 2: Gale.

Hannie Rayson

Australian, 1957–

Born in Melbourne, Rayson was co-founder of Theatreworks in 1981. Her plays are witty, pointed and highly contemporary, engaging issues of feminism, frequently alongside investigations of Australian identity in works such as *Mary*, which addresses mother–daughter relationships, juxtaposing a Greek-Australian family with an Anglo-Australian one. The award-winning *Hotel Sorrento* (filmed in 1995) movingly explores the conflicts reawakened within a family when Meg, now living in England, publishes a Booker-nominated novel that draws on events in her and her two sisters' youth in Sorrento, Victoria. The piece also engages issues of masculinity, especially Australian male identity. Men's responses to the women's movement are central to *Room to Move*, in which events are triggered by a 'new man' who moves as lodger into widowed Peggy's home and becomes the catalyst for crises in her children's relationships. *Falling from Grace* focuses on the conflicts between women and their personal, political and ethical responsibilities when journalists on a magazine are confronted with evidence suggesting that a woman doctor's pioneering research on a pre-menstrual syndrome drug may have ignored its causing serious birth defects.

Plays include: *Please Return to Sender* (MS); *Leave it till Monday* (MS); *Mary* (5f, 1985) and *Room to Move* (3f,3m, 1985) – both Yackandandah; *Hotel Sorrento* (4f,4m, 1990); *Falling from Grace* (6f,2m, 1994); *Competitive Tenderness* (4f,4m, id, 1996); *Life After George* (4f,2m, 2000) – all Currency.

Christina Reid
Irish, 1942–

Family is the first site of the 'Troubles' in Belfast-born Reid's work, which focuses with power, wit and compassion on the prejudices of a divided community fallen to the desperation of poverty and the consequences of militarism. Reid's first play, *Did You Hear the One about the Irishman?*, juxtaposes a comedian's increasingly abusive anti-Irish jokes with the love affair between a Protestant girl and Catholic boy, their mirror-image families and their eventual killing, attributed to the gunmen of both sides. Young people from the notorious Divis flats undergo a Youth Training programme in the 1986 *Joyriders* (whose sequel is the equally acute and witty *Clowns*, 1996).

Experience across generations, especially that of women, is central for Reid. *Tea in a China Cup* traces the lives of three Protestant women from 1939 to 1972 for whom respectability is bone-china cups and contempt for the 'dirty, feckless' Catholics. The mould is broken by the grand-daughter, Beth, who ends taking her first steps towards independence. The bawdy 77-year-old heroine of *Belle of Belfast City*, which won the George Devine award, is a former music hall child star celebrating the first visit of her mixed-race grandchild on the eve of a National Front-supported rally against the Anglo-Irish agreement.

Plays include: *Tea in a China Cup* (6f,3m,id, 1983); *Joyriders* (3f,2m, 1986); *The Belle of Belfast City* (5f,2m,id, 1989); *My Name, Shall I Tell You My Name?* (1f,1m, 1v, 1989) and in Tylee; *Did You Hear the One about the Irishman?* (3f,4m,id); *Clowns* (4f,3m, 1996) in *Christina Reid Plays One*, Methuen, 1997; *The Last of a Dyin' Race* (7f,7m) in BBC Radio, 1986.

See also: Roll-Hansen in MD 30, 1987.

Gerlind Reinshagen

German, 1926–

Reinshagen was born in Königsberg and studied pharmacy before becoming a writer, commencing with radio plays then moving to the stage. A highly esteemed author of poetry, prose pieces and novels as well as numerous stage plays, she now lives in Berlin. Her work addresses issues of female identity in conjunction with questions of nationality, history and ecology.

The Clown focuses on the crisis of an actress and, like many of Reinshagen's plays, deals with the construction of self and limitation of socially acceptable roles and representations. Using the device of photos from the family album to frame scenes, *Sunday's Children*, the first play of a trilogy examining the lives of German women since the Nazi period, focuses on a young girl's self-suppression, encountering the dynamics of fascism in everyday life and female complicity and guilt in its perpetuation. *Ironheart* presents a ritualized, repetitive image of alienated labour in an office world of stagnation, submission and sterile efficiency, where language is fragmented, humanity only able to find expression in escapist fantasies and moments of sympathy.

Untranslated plays include: *Doppel Kopf*; *Himmel und Erde*; *Elsa's Nachtbuch*; *Fruhlingfest*; *Tanz Marie!*

Translated plays include: *Ironheart* (5f,2m, 1982) tr. Sue Ellen Case & Arlene Teraoka, in Case; *Sunday's Children* (1982); *The Clown* (1985, both MS) all tr. Tinch Minter; *The Life and Death of Marilyn Monroe* (MS, 1971) tr. Anthony Vivis.
See also App. 2: Sieg.

Renee

New Zealand/Aotearoan, 1929–

New Zealand's leading woman playwright was born in Napier of Ngati Kahungunu and Irish/English descent. A socialist and feminist, her plays explore such issues as domestic violence and rape but particularly women's resistance to injustice, from revues like *Asking for It* (MS) to *Groundwork* (MS), which addresses divisions between Maori and pakeha women during protests against the 1981 Springboks tour.

Renee's best-known work, the 1985–91 trilogy, maps the lives and battles of working-class women across four generations of one family. *Wednesday to Come* and *Pass It On* are narrowly focused detailed realist pieces. The first, set in the 1930s Depression, follows the Kaye household as the family await the arrival of the father's body, a suicide in the relief camp after being forced to haul a plough, reduced to the level of a beast. Where his giving up in the face of hardship is condemned by his wife, the women of the family continue to struggle, and teenage Jeannie and Cliff are galvanized into political action, insisting on joining the hunger march to Wellington. Their activism is central to the second play, focused on the Waterfront Lockout of 1951. *Jeannie Once* tackles a broader frame of reference, including touring theatre, Puritanism, repression and mental illness, in re-creating the life of an earlier Jeannie, who appears as the great-grandmother of *Wednesday* . . . The young immigrant widow, eager to establish herself as a dressmaker in 1879 Dunedin, is drawn into helping a part-Maori servant escape her oppressive master.

Plays include: *Wednesday to Come* (6f,2m, 1986); *Pass It On* (4f,4m,id, 1986); *Jeannie Once* (6f,3m, 1991) – all Victoria UP; *Te Pouaka Karehe: The Glass Box* (4f,4m, 1f/m) in Jansen, 1991; *Tiggy Tiggy Touch Wood* (3f,1m) in Dean and M. G. Soares, and in Prentice and Warrington; *Born to Clean* (MS, 1987).

See also: Warrington in ADS, April 1991; App. 2: Tompkins and Holledge.

Yasmina Reza

French, 1957–

Daughter of a Hungarian mother and an Iranian father, Reza studied sociology before taking up theatre and becoming a playwright, actress and director. *'Art'* has been internationally successful, a witty and perceptive study of the unravelling of the relationship of three male friends after the purchase by one of them of a piece of modern art exposes hidden levels of disagreement and mutual bewilderment. Reza anatomizes the threat posed by a radical difference of opinion and the hostility arising from incomprehension. *The Unexpected Man* follows the journey of a man and woman, writer and reader, across Europe by train solely through the interior monologues of their drifting consciousness. *Life x 3* continues to explore the divergence of perceptions between individuals, presenting three different versions of the same evening's dinner. Reza has also written the novel *Hammerklavier* (Faber, 2000).

Untranslated plays include: *Jascha*.

Translated plays: *'Art'* (3m, 1996); *The Unexpected Man* (1f,1m, 1998); *Conversations after a Burial* (3f,3m, 2000); *Life x 3* (MS, 2000). All tr. Christopher Hampton, Faber.
See also App. 2: Sierz.

Anne Ridler
English, 1912–

Poet, editor and critic, Ridler was an editor at Faber from 1935 to 1940. Her theatrical works also include numerous opera libretti and translations. Like Christopher Fry, T. S. Eliot and other contemporaries, her work forms part of the revival in the mid-twentieth century of verse drama and is marked by its allegorical and Christian themes, centring on the quest for salvation. Several plays confront Christian precepts with the dehuman-ization of the industrial machine and the exploitation of workers by own-ers. While the arrogant behaviour of the factory owner, Brace, in *Who is My Neighbour?*, is blamed, it is ultimately those who stood by when he was beaten to death who are condemned, while Nello, the Italian barman and outsider, plays Good Samaritan, attempting to intervene. In *The Shadow Factory* the boss is confronted with his abuse of his employees in the image painted by a mural artist, and reformed when he participates with his workers in a nativity play. Other plays subtly and evocatively re-work songs and fables from folklore or, with *Henry Bly*, from Grimm, in which a rascally demobbed soldier attaches himself to an old tramp, a miracle worker, and attempts to exploit his powers for gain.

Plays include: *The Shadow Factory*: a nativity play (5f,6m, 1946); *Henry Bly* (2f,4m); *The Mask* (2f,3m); *The Missing Bridegroom* (4f,4m, all 1950); *The Trial of Thomas Cranmer* (2f, 15m+, 1956, 1961); *Who is My Neighbour?* (3f,5m) and *How Bitter the Bread* (3f,3m, both 1963) – all Faber; *The Jesse Tree* (1f,3m+chorus) London: Lyrebird Press, 1972.

Mary Roberts Rinehart
American, 1876–1958

Prolific novelist, journalist and war correspondent, Rinehart also wrote extensively for stage, television, radio and screen, many of her works being adapted for every medium. *Seven Days* started as a story, was extended to a novel, adapted as a play (1909), a film and a musical (1919). The classic thriller, *The Bat*, based on her story 'The Circular Staircase', was adapted by herself and Avery Hopwood as a long-running Broadway success. Centred on an apparently haunted house rented by a feisty middle-aged woman, it concerns the police's hunt to identify the blood-thirsty killer 'The Bat', who nightly seeks out new victims.

Plays include: *What Happened to Father* (screen); *The Doctor and the Woman* (screen); *Take This Woman* (screen); *The State vs Elinor Norton* (screen); *Spanish Love* (MS); *The Bat* (3f,7m+, 1931) and in Cerf and Cartmell; *Seven Days* (1931) – all with Avery Hopwood, both French; *A Double Life* (MS); *The Breaking Point* (MS).

See also: *Improbable Fiction: the Life of Mary Roberts Rinehart* by Jan Cohn, Pittsburgh: Pittsburgh UP, 1980; App.2: Jansen in Brask.

Gwen Pharis Ringwood
Canadian, 1910–84

After growing up in Alberta, Ringwood studied at Frederick Koch's Carolina Playmakers, the influential promoter of folk plays in the 1940s, and began writing works for stage and radio with a strong regional flavour (cf. **Gowan**). She deals with the realities of a vast dry landscape where farming is a struggle to survive through the next season and waiting for rain becomes desperation. Folk heroes are often central to her plays, whether the dowsers of *The Rainmaker* and *Widger's Way* or historical characters like 'Nigger John' Ware in *Stampede*. Central also are the passions that animate individuals in isolation or small communities: frustrated desires, emotions dried up with the land. Ringwood draws on a range of dramatic techniques, including expressionist-style choral speech, music, choreographed movement and images that become freighted with symbolism, such as the wheat field of *Dark Harvest*, destroyed by the man who loves it when his wife rejects him.

Ringwood's work (more than 20 plays) depicts a great range of Canadian life: gold miners in Saskatchewan, cowboys, social activists, immigrants and Indians in pieces like *Maya* (*Lament for Harmonica*) which deals with the identity conflict of a mixed-race girl, grown self-destructive after her white lover abandoned her, leaving her pregnant. Later plays are satirical or directly critical of social wrongs, such as *A*

Remembrance of Miracles, which defends the freedom of the poetic imagination against the efforts of conservatives to ban books. Best known is *Still Stands the House*, the struggle of two women, one of whom wants to leave, the other to stay on the land, which is still one of the most widely produced Canadian plays.

Plays include: *One Man's House* (3f,3m, 1937); *Dark Harvest* (2f,5m, 1945) in CTR 5; *Maya (Lament for Harmonica)* (5f,2m, 1959); *Still Stands the House* (2f,2m, 1938); *Pasque Flower* (1f,2m) in Wagner; *Stampede* (6f, 17m, 1946), *The Rainmaker* (5f, 15m+, 1944) also Playwrights Co-op, 1975; *The Courting of Marie Jenvin* (2f,5m, 1942) in Mayorga, 1943; *A Remembrance of Miracles* (4f,4m, 1975–9); *The Lodge* (5f,5m, 1975); *Widger's Way* (2f,9m, 1952). All in *The Collected Plays* ed. Enid Delgatty, Ottawa: Borealis Press, 1983.

See also: *The Gwen Pharis Ringwood Papers* compiled Marlys Cherrefils, Calgary: Calgary UP, 1989; *Gwen Pharis Ringwood* by Geraldine Anthony, Boston: Twayne, 1981; Lynde in *Ariel* 18, 1987; Conolly in CD 11:1, 1985; App. 2: Anthony.

Anna Cora Ritchie *see* Anna Cora Mowatt

Erika Ritter
Canadian, 1948–

Author of numerous comic sketches, Ritter also focuses on a comedian in her best-known play, *Automatic Pilot* (cf. **Hayes**). After a failed marriage and series of short sexual encounters, the heroine Charlie rejects the chance of a meaningful loving relationship in favour of a self-destructive independence which, however, fuels her bitter comedy. Several of Ritter's other plays also focus on marital collapse and forms of escapism, such as the heroine's in *A Visitor from Charleston* who takes refuge from emotional confusion in her obsession with Scarlett O'Hara.

Plays include: *A Visitor from Charleston* (1f,4m, 1974), *The Splits* (1f,3m, 1976) both Toronto: Playwrights Canada, 1994; *Miranda* (3f,3m,id, radio) in CTR 47, Summer 1986; *Automatic Pilot* (1f,3m, 1980) in Wasserman.

See also App. 2: Zimmerman; Wallace and Zimmerman.

Elizabeth Robins

American, 1862–1952

Although American-born, Robins spent most of her career in London, establishing herself as a major actress, novelist and active member of WSPU and AFL. A pioneer of Ibsen's work (publishing *Ibsen and the Actress*, 1928), she produced and was influenced by his plays. Her and Florence Bell's controversial *Alan's Wife* is a forceful and moving exploration of grief and infanticide in which a woman's rejection of Christian 'acquiescence in the ways of God' and murder of her disabled child are portrayed with compassion (although the piece expresses eugenicist sympathies, popular at the time). Robin's *Votes for Women* involves the equally controversial issue of abortion. It focuses on the education of sheltered, idealistic young heiress Jean Dumbarton, engaged to the prominent MP Geoffrey Stonor, and the revelation that he was the father of campaigning suffragist Vida Levering's aborted child. Jean discovers both the humanity and integrity of the fearful suffragettes and the sexual double standard. In a reversal of contemporary dramatic convention Vida demands political rather than personal reparation: his support for the suffrage cause.

Plays include: *Alan's Wife* (with F. Bell, 5f,5m, 1893) in Fitzsimmons and Gardner, and in Scullion; *Votes for Women* (7f,7m+, 1909) in Spender and Hayman, and in Kelly.

See also: *Elizabeth Robins: Staging a Life 1862–1952* by Angela V. John, Routledge, 1995; App. 2: Stowell.

Gertrude Robins

British, 1871–1917

Robins, an actress, was one of a number of playwrights encouraged by producer Annie Horniman to write for the Gaiety Theatre in Manchester in the 1900s. Most histories of the Manchester School of Drama have neglected the women playwrights such as Robins, whose work engaged with contemporary social realities of women in a world of limited options: stuck in grinding work from which the only possible escape is marriage (*Makeshifts*), the social costs of divorce (*After the Case*) and female sexual ignorance (*The Point of View*).

Plays include: *Makeshifts* (2f,2m, 1908); *The Exit* (2f,1m); *Lancelot and the Leading Lady* (2f,1m); *Old Jan* (2f,2m); *The Point of View* (2f,1m) in *Makeshifts and Other Short Plays* (1909); *Realities* (2f,2m, 1912); *Loving as We Do* (1f,2m, 1910); *The Return* (1f,2m); *'Ilda's Honorable* (2f,1m); *After the Case* (3f,1m) in *Loving as We Do and Other Plays* (1912) – both London: Werner Laurie.
See also App. 2: Gardner and Rutherford.

Betty Roland
Australian, 1903–96

Journalist and novelist as well as playwright, Roland's first play, *Feet of Clay*, is a contemporary reworking of the Pygmalion myth. She found a more powerful direction in *Morning*, in which a couple struggle to survive in the Australian outback during the Gold Rush. *The Touch of Silk* has become an Australian classic. Originally produced by the Little Theatre movement it exists in two stage versions: 1928 and a 1955 revision. It takes place in an Australia of poor farms and small towns, isolated in a drought-stricken land and suspicious of outsiders. Sheep farmer Jim Davidson has returned from the war in Europe with a young French wife, Jeanne, whose vivacious and open manners, so different from the dour restraint of local women, have tainted her with the suggestion of sexual looseness. When, burdened with debt and about to lose the farm, her shell-shocked husband attacks and kills the man with whom Jeanne has shared memories of Paris, she resolves to allow the town to believe he was her lover to save her husband on a plea of provocation. Prejudice against difference is also central to *Granite Peak* (1955) which deals with generational conflict and the struggles of an Aboriginal for acceptance by white society.

Many of Roland's mid-career plays – such as *Are You Ready Comrade?* (MS, 1938) addressing military aggression, communism, male–female relationships, *Vote No!* (MS, 1938) and *It isn't Possible* (MS, 1939) – reflect the political radicalism she shared with contemporaries like Katherine Susannah **Prichard**, **Gray** and **Devanney**. Roland also wrote many radio plays, including *The Spur of the Moment* (1931), later filmed.

Plays include: *Morning* (1f,2m, 1932) in W. Moore; *The Touch of Silk* (5f,7m, 1928); Currency, 1974; 1955 revision with *Granite Peak* (6f,7m) Currency, 1988; *Feet of Clay* (2f,2m, 1924) in Kilner and Tweg; *Daddy was Asleep* (radio, MS)
See also: *An Improbable Life* (autobiography) Sydney: Angus and Robertson, 1989.

Rachel Rosenthal

American, 1926–

In her performance work Rosenthal draws on sources as various as her Russian-Jewish immigrant heritage, Artaud, history, New Age philosophies and John Cage. She is a rare creature, an older woman performance artist making work that has been called auto-biological, exploring the connections between the physiology of her ageing female body, breaking down, the site of pain and deterioration, and planetary geology, excavating the marks of destruction inflicted on the earth by human beings. Drawing on the Gaia hypothesis of James Lovelock, which sees earth and its inhabitants as one self-regulating organism, her works explore the interconnectivity of living creatures. *The Others* (MS, 1984) addresses human relationships with other creatures in a performance that features animals and the dilemmas and contradictions of modern existence, the desire for consumer comforts and the catastrophic planetary cost of irresponsibility. Her performance texts draw on mythology, especially the image of the Old Crone and Native American legends. By turns anecdotal and invocatory, they are shot through with flashes of humour, combining ritual devices, sophisticated performance skills and technology – slides, taped sound, video – in their enactment.

Plays include: *My Brazil* (1979) in Champagne; *Gaia, mon amour* (MS, 1983); *L.O.W. in Gaia* (1986) in PAJ 30; *Was Black* (video, 1989); *Pangaean Dreams: a Shamanic Journey* (1990, also video) in Marranca; *Rachel's Brain* in Roth (below) (all 1f).

See also: TDR 117; *Rachel Rosenthal* ed. Moira Roth, Baltimore, MD: Johns Hopkins UP, 1997; App. 2: Marranca; Forte in Case ed.

Susanna Rowson

American, 1762–1824

One of the earliest American women playwrights, Rowson was born in Portsmouth, England, and began writing novels before travelling to the USA as an actress with a touring theatre company. While her novels, including the hugely successful *Charlotte Temple* (1790), have survived, only one of seven plays still exists. *Slaves in Algiers*, set in an attractively exotic stage locale, focuses on the plight of women captives imprisoned by Muley Moloc, the lustful Dey of Algeria. The women characters are active and resourceful and the piece equates their white slavery with the struggle of women against subjugation. It also celebrates America: 'that land, where virtue in either sex is the only mark of superiority', though making no mention of the practice of black slavery closer to home.

Play: *Slaves in Algiers or A Struggle for Freedom* (5f, 10m+, 1794) NY: Scholarly Facsimiles, 1976 and in Kritzer.

See also: *Susanna Rowson* by Patricia L. Parker Boston: Twayne, 1986; App. 2: Schofield and Macheski.

Banuta Rubess
Canadian, 1956–

Born to Latvian parents, Rubess's work includes translations of plays by the Latvian woman playwright, Aspazija (1865–1943) and addresses the experience of European émigrés in plays such as *Tango Lugano* and *Boom, Baby, Boom!* against a background of the Cold War and incipient nuclear threat, *Boom* is set in a Fifties Toronto jazz club, financially ailing but artistically vibrant, where real-life character Clem Hambourg attempts to realize his musical vision and a young immigrant, Austra Mednis, hopes to find her dreamed-of world of beatnik bohemia. Rubess's text invites a collaborative approach reflecting both the world of improvised jazz it re-creates and her own beginnings as a writer as a collective member on **The Anna Project** (along with Ann-Marie **Mac-Donald** whose *Goodnight Desdemona* she later directed). *Smoke Damage*, reflecting a similar origin in women's theatre practice, juxtaposes witch-hunting of the past with a modern-day tour of the witch sites and a commentary from historical witch-hunters Kramer and Sprenger.

Plays include: *Pope Joan* (MS, 1984); *Boom, Baby, Boom!* (3f,3m+band, 1988) in CTR 58 + *CTR Anthology*; *Smoke Damage* (5f, 1985) – both Playwrights Canada. *Thin Ice* (with Beverley Cooper, 2f,2m, 1987) in *Wanna Play?*, Playwrights Canada Press, 1993; *Oblivion: a Story of Isabelle Eberhardt* (4f,6m, radio) and *No. Here Comes Ulrike Meinhoff* (7f,10m, radio) in Jansen 1993.

See also App. 2: Jansen in Brask.

Jacqueline Rudet

British/Dominican, 1962–

Born in east London, Rudet grew up in Dominica and began her career as an actress with London-based alternative theatre companies CAST and Belt and Braces, before forming Imani-faith, a group founded to present theatre for and by black women. Her plays sensitively explore issues of black, especially female, identity and life choices. The process of self-naming is central to *Basin*, where Susan and Mona identify themselves as 'Zammies', a Dominican word that implies a spiritual bond which may be lesbian or that of close friendship. Coming out is also at the core of *God's Second in Command* as Leo clashes with his father, rejects the crass macho images of masculinity available to him and struggles to accept his homosexuality. *Money to Live* centres on the experience of women working in the sex industry and the reactions of Charlene's family to her decision to work as a stripper.

Plays include: *God's Second in Command* (MS, 1985); *Take Back What's Yours* (MS, 1989); *Basin* (3f, 1985) in Brewster 1 and in Busby; *Money to Live* (4f,2m, 1984) in Remnant 5.

See also App. 2: Croft in Griffiths and Llewellyn Jones.

Ulla Ryum

Danish, 1937–

Prose writer and playwright, Ryum is also a teacher, director and dramaturge who has worked particularly with the Sami people of northern Scandinavia to encourage development of new work expressing their culture. Her own work has been described as often ironic and dream-like, mixing psychoanalytic symbolism, religious allegory and mysticism with realism, grotesquerie and farce. The prize-winning *And the Birds are Singing Again* is one of a series of radio plays investigating the collapse of Western civilization and values following major planetary devestation. Three soldiers, two women and a man, have been sent to report on the status of a former amusement park. They listen to tapes from the 'white box' that recorded the last hours of the fairground stall-holders from a recent past 'before the efficiency of human nature was radically improved', and despite their rationality and rigorous training, find themselves exposed to the dangerous influences of concepts such as love, sexual attraction, beauty and nature.

Translated plays include: *And the Birds are Singing Again* (4f,3m, radio) tr. Per Brask, in Brask; *The Faces of the Hunter* (MS, 1978, DDF) tr. Brask; *The Sad Ventriloquist* (MS, 1972, DDF) tr. David Hohkien.

See also: Interview in PAJ 1989.

Nawal el Saadawi
Egyptian, 1930–

As a novelist, doctor and activist, Saadawi's feminist questioning of Islamic and political orthodoxies and condemnation of patriarchal family laws, female circumcision, censorship and other abuses have brought her into frequent conflict with the Egyptian authorities. Her imprisonment in 1981 under Sadat became the source for her play *Twelve Women in a Cell*. The prisoners in the play, as in Saadawi's experience, are women of disparate beliefs and backgrounds, united only by the fact of their sex and audacity in having opinions and in the eyes of a government grown paranoid about all opposition. They include devout fundamentalist Muslims, students who have dared wear the oulawed veil in school, free-thinkers, Westernized women, divorcees and a girl from the streets accidentally swept up in the arrest, living cheek by jowl with despised prostitutes, beggars and thieves. The play explores the dynamics of their developing relationships and of new understanding growing across prejudice and despite disagreement.

Play: *Twelve Women in a Cell* (16f,4m, 1982) in Baraitser.
See also: Shteir in *Theater*, Winter 1983.

Nina Sadur
Russian, 1950–

Of part Tatar extraction, Sadur was born in Novosibirsk, Siberia, but lives in Moscow. The folklore of her birthplace combine with the influences of Gogol and Beckett in plays characterized by a sense of a macabre absurdism. They feature figures, often female, who are socially marginal: peasant women, cleaners, witch-like old women, or those caught up in strange circumstances, which both produce and express inner anxieties. Sadur's plays are haunted by ghosts and portents and take place in landscapes lacking solidity, where reality borders on surreal nightmare. In *Weird Woman*, Lydia, a volunteer helping with the potato harvest, is trying to cross a field when she encounters a strange peasant woman who threatens to eat her and from whom she seems unable to escape, as the solid land itself begins to collapse beneath her and her Moscow life, job and children start to appear increasingly illusory. In *Frozen* a theatre cleaner is terrified when she believes she sees the face of God in a piece of stage scenery. In *My Darling Red-Haired Boy*, student Natasha's landlady becomes a fairytale grandmother character in the borderland of reality, insomnia and dream, terrifying Natasha with strange voices, delusions of grotesque apparitions and the room apparently filling up with dough.

Translated plays include: *Frozen* (3f,1m, 1989) tr. Catriona Kelly *et al.* in C. Kelly; *The Field*; *A Group of Friends*; *Weird Woman*; *Drive On* (all MS one-acts tr. Cathy Porter); *The New Acquaintance* (MS tr. Nina Froud); *My Darling Red-Haired Boy* (MS tr. Stephen Mulrine).

Diane Samuels
British, 1960–

Samuels trained as a teacher and has worked extensively in youth and children's theatre for which her many early plays, including *Salt of the Earth* and *The Bonekeeper* (both MS), were written. Also unpublished is her exploration of the dilemmas of maternity, *Watch Out for Mr Stork*.

Mother–daughter relationships are central to the moving *Kindertransport*, joint winner of the Verity Bargate award 1992, which is based on verbatim accounts by some of the *kinder* evacuated by their Jewish parents from Germany in 1938 to save them after the pogroms of Kristallnacht and the ever-worsening persecution. Faith discovers from old letters in the loft that her mother, Evelyn, was one of the children sent away. She has dealt with her grief and guilt at survival by changing her name from Eva, denying her identity and concealing all evidence of her past. As she is forced to face her memories, the confrontation between Faith and Evelyn is juxtaposed with Eva's parting from her own mother, her arrival in Manchester and her meeting with her adoptive mother, Lil. Nightmarish visions of the Ratcatcher from her German storybook, transmuted for her into an ominous Nazi official and later into her real mother, whose reappearance, having survived the camps, threatens Eva's self-protective amnesia. *Swine* also addresses racist horrors as a woman rabbi and a young Asian girl confront the desecration of both the local mosque and the Jewish cemetery.

Plays include: *Kindertransport* (5f,1m) NHB, 1995; *Swine* (12f, 17m) London: BBC Radio Five in July 1996; *100 Million Footsteps* (MS, 1997).
  See also App. 2: Edgar.

Sonia Sanchez
  American, 1934–

Born in Birmingham, Alabama, Sanchez studied at Hunter College and New York University and is a poet and teacher. In the late 1960s and early 1970s she was one of the earliest women playwrights working within black theater to reflect and celebrate the Black Power movement and condemn those seen to betray the race. However, she also criticizes the movement's often destructive male-dominated politics and misogynist attitudes and, centrally, celebrates the achievements and continuing struggle and advancement of black women in plays such as *Sister Son/ji*. A woman sits at a dressing table and makes herself up as the person she was at different stages in her life: from the old woman reminiscing and preparing for death to the young girl making her first act of protest in the struggle against white oppression. *Uh, Uh* ... presents a set of critical pictures of the relationships of black men and black and white women: two rival wives struggle for their black Muslim husband's attention, a sister in the movement is neglected by her man for a white 'devil woman', a whore is abused by drug-dealing criminals but gropes towards discovering her true status as black woman.

Plays include: *Sister Son/ji* (1f, 1967) in Bullins, 1967 and in Brown-Guillory; *Uh, Huh, But How Do It Free Us* (8f,9m, 1971) in Bullins, 1974; *Malcolm/Man Don't Live Here No Mo*, in *Black Theatre* 6, 1972; *The Bronx is Next* (2f,5m) in TDR 44; *Dirty Hearts* (1f,4m), in *Scripts* 1, Nov. 1971.

Milcha Sanchez-Scott
  American, 1955–

Daughter of an Indonesian mother and a Colombian father, Sanchez-Scott grew up in Bali and England, moving in her teens to California where she first encountered racism. An often unemployed actress, her experience working in an employment agency for latina maids, most of them illegal immigrants exploited by the owner and by the families who hired them, became the basis of her first play. Written in a mixture of Spanish and English *Latina* vividly creates the pressures, desperation and comedy of the women's lives and of chicana actress Sarita's attempts to find work more challenging than endlessly playing wives of Barrio gang members.

Many of Sanchez-Scott's plays explore issues around Hispanic masculinity. *Roosters* uses the image of cock-fighting as a parallel to family machismo: the cockerel and the father both strutting with ritual arrogance while his wife identifies with a little grey hen, his daughter takes refuge in religious obsession and his son yearns for escape. *Stone Wedding* (MS), developed with the Los Angeles Latino Theatre Lab, weaves together ancient Aztec myth in the guise of Huitziopochli, the god of war, blood and sacrifice, with recent history in a form of magic realism. The play is set in the head of a Hispanic American soldier wounded during the Korean War, as he undergoes a brain operation and dreams of his doomed, grief-stricken town in Southeastern USA where all the men have died. Sanchez explores the idea of the warrior and a Chicano inheritance of a culture of fighting and sacrifice, touching on the LA street gangs.

Plays include: *Latina* (with Jeremy Blahnik, 18f,2m, 1980) in Huerta; *Roosters* (3f,3m) in AT Sept. 1987 and in Osborn; *Dog Lady* (5f,2m, 1984) in Delgado 1986; *The Cuban Swimmer* (3f,2m, 1984) in Halpern; *Evening Star* (4f,3m) DPS, 1989.

Nathalie Sarraute
French, 1900–99*

Pioneer of the Nouveau Roman group of writers and author of numerous experimental fictions including novels such as *Martereau* (1953) and *The Planetarium* (1959) and the short pieces *Tropisms* (1939), Sarraute was encouraged to write for theatre by Jean-Louis Barrault, who convinced her of the theatricality of her fictional world. Her plays, originally written for radio and then adapted for the stage, are subtle and compelling pieces, exploring the minute movements and rhythms of ordinary conversation, the rituals of alliance and passions of disagree-

*Sarraute officially gave her year of birth as 1902. After her death it was revealed as 1900 or possibly even 1899.

ment. In *It's There* two men plot how to convince a woman who disagrees with them, horrified at the disruptive potential of her ability to think differently from them and threaten their ideas. Even murder seems an imaginable solution to their difference. In *Over Nothing At All*, two male friends, one confident, aggressive, the other passive and rather dreamy, have fallen out 'over nothing at all' and call in two neighbours as arbiters of the grievance. Their exchange reveals the long-felt hidden hostility beneath their professions of friendship.

Plays include: *It's There* (3m, 1f, 1978) tr. Barbara Wright; *It's Beautiful* (1f,2m+, 1972); *Izzum* (4f,4m, 1970); *The Lie* (5f,4m, 1966); *Silence* (4f,3m, 1966) all tr. Maria Jolas in *Collected Plays*, Calder, 1980; *Over Nothing At All* (1f,3m, 1982) tr. Philippa Wehle in Wehle.

See also: *Sarraute* by Ruth Z. Temple, NY: Columbia UP, 1968; Henderson in *Theater* Winter 1983. App.2: Bradby and Sparks.

Dorothy L. Sayers
English, 1893–1957

Born in Oxford, where she later attended Somerville College, Sayers is best known for detective stories, latterly much adapted for television and radio, featuring the aristocratic Lord Peter Wimsey. The final part of his story, *Busman's Honeymoon*, appeared first as a well-received play, a collaboration with Muriel St Clare Byrne, that interwove comedy, thriller and love story as Wimsey and his new wife, writer Harriet Vane, discover a body in their honeymoon cottage. Sayers' concern, in the four novels in which Vane appears, with the cost of unequal marriage for women – Harriet initially resists a relationship with Lord Peter based on dependence and gratitude – is also explored in the witty 'comedy of manners' *Love All* (1941). Writer Godfrey Daybrook's actress lover, frustrated by his insistence that she give up her career to give him emotional support, encourages him to return to his docile wife but discovers the latter, in the new guise of successful playwright, is equally unwilling to shoulder her former duties.

Sayers's main reknown as a playwright rests on her poetic religious plays for stage, commissioned by cathedral cities such as Lichfield and Canterbury (*Zeal*, on the building of the cathedral; *Devil to Pay*, a reworking of *Faust*) and her radio sequence on the life of Christ, *The Man Born to be King*. Controversial in its use of contemporary colloquial language and its immediacy, situating biblical events in a 'confused passionate world' rather than a 'remote, symbolical life', it provoked questions in Parliament but won enormous acclaim for the BBC.

Plays include: *Busman's Honeymoon* (with M. St Clare Byrne, 3f,10m) also in Famous, 1937 and *Love All* (5f,3m) ed. Alzina S. Dale, Kent, OH: Kent State UP, 1984; *The Zeal of His House* (1f,25m+, 1937) also in Famous 1938–9; *The Devil to Pay* (3f, 13m+, 1939); *He That Should Come* (2f, 13m, nativity, 1939) *The Man Born to be King* (1943) – all London: Gollancz.

See also: *British Radio Drama* ed. John Drakakis, Cambridge: CUP, 1981.

Joan Schenkar
American, 1946–

Seattle-born Schenkar is the author of grotesque, highly visual and theatrical comedies of menace. In structuring her pieces she draws on images from popular culture: comic strips in *Fulfilling Koch's Postulate*, Thirties radio shows in *Hitler*, Fifties sitcoms (staged within a giant television set) in *Family Pride*, then explodes their conventions with outrageous parody, foregrounding their repressions and discontents.

Central to her work are images of food, disease and cannibalism. *Koch's Postulate* recreates the Typhoid Mary story (cf. **Gee**), centring on an obsessive cook and conflating images of sexual desire, appetite and sickness as her unwitting victims burn with hunger for her infected food. The all-American patriarch is obsessed with castration anxieties and eating his young in *Family Pride*, while *The Universal Wolf* deconstructs Little Red Riding Hood and its imagery of eating women. *Cabin Fever* is set on a porch during an endless Vermont winter, where three old-timers gleefully recount stories of neighbourhood madness, in-breeding and murder and plot eating each other. Tellingly, her most obviously feminist play, *Signs of Life,* draws parallels between P. T. Barnum, exhibitor of freak-shows; Henry James, drawing material for his novels from his dying sister, Alice (cf. **Sontag**); and a doctor devoted to remaking an Elephant Woman as a proper female through reconstructive surgery. As all three diagnose the feminine as deformed, and feed off and exploit that deformity, they toast 'the ladies', in a recurrent scene of distorted sacrament, in tea that tastes of blood and biscuit that smacks of bone.

Plays include: *Signs of Life* (5f,3m+, 1979) in Miles 1980; *Cabin Fever* (1f,2m, 1980) – both French; *The Universal Wolf* (2f,1m, 1f/m) in Lamont and in KR Spring

1991; *The Last of Hitler* (3f,6m, 1fv,1mv, 1982); *Fulfilling Koch's Postulate* (2f,2m, 1985); *Burning Desires* (9+f,6+m, 1995) – all in *Signs of Life: Six Comedies of Menace*, Wesleyan/New England Press, 1998; *The Lodger* (2f, 1988) in Curb; *Family Pride in the Fifties* (4f,4m) in KR Spring 1993.

See also: SAD ; TA 1985; App. 2: Patraka essays in Case ed.; Hart.

Carolee Schneeman
American, 1939–

Performance artist, painter, writer, film-maker, Schneeman's work engages with feminism, eroticism and transcendence, and has remained consistently challenging. In 1964, her *Meat Joy*, which she describes as an 'assault on a repressive culture', a celebratory happening, influenced by her reading of Artaud, became much celebrated. Using raw fish, plucked chickens, blood, and revelling in flesh, human and animal, as sex and food, it seemed the quintessential performance of the sexual revolution. Her published scripts are blueprints for and documentations of action. A later performance, *Snows*, responded to the political situation in Vietnam with a juxtaposition of newsreels, victim–pursuer games and ritually enacted body sculpting, trapping the performers in individual cocoons. With the postmodern, 1990s critical obsession with the explicit body and its performance (cf. Annie Sprinkle, **Hughes**), Schneeman has attracted new interest, particularly for pieces such as *Interior Scroll* where she read from a text extracted from her vagina, a male 'structuralist film-maker's' censure of her films for their (feminine) 'diaristic indulgence' and 'personal clutter'.

Plays include: *Meat Joy* (various) in *Mirrors for Man* ed. Leonard Ashley, NY: Winthrop/Prentice Hall, 1974 and in Benedikt; *The Queen's Dog*; *Snows*; *ABC – We Print Anything on the Cards* (all group pieces) *et al.* in *More than Meat Joy*, New Paltz, NY: Documentext, 1979.

Related texts: *Parts of a Body House Book*, Devon: Beau Geste Press, 1972; *Cézanne, She was a Great Painter*, NY: Trespass Press, 1976.

See also App. 2: Juno and Vale; Sayre; Schneider.

Florida Scott-Maxwell

American, 1883–1979

Florida Scott-Maxwell was born in Orange Park, Florida and worked as an actress and journalist before emigrating to Britain on her marriage. She had four children and was active in the suffrage movement. The frustrations of bourgeois marriage led to her divorce in 1929 and is a central theme in her first play, *The Flash Point*. It is a powerful and passionate study of an intelligent woman's entrapment in respectability. Unable to marry because her fiance must support his mother and sister, and unable to seek paid work, as this is unacceptable for a well-brought up young girl, she is surrounded by silly, narrow-minded women. Scott-Maxwell presents a mother–daughter relationship of emotional manipulation, quarrelling and misunderstanding, in a way rare for its time, and explores the damage inflicted by the family on those who fail to fit in. Scott-Maxwell's later training as a Jungian analyst informs both her non-fiction writing, such as *Women and Sometimes Men* (1957), and her later play, *I Said to Myself* (MS, 1946), where the characters' alter egos appear on stage. She is best-known for the meditation on old age, *The Measure of My Days* (1968).

Plays include: *The Flash Point,* London: Sidgwick & Jackson, 1914; *Many Women* (MS, 1933).

Simone Schwartz-Bart

Guadeloupean, 1938–

Schwartz-Bart is a novelist and theorist *(In Praise of Women of Colour,* 1989) born in France and brought up in the Caribbean; she married Jewish novelist Andre Schwartz-Bart. In her play, Wilnor, a Haitian migrant forced to earn his living in Guadeloupe, exchanges letters on cassette with his wife back home, including, eventually, her confession of infidelity with a man who reminded her of him. Schwartz-Bart's use of Wilnor's onstage presence and his absent wife's voice movingly reinforces the isolation of the migrant worker and the poignant reality of exile forced by economic circumstances.

Translated play: *Your Handsome Captain* (1fv,1m, 1987) tr. Jessica Harris & Catherine Temerson in Ubu 1 and 3.
   See also App. 2: Miller in Laughlin and Schuler.

Djanet Sears

Canadian, 1959–

Sears was born in England of Jamaican and Guyanan parents who moved to Saskatoon, Canada, when she was 15. Her first play, the prize-winning *Afrika Solo,* which she calls 'an autobio-mythography', is an exploration of her hybrid identity framed by a narrative of an extended journey through Africa as Janet discovers a new self in Djanet. Inter-weaving accounts of her experiences with childhood memories of tele-vision shows and schooldays, casual racism and black invisibility, the piece uses rapping, songs, monologues, chants, drumming and dialogue in a form Sears identifies as 'Sundiata', a West African tradition of story-telling through narrative, music and dance.

Who Killed Katie Ross?, part of the collective project *Stolen Lands* (1994) addressing the oppression of indigeneous Canadians, tells the true story of Katie Ross, who was shot by a drunk and then died from neglect by white doctors. *Harlem Duet,* winner of the Governor Gen-eral's Drama award, uses an aesthetic structure drawn from the blues to re-examine Shakespeare's *Othello* from the point of view of a black woman, looking at same-race and cross-race relationships and the ten-sions, creative or otherwise, between black cultures and dominant white Western culture.

Plays include: *Afrika Solo* (1f,2m) Toronto: Sister Vision Press, 1990 and extract in Brennan; *Stand Off* (screen, 1993); *Survivors* (1992, screen, co-scripted, on AIDS); *The Mother Project* (MS); *Double Trouble* (MS); *Who Killed Katie Ross?* (6f,5m+ chorus) in Zimmerman; *The Madwoman and the Fool: a Harlem Duet* (2f,2m) in Nolan, Quan, etc.; *Harlem Duets* (5f,1fv,4m, 1997) in Sears and in Fischlin and Fortier.

See also App. 2: Tompkins and Holledge; Bennett in Brask; Sears in Much; Gilbert and Tompkins.

Ntozake Shange

American, 1948–

Probably the most influential black woman writer for theatre, Shange is also a poet and novelist whose acclaimed work includes *Nappy Edges* and *A Daughter's Geography* and the novels *Sassafrass, Cypress and Indigo* and *Betsey Brown.* Her work crosses boundaries in itself and has often been adapted: *Liliane* is both a novel and a play about a black woman's psychoanalysis.

Shange allows her material to generate its own original form, which may not conform to received notions of performance structure. *for colored girls who have considered suicide/when the rainbow is enuf* started life as a series of poems that Shange worked on with dancers, musicians and actresses and presented in bars and cafés, before it developed its full theatrical form, becoming both a Broadway success and a modern classic. Seven black women, described only by the colour each is dressed in, talk, sing, tell stories about their lives, dreams, desires, betrayals, struggles; about black men, their children, their history and their future. *Spell # 7*, set in a Manhattan bar, hang-out for out-of-work actors and musicians, uses poetry, music, clowning and sketches to explore the experience of nine friends and, through their frustration, fantasies and play, the joy, pride, and the pain and limitations of the on- and off-stage roles for blacks in white America. *The Love Space Demands* again uses words, music and dance to explore 'the extremes of rapture and desperation in contemporary African-American life' in a piece for one or more performers. *Betsey Brown* was a collaboration between Shange, Emily **Mann** and jazz trumpeter Baikida Carroll, based on Shange's novel about the coming of age of a teenage black girl in 1950s St Louis.

Plays include: *for colored girls . . .*: a choreopoem (7f, 1974) Methuen, 1977 and in Hatch and Shine, and with *Spell # 7* (5f,4m, 1979) and *The Love Space Demands* (1f, 1987–92) in *Shange: Plays One*, Methuen, 1992; *Spell # 7, A Photograph: Lovers in Motion* (3f,2m, 1977), *Boogie Woogie Landscapes* (4f,3m, 1978) in *Three Pieces* NY: St Martin's Press, 1981; *From Okra to Greens/a Different Kind of Love Story* (7f,7m) St Louis: Coffee House Press, 1984/French. Extract from *Betsey Brown* (with Emily **Mann**, 4f,4m, 1985) in *SAD; Daddy Says* (3f,1m) in King Jr 1989; *The Resurrection of the Daughter: Liliane* (1f,1m) extract in Mahone.

See also: *See No Evil: Prefaces, Essays and Accounts 1976-1983*, SF: Momo's Press, 1984; Timpane in SAD 1989; App. 2: Schlueter; Cronacher in Keyssar ed.; Geis in Brater; Deshazer in Hart; Bloom; Betsko and Koenig; Brown-Guillory.

Adele Edling Shank

American, 1940–

Born in rural Minnesota, in 1954 Shank moved with her family to California, the state whose chronicler she has become. Critic, dramaturg and director Theodore Shank became her husband in 1967 and influenced or collaborated on much of her work. She leads the Playwriting Program at the University of California, San Diego.

Her plays are based on an aesthetic of hyper-realism, adapted from the visual arts practice of Duane Hansen and others. They reject exposition, focusing on the surface observation of characters, emphasizing audience detachment, dealing with mundane situations and incorporating details of life usually left out of stage representation, such as background conversations continuing half-audibly behind the central action. Her focus tends to be on suburban dwellers, like the family gathered for Christmas in *Winterplay* or at a backyard barbecue in *Sunset/ Sunrise*, while other characters overlap from play to play. Anemone, the call-girl's daughter from the beach comedy *Sand Castles*, marries hippie poet Moon Hawk in a New Age ceremony in *The Grass House*. Ordinariness abuts mild eccentricity adjoins the surreal in the image of Anne, the 17-year-old girl allergic to everything but plastic, confined in a sealed room, communicating on video and fascinated by the physical details of her brother's relationship with his gay lover in *Winterplay*. The everyday strangenesses of California lives and landscapes are reflected in *Stuck*, set in the cars in a freeway traffic jam, a routine occurrence which drivers have learnt rituals to cope with. Shank has also translated Fernando Arrabal and adapted Ben Jonson.

Plays include: *Winterplay* (4f,4m, 1980) in TCG 1; *Sunset/Sunrise* (8f,5m, 1979) in WCP 4; *Stuck* (6f,6m) NY: PiP, 1983; *The Grass House* (5f,3m) PiP, 1983; *67201* (1f,1m) and *Dry Smoke* (1f,1m, 1995) in Frank; *Sand Castles* (6f,5m,1d, 1982) in WCP 15/16, 1983.

See also: Jenner in *Contemporary Review*, 1985.

Frances Sheridan
Irish, 1714–66

Largely forgotten except as the mother of the playwright and manager Richard Brinsley Sheridan (1751–1816), Frances Sheridan was a highly successful novelist and playwright in her own right. David Garrick thought *The Discovery* (1763) one of the best plays of the age; the loquacious, over-ceremonious Sir Anthony Branville was his favourite role.

Like many contemporary women playwrights Sheridan's prologue opens with her pleading 'at the bar' before men for the crime of trespassing on the male preserve of playwriting. Sheridan's plays are concerned with the question of what makes a good marriage. She creates strong, witty, likeable characters and a skilfully convoluted plot, both pointed and funny. *The Discovery* centres on cynical Lord Medway's need for money, for which he is prepared to anger his wife by marrying his son and daughter off to a rich widow, Mrs Knightley, and ageing Sir Anthony. Meanwhile, under the pretence of giving avuncular advice, he is encouraging disagreements between the recently married Flutters so as to alienate them and pursue his own amours with Mrs Flutter. *The Dupe* (1764), criticized by contemporaries for the indecorum of its subject matter, also examines marriage and in particular the folly of an old man in marrying a silly and manipulative young woman for lust.

Plays: *The Discovery* (5f,4m), *The Dupe* (4f,4m), *A Journey to Bath* (6f,6m) in *The Plays of Frances Sheridan* ed. Robert Hogan and Jerry C. Beasley Newark: Delaware UP/London and Toronto: Associated University Presses, 1984.

Sandra Shotlander

Australian, 1941–

Writer, director and teacher, Shotlander has worked in TIE and theatre of the deaf. Her work explores lesbian identities and women's search for a spirituality and history beyond the limitations of patriarchal mythologies. *Blind Salome* uses the metaphor of a journey across Europe made by four Australians in a psychological quest for self, while *Framework* explores the developing relationship between two women meeting in a New York art gallery between Georgia O'Keefe's 'Black Iris' and Picasso's 'Gertrude Stein', excavating the suppressed history of lesbian culture.

Plays include: *Chronicles of the French Revolution* (MS); *The Crimson Firefly Circus* (MS); *Blind Salome* (3f,2m, 1985) and *Framework* (2f, 1983) Winter Park, FL: Wild Iris Press, 1989; *Is that You Nancy?* (3f, 1991) in Parr; *Angels of Power* (4f,3m, 1991) Melbourne: Spinifex Press, 1985.

See also App. 2: Curb in Hart; Shotlander in Laughlin and Schuler; Tompkins and Holledge.

Maria Martinez Sierra

Spanish, 1874–1974

Half of a successful writing partnership with her husband Gregorio (1881–1947), Maria's contribution has often been marginalized and forgotten – even many of the couple's acknowledged collaborations are published under his name alone. Patricia O'Connor's research has underlined how key was Maria's contribution to their numerous dramatic works: she probably wrote most of the plays, while he, in effect, supplied dramaturgical comment alongside directing a theatre company and running journals and publishing concerns. Despite the break-up of the marriage, they continued to collaborate though she became strongly politicized, increasingly involved in socialism, Republicanism and feminism and writing several books on the topic.

Clearly identified as Maria's are the series of convent plays in which arguments for Christian charity are allied to a socialist politic. These include *Lily among the Thorns* and the highly successful and acclaimed *Cradle Song*, which explores the forces that propel women into the convent and both the nurturing love and frustrated desires that inhabit it. Notable for realistic portrayals of women, in contrast to the idealized symbolic females in earlier experimental modernist plays and allegorical poetic dialogues, they presage the independent heroines of *Cano uno y si vida* and *Sueño de una de agosto*. Several plays focus on themes of maternal sacrifice or domestic responsibility, such as *Mistress of the House* (1910), where a young stepmother struggles to be accepted.

Numerous translated plays include: *The Cradle Song* (10f,4m+, 1911); *The Lover* (2f,1m, 1913) in Martin; *Love Magic* (3f,4m, 1908); *Poor John* (5f,5m, 1912); *Madame Pepita* (6f,5m, 1912) all tr. John Garrett Underhill in *Plays of Sierra*, London: Chatto and Windus, 1923; *The Kingdom of God* (17f,12m,dp, 1916); *Take Two from One* (17f,5m); *The Romantic Young Lady* (6f,5m). All tr. Harley and Helen Granville-Barker, *Collected Plays vol. 2*, London: Sidgwick and Jackson, 1929.

See also: *Gregorio and Maria Martinez Sierra* by Patricia O'Connor Boston: Twayne Publishers, 1977.

Beverley Simons
Canadian, 1938–

Described in 1975 as Canada's 'most ignored, important writer', Simons is studied, but her work remains under-produced, often seen as 'difficult'. Her plays are highly stylized, self-reflective and theatrical, drawing on Oriental theatre traditions from Noh or Bunraku and the theories of Antonin Artaud. Often called Absurdist, they centre on death and its human evasions, but are fuelled by passion, splintered by multiple perspectives and marked by highly coloured language that is anything but minimal. At their heart is the image of games played with time, space, costume, audience perceptions and metaphor. *Leela* deconstructs the life of a judge, investigating the contradictions of power, personal interaction, loss and responsibility. *Crabdance* centres on Sadie Golden, an isolated, middle-aged woman, a powerful role for an actress, visited by three salesmen. Their regular visits for tea become a ritual re-enactment in which they play son, husband and lover in a fantastical family drama, refracted through a distorting mirror in which she becomes the quintessential projection of the Great Mother, all-nourishing and all-devouring, and need, appetite, desperation, desire and rejection appear in comic and grotesque proportions.

Plays include: *The Elephant and the Jewish Question*, Vancouver: New Play Centre, c.1962; *Crabdance* (1f,3m, 1969); *Preparing* (1f) with *Prologue* (2f,1m); *Triangle* (3m); *The Crusader* (1f,2m); *Green Lawn Rest Home* (2f,1m) in *Preparing* (1975) – both Talonbooks; *Leela Means to Play* (3f,9m) in CTR 9 Winter 1976; *If I Turn Round Quick* in *Capilano Review* Summer 1976.
   See also: Casebook in CTR 9, 1975; Herzberg in CD 10:2, 1984.

Sistren
Founded Jamaica, 1977

Sistren was founded by a collective of director Honor Ford-Smith and 13 working-class women who worked collaboratively and improvisationally through popular drama workshops to create acclaimed theatre pieces dealing with such issues as women's history, violence, sexuality, relationships, domestic violence, motherhood and women's struggles to achieve autonomy, as well as experiences of migration, poverty and single parenthood. Among many plays produced are: *Depression Get a*

Blow, Bellywoman Bangarang (1978), *Bandoolu Version* (1979), *Nana Yah* (scripted by Jean Smith, 1980), *QPH* (scripted by Hertencer Lindsay, 1986) and *Muffet Inna All a Wi* (1985, all MS). Working in Jamaican patois and drawing on story-telling traditions, their acclaimed work is moving, fierce and comic; it has toured to women's groups throughout the country and internationally. Though individual scripts are largely unpublished, they have produced a number of videos, oral history documentations and educational materials. Their lively comic strip book, *Wid dis ring*, was designed to draw attention to the history of working-class women in Jamaica from the 1938 uprising onwards and the government's encouragement of women to stay at home as a means of manipulating them and exploiting their labour. *Lionheart Gal* consists of vivid first-person accounts based on both company members' lives and interviews with other women.

Plays: extract from *Buss Out* (various) scripted with Pat Cumper, 1989, in *(Post) Colonial Stages* ed. Helen Gilbert, Hebden Bridge: Dangaroo Press, 1999. Videos include: *Miss Amy and Miss May* (Women Make Movies, 1990); *Muffet Inna All a Wi* (1986). Books include: *Lionheart Gal: life stories of Jamaican women* ed. Honor Ford-Smith, London: Women's Press, 1986; *Wid dis ring* by Joan French with Honor Ford-Smith, Toronto: Sister Vision, 1987.

See also: Bennett and Di Cenzo in *Ariel* v23, no.1, 1992; App. 2: Tompkins and Holledge; France and Corso; Gilbert and Tompkins.

Anna Deavere Smith
American, 1950–

African-American actress, teacher, playwright and director, since 1982 Smith has been developing a series of one-woman documentary performances, *On the Road: a Search for American Character*. Based on oral history interviews with a range of people in a given locality, typically coalescing around themes related to race and gender identities, her earlier performances were shown within the community in which they were made. They spoke of 'a desire for community ... while dramatizing the fractured quality of contemporary social networks' (Richards). Later pieces have focused on events anchored in specific communities but with larger public resonance. The events in *Fires in the Mirror* – the death of a young black boy in Crown Heights, Brooklyn, struck by the Lubavitch rabbi's speeding motorcade, and the retaliatory killing by blacks of a Jewish student – become the flashpoint for smouldering tensions within the two communities. Smith's technique collects testimony from eyewitnesses, victims, cultural commentators, reproducing the precise vocabulary and speech rhythms of speakers to create a complex, contradictory mesh of voices, articulating the tensions of contemporary American experience. The equally acclaimed *Twilight, Los Angeles, 1992* dissects the bitterness, fear, rage and pain of a Los Angeles where enormous wealth and poverty are neighbours, where pent-up frustration at police racism and material deprivation exploded in riots following the not guilty verdict on police officers accused of the beating of Rodney King, a black man, despite the graphic video evidence against them.

Plays include: *Piano* (4f,4m) PiP, 1988; *Twilight, Los Angeles, 1992,* also excerpts in Perkins and Uno (1994); *Fires in the Mirror: Crown Heights Brooklyn and Other Identities* (1993) and extract in Mahone, and in Hatch and Shine (all 1f) – both NY: Anchorbooks/Doubleday; *Chlorophyll Postmodernism and the Mother Goddess* (1f) in *W&P* 8; *Aye Aye Aye I'm Integrated* (2f, 1984), in Miles 1997.

See also: JDTC Fall 1994; App. 2: Richards in Hart and Phelan; Martin in Martin.

Dodie Smith (a.k.a. C. L. Anthony)
English, 1896–1991

A quintessential boulevard dramatist, Smith had a series of West End successes in the 1930s, culminating in *Dear Octopus*, which celebrates the family despite its tendency to smother and control. As four generations gather to prepare for the golden wedding of matriarch Dora Randolph and her husband, Nicholas's admission of his love for his mother's companion, Fenny, is engineered by the family, while Cynthia, daring to acknowledge to her mother the six-year affair she had with a married man in Paris, discovers understanding and forgiveness where she expected condemnation. It is one of many endorsements of liberal sexual values advanced in Smith's work. Aspiring actress Janet Jason, in *Bonnet Over the Windmill*, is encouraged by actor-knight Rupert Morellian to gain experience and her brief relationship with a womanizing playwright, Kit Carson, is presented as offering her a deeper understanding of her art through suffering. In *Autumn Crocus* it is her shocked and conventional friend's insistence on the sordidness of stealing another man's wife, not the act itself, that persuades Fanny to leave the young German hotel-keeper she loves and return to her repressed life as a schoolteacher, while her torment is contrasted with the blithe insouciance of a young couple flaunting their trial marriage. *Lovers and Friends* presents with sympathy the situation of the other woman, who interrupts the domestic routine with her demand for a hearing.

Plays include: *Autumn Crocus* (8f,4m) in Famous 1931; *Service* (16f, 14m) in Famous 1932–3; *Touchwood* (6f,7m) in Famous 1934 and in *Three Plays*, 1939; *Dear Octopus* (12f,5m, 1938); *Call it a Day* (11f,5m) in Famous 1935–6; *Bonnet Over the Windmill* (1937); *Lovers and Friends* (4f,2m, 1943) – all: London Heinemann; *Those People, Those Books* (MS, 1958); *Amateur Means Lover* (MS, 1962).

See also: Autobiographies: *Look Back . . . with Love* (1974), *. . . with Mixed Feelings* (1978), *. . . with Astonishment* (1979), *. . . with Gratitude* (1985). All London: Muller, Bland, White; App. 2: Gale.

Zulu Sofola

Nigerian, 1935–96

Sofola was the first major Nigerian woman playwright, producing numerous works. Often her plays focus on the political conflicts between generations and between traditional and Western values *(King Emene,* 1975; *Old Wines Are Tasty, The Sweet Trap)*, the status of women, the conflict between individual love and the demands of family and community. They draw on African myth, ritual and magic as well as Western theatre styles in their presentation. *The Disturbed Peace of Christmas* uses a theatrical metaphor of the rehearsals for a nativity play to confront the problems of teenage pregnancy. *Queen Omu-Ako of Oligbo* (MS) addresses the dilemmas of women attempting to bring a voice for change within African patriarchal structures. Sofola also published critical essays on theatre and tragic theory.

Plays include: *The Operators* (1973); *Lost Dreams; The Love of Life; The Showers* all in *Lost Dreams and Other Plays* 1992*; *The Disturbed Peace of Christmas* (6f,9m+, chorus) Ibadan: Dayster Press, 1971; *Wedlock of the Gods* (1972); *The Wizard of Law* (1f,4m) – all London: Evans Brothers; *The Sweet Trap* (10f, 15m+) Ibadan: Oxford UP, 1977 and in Busby; *Old Wines Are Tasty* (5f, 14m+, 1979); *Song of a Maiden* (16+f, 14m, 1991) – both Ibadan: Ibadan UP; *Maternity Series* (TV, MS).

See also: Asagma in *Kunapipi,* 8, iii, 1986; Fido in *Ariel,* 18, iv, 1987; App. 2: Dunton; James.

* Detailed cast and publication information not available.

Susan Sontag

American, 1933–

Influential novelist, essayist and theorist, Sontag's work includes both writings for and on performance: theatre criticism, the influential essay 'Notes on Camp' and a major edition of Antonin Artaud's writings, among others. She has also directed, including a production of Beckett's *Waiting for Godot* under shellfire in Sarajevo. Parone's arrangement of her short story, *The Way We Live Now*, is a moving and harrowing exchange between friends who, metaphorically encircling the bed of a man dying of AIDS, exchange messages, memories, speculations, gossip, hope, desperation and love. *Alice in Bed* also concerns early death, that of Alice James, brilliant younger sister of Henry and William, confined to bed by a series of mysterious, possibly hysterical ailments, who in Sontag's piece becomes conflated with her nineteenth-century counterpart, Alice in Wonderland, in a piece like a fantastic laudanum dream, featuring a Mad Hatter's tea party attended by Margaret Fuller, Emily Dickinson and the queen of the wilis from *Giselle*.

Plays include: *Duet For Cannibals* (screen) NY: Farrar, Strauss and Giroux, 1969; *Brother Carl* (screen); *Promised Land* (screen); *Unguided Tour* (screen); *The Way We Live Now* (arranged by Edward Parone, 5f/m) in Osborn, 1990; *Alice in Bed* (8f,4m) NY: Farrar, Strauss and Giroux, 1993.

Sor Juana (Inez De La Cruz)

Mexican, 1648–95

Sor Juana was the first woman and the first American-born (in San Miguel de Nepantla) playwright. In 1669 she entered the convent of the Order of St Jerome. She wrote poems as well as both religious and secular theatre, the latter including *loa*s (dramatic poems), *sainete*s (skits) and comedies on themes of love, jealousy and honour. Her religious plays include *The Divine Narcissus*, a reworking of the classical myth which she uses as an allegory in which Narcissus/Christ can no longer see himself clearly in the mirror of human nature, presented as female, so muddied is her clarity by sin. Attacked for her writing, Sor Juana produced a brilliant defence of women's intellectual and artistic endeavours. As well as songs from various plays, a few other extracts have been published in translation. Sor Juana's life and work have inspired at least two plays by later American women writers, Diana Ackerman's dramatic poem *Reverse Thunder* (1988) and Estela Portillo Tremblay's *Sor Juana* (1983).

Translated plays include: *The Divine Narcissus* (extracts) in *A Sor Juana Anthology* ed. Alan S. Trueblood, Cambridge, MA: Harvard UP, 1988; *Las empenos de una casa* (*A Household Plagued By Love*) tr. James C. Bardin extracts in *Literature in Pan-America* Washington, DC: Pan American Union, 1950 and as *The House of Love* tr. Peter Oswald (MS, 1997 UK).

See also: *Sor Juana Inez de la Cruz* by Gerard Flynn, NY: Twayne Publishers, 1971, *A Woman of Genius: the Intellectual Biography of . . .* tr & intro Margaret Sayers Peden, Salisbury: Lime Rock, 1982.

Githa Sowerby
English, 1876–1970

Born near Gateshead, Northumberland, Sowerby was the daughter of a glass manufacturer who became the model for the patriarchal father in her most famous play, *Rutherford and Son*. Produced in 1912, it was quickly recognized as a remarkable piece of work: passionate, uncompromising, incisive (Sowerby is the only woman discussed by Emma Goldman – see below – alongside Chekhov, Ibsen, *et al.*), but fell unaccountably into neglect until its rediscovery by feminist companies and subsequent productions at the RNT and elsewhere. John Rutherford is Master of the Works and of his family, presiding over both with dour Northern tyranny, seeing all human beings as commodities to be used and exploited, all relationships as contracts. He entraps his children in a sense of infantile powerlessness and fear, his daughter caught in the frustration of respectable idleness, while he is prepared to swindle his eldest son out of the new manufacturing technique he has invented for the good of the Works. Only his daughter-in-law, realizing his weakness – his need for an heir – and how to exploit it, defies him.

Plays include: *Rutherford and Son* (4f,4m, 1912) in Dickinson and in Fitzsimmons & Gardner.

See also: *The Social Significance of Modern Drama* (1914) by Emma Goldman, reissue, NY: Applause, 1987; App. 2: Stowell; Holledge.

The Sphinx *see* Women's Theatre Group

Spiderwoman Theatre
Founded United States, 1975

The core members of Spiderwoman (they have sometimes worked with other women: African-American, native or white) are sisters: Lisa Mayo, Gloria Miguel and Muriel Miguel, Native Americans of Kuna-Rappahannock ancestry. Large, brown-skinned, middle-aged women dressed with vivid individualism, their physical presence is a vital part of work that is playful, irreverent, challenging and celebratory, exploring gender, sexual and, especially, native identities. They take their name from the Hopi goddess, Spiderwoman, who taught her people to weave, and their work knits together snatches of songs ('Indian Love Call', Kurt Weill's 'September Song'), memories, pastiche, games, rituals, deconstructed fragments of classic texts (Chekhov's *Three Sisters*), laced through with exchanges reflecting their relationship as sisters. They joke, contend for prominence, collude in shared fantasies or counter one's escapist version of the past with another's harsher account.

In *Winnetou's Snake-Oil Show* they address whites' latest appropriation of native property, the phenomenon of 'plastic shamanism' – New Age teachers who purport to sell Indian spirituality at $600 weekend workshops. The piece parodies such sessions as an audience member undergoes an initiation that will 'turn him into an Indian', culminating in his presentation with a photocopied picture of an Indian face and instructions to wear it always. *Winnetou* ends with Muriel's ironic thanks to the audience for discovering her and 'knowing more about me than I do'. The group returned to the theme of spirituality in a piece about 'receiving messages', *Reverb-ber-ber-rations*, a first attempt to explore their own relationship to sacred traditions and the interconnection of their work as communicators with the role of healer.

Plays include: *Winnetou's Snake-Oil Show from Wigwam City* (1991), in CTR 68; *The Banana Bunch* (MS); *Sun Moon and Feather* (1981), in Perkins and Uno; *Reverb-ber-ber-rations* (1990) in W&P 10 (All 3f); *Power Pipes* (6f, 1993) in D'Aponte.
See also: interview in W&P 10; App. 2: Schneider, Tompkins and Holledge.

Split Britches
Founded United States, 1980

Begun by deviser-performers Peggy Shaw and Lois Weaver and writer-performer Deb Margolin, Split Britches has consistently presented some of the most radical contemporary 'queer' performance, questioning gender constructions, reclaiming 'politically incorrect' areas of sexuality such as butch–femme and sexual role-playing. Coming out of the irreverent WOW (Women's One World) Café in NYC's East Village and from a break-away lesbian sub-group of the then ethnically mixed **Spiderwoman** company, their name came from their first show. *Split Britches* was an excavation of the histories of the women of Weaver's family, poor farmers in rural Virginia: the name came from the clothing they wore to allow them to urinate standing up in a field. The performers' use of tableaux of 'old photographs' as framing device commented on both their distance from and identification with the women portrayed.

It was a first example of the self-reflectivity of the company's work, commenting on its theatricality and incorporating within the shows aspects of their self-identities as struggling artists on the East Village poverty line, and on Weaver's and Shaw's on/off-stage relationship, along with parody of contemporary cultural concerns, mainstream and lesbian, and multiple role changes. Their work deconstructs texts from Louisa May Alcott to fairy tales to the media response to serial killer Aileen Wuornos. *Belle Reprieve* deconstructs Tennessee Williams's *A Streetcar Named Desire* in a delicious – and disturbing – collaboration with the 'radical sissy' men of Bloolips, Bette Bourne playing Blanche to Peggy Shaw's Stanley Kowalski.

Plays include: *Split Britches* (1980) in W&P 10; *Beauty and the Beast* (1982); *Upwardly Mobile Home* (1984); *Little Women* (1988) also in *The Kenyon Review*, Spring 1993 (all 3f); *Lesbians Who Kill* (1992); *Lust and Comfort* (1995, both 2f); *Belle Reprieve* (with Bourne and Paul Shaw, 2f,2m) also in Helbing. All in *Split Britches: Lesbian Practice/Feminist Performance* ed. Sue-Ellen Case, Routledge, 1996; *Faith and Dancing* (1f, 1996) in Goodman 2000.

See also App. 2: Patraka in Hart and Phelan.

Gertrude Stein
American, 1874–1946

The most linguistically and formally inventive of American writers for performance, Stein's inter-war texts needed the post-war avant garde to explore their theatrical possibilties. A list of her directors and successors reads like a roll-call of experimental theatre: Julian Beck, Judith **Malina**, Richard Foreman, Robert Wilson, Anne Bogart, Suzan-Lori **Parks.** Stein works with words musically, using simple constructions over and over in different combinations, creating patterns of sound and rhythm, suggesting layered nuances of meanings, eluding fixity.

Stein's pieces (almost 80 in total) vary hugely in length and rarely have obvious cast lists, characters or dialogue, but play with the form and layout of the play, inviting interaction, incorporating self-parody and commenting on their status as theatrical and literary constructs. Early works focused on moments of relationships fragmented, decontextualized, capturing mood and image. Mid-career works such as *Geography and Plays* (1922) have been the focus of recent analysis with their emphasis on the spatial landscape of performance as the locus for multiple concurrent actions, words, images, levels of consciousness. Later works, including the operatic collaborations with Virgil Thomson *Four Saints in Three Acts* (1927) and *The Mother of Us All* (1947), a meditation on the career of Susan B. Anthony, are more accessible and conventional in form and continue to be the most produced works. but Stein is still the most under-performed major American playwright.

Plays include: *Ladies Voices*; *Please Do Not Suffer*; *He Said It*; *Counting her Dresses*; *I Like it to Be a Play*; *IIIIIIIII*; *The King or Something (The Public is Invited to Dance)* in *Geography and Plays*, NY: Haskell House Publishers, 1922, reissued 1967; *Four Saints in Three Acts*; *They Must be Wedded to Their Wife*; *Turkey Bones and Eating and We Liked It*; *What Happened*, also in Benedikt and in Poland, in *Selected Operas and Plays* ed. J. M. Brinnin, Pittsburgh: Pittsburgh UP, 1970; *Three Sisters Who Are Not Sisters*; *The Maids*; *In a Garden* in *The Gertrude Stein First Reader and Three Other Plays*, Dublin: Fridberg, 1946; *Yes is for a Very Young Man*, London: Pushkin, 1946; *Dr Faustus Lights the Lights*; *Byron*; *The Mother of Us All* (10f, 14m) also in Barlow 1994 and in France; *A Play called Not and Now*; *A Play of Pounds*; (casts various) in *Last Operas and Plays* NY: Vintage, 1975; *Please Do Not Suffer* and *Accents in Alsace* – both in Tylee.

See also: *Gertrude Stein's Theatre of the Absolute* by Betsy Alayne Ryan, Ann Arbor: UMI Research Press 1980; App. 2: Marranca; Pladott in Schlueter; Donkin and Clement.

Barbara Stellmach

Australian, 1930–

Stellmach, born in Warwick, Queensland, was taught speech and drama before beginning writing, gaining great success with the Australian amateur theatre movement. She was one of the founders of Brisbane's Playlab, where she has had several first productions. Her work ranges from thrillers and romantic comedies (*From the Fourteenth Floor* involves two people thrown together by a double-booked hotel room) to plays exploring the legacy and impact of the Australian bush. *Legend of the Losers* alternates blank verse narration by a chorus with naturalistic scenes in its account of the life and legends of a bushranger, Captain Thunderbolt, in the mid-nineteenth century. *Dust is the Heart* is influenced by the writings of Henry Lawson (cf. **Gray**) in its plot of a young girl's struggle to free herself from the social alienation to which the family's criminal past and the father's drunkenness condemn her, and to save her simple-minded brother from a future in jail. The judgement of an intolerant society is also central to *Dark Heritage* (1964), in which the young English wife of 'coloured' doctor Neil Harrison encourages him to defy the prejudice he encounters, but discovers the most deep-seated problem is in his internalized hatred of his Aboriginal self.

Plays include: *Not Even a Mouse* (4f,3m, 1978); *From the Fourteenth Floor You can See the Harbour Bridge* (2f,2m, 1980) – both Brisbane: Playlab; *Dark Heritage* (3f,4m, 1964); *Dust is the Heart* (2f,2m, 1961); *Hang Your Clothes on Yonder Bush* (9f,3m, 1969); *Legend of the Losers* (6f, 16m, 1970) in *Four Australian Plays*, Queensland UP, 1973.

Shelagh Stephenson

English, 1955–

Stephenson first won acclaim for her radio plays, culminating in the award-winning *Five Kinds of Silence* (since adapted for stage, 2000). The chilling voice-over of the dead father and the statements of the wife and daughters who killed him, reveal a family life ruled by strict order and ritual, governing food preparation, the storage of provisions and the service of sexual needs; deviations punishable by brutal violence. Stephenson was called a 'mistress of comic anguish' for her first stage play, *The Memory of Water*, which explores the conflicts, evasions and divergences of memory, shared and individual, as three sisters meet in the depths of winter to bury their mother. The piece centres on rage, loss and betrayal as Mary, the middle daughter, confronts the anguish of her childlessness and the loss both of her mother and the baby she was forced to give up for adoption. *An Experiment with an Air-Pump* addresses ethical dilemmas about science and genetic experimentation over two time frames, while *Ancient Things* explores the nature of celebrity.

Plays include: *The Memory of Water* (4f,2m, 1996); *Five Kinds of Silence* (3f,1m, 1996) – both 1997; *An Experiment with an Air-Pump* (4f,3m,id, 1998); *Ancient Things* (MS, 2000). All Methuen.

See also App. 2: Sierz.

G. B. (Gladys Bronwen) Stern
British, 1890–1973

Daughter of Jewish Londoners, Stern's play *The Matriarch*, like several of her novels focusing on the Rakonitz family, compellingly explores the bonds and constraints of Jewish family life, the demands made by family honour, on preserving the bloodline and 'fitting in' under the despotic rule of the matriarchal grandmother. Women and power are also central to *The Man Who Pays the Piper*, which addresses the experience of a generation of women made heads of families by the death of fathers and brothers in the First World War. A prologue shows Daryll as a witty and rebellious 18-year-old, coming home late and defying her father, a scene later tellingly reversed as she castigates her frivolous and irresponsible younger sister. Daryll is now running the fashion-house 'Alexia' and is tired and oppressed by the demands of management, financial responsibility for supporting an extravagant family and being feared and resented for it. The piece does not present easy answers. When she does stop working and marry, she finds herself bored by idleness and frustrated by her wasted abilities, while the validity of her husband's proposed solution, that they have children, is left open to question.

Plays include: *The Man Who Pays the Piper* (6f, 10m, 1929), Heinemann, 1931; *The Matriarch* (8f,9m) French, 1931.

See also App. 2: Gale.

Ena Lamont Stewart

Scottish, 1912–

Stewart is the major woman Scottish playwright of the inter-war period. Her work, long forgotten, was rediscovered in the 1980s with 7:84 company's revival of *Men Should Weep* (1947), written in Scots and originally produced by the influential left-wing Unity Theatre.

Her work emerged from a 'red-hot revolt against cocktail time, glamorous gowns and under-worked, about-to-be-deceived husbands', a desire to see real life and ordinary people on stage. She based *Starched Aprons* on her observation of conditions at the children's hospital where she worked as receptionist. Her work focuses on the realities of struggling to survive in Depression Glasgow, especially on the experience of women like Maggie, the mother in *Men Should Weep*: charring to support her family, then coming home to slave for them, while her unemployed socialist husband sees housework as beneath his dignity, her son wheedles money from her to support his manipulative wife and her daughter becomes a kept woman to get a better life. Moving, fiercely realistic yet funny, it asks pointed questions about the economic bargain of married virtue versus prostitution. Later plays such as *Walkies Time* and *Towards Evening* present sharp vignettes of encounters across social or family divides, communication or its failure.

Plays include: *Distinguished Company* (MS, 1942); *Kind Milly* (MS); *Business in Edinburgh* (MS); *Knocking on the Wall* (MS); *Starched Aprons* (17f,9m) n.p.: New Theatre Play Service with Unity Theatre Society, c.1945; *Men Should Weep* (10f,7m, 1947) Glasgow: SSP, 1981 and Edinburgh: 7:84, 1983; *Walkies Time* (2f) and *Towards Evening* (1f,1m, 1985) in Remnant 8.

Harriet Beecher Stowe

American, 1811–96

Stowe published her great novel, *Uncle Tom's Cabin*, in 1851. It rapidly became massively influential in the fight against slavery, selling 3 million copies, and was immediately pirated for dramatic presentation. George Aiken's version was enormously successful both before and after the Civil War, to the extent that actors spent whole careers 'Tomming', that is, touring in the show. The stage version, with its wide exposure to new audiences, also played a key part in reinforcing the pressure for abolition. In his *History of the American Drama* (1923), Arthur Hobson Quinn wrote:

> *Read in cold blood, Aiken's play seems cheap and melodramatic in the extreme . . . Eva dies on stage and is transported bodily by angels to a better world. The play is hopeless from the standpoint of dramatic criticism, and yet in the catalogue of social forces it remains probably the most potent weapon developed by the literary crusade against slavery.*

While later Stowe works also appeared on stage, none was as hugely successful as *Tom*.

Plays include: *Dred: a Tale of the Dismal Swamp* (7f,8m) adapted by W. E. Suter, French, c.1856. *Uncle Tom's Cabin* (5f, 11m+, 1852), dramatized by George Aiken in *American Melodrama* ed. Daniel Gerould, PAJ Publications, 1983 and in Moses v. 2.

Efua T. Sutherland
Ghanaian, 1924–96

A major contributor to the development of Ghanaian drama as both playwright and director, Sutherland was also developer of projects setting up performance spaces such as the Atwia village 'story-house'. In 1958 she established the Experimental Theatre Players which became Ghana Drama Studio and the site of much of her work. She co-founded the literary magazine *Okeyame* and led research on traditional performance at Ghana University.

Her plays include rhythm and story works aimed at children, such as *Vulture! Vulture. Foriwa* links the love story of a university-educated outsider and a young local woman trained as a teacher with an argument for progress and development, while including the rejection of tribalism which prevents their marriage. Like the tragic *Edufa* it focuses on the role of women. *Anansewa* uses song, ritual and audience participation, drawing on the classic story-telling performance tradition built round the stories of Ananse the trickster spider, 'artistically a means for society to criticize itself', confronting questions of social and personal behaviour.

Plays include: *Odasani* (MS); *Edufa* (3f,4m+) Longman, 1975 and in Branch; *The Marriage of Anansewa* (19f, 12m+) Longman, 1975 also ext. in Arkin and Shollar; *Foriwa* (9f, 19m, 1967); *Vulture! Vulture* (2 f/m,+chorus) – both Accra: Ghana Publishing House, 1968; *The Pineapple Child* (MS).

See also: Pearce in *African Literature Today* No 15.

Elizabeth Swados

American, 1951–

Director, playwright, composer, Swados's work encompasses travels with Peter Brook to Africa to explore the possibilities of a universal theatre language and composing. Her work ranges from song cycles (*Bible Women*) to scores for ballet and for Andrei Serban's productions of *Medea* (1972) and *Agamemnon* (1977) to music for PBS television. She has also written both book and lyrics for several musicals, including *Nightclub Cantata* (MS, 1977), based on the writings of Sylvia **Plath**, Carson **McCullers**, Pablo Neruda and others, and the influential *Runaways*, addressing the alienation of young people, child prostitution, bullying and adult indifference.

More recently she has addressed Jewish identity and cultural inheritance. In *Jerusalem* she sets to music poems by Yehuda Amichai, conjuring up the religious diversity and conflicts of the holy city, focusing on the wanderers and refugees who find their way there. In *Esther* she draws on the Purim tradition of slapstick and broad comedy, presenting Esther as 'a Jewish Mata Hari – a working wonder woman'.

Plays include: *Under Heat* (screen); *Cosmic Eye* (screen); *Dispatches* (MS, 1979); *Runaways* (9f, 11m) NY: Bantam, 1979; *Alice in Concert* (7f,6m+band, 1981); *The Haggadah* (19m/f, 1982); *Doonesbury* (with Gary Trudeau 2f,7m, 1986) – all Samuel French; *Esther, a Vaudeville Megillah* (3f,3m+6, 1988) in Schiff 1996; *Jerusalem* (10f, 19m,dp) – both BPP, 1988; *Jonah* (MS, 1990).

Meera Syal

British, 1963–

As a writer, actress and deviser, much of Syal's work draws on autobiographical experiences. Her novels *Anita and Me* – vividly charting an Asian girl's growing up in 1960s Wolverhampton – and *Life Isn't All Ha Ha Hee Hee*, have been widely acclaimed. Her play *One of Us* is a pointed and comic piece about a young Asian girl's ambition to become an actress. Her dramatic work gleefully subverts stereotypes of submissive Asian women, arranged marriages and addresses issues of British Asian cultural identity. She has also written extensively for Asian comedy series *Goodness Gracious Me*, first for radio then television, in which she also performs.

Plays include: *One of Us* (with Jacqui Shapiro, MS); *My Sister Wife* (19f,9m+, 1993, screen) in George; *Bhaji on the Beach* (screen); *The Real McCoy* (radio).

See also: 'Finding My Voice' in *Passion: Discourses on Blackwomen's Creativity* ed. Maud Sulter, Hebden Bridge: Urban Fox Press, 1990.

Violet Targuse

New Zealand/Aotearoan, ?–1937

Targuse lived in Canterbury and was three times winner in the British Drama League (NZ Branch) competitions for amateur one-act plays. While some of her plays, such as *Fear* (in which a woman is terrorized by memories of her former husband) lapse into melodrama, her best works, such as *Rabbits* and *Ebb and Flow*, describe a New Zealand of sparse population and isolation where women are desperate to escape their entrapment or project their desires for a fuller life onto children or siblings. Peter in *Mopsey* is also trapped by loyalty and guilt to staying with his mentally handicapped but manipulative sister, while *The Touchstone* and *Men in Pieces* also explore the limits and conflicts of loyalty.

Plays include: *The Touchstone* (3f,3m); *Fear* (3f,2m); *Rabbits* (2f,2m) in *Seven One Act Plays* (1933); *Ebb and Flow* (2f,1m) in *Seven One Act Plays 1934* (1934) – both Wellington: Radio Publishing Co.; *Mopsey* (3f,1m) and *Men for Pieces* (3f,1m) in *Further One Act Plays 1935*, Wellington: National Magazines Ltd, 1935.

Fiona Templeton

Scottish, 1951–

Templeton's *You – the City*, which has been performed in New York, London, Amsterdam and other cities, was described as an intimate city-wide perfomance for an audience of one. The audience member was led through streets, spoken to in a strange and cryptic series of monologues by a sequence of guides: businesswomen, therapists, lovers, drivers, 'old friends', each addressing 'you' in what became a second person singular meditation on self, others, reality, illusion, perception and performance. Overheard snatches of conversation in the action of the streets mingled seamlessly with the staged action and with encounters with fellow audience members, momentarily transformed into performers in each other's sight. It was described as entering 'a parallel universe that looked, shook and smelt like Times Square'.

Following early work in Cardiff with the performance art company Theatre of Mistakes (founded 1974) investigating the complexities within simple actions, repeated and then modified, Templeton has spent much of her career in the USA. Her writing also, beneath a surface of delusive clarity, constantly plays with ideas of knowledge and power, questions its own strategies and language, plays games with meaning, queries and contradicts.

Plays include: *You the City* (13f/m, 1988) NY: Roof Books, 1990; *Realities* (2f,4m) extract in cheek 1; *Strange to Relate* (1f,1m, 1988) in Champagne.

See also: TDR 123 and 126; App. 2: Carr.

Megan Terry
American, 1932–

Terry pioneered methods of writing collaboratively with a company with Joseph Chaikin's Open Theater in the 1960s. She then moved, with actor/director JoAnn Schmidman, to Nebraska to establish an experimental theatre space outside the unreality of the New York theatre scene: the Omaha Magic Theatre. Her early plays used techniques of transformational acting involving the performers in rapid shifts from one role to another and employed a range of performance resources: *Viet Rock* was the first rock musical; later works are made in conjunction with local visual artists and composers.

Terry has been called the 'mother of American feminist drama' and female experience is central to many of her plays. *Hothouse* explores three generations of women in Terry's home town, Seattle; *Willa Willie-Bill's Dope Garden* is a meditation on Nebraska-born Willa Cather and *Ex-Miss Copper Queen*... is discovered by two fiercely territorial bag ladies, doped out on their turf. Verbally and visually extremely vivid, plays such as *Babes in the Bighouse*, set in a women's prison, evoke a sense of immediacy, flux and uncertainty and a great breadth of experience through rapid switches from humour to pain. Like many of Terry's plays, such as *Kegger* (on alcohol abuse, 1982) and *Goona Goona* (domestic violence, 1979), it was closely based on interviews and community workshops and designed as an environmnental piece in which the audience plays an active role. In *Babes*, they are visitors to the prison, kept behind a rope and under continual scrutiny as the prisoners act out their daily lives, their fantasies and imaginative escapes.

Plays include: *Viet Rock* (group, 1966); *The Gloaming Oh My Darling* (6f,4m); *Comings and Goings* (1f,1m, 1967); *Keep Tightly Closed in a Cool, Dry Place* (3m, 1965) in *Viet Rock and Other Plays* NY: Simon and Schuster, 1967; *Massachusetts Trust* (5f, 10m+, 1968) in Poland; *Calm Down Mother* (3f, 1965) in Sullivan and Hatch; *Ex-Miss Copper Queen on a Set of Pills* (3f, 1959) in France and in Ballet 1; *Approaching Simone* (4f,8m, 1970) in Kriegel; *Hothouse* (4f,4m) DPS, 1974; *AMTRAK* (2f,2m+1, 1989) in *SAD*; *Babes in the Bighouse* (12f,2m+, 1974); *American Kings English For Queens*, (6f,2m, 1978) in *High Energy Musicals from Omaha Magic Theatre*, BPP, 1983 and *Molly Bailey's Travelling Family Circus* (12f, 10m+) – both BPP, 1983; *Willa Willie Bill's Dope Garden* (4f, 1977) in Curb; *Breakfast Serial* (1f,3m, 1989–95) in Frank; *Body Leaks* (3f, 1f/m+) with Sora Kim and JoAnn Schmidman, in Bert.

See also: Babnich in *Centennial Review* 32 1988; SAD 1989; App. 2: Breslauer and Keyssar in Hart; Keyssar; Schlueter; Savran; Betsko and Koenig.

Josephine Tey *see* Gordon Daviot

Heidi Thomas
British, 1963–

Born into a large Liverpool-Irish family, Thomas's teenage years were marked by the death of a Down's syndrome brother and, devastatingly, by her father's suicide when she was 18. She revisited this experience in the acclaimed *Shamrocks and Crocodiles*, in which the father's death lays bare the web of lies he has spun for his family to disguise his involvement in a seedy semi-criminal underworld where selling 'insurance' is mass trading in condoms in Ireland.

Thomas's plays are marked by the characters' dense poetic internal monologues, that have divided critics, some condemning a 'parade of ostentatious emptiness' while others praised their 'delicate power' and 'restless landscape of imagery'. *Indigo* parallels the struggles between two fathers, an African king and a Liverpool slave trader, and their rebellious sons' different discoveries of moral complicity and the limits of power. William the would-be liberal becomes the thing he claimed to hate, a slaver, his human cargo dying in filth, while Ide learns the impotence of his desired sacrifice to save his people. Thomas's plays have settings as diverse as the Irish potato famine and 1990s Zimbabwe, themes as various as love, prostitution and family history, though death remains a constant theme.

Plays include: *All Flesh is Grass* (MS); *Some Singing Blood* (MS); *Our Lady Blue* (TV); *Mr Wonderful* (TV); *Shamrocks and Crocodiles* (2f,3m,id), *Indigo* (1f,8m). Both Amber Lane Press, 1988; *Madame Bovary* (TV, 2000).

See also: Griffiths and Llewellyn-Jones.

Judith Thompson
Canadian, 1954–

One of the most significant and exciting contemporary Canadian playwrights, Thompson was born in Montreal and grew up in Kingston, Ontario. Long-term playwright-in-residence at the Tarragon Theatre, she describes her work as dealing with the walls we erect to keep out 'the monster that's hovering around the periphery of civilization'. Her haunting, harrowing plays have twice won her the Governor General's Award for English language drama, while critics praise her 'orgiastic and poetic . . . use of language' and extraordinary theatricality.

The Crackwalker, set in Kingston, explores the psyche of an urban underclass through Therese and her friends, caught in a downward spiral of ignorance, poverty and frustration. Thompson's plays are less about social problems, however, than about the psychological and spiritual consequences of emotional and physical violence, constricted lives, broken communication. Scenes of blistering realism swell into nightmarish horrors. *The Lion in the Streets* that stalks her characters is the memories, desires, urban terrors and fantasies that possess their and our imaginations – murder, torture, jealousy, insanity, revenge – and invade reality. The piece is haunted by a seven-year-old Portuguese girl murdered years before, a lost soul and guardian spirit whose final forgiveness of her murderer suggests the possibility of deliverance. The desire for transformation is a central concern of Thompson's work. Pony in *White Biting Dog* is obsessed by the need to save his father from death – and himself from Hell – after he has a vision of a white dog that speaks, giving him a mission; Dee in *I Am Yours* feels possessed by a 'beast' when she becomes pregnant and struggles to find redemption.

Plays include: *The Lion in the Streets* (4f,2m,id, 1992); *Sled* (3f,4m, 1996) – both Playwrights Canada; *White Biting Dog* (2f,3m, 1984); *The Crackwalker* (2f,3m, 1980) – both also Playwrights Canada; *Pink* (1f, 1986); *Tornado* (9f,9m,id, 1987); *I Am Yours* (3f, 3m, 1987) also in Wasserman, also Faber 1998 – all in *The Other Side of the Dark*, Coach House Press, 1989; *White Sand* (3f,1m) in Jansen, 1991; *Perfect Pie* (1f) in Sherman.

See also: CD 16:2, 1990; George Coles in *Canadian Literature*, Autumn 1988; App. 2: Zimmerman; Adam in Much; Ann Wilson in Brask; Gilbert and Tompkins; Sierz.

Jane Thornton
British, 1961–

A runner-up in the *Sunday Times* Playwriting Competition, Thornton has worked extensively with John Godber (often as co-writer) and the Hull Truck Theatre Company, as both actress and playwright. Like Godber's successful *Bouncers*, to which their consistently popular *Shakers* is a companion piece, Thornton's plays tend to focus on groups of women in the workplace: hairdressers in *Cut 'n' Dried*, models in *Catwalk* (both MS), switching roles to play customers, boyfriends and others. In the much-praised *Amid the Standing Corn* (MS) she used a similar documentary technique to focus on women in a pit-town during the 1984 miners' strike and in *Handle with Care* (MS) explored the lives of four socially dispossessed teenagers. *Shakers* (1984, revised 1991) wittily examines the dreams behind the fixed smiles of four waitresses in a plush cocktail bar, oozing glamour and sophistication. It alternates monologues with group scenes at the club between the girls or the customers: supermarket check-out operators on a 21st birthday spree, the lads trying their chat-up lines, the jilt crying in the toilets.

Plays include: *Back to the Walls* (MS); *Everyday Heroes* (MS); *Shakers* (4f, 1987) and *Shakers Restirred* (4f, 1993) – both with John Godber, both Chappell.

Marta Tikkanen
Finno-Swedish, 1935–

A member of the Swedish-speaking minority in Finland, Tikkanen is a poet and experimental novelist (*now tomorrow*, *Manrape*) many of whose works re-examine myths or fairy tales like *Little Red Riding Hood* (1986). *Love Story of the Century* is a poem that was translated and adapted for production by the British feminist theatre company Monstrous Regiment. A brutally honest account of the experience of a woman and her family where the husband and father is an alcoholic, the play divides the role of the woman between two actresses as it traces the complexities and contradictions of feeling as someone once loved becomes a stranger – 'love's despair'.

Plays: *Love Story of the Century* (2f, 1990) tr. Stina Katchadourian, adapted by Clare Venables in Hanna.

Claire Tomalin
English, 1933–

Journalist and biographer Tomalin's works include *Mrs Jordan's Profession* (1994) on the eighteenth-century actress (and possibly playwright) Dora Jordan, and *Katherine Mansfield: a Secret Life* (1988) on which she based her highly praised play. Set in Menton near the end of **Mansfield**'s life, it movingly re-creates her relationship with her faithful, much put-upon friend, Ida Baker, who dedicated herself to nursing Mansfield and enraged her with her zealous devotion. Tomalin was praised for her exploration of 'the contradictions within each woman and the strange love that grew out of Katherine's furious need and Ida's compulsion to serve'.

Play: *The Winter Wife* (1m,3f), NHB, 1991.

Sue Townsend
English, 1946–

Born in Leicester, Townsend left school at 15 and worked at a variety of jobs, finally training as a community worker. She achieved immense success with her bestselling *The Secret Diary of Adrian Mole Aged 13¾* and its sequels, later adapted for television and stage. They present suburban English life, teenage crushes, sex and marital difficulties, problems of school, all hilariously seen through the eyes of an adolescent boy.

Her plays, at once comic and humane, often feature groups of oddly assorted characters and their awkward attempts at communication. In *Bazaar and Rummage* three agoraphobics are persuaded out of their homes to run a jumble sale with a neurotic do-gooder and a trainee social worker, with predictably dire consequences. In *Groping for Words* the setting is an adult literacy class where a nanny, a divorcee with a daughter down-under and a school caretaker must confront their terror of admitting their ignorance of reading in a piece that looks deeply into the politics of access to knowledge. *The Great Celestial Cow*, originally developed with the Joint Stock Theatre Company (cf. **Churchill**), addresses the lives of Asian women coping with British prejudice and family restictions. It focuses on Sita, who leaves India for Leicester, where her husband and his friends reproduce the strictest Hindu mores to protect their women and themselves against the threat of an alien world. In the satirical musical *The Queen and I*, the deposed Queen of England is relocated by a republican government to a Leicester council estate and forced to confront the inadequacies of a rundown welfare state.

Plays include: *The Ghost of Daniel Lambert* (MS, 1981); *Dayroom* (MS, 1983); *Bazaar and Rummage* (6f, 1982); *Womberang* (10f, 1979); *Groping for Words* (2f,2m, 1983); *The Great Celestial Cow* (8f,id, 1984); *The Secret Diary of Adrian Mole Aged 13 1/4* (8f,8m+, 1986) in *Sue Townsend Plays 1*, (1996); *Ten Tiny Fingers, Nine Tiny Toes* (3f,4m,id, 1990); *The Queen and I* (4f,4m, 1994). All Methuen.

Sophie Treadwell
American, 1885–1970

In recent years Treadwell has received new acclaim as feminist critics have rediscovered her work, and with the success of productions such as the British RNT's 1993 *Machinal* and the BBC radio adaptation of *Intimations for Saxophone* (1999). Both plays use the stylized vocabulary of expressionist theatre to focus on women trapped in a soulless, mechanistic age, conveyed in *Machinal* by the bleak rituals of office life, the ceaseless clamour of the city whence a nameless Young Woman seeks escape, first into a loveless marriage then a brief desperate affair before murdering her husband and going to the electric chair. Both plays employ rhythmic, telegraphic language. In *Intimations for Saxophone* it is used to convey the empty, conventional utterances of a polite society marriage, praising the trousseau, the bride's looks, the honeymoon plans, while the haunting strains of the saxophone weave in and out of the action, the voice of Lily's unfulfilled longing as she aches for escape into something other than her 'empty, vulgar ... nice, slick, smooth' life, a longing which drives her away from her sexually repressed husband into the compulsion of a self-destructive passion.

More optimistic is the naturalistic *Hope for a Harvest*, its heroine an older woman returning from war-torn Europe to her native California. She challenges the lassitude of her family and a society that has abandoned the land and the values that built a community in favour of self-pity, debt, consumer goods and racial prejudice against hard-working immigrant Italians.

Plays include: *Intimations for Saxophone* (MS, 1930); *Million Dollar Gate* (MS, 1930); *Promised Land* (MS, 1933); *The Last Border* (MS); *Machinal* (1of, 17m+, 1928) NHB, 1993 and in Barlow 1981; *Hope for a Harvest* (5f,5m) French, 1942.

See also: *Sophie Treadwell: a Research and Production Sourcebook* by Jerry Dickey, Greenwood, 1997; Jones in MD 37, 1994; App. 2: Bywaters in Schlueter; Shafer, Sierz.

Catherine (Cockburn) Trotter
English, 1679–1749

Third of the triumvirate of 'female wits', with Delarivier **Manley** and Mary **Pix**, Trotter was intellectually precocious and wrote her first play, *Agnes De Castro*, aged 18. It has been read as an early lesbian play, in which the heroine's passionate devotion to the wife of the prince who is trying to seduce her is the strongest emotion and most fully developed relationship in the piece. In *The Fatal Friendship*, Gramont makes a big-amous marriage in a desperate attempt to gain money to free his friend from captivity, only to discover he has married the friend's lover. Trotter explores the conflicting loyalties, desperate discoveries and both wives' sense of betrayal with subtlety and complexity.

Trotter's other tragedies are less effective than her brilliant comedy *Love at a Loss*, which examines attitudes to marriage through three betrothed couples and their rival suitors. Central is the strikingly modern predica-ment of Lesbia who, on the rebound from Grandfoy, has started a sexual relationship before formally being married to Beaumine and is faced with the choice to believe his protestations that he will – eventually – marry her and those of the returned loyal lover she has betrayed. The cynical Beau-mine is matched by Miranda, an unconventional woman in charisma, wit, mockery of love and incisive analysis of the pitfalls of marriage.

Plays: *Agnes De Castro* (4f,6m+, 1696); *The Fatal Friendship* (3f,5m+, 1698) also in Morgan; *The Unhappy Penitent* (3f, 10m+, 1701); *Love at a Loss* or *Most Votes Carry It* (4f,6m+, 1701), also in Kendall; *The Revolution in Sweden* (4f,6m+, 1706) all in *The Plays of Mary Pix and Catherine Trotter* ed. Edna Steeves, NY: Garland, 1982.

See also: *Three Augustan Women Playwrights* by Constance Clark, NY: Peter Lang, 1986; App. 2: Cotton; Pearson; Kendall in Donkin and Clement.

Lesya Ukrainka (Lesya Kosach)
Ukrainian, 1871–1913

Lesya Kosach, known as Ukrainka, is recognized as one of the three most important Ukrainian writers. She grew up in Kiev surrounded by major figures in theatre, arts and sciences, and spoke several European languages. Because of poor health she travelled widely for treatment in Europe and to the Middle East. Her many poetic dramas draw on 'the spiritual history of the world, examining the historical process and how human aspirations operate within it'. Several use biblical themes to symbolize Ukrainian suffering and struggle against Tsarist oppression. *The Forest Song* (1911) has remained her most popular and most translated work. Based on the legends and songs of Polissia, the wetland area of northern Ukraine, it centres on the love of a sylph for a young man over the course of the changing seasons and explores the shifting boundaries between wilderness and civilization, as the forest spirits are threatened by the arrival of human interlopers.

Translated plays: *On the Ruins* (4f,6m+, 1902); *The Babylonian Captivity* (5f, 13m, 1902); *The Noblewoman* (4f,5m, 1916); *Forest Song* (4f, 10m+, 1911); *Martianus the Advocate* (3f,8m+, 1911) all tr. Percival Cundy in *Spirit of Flame: a Collection of the Works of Lesya Ukrainka*, NY: Bookman Associates, 1950. Also *Forest Song* (7f,8m+) tr. Virlana Tkacz & Wanda Phipps, 1993, MS from Yara Arts Group.

Judy Upton
British, 1967–

Many of Upton's plays take place in British seaside towns or beaches, places on the edge where she explores relationships on the edge, where language runs out and is replaced by violence. As Upton says in the afterword to *Ashes and Sand* (1994 winner of the George Devine New Writing Award), the rage and frustration of the girl gang she depicts was a reflection of her own anger 'for myself and my friends, dragged kicking and screaming through a hell-hole of a comprehensive school to end up living lives that fell well short of our dreams'.

In other plays violence is compulsively repeated across generations or becomes the cement of relationships that should have ended years before. *Bruises* won the 1994 Verity Bargate Award and critical acclaim for its shocking exploration of the entrapment of a father and son who run a Worthing bed-and-breakfast. A cycle of casual battery is extended to their frighteningly docile women friends, seduced by the neediness of men who claim they can't explain their actions. Less successful is the rather mannered triangular relationship of *The Shorewatcher's House*, although the bleakness of its contaminated landscape in the shadow of a nuclear power station becomes an apt image for sterile lives.

Plays include: *Sunspots* (MS, 1996); *Temple* (MS, 1995); *People on the River* (MS, 1997); *To Blusher with Love* (MS, 1997); *Confidence* (MS, 1998); *Know Your Rights* (MS, 1998); *The Girlz* (1998); *Ashes and Sand* (4f,3m,id, 1994) in Edwardes 3; *Bruises* (2f,2m, 1995) with *The Shorewatcher's House* (2f,2m, 1995) Methuen, 1996; *Everlasting Rose* (1f,2m, 1992) in Setren.
See also App. 2: Sierz.

Barbara Vernon
Australian, 1916–78

Born in Inverell, NSW, Vernon worked as a radio announcer and ran an amateur theatre group, later moving to ABC's radio drama department. Several plays focus on the lively Donnelly family, newly middle-class bookmakers. They feature in the trilogy *The Growing Year* and the prize-winning *Multi-Coloured Umbrella*, which dissects social and marital tensions between their inhibited sophisticated daughter-in-law and the rest of the family. Vernon's TV series about ordinary lives in a small country town, *A Big Day at Bellbird* (1971), was a long-running popular success.

Plays include: *Dusty Frangipani*; *Enough to Make a Pair of Sailor's Trousers*; *The Questing Heart* (all MS); *The Passionate Pianist* (1f,4m 1957) in Duncan 1958; *The Multi-Coloured Umbrella* (3f,3m) in *Theatregoer* Feb.–Apr. 1961; *King Tide Running* (with Bruce Beaver, 2f,3m) in Horner, 1967.
See also App. 2: Rees.

Anca Visdei
Romanian, 1954–

Visdei studied theatre and wrote her first play in Bucharest before emigrating at 19 to Switzerland, where she began writing in French, translating her work into her native Romanian. *Always Together* movingly reflects the experience of exile and loss of identity, structured as a series of letters exchanged between the sister who left and the one who stayed behind under the communist regime.

Untranslated plays include: *Atroce fin d'un séducteur* (1985); *Dona Juana* (1987); *Femme-Sujet* (1990).

Translated plays include: *Always Together* (2f, 1994) tr. Stephen J. Vogel; Montreuil: La Femme Pressée (bilingual edition), 1997 and in Ubu 3.

Paula Vogel
American, 1951–

One of the most inventive contemporary American playwrights, Vogel has both, as a critic has said, 'a gift for sustaining humour and pathos ... without trivializing either emotion' and an ability to deal with disturbing issues such as paedophilia (*How I Learnt to Drive*) or sexual violence, with compassion and complexity.

Her best-known play, *The Baltimore Waltz*, explores the alienation of medical language and the poignancy of loss. Written as a tribute to her brother, Carl, who died of AIDS, it is a surreal fantasy of a trip across Europe, taken by brother and sister, in which she becomes the one sick – with ATD, 'Acquired Toilet Disease', a plague striking down single schoolteachers across the country. In the both wildly comic and deeply disturbing *And Baby Makes Seven*, Ruth, heavily pregnant Anna and Peter share a flat and enact the lives, deaths and resurrection of their imaginary children – a wild child raised by wolves, an eight-year-old philosopher and a French boy who believes he is the protagonist of the film *The Red Balloon*.

Vogel's plays use filmic devices such as *Desdemona*'s 30 cinematic 'takes' or intercut voice-overs, or make re-takes on familiar themes. Like the protagonist of *Hot 'n' Throbbing*, they attempt to rewrite established narratives. She scripts women's 'erotic' films, a job that seems to offer economic and sexual control. But her version of events is contradicted by the onstage horror movie her husband wants to enact, in which, as a woman, she is inevitably cast as victim.

Plays include: *The Baltimore Waltz* (1f,2m, 1990) in Osborn, 1990 and in Goodman and Smith, 1992 and in Lake and Shergold; *Hot 'n' Throbbing* (3f,3m, 1993) in Smith 1994; *Desdemona* (3f, 1993) in Curb and in Fischlin and Fortier; *The Oldest Profession* (5f, 1981); *And Baby Makes Seven* (2f,1m, 1984) – all TCG, 1996;

The Mineola Twins: a Comedy in Six Scenes, Three Dreams and Five Wigs (1f,1m) in Guare; *How I Learnt to Drive*, (3f,2m, 1996) DPS, 1997 – both in *The Mammary Plays*, TCG, 1998.

Jane Wagner
American, 1935–

Born Morristown, TN, Wagner is a director and producer/co-writer with her partner, comedienne Lily Tomlin, of many of Tomlin's shows and films. *The Search for Signs of Intelligent Life . . .* was a Broadway success that addressed feminist issues in a form at once accessible and uncompromising . Tomlin's celebrated virtuoso performance introduced Wagner's bag-lady heroine, Trudy, who, drawing on a transformational acting style influenced by **Terry**, becomes a sequence of 12 other characters: punks, feminists, housewives, prostitutes, presented with sympathy, complexity and wit. Trudy, a marginal figure, on the borders of society and its definitions of sanity, believes herself visited by aliens and appointed their 'creative consultant'. Her search for intelligent life discovers some of the myriad possibilities of women's lives, the points of meeting and human connections that link them.

Plays include: *The Search for Signs of Intelligent Life in the Universe* (1f) NY: Harper and Row, 1986; *Appearing Nightly* (with Tomlin, MS, 1977).

Cicely Waite-Smith (Howland)
Jamaican, 1910–78

Canadian by birth, Jamaican by marriage, Waite-Smith was author of at least 11 plays. Her subjects range from the desire to emigrate to the hardship of female domestic workers unable to find work *(Return to Paradise)* or mistreated by employers – Bertice in *The Impossible Situation* is the object of abuse from her light-skinned employer because of her darker colour. She draws on a range of Caribbean linguistic styles including patois and, in *Africa Slingshot*, the ritual story-telling and drumming of a Stranger who entrances the villagers with dreams of Africa before being revealed as an escaped prisoner and recaptured.

Plays include: *Grandfather is Dying* (1943) in *Focus Jamaica* 1943, ed. Manley;

Uncle Robert (8f, 11m, 1967); *Africa Slingshot* (2f,8m+, 1958) also in Lee Wah; *The Creatures* (6f,5m+, 1966); *The Impossible Situation* (2f,1m, 1966); *Return to Paradise* (3f,1m, 1966) – all Caribbean Plays Series, Trinidad and Tobago: University of West Indies Extra-Mural Dept.

See also: *The Theatrical into Theatre* by Kole Omotoso, London: New Beacon, 1982; *The Long Run* (autobiography), 1967.

Naomi Wallace
American, 1960–

Kentucky-born Wallace's major works have been produced in Britain, a situation she sees as reflecting the lack of a tradition for political theatre in the USA. Her work addresses the politics of desire and, in particular, relationships between men, especially in wartime. In *The War Boys* she explored the dynamics of macho power games as three young men, members of a para-military organization, watch for illegal immigrants on the Texas/Mexico border. *In the Heart of America*, which won the Susan Smith Blackburn Award, focused on the Gulf War: a vow of love between two men is made 'while chanting a litany of the hi-tech weapons of mass destruction ... [its] effect both appalling and erotic ... a reminder of how far the language of love has been appropriated by the language of war', wrote one critic. Her acclaimed and imaginative adaptation of Wharton's *Birdy* splits the roles of friends Birdy and Al between their younger selves and the damaged men who have undergone the dehumanizing process of war. *One Flea Spare*, set in a house in the plague-stricken London of 1665, explores a society in extremis, the sexuality, suffering and tenderness between human bodies, while, in *Slaughter City*, the butchery of animal bodies become a metaphor for that of human lives in a piece about the exploitation and plunder of bodily labour.

Plays include: *The War Boys* (MS, 1993); *In the Heart of America* (1f,4m, 1994) in AT, Mar. 1995 and *Staging Gay Lives* ed. John M. Clum, NY: Westview, 1996; *The Girl Who Fell Through a Hole in Her Jumper* (with Bruce McLeod, 1f,2m,3f/m, 1995) in Goldsworthy; *In the Sweat* (with Mcleod, 1f,2m,3f/m, 1995); *One Flea Spare* (2f,3m, 1995) BPP, 1997 and in Dromgoole; *Slaughter City* (3f,5m, 1996); *Birdy* (6m) based on the novel by William Wharton, 1997, both Faber; *Lawn Dogs* (screen, 1997); *In the Fields Aceldama* (2f, 1m, 1993) in Setren.

See also: *Guardian*, 24 Jan. 1996; App. 2: Stephenson and Langridge, Sierz.

Michelene Wandor

British, 1940–

The first historian of the post-1970 women's movement in British theatre, Wandor was also its first anthologist, editing volumes of scripts and
devised work, particularly the Methuen *Plays by Women* volumes 1–4.
Influentially she suggested (in *Drama*, Summer 1984) that feminist
theatre is of three types – bourgeois, socialist or radical, depending on
the play's assumptions made and conclusions drawn about the nature of
the problems facing women and the strategies for change proposed. Her
own work, informed by a socialist feminist perspective, encompasses
original plays scripting from a company devising process and numerous
adaptations for radio and stage, including Eugene Sue's *Wandering Jew*
for Shared Experience and Elizabeth Barrett Browning's verse-novel
about the making of a woman writer, *Aurora Leigh*, for WTG.

Wandor's plays combine feminist exploration of 'issues', including
beauty contests, prostitution, marriage, with a range of forms from naturalism and domestic comedy to satire and allegorical fable. She incorporates poetry, startling and surreal images: two prostitutes floating
down the Thames on a raft, or biblical figures – angels, Mary and Joseph
or, in the dialogue sequence of poems *Gardens of Eden* (1990), Eve and
Lilith. Several plays (*Wanted, Aid Thy Neighbour, Care and Control* – see
Gay Sweatshop) address women's desire to have babies, surrogacy, the
role of medical technology and societal attitudes to 'correct' and 'incorrect' contexts and methods of female reproduction.

Plays include: *Aurora Leigh* (4f,1m, 1979) in Wandor 1; *To Die Among Friends*
(4f,2m,1d, 1973 and in *Sinksongs*), *Whores D'Oeuvres* (2f, 1978), *Scissors* (2f,3m,
1978), *Aid Thy Neighbour* (7f,1m,dp, 1978), *The Old Wives Tale* (4f, 1977) in *Five
Plays* London: Journeyman/Playbooks, 1984; *Wanted* (2f,1m) London: Play-
books, 1988; *The Wandering Jew* (with Mike Alfreds, 6f, 10m,1d) Methuen, 1987.
See also App. 2: Wandor 1981 and 1987; Reinelt in Hart; Betsko and Koenig.

Mercy Otis Warren

American, 1728–1814

Married to one key participant of the American Revolution, sister of
another, close friend of two more (John and Abigail Adams), Warren made
her home a centre of literary and political debate. She became the historian

of the Revolution while her satirical plays, published as pamphlets, mocked the absurdities of British rule and lampooned its leaders. She reserved her bitterest satire for wealthy and aristocratic American Tories who continued to support the British against the elected assembly of the colony. Figures such as Governor Thomas Hutchinson appear thinly disguised as Rapatio alongside Sir Sparrow Spendall and Scriblerius Fribble. Warren's fervid indignation at tyranny fuels fierce political speeches, celebrating the heroic idealism of freedom-loving colonial patriots given Roman names like Brutus and Cassius and drawn from Adams, her brother and other real figures. Tyrannical government is linked to oppression of women through characters like the wife-beater, Brigadier Hateall, in *The Group*.

The authorship of some plays (*The Blockheads* and *The Defeat*) remains disputed: most were published anonymously, most probably unperformed. Warren, like her Boston Puritan society, expressed ambivalence about the stage, though *The Group* was acted and she later sought production for one of her verse tragedies. They centre on forceful, complex and morally ambiguous female characters such as Edoxia in *The Sack of Rome* who, fiercely loyal to her husband, refuses to be transferred to his conqueror, despite the danger this presents to the country's security.

Plays: (all Boston unless marked) *The Blockheads* or *The Affrighted Officers* (3f, 10m 1776) in Philbrick; *The Defeat* (12m, 1773); *The Adulateur* (14m+, 1773) and in NY: *Magazine of History*, 1905; *The Group* (16m, 1775) and in Moses VI, in Rogers and in Kritzer; *The Ladies of Castille* (2f,6m) and *The Sack of Rome* (3f,9m) in *Poems Dramatic and Miscellaneous*, Boston: I. Thomas and E. T. Andrews, 1790; *The Motley Assembly* (9f,6m, 1779) and in Philbrick. All in *The Plays and Poems of Mercy Otis Warren*, NY: Scholars Facsimile, 1980.

See also: *First Lady of the Revolution* by Katherine S. Anthony, Garden City, NY: Doubleday, 1958 (rpr 1972); Baym in *South Atlantic Quarterly*, Summer 1991; App. 1: Philbrick; App. 2: Kern in Schofield and Macheski.

Wendy Wasserstein
American, 1950–

Laced with contemporary songs, jokes, cliquey allusions and acerbic *bons mots*, Wasserstein's plays wittily chart the progress of educated middle-class women in the wake of the women's movement. *Uncommon Women and Others* stages the reunion of five graduates of a women's college six years on, as they reminisce on the misdeeds of their youth and share their subsequent experiences. Another reunion is at the heart of *The Sisters Rosensweig*, bringing together, with a nod towards Chekhov, three sisters: an itinerant travel writer, a housewife turned radio phone-in shrink, and the eldest, a wealthy divorced banker. Meeting at the latter's London home, together with her daughter and various attached men, they compare the state of their lives, loves or the lack of them, aspirations and relationship to their Jewishness.

In 1989 *The Heidi Chronicles* won a Tony Award, the Pulitzer Prize for Drama and the Susan Smith Blackburn Award. The most poignant and candid of Wasserstein's works to date, it is a comedy that surveys two decades of social change through the eyes of a woman art historian and her circle of friends. It charts the struggles, compromises, pain and achievements of a generation, trying to do it all, have fulfilling careers, maintain political commitment and, maybe, impossibly, even find love, have babies, achieve happiness. Wasserstein has also written a collection of witty essays on similar themes: *Bachelor Girls* (1990).

Plays include: *Uncommon Women and Others* (9f, 1975) NY: Avon, 1978 and with *Isn't it Romantic?* (4f,5m, 1981); *The Heidi Chronicles* (5f,3m, 1988) in *The Heidi Chronicles and Other Plays*, Penguin, 1990; *Tender Offer* (1f,1m) in Halpern; *Antonia and Jane* (5f,6m) in Guare; *The Sisters Rosensweig* (4f,4m) NY: Harcourt, Brace and Co., 1993; *Workout* (1f, 1995) in Frank.

See also: Cohen in Women's Studies 15 1988; App. 2: Carlson in Schlueter; Keyssar ed.; Betsko and Koenig; Giociola, 1998.

Maurine Watkins
American, 1900–68

Watkins is the often-forgotten woman behind the celebrated musical *Chicago*, the fame of which has overshadowed the success of Watkins's original play on which it was based. A romping, melodramatic satire, it centres on a gold-digging wife who has killed her husband, and presents a picture of a justice system mired in corruption. With rival murderesses competing for prominence and to get their story in the papers, Watkins mocks a newspaper industry readily manipulated by theatrics and willing to see women as wronged victims and suffering madonnas.

Plays include: *Chicago* (8f, 18m) NY: Knopf, 1926; *Gesture* (MS, 1926); *Strictly Dynamite*; *Professional Sweetheart*; *No Man of Her Own*; *Play Girl*; *Doctor Wives* (all screen). See also App. 2: Shafer.

Fay Weldon

English, 1931–

Best known as a novelist, Weldon has punctuated her career with plays for stage, radio and for television – numerous original works from *The Fat Woman's Tale* (1966) onwards, plus adaptations of novels, including **Austen**, Elizabeth Bowen and her own *Lives and Loves of a She-Devil*. Sharply observant comedies of social and marital interactions, Weldon's juxtapositions of different households – such as those of mother and daughter in *Moving House* (MS, 1978) – point up differences, subtle alterations and repetitions of behaviour. In *Action Replay* she uses the constant replay of variant actions to investigate changes in the developing relationships between each of three couples over twenty-five years, while *I Love My Love* uses the device of a life- (and eventually husband-) swap between whizz-kid advertising executive Cat and country bumpkin Ann to explore contemporary social and sexual mores. Environmental issues are central to the youth opera *A Small Green Space*, about the defence of derelict land gone wild in the inner city. *Hole in the Top of the World* draws parallels between scientific pragmatism in its relation to the exploitation of the planet and of other people in human relationships.

Plays include: *I Love My Love* (3f,2m, 1981); *Action Replay* (3f,3m, 1979); *Word of Advice* (4f,2m, 1974) French; *Polaris* (3f,7m,id) in BBC, 1978; *A Small Green Space* (3f,2m,2f/m+chorus, libretto) in *Storia* 4, 1990, *Mr Director* (MS, 1977); *The Hole in the Top of the World*; *Friends* (MS, 1984); *Woodworm* (MS, 1984); *The Four Alice Bakers* (MS, 1999).

Vivienne Wellburn

English, 1941–

Wellburn's plays encapsulate a youth culture of frustration, search, fantasy, sexual desire and rebellion in a style distinctly of their 1960s era. Playful, intermittently disturbing, self-reflective – characters are always aware of their theatricality. *The Drag* was Wellburn's early attempt (in 1962) to write a feminist play. Opening with the rape of its central character, it traces her disintegration, attempt to find self and freedom and gradual entrapment by social confines, literalized in the image of a cage of metal frames that finally closes around her. It was unusual for its time and among Wellburn's work, in which most protagonists in search of life's meaning and direction are, more conventionally, male. Sammy in *The Treadwheel* is a young northerner, an illegitimate child who leaves home on a ritualized journey from innocence to experience through encounters with first love, London sophisticates, sinister gangland types, the death of his stepfather and finally with his own inadequacies. The real hero of *Johnny So Long* never appears – only his adolescent acolytes, paralysed in indecisiveness, unable to go to the symbolically weighted fair without him. They fill the space with rituals, games, stylized exchanges and story-telling, characteristic features of all Wellburn's plays.

Plays include: *Clearway* (2f,4m, 1967); *Johnny So Long* (3f,3m, 1967) and *The Drag* (9f, 15m,+8,dp, 1967); *The Treadwheel* (8f, 13m,dp, 1975) and *Coil Without Dreams* (2f,2m, 1975). All Calder & Boyars.

Timberlake Wertenbaker
American/French, 20th century

Multi-lingual and multi-cultural, Wertenbaker grew up in the French Basque country, studied in England and New York, taught in Greece and is a successful translator of Sophocles, Marivaux, Anouilh, Maeterlinck and Ariane **Mnouchkine**'s *Mephisto* and adaptor (a grim Brothers Grimm in *The Ash Girl*). Her plays are highly intelligent, complex and feminist interrogations of history and literary convention.

New Anatomies explores the life of Isabelle Eberhardt, the rebellious female explorer who dressed in men's clothing, and of her music-hall counterpart, Vesta Tilley. Wertenbaker's first major success was *The Grace of Mary Traverse*, a picaresque play that traces its heroine's passage from innocence to experience in an eighteenth-century London of political intrigue and sexual dissipation. A traditional landscape for a male character's search for self is here explored to discover the possibilities for knowledge and wisdom it might offer a woman. *The Love of the Nightingale* uses the myth of Philomel and Procne to focus on the silencing of women in history but was less successful in allowing ideas to arise out of the action, instead giving them direct expression through a chorus. The highly successful *Our Country's Good* adapted Thomas Keneally's novel *The Playmaker* to brilliantly theatrical effect, addressing issues of the use and redemptive possibilities of drama through the story of the first performance of a play in colonial Australia, when a young lieutenant directs the convicts in Farquhar's *The Recruiting Officer*.

More recently, Wertenbaker has focused directly on contemporary Britain. *Three Birds* is a satire on the contemporary art market and the ethical bankruptcy of Eighties values. *The Break of Day*, a rewriting of Chekhov's *The Three Sisters*, interrogates the visions and hopes of women who had struggled for careers and feminism, now trying both to conceive children and conceive of futures to aspire to at the end of a century, under a moribund government and in a climate of moral and political sterility.

Plays include: *The Third* (MS, 1980); *New Anatomies* (5f,id) in *Plays Introduction* Faber, 1984; *Abel's Sister* (with Yvonne Bourcier, MS, 1984); *The Grace of Mary Traverse* (3f,5m+, 1985); *The Love of the Nightingale* (8f,8m,id, 1988); *Three Birds Alighting on a Field* (5f,4m, 1991) – all in *Plays One*, 1996; *The Break of Day* (5f,8m,id, 1995); *After Darwin* (1f,2m, 1998); *The Ash Girl* (8+f,4+m, 2000); *Credible Witness* (3f,8m, 2001) – all Faber. *Our Country's Good* (4f, 6m,id) Methuen, 1988.

See also: Ritchie in MD 39, 3, 1996; App. 2: Cousin; Davis in Reynolds; Griffiths and Llewellyn-Jones; Stephenson and Langridge; Edgar; Sierz.

Mae West

American, 1892–1980

Actress, novelist and screenwriter, sex symbol and mistress of innuendo, West's career as a playwright has remained little known until recently and her plays only available in manuscript. Despite being melodramatic, raggedly plotted and sensationalist, West's plays are nevertheless fascinating both in their spirited defence of socially unacceptable and deviant sexualities and their picture of gay sub-cultures in the 1920s. Margy, her prostitute heroine in *Sex*, is not only allowed to win love and marriage (with her loyal lieutenant, if not her young millionaire lover) but to castigate the latter's mother for hypocrisy, condemning her for choosing to engage in sordid sex where Margy and her like are forced into it for economic reasons. The judge in *The Drag* condemns homosexuality as degenerate until forced to realize that his son was killed by his gay lover. Both it and *The Pleasure Man* present a world of camp drag queens, preening, bitchy and very funny, while not shying away from the dangers and persecution of a homophobic world. West exploited audience voyeurism, offering the frisson of a peek into underworlds usually hidden from mainstream spectators. She also conducted a spirited defence of her work against a legal system determined to censor her for presenting 'obscene, indecent, immoral and impure' performances, gaining fines but also increased notoriety and box-office takings in the process.

Plays include: *Sex* (6f, 15m, 1926); *The Drag* (4f, 13m+, 1927); *The Pleasure Man* (17f,28m, 1928) ed. Lillian Schlissel, NHB, 1997; *The Hussy* (MS, 1922); *Diamond Lil* (MS, 1928); *The Constant Sinner* (MS, 1931).

See also: *The Queen of Camp* by Marybeth Hamilton London/NY: Harper-Collins, 1996; App. 2: Curtin.

Valerie Windsor
   English, 1946–

Windsor trained as an actress, worked as a teacher and began writing for radio, for which she won several awards for plays such as *Myths and Legacies*, exploring the conflict between two brothers, artist and industrialist, and the values they espouse in an increasingly materialist, repressive Edwardian world.

Windsor's first stage piece, *Effie's Burning*, movingly charts the developing relationship between a 64-year-old woman admitted to hospital with extensive burns and her doctor, insecure and patronized by the senior surgeon. The woman, Effie (short for 'effin' brat'), was committed to mental hospital at 13 for being 'morally defective' following a series of sexual assaults and pregnancy. Released into the community after decades of incarceration, due to the latest cost-saving change in government policy, Effie attributes the fires that start in her wake to spontaneous combustion. Critics praised the 'density, discipline and graphic power' Windsor brought from her radio experience. Windsor also writes for the TV soap *Brookside*.

Plays include: *Myths and Legacies* (4f,7m) in BBC Radio, 1986; *Variations on a Snow Queen* (radio); *Effie's Burning* (2f) in Remnant 7; *Twopence to Cross the Mersey* (from Helen Forrester, 14f, 15m+,dp) London: Collins Educational, 1987.

Christa Winsloe
   German, 1888–1944

Born in Darmstadt into a military family, Winsloe was educated at the Potsdam School under the kind of strict, repressive regime she presents in her best-known play. During the war she and her lover Simone Gentet worked for the Resistance in southern France; they were murdered by fascists in 1944. Famously filmed in 1931 as *Mädchen in Uniform*, Winsloe's play presents a school run on military lines, spartan and heartless, dedicated to stamping out all expression of individuality and producing mothers of soldiers for a Prussia about to rise again from the ashes of defeat. For a new student, the sensitive, motherless Manuela, the schoolmistress dedicated, just, sympathetic, Fräulein von Bernberg, becomes a heroine but when in a fervour of love Manuela announces her feelings to the world, the implacable headmistress is determined to crush such dangerous emotions. Winsloe's play is both a mirror of the operation of fascism and an exploration of youthful lesbian passion. In later plays she also explores 'deviant' gender and sexuality, as in *Aiono*, in which the heroine lives her life in drag.

Untranslated plays include: *Aiono* (1943).

Translated plays: *Children in Uniform* (29f) in Famous 1932–3 and French, 1933. See also App. 2: Curtin.

Jane Wiseman
British, 18th century

One of the few early British women playwrights of working-class origins, Wiseman appears to have been a servant in the family of the Oxford Recorder. Allowed access to his library, she read widely and probably also saw plays, as she knew Susannah **Centlivre** and George Farquhar. Her own play, *Antiochus the Great* (1701), is a moving, poetic tragedy focusing on Leodice, Antiochus' cast-off mistress and mother of his child, and his new wife, Berenice, forcibly married to him by her father for political reasons. Wiseman presents both women with great sympathy: Berenice, separated from the man she loves, and the Egyptian (and therefore, it is suggested, black) Leodice, driven by the wish for revenge on the white rival who has supplanted her.

Play: *Antiochus the Great* (5f,6m+) London: n.p., 1702 and in Kendal.

Women's Theatre Group (The Sphinx)
Founded Britain, 1974, renamed 1991

The earliest surviving feminist theatre company of the post-1970 women's movement (it now operates as The Sphinx), WTG's first shows were group devised, but later they commissioned individual writers or worked jointly with them. Early plays were deliberately educational, aimed at raising awareness of women's oppression. *My Mother Said*, on sex, contraception, abortion, toured to schools and youth clubs. *Double Vision*, devised through the tensions of collaborative workshops, explored a lesbian relationship between two women from different class backgrounds, from meeting to break-up and eventual friendship. *Time Pieces*, tracing 'ordinary' women's histories through the twentieth century – wars, suffrage agitation, strikes, etc. – aimed to attract an audience across generations. Later plays became more subtle, individual and complex, reflecting a movement excavating more deeply the contradictions of women's experience.

Griffin and Aston's *Herstories* volumes collect plays re-examining history and myth from feminist perspectives, including plays by Julie Wilkinson (the Crusades), Joyce Holliday (Second World War women aviators), **Lavery**, Elizabeth Bond (Alexandra Kollontai and the Russian Revolution) and Tierl Thompson and Libby Mason (women's friendship in 1897). *Lear's Daughters* deconstructs Shakespeare's play, going beyond the women's division into bad and good daughters to explore choices in their relationships to patriarchy and their own access to power. Other WTG-commissioned writers include **Pinnock**, **Levy** and **Wertenbaker**.

Plays include: *My Mother Said I Never Should* (with **Wandor**, 7f, 1975) in *Strike While the Iron is Hot* London: Journeyman, 1980; *Double Vision* (with Libby Mason,3f, 1982) in Davis 1; *Time Pieces* (with Lou Wakefield, 7f, 1982) in Wandor 3; *Lear's Daughters* (with Elaine Feinstein, 5f, 1987) in Griffin and Aston 1 and ext. in Goodman 2000 and in Fischlin and Forker.

See also App. 2: Itzin; Wandor; Griffiths and Llewellyn-Jones; Reinelt in Case ed.; Sierz.

Elizabeth Wong
American, 1958–

Born in Los Angeles, Wong's plays explore the experience of Chinese-American women, issues of identity, the experience of racial prejudice, personal and family history. *Letters* was written in commemoration of the Tiananmen Square massacre, structured as an exchange of letters between a Chinese woman and her American friend, a communication across the barriers of mutual cultural incomprehension. A chorus comments on the action and plays small roles. *China Doll* is the caustic monologue of a 1940s

Chinese-American actress, reminiscing on her struggles to become an actress and on movie fantasies of Asian women as she acidly coaches the white American woman who is to play the first sympathetic Asian part in the movies. She instructs her in the proper manner to play 'B' movie temptress, Oriental seductress and the necessary swooning death scene – a Chinese woman is allowed to love the white hero provided she conveniently dies.

Plays include: *Assume the Position* in *Script Magazine*, NYU, 1990; *Letters to a Student Revolutionary* (3f,3m,id, 1989) in Uno and in Lamont; *China Doll* (1f, 1990) in Perkins and Uno; *Kimchee and Chitlins* (4f,5m,id, 1990) in Houston, 1997.

Ellen (Mrs Henry) Wood
English, 1814–87

'Dead! dead! And never called me mother!' intones the anti-heroine of Wood's *East Lynne*, at least in the popular stage version which, like **Braddon**'s and **Stowe**'s bestsellers, became even more popular than the novel. Mrs Henry Wood, née Ellen Price, was immensely successful with her sentimental novels preaching gospels of religious stoicism, domestic morality and temperance. With 16 stage versions (only two of which are listed below) appearing before 1900 in Britain alone, the popularity of *East Lynne* reflects the nineteenth-century fascination with the fallen woman. Still sometimes produced on the amateur stage, its central character is Lady Isobel who, having eloped with her lover, deserts her family but, tortured by remorse, returns to East Lynne disguised as governess to her own children.

Play: *East Lynne*: a melodrama (7f,8m, c.1883) in *British Plays of the Nineteenth Century* ed. J. O. Bailey, NY: The Odyssey Press, 1966 and adapted by T. Palmer (1874), in Scullion.

Victoria Wood
English, 1953–

The most popular British woman comedian, whose television specials attract enormous audiences, Wood's brilliance lies in her piquant character observation, linguistic verve, caustic songs and affectionate satire on suburban pretensions, male vanity and her native north of England, among other topics.

Her career was first launched by the success of her stage plays, exploring the margins of the entertainment world, loneliness, friendships between women, everyday betrayal and despondency. *Talent* is set in a northern club where the heroine, an aspiring singer, dreams of escape from a dull marriage and boring office job through winning the talent contest, but discovers the outcome's been rigged. Laced with Wood's usual hilarious one-liners, it is punctuated with songs (accompanied by fat and frumpy pianist, Maureen, a typically strong female role originally played by Wood herself) and describes a world of mundane desperation and circumscribed futures. *Good Fun* takes place in a community arts centre as its gullible do-gooding misused administrator attempts to deploy a motley crew of entertainers to organize a party for cystitis sufferers. Wood's sardonic humour combines with finely developed parts for women.

TV scripts include: *Up to You Porky* (1985); *Lucky Bag: the Victoria Wood Songbook* (1984); *Mens Sana in Thingummy Doodah* (1990); *Chunky* (1996).

Plays include: *Talent* (2f,4m, 1978); *Good Fun* (5f,4m, 1980); *Pat and Margaret* (TV) in *Plays One* (1998) – all Methuen; *Nearly a Happy Ending* (TV, MS).
   See also App. 2: Banks and Swift.

Virginia Woolf
English, 1882–1941

Woolf's novels have several times been adapted for stage and screen, especially *Orlando*, its themes of shifting gender and identity lending themselves to performance. Most famous is the film by Sally Potter (1993), but it has also been scripted by Robert Wilson and Darryl Pinckney and by Angela **Carter**. *The Waves* was performed in Paris and *To the Lighthouse* has been filmed.
   Woolf and her circle enjoyed dressing up and playing roles, on one occasion publicly masquerading as an Abyssinian delegation, and they regularly staged skits and amateur theatricals, ranging from the classical to the 'sublimely obscene'. *Freshwater* was written for such a performance by Bloomsbury friends. Set at the home of Woolf's great-aunt, the notable photographer Julia Margaret Cameron, the whimsical piece fields a cast of great Victorian artistic luminaries and eccentrics, including Tennyson, George Frederick Watts and his 16-year-old wife, Ellen Terry, who feeds her wedding ring to a porpoise and elopes with a handsome lieutenant.

Play: *Freshwater* (5f,4m, 1923) San Diego/NY: Harcourt, Brace, Jovanovitch, 1976. See also App. 2: Sierz.

Frances Wright (D'Arusmont)
Scottish/American, 1795–1852

Born in Dundee into a radical family, Wright emigrated to America where she was converted to Owenite socialism and established a community of freed slaves. In 1825 she married a physician, William D'Arusmont, but continued to make extensive lecture tours speaking against slavery and religious authority and in favour of female suffrage and marriage based on 'mutual inclination'.

Her only surviving play, *Altorf*, dates from her first US visit and the preface praises America's democracy and freedom from stage censorship as fertile ground for a revival of the drama. The play uses the history of a fourteenth-century insurrection of Swiss peasants to condemn both tyrannical regimes and patriarchal authority. Wright explores the personal costs of such political convictions as the hero, Altorf, a leader in the Swiss army, is forced for strategic reasons into a marriage with the sister of a military ally despite his former betrothal to the woman he loves. Skilfully plotted, the play presents the conflicts of love, duty and political commitment with enormous sympathy, and develops complex characters in the 'melancholy, visionary and enthusiastic' hero and both his resolute wife, Giovanna, and resourceful lover, Rosina.

Play: *Altorf: a tragedy* (2f,4m) Philadelphia: M. Carey & Son, 1819 and in Kritzer.

Hella Wuolijoki
Finnish, 1886–1954

Estonian-born, Finnish-educated Wuolijoki was inheritor of a long-standing Finnish tradition of major women dramatists that includes Minna Canth and Maria Jotuni. She wrote 23 plays in all, many focusing on strong, independent, questioning women. She was also a political radical, her later work influenced by Brecht, whom she sheltered on her country estate during the early 1940s and with whom she collaborated on *Mr Puntila and His Man Matti*. She also providing its source narrative in her play

The Sawdust Princess (1940), a debt he rarely acknowledged.

Her first success came with *The Women of Niskavuari*, a cycle of five naturalistic folk plays set in her beloved Finnish countryside. *Hulda Juuraako* (1937) combines romance and realism in tracing the progress of a vivacious young country girl, jokingly taken up as a representative of the people by a group of MPs who treat her as a social demographic to be saved from the statistical danger of ending up a prostitute. Hulda has her own ideas and, working as parlourmaid for one of them, struggles to get an education and become a socialist party representative on behalf on her people. *Law and Order* (1933) explores the 1917–18 Finnish Civil War from the perspective of an idealistic socialist congresswoman whose rejection of violence makes her suspect by both Reds and Whites.

Untranslated plays include: *Justina* (1937); *Women and Masks* (1937); *Green Gold* (1938).

Unpublished translations include: *Women of Property* (adapted, Frank Davison, MS, LCP 1937).

Published translations: *Hulda Juuraako* (8f,8m, 1937) tr. Ritva Poom in K. Kelly; *Mr Puntila and His Man Matti* (8f, 13m+, 1951) with Bertolt Brecht tr. John Willett, Methuen, 1987; *Law and Order* (4f, 13m, 1933) tr. Marja and Steve Wilmer in Wilmer.
    See also: introductions to published editions.

Olwen Wymark
American, 1932–

California-born Wymark moved to Britain on her marriage in 1951. Prolific in output, her work covers a wide range of styles including numerous original plays and adaptations for stage, television and radio, including **Rame** and Zola's *Nana*. Victimization, manipulation and imprisonment are frequent themes and the figures of interrogators, 'technicians' or the Examiner of *Jack the Giant Killer* are a presence throughout Wymark's career. In early pieces such as *Stay Where You Are*, in which Ellen becomes the butt of a series of games designed to shake her out of her restrained politeness into authentic emotion, the collusion of the victim in their own abuse as a means of evading responsibility is central. In later works like *The Twenty-Second Day*, differences between controlling friend and well-meaning foe are blurred and apparent reality melds into disturbing fantasy, a technique used, less malevolently, in *Best Friends*, in which playwright Baba's fictional characters intrude on her life. Incarceration, both within madness and within mental institutions, is also central to *Find Me*, as understanding of Verity's illness eludes family, psychiatric professionals and herself, imaged by the splitting of her role among five performers. In *Brezhnev's Children* seven women, quarantined and separated from their babies in a post-natal ward, eventually rebel against their confinement by a hostile system.

Plays include: *Lunchtime Concert* (1f,1m); *Coda* (2f,1m); *The Inhabitants* (1f,2m +1, 1967); *The Gymnasium* (2m, 1967); *The Technicians* (4m, 1969); *Stay Where You Are* (2f,2m, 1969); *Jack the Giant Killer* (1f,3m); *Neither Here nor There* (8f,1m) in *The Gymnasium and Other Plays*, 1971 – both Calder & Boyars; *Find Me* (5f,3m,id, 1977) in Wandor 2; *Buried Treasure* (MS, 1983); *Best Friends* (3f,3m+, 1981); *The Committee* (2f,1m); *The Twenty-Second Day* (2f,2m) Calder, 1984; *The Child* (4f,1m) in BBC Radio, 1979; *The Winners* (8f, 15m) in Robinson; *Brezhnev's Children* (7f,3m, 1992) from Julia Vosnesenskaya's *Woman's Decameron*; *Strike Up the Banns* (3m,3f, 1990) – all French.

Wakako Yamauchi
American, 1924–

Born in Imperial Valley, California, Yamauchi grew up through the Depression, daughter of first-generation immigrant Japanese. Her familiar reality, the family farm and her education, came to a sudden end in 1939 when Japanese-Americans were sent to internment camps. This grim experience, and a sense of anxiety of people striving to fit into an alien society that fails to understand them and may at any point reject them, haunt her plays. These anxieties are often articulated through women, especially adolescent girls. Their borderline position, neither child nor adult, neither wholly Japanese nor American, focuses questions of identity as they explore love, developing sexuality and choices for the future.

In *And the Soul shall Dance*, events are observed through the eyes of young Masako Murata. She sees the clashes between the neighbouring couple, farmer Oka and his wife Emiko, rejected by her family for having sullied herself with a lover and sent out to Oka as a replacement wife after her sister has died. Burdened with an education in Japanese feminine graces, she finds herself exiled in a strange land with an indifferent husband. While she nurses dreams of returning to Japan, her stepdaughter Kiyoko, struggling with American pronunciation, clothes, permed hair, tries desperately to fit in. *12-1-A* is the barrack number assigned to the Tanaka family in a desert internment camp. With new friends and neighbours they try to cope with grim living conditions, lack of freedom and the sense of their betrayal by an America that has taken from them everything they struggled for.

Plays include: *The Memento* (MS, 1984); *What For?* (1992); *And the Soul shall Dance* (4f,2m, 1977) in Berson and in WCP 11/12 and in Madison; *12-1-A* (5f,7m, 1982) and *The Chairman's Wife* (3f,6m, 1990) in Houston; *The Music Lessons* (3f,5m, 1980) in Uno.
    See also App. 2: Arnold in Hart.

Susan Yankowitz
    American, 1941–

Born in New Jersey, Yankowitz's first works grew out of the ferment of collaborative work in 1960s New York. She was one of several writers who worked with the acclaimed experimental Open Theater under the direction of Joe Chaikin to create *Terminal*, an exploration of the rituals and terrors of dying. Yankowitz both wrote text and contributed to structuring a scenario and devising physical and visual images, processes also true of her early individual work such as *Boxes*. This study of the multiple social rituals and interactions of suburban America, each within their separate boxes, where ecstasy must be straitjacketed and birth is a military exercise, is observed by a vagrant outsider. The musical *Slaughterhouse Play* presents a gruesome image of white exploitation of blacks as an abattoir where blacks are castrated and butchered for white consumption, a process which eventually ignites violent reprisal and counter-reprisal in an 'endless loop' of carnage. Later plays, more formally conventional, continue to draw on vivid expressionist devices such as the constant interplay of images and of mythic and contemporary roles in *Alarms*, in which Cassandra becomes a doctor, horrified at environmental contamination and nuclear threat. The linguistic play of *Night Sky* draws parallels between the mysteries of cosmology and those of human communication, as a woman astronomer struggles to recover from aphasia, a piece made in tribute to Chaikin's recovery/rediscovery of language after a stroke.

Plays include: *Rat's Alley* (MS); *The Lamb* (MS); *Terminal* (3c.1f,3m, 1971) in Sainer and in *Three Works by the Open Theatre* NY: Drama Book Specialists, 1974; *Boxes* (6f/m, 1972), in Ballet 11; *The Ha-ha Play* (2f,3m+) in *Scripts* 10, Oct.

1972; *Slaughterhouse Play* (6f,22m+, 1971) in Hoffman 4; *Alarms* (3f,1m, 1986) in *Female Voices*; *Night Sky* (3f,3m, 1991) in Miles 1993; *Phaedra in Delirium* (MS, 1998).

See also App. 2: Betsko and Koenig.

Sheila Yeger
British, 1941–

Bristol-based Yeger's development as a writer paralleled the feminist movement in Britain. Her early work tends towards a rather formulaic feminism, reflecting the politics of 'positive images' of the early 1980s in works such as *Free 'n' Lovely*. Set in the tacky back room of an East London ballroom, the contestants in a beauty contest prepare to go on, desperate to win the chance of escape from unemployment, dead-end jobs or violent husbands. The primary concern of the contests's sponsors, makers of Free 'n' Lovely hair-remover, however, is with sanitizing the public image of a product revealed as carcinogenic.

Later Yeger plays tend to be biographical in subject but mesh their exploration of the lives of women like artist Gwen John and composer Clara Schumann with those of modern women. In *Self Portrait*, set at a retrospective exhibition of John's work, the gallery owner, exhibition organizers and sundry hangers-on double as figures in John's life, mirroring their conflicts, most centrally John's struggle between the demands of love and work. In *Variations* Louise's fascinated pursuit of Schumann is interwoven with her own search for self on a train journey across Europe, haunted by memories of her parents and psychoanalyst, ghosts of earlier lovers, earlier trains – Anna Karenina, Laura from *Brief Encounter*, Marilyn Monroe in *Some Like It Hot*, offering alternative possible versions of her story. A complex psychological investigation, it confronts issues of patriarchal authority, sexual abuse and repression.

Yeger has also written extensively for community plays, including Ann **Jellicoe**'s Colway Theatre Trust.

Plays include: *Ophelia* (MS); *A Quieter Sex* (MS); *Watching Foxes* (MS); *Free 'n' Lovely* (5f,2m) London: Theatre Venture, 1984; *Variations* (5f,2m,id) in Castledine 9; *Self Portrait* (6f,3m+,id) Amber Lane Press, 1990; *A Better Day* (MS, 1992); *Geraniums* (8f, 11m+,dp, 1995) in Goldsworthy.

See also: *The Sound of One Hand Clapping: a Guide to Writing for the Theatre* by Yeger, Amber Lane, 1990; App. 2: Griffiths and Llewellyn-Jones; Cousin.

278

Appendix 1: Anthologies and Series

Addresses of major publishers are given in Appendix 3

Arkin, Marian and Barbara Shollar, *Longman Anthology of World Literature by Women 1875–1975*, NY & London: Longman, 1989

Ballet, Arthur H., *Playwrights For Tomorrow*, Minneapolis: Minnesota UP, 1969 (several vols)

Baraitser, Marion, *Plays by Mediterranean Women*, London: Aurora Metro, 1994

Baraka, Amiri and Amina, *Confirmation: an Anthology of African American Women*, NY: Quill, 1980

Barlow, Judith, *Plays by American Women: the Early Years*, NY: Avon/Bard, 1981 (and Applause, 1988)

Plays by American Women: 1930–60, NY: Applause, 1994

BBC Radio, Best Radio Plays 1978–1989 (*Giles Cooper Award Winners*)

Bell's British Theatre, 34 vols, London: published for George Cawthorn, 1797

Benedikt, Michael, *Theatre Experiment: an Anthology of American Plays*, NY: Anchor/Doubleday, 1968

Benmussa, Simone, *Benmussa Directs*, London: John Calder, 1979

Berson, Misha, *Between Worlds: Contemporary Asian American Plays*, NY: TCG, 1990

Bert, Norman A. *Theatre Alive! an Introductory Anthology of World Drama*, Colorado Springs, CO: Meriwether Publishing, 1995

Bessai, Diane and Don Kerr, *NeWest Plays by Women*, Edmonton: NeWest Press, 1987

Bourne, John, *Seven Short Plays for Amateur Societies*, London: Harrap, 1935

Five New Full-Length Plays for All-Women Casts, London: Lovat Dickson Thompson, 1935

Box, Sydney, *One Act Plays for Players Second Series*, London: George Harrap, 1936

Bradwell, Mike, *The Bush Theatre Book*, London: Methuen, 1997

Branch, William B., *Crosswinds*, Bloomington, IN: Indiana UP, 1993

Branson, Greg, *Australian One-Act Plays Book Two*, Adelaide: Rigby, 1962

Brask, Per, *Drama Contemporary: Scandinavia*, NY: PAJ Publications, 1989

Brennan, Kit, *Going It Alone: Plays by Women for Solo performers*, Winnipeg: Nuage, 1997

Brewster, Yvonne, *Black Plays 1–3*, London: Methuen, 1987–1993

Browne, Martin, *Penguin Plays*, Harmondsworth: Penguin, 1958

New English Dramatists, Harmondsworth: Penguin, 1959 and 1969

Brown-Guillory, Elizabeth, *Wines in the Wilderness: Plays by African American Women from the Harlem Renaissance to the Present*, Westport, CN: Greenwood, 1990

Bullins, Ed, *New Plays from the Black Theatre*, NY: Bantam, 1969

Bullins, Ed, *The New Lafayette Theatre Presents . . .*, NY: Anchor, 1974

Busby, Margaret, *Daughters of Africa*, London: Virago, 1993

Cameron, Alastair, *Scot Free: New Scottish Plays*, London: NHB, 1990

Caribbean Plays Series, Port of Spain: Extra-Mural Dept, University of West Indies, 1966

Case, Sue-Ellen,*The Divided Homeland: Contemporary German Women's Plays*, Ann Arbor: Michigan UP, 1992

Castledine, Annie, *Plays by Women vols 9 and 10*, London: Methuen, 1991

Cerf, Bennett, and Van H. Cartmell, *Sixteen Famous American Plays*, NY: The Modern Library, 1941

S. R. O. the most successful plays of the American stage, Garden City, NY: Doubleday, 1944

Champagne, Lenora, *Out from Under: Texts by Women Performance Artists*, NY: TCG, 1990

Chavez, Denise and Linda Feyder, *Shattering the Myth: Plays by Hispanic Women*, Houston, TX: Arte Publico Press, 1992

Cheek, Cris, *Language Alive 1*, Lowestoft: Sound and Language, 1995

Clark, Barrett H., *Representative One-Act Plays by British and Irish Authors*, Boston: Little Brown and Co., 1921

Clements, Colin Campbell, *Sea Plays*, London: Holden, 1923

Considine, Ann and Robyn Slovo, *Dead Proud: from Second Wave Young Women Playwrights*, London: The Women's Press, 1987

Cook, George Cram and Frank Shay, *The Provincetown Plays*, Cincinnati: Stewart Kidd, 1921

The CTR Anthology (Canadian Theatre Review), Toronto: Toronto UP, 1992

Curb, Rosemary, *Amazon All Stars*, NY: Applause, 1996

Curran, Colleen, *Escape Acts: Seven Canadian One-Acts*, Winnipeg: NuAge Editions, 1992

D'Aponte, Mimi Gisolfi, *Seventh Generation: an Anthology of Native American Plays*, NY: TCG, 1999

Davis, Jill, *Lesbian Plays 1* and *2*, London: Methuen, 1987 and 1989

Dean, Nancy and M. G. Soares, *Intimate Acts: Eight Contemporary Lesbian Plays*, NY: Brito and Lair, 1997

Delgado, Ramon, *The Best Short Plays of the Year*, Garden City, NY: Fireside Theatre, 1981, 1983 and 1984

De Nobrigo, Kathie and Anderson, Valetta, *Alternate Roots: Plays from the Southern Theater*, Portsmouth, NH: Heinemann, 1994

Dickinson, Thomas and Jack Crawford, *Contemporary Plays*, NY: Houghton Mifflin, 1925

Dromgoole, Dominic, *Bush Theatre Plays*, London: Faber, 1996

Duncan, Catherine, *The Derwent Series of One Act Plays*, Hobart: Tasmanian Adult Education Board, 1958

Durband, Alan, *Playbill Two*, London: Hutchinson, 1969

Second Playbill Two, London: Hutchinson, 1973

Edwardes, Pamela, *Frontline Intelligence 1, 2* and *3 – New Plays for the Nineties*, London: Methuen, 1995

Eight Plays by Australians, Melbourne: The Dramatists Club, 1934

Elam, Harry J. and R. A. Alexander, *Colored Contradictions: an Anthology of Contemporary African American Plays*, NY: Plume/Penguin, 1996

Embassy Successes 2 (1945–6), London: Sampson, Marston, Low, 1946

Famous Plays of . . . , London: Victor Gollancz, 1931–9

Famous Plays of Today, London: Victor Gollancz, 1953 and 1954

Female Voices, London: Playwrights' Press, 1987

Fifty One Act Plays, London: Victor Gollancz, 1934

Filewod, Alan, *The CTR Anthology*, Toronto: Toronto UP, 1993 (2 vols)

Filichia, Peter, *New American Plays*, Portsmouth, NH: Heinemann, 1992

Fischlin, Daniel and Mark Fortier, *Adaptations of Shakespeare: a critical anthology of plays from the seventeenth century to the present*, London: Routledge, 2000

Fitzsimmons, Linda and Viv Gardner, *New Woman Plays*, London: Methuen, 1991

Five Plays of 1940, London: Hamilton, 1940

France, Rachel, *A Century of Plays by American Women*, NY: Richard Rosen Press, 1979

Frank, Leah D., *Facing Forward: One-Act Plays and Monologues by Contemporary American Women at the Crest of the 21st Century*, NY: BPP, 1995

Frontline Drama 4: Adapting Classics, London: Methuen, 1996

Fuchs, Elinor, *Plays of the Holocaust: an International Anthology*, NY: TCG, 1987

Further One-Act Plays 1935, Wellington: National Magazines Ltd, 1935

Gardner, Viv, *Sketches from the Actresses Franchise League*, Nottingham: Nottingham Drama Texts, 1985

Garton, Janet and Henning Sehmsdorf, *New Norwegian Plays*, Norwich: Norvik Press, 1989

Gassner, John, *Best American Plays Fifth Series 1957–1963*, NY: Crown, 1963

George, Kadija, *Six Plays by Black and Asian Women Writers*, London: Aurora Metro Publications, 1993

Glenny, Michael, *Stars in the Morning Sky: New Soviet Plays,* London: NHB, 1989

Goldsworthy, Sally, *Young Blood: Five Plays for Young Performers*, London: Aurora Metro, 1997

Goodman, Lizbeth, *Mythic Women/Real Women*, London: Faber, 2000

Goodman, Robyn and Marisa Smith, *Women Playwrights: The Best Plays of 1992* and *1993* Newbury, VT: Smith and Kraus, 1992 and 1994

Grant, David, *The Crack in the Emerald: New Irish Plays*, London: NHB, 1990

Gray, Frances, ed., *Second Wave Plays: Women at the Albany Empire*, Sheffield: Sheffield Academic Press, 1990

Griffin, Gabrielle & Elaine Aston, eds., *Herstory vols. 1 and 2*, Sheffield: Sheffield Academic Press, 1991

Guare, John, *Conjunctions 25: The New American Theater*, Annandale on Hudson: Bard College, 1995

Halpern, Daniel, *Antaeus: Plays in One Act* Spring 1991, NY: The Ecco Press

Hanna, Gillian, *Monstrous Regiment; A Collective Celebration*, London: NHB, 1991

Harwood, Kate, *First Run: New Plays by New Writers*, London: NHB, 1989–91 (3 vols)

Hatch, James and Leo Hamallian *The Roots of African American Drama 1858–1938*, Detroit, MI: Wayne State University, 1991

Hatch, James & T. Shine, *Black Theatre USA: 45 Plays by Black Americans 1847–1945* *Black Theatre USA: The Recent Period 1935–Today*, NY: Free Press, 1996

Hayman, Carole & Dale Spender, *How the Vote was Won & Other Suffragette Plays*, London: Methuen, 1984

Haynes, Jim, *Traverse Plays*, Harmondsworth: Penguin, 1966

Helbing, Terry, *Gay and Lesbian Plays Today*, Portsmouth, NH: Heinemann, 1993

Hill, Philip, *Our Dramatic Heritage vol. 1*, London: Associated University Press, 1983

Hoffman, William, ed., *Gay Plays: the First Collection*, NY: Avon, 1979 *New American Plays vols 1–4*, NY: Hill & Wang, 1968

Horin, Ros, *Passion: Six New Short Plays by Australian Women*, Sydney: Currency Press with Griffin Theatre Co, 1994

Horner, Musgrave, *Australian One-Act Plays Book Three*, Adelaide: Rigby, 1967

Houston, Velina Hasu, *The Politics of Life: Four Plays by Asian American Women*, Philadelphia, NJ: Temple UP, 1993 *But Still, Like Air, I'll Rise: New Asian American Plays*, Philadelphia, NJ: Temple UP, 1997

Huerta, Jorge, *Necessary Theatre: Six Plays about the Chicano Experience*, Houston, TX: Arte Publico Press, 1989

Introduction (Plays), London: Faber, 1984

Jansen, Ann, *Airborne: Radio Plays by Women*, Winnipeg: Blizzard Publishing, 1991 *Adventures for (Big) Girls: Seven Radio Plays*, Winnipeg: Blizzard Publishing, 1993

Jenness, Morgan, John Richardson and Mac Wellman, *Slant Six: New Theater from Minnesota's Playwrights' Center*, Minneapolis: New Rivers Press, 1990

Kelly, Catriona, *An Anthology of Russian Women's Writing*, Oxford: OUP, 1994

Kelly, Katherine, *Modern Drama By Women: an International Anthology*, London: Routledge, 1996

Kendall, *Love and Thunder: Plays by Women in the Age of Queen Anne*, London: Methuen, 1988

Kilgore, Emilie S., *Landmarks of Contemporary Women's Drama*, London: Methuen, 1992

Kilner, Kerry and Sue Tweg, *Playing the Past: Three Plays of Australian Women*, Currency, 1995

King Jr, Woodie, *New Plays for the Black Theatre*, Chicago: Third World Press, 1989

Kohut, George Alexander, *A Hebrew Anthology*, Cincinnati, OH: Bacharach, 1917

Kritzer, Emelia Howe, *Plays by Early American Women 1775–1850*, Ann Arbor, MI: Michigan UP, 1995

Kriegal, Harriet, *Women in Drama*, NY: Mentor, 1975

Lake, Eric and Nina Shergold, *The Actor's Book of Gay and Lesbian Plays*, NY: Penguin, 1995

Lamont, Rosette, *Women on the Verge: Seven Avant Garde American Plays*, NY: Applause, 1992

Lane, Eric, *Telling Tales: New One Act Plays*, NY: Penguin, 1993

Lee Wah, James, *Carray!: a Selection of Plays for Caribbean Schools*, London and Basingstoke: Macmillan Caribbean, 1977

Leverett, James, *New Plays USA 1*, NY: TCG, 1982

Leverett, James and M. Elizabeth Osbourn, *New Plays USA 3*, NY: TCG, 1986

Levy, Deborah, *Walks on Water*, London: Methuen, 1992

Linden, Sonia, *Bottled Notes from Underground*, London: Loki Books, 1998

Louisville, Plays from the Actors Theatre of . . ., NY: BPP, 1989

Lyons, Paddy and Fidelis Morgan, *Female Playwrights of the Restoration*, London: Everyman, 1991

Madison, D. Soyini, *The Woman that I Am: the Literature and Culture of Contemporary Women of Color*, NY: St Martin's Press, 1994

Making Scenes – Short Plays for Young Actors vol 1–3, London: Methuen, 1994

Makward, Christiane and Judith G. Miller, *Plays by French and Francophone Women*, Ann Arbor: Michigan UP, 1994

Mahone, Sydne, *Moon Marked and Touched By Sun: Plays by African American Women*, NY: TCG, 1994

Marranca, Bonnie and Gautam Dasgupta, *Wordplays 1–5: New American Drama*, NY: PAJ, 1982–7

Marranca, Bonnie, *Plays for the End of the Century*, Baltimore, MD and London: PAJ/Johns Hopkins Press, 1997

Marriott, J. W. *One Act Plays of Today: Third Series*, London: Harrap, 1926
   One Act Plays of Today: Fourth Series, London: Harrap, 1928
   The Best One-Act Plays of 1931, London: Harrap, 1932

Martin, Carol, *A Sourcebook of Feminist Theatre and Performance*, London: Routledge, 1996

Martin, Constance M., *Fifty One Act Plays*, London: V. Gollancz, 1934
   Fifty One Act Plays Second Series, London: V. Gollancz, 1940

May-Days Dialogues, The, London: Royal Court Theatre, 1990

McDermott, Kate, *Places Please: the First Anthology of Lesbian Plays*, Iowa City, IO: Aunt Lute Books, 1985

McGuinness, Frank, *The Dazzling Dark: New Irish Plays*, London: Faber, 1996

Mednick, Murray, Bill Raden and Cheryl Slean, *Best of the West*, Claremont, CA: Padua Hills Press, 1991

Miles, Julia, *The Women's Project 1*, NY: PAJ Publications, 1980
   The Women's Project 2, NY: PAJ Publications, 1984
   Women Heroes: Six Short Plays from the Women's Project, NY: Applause, 1987
   Women's Work: 5 New Plays from the Women's Project, NY: Applause, 1989
   Playwriting Women; 7 Plays from the Women's Project, NY: Portsmouth, NH: Heinemann, 1993
   Here to Stay! 5 Plays from the Women's Project, NY: Applause, 1997
Moore, Honor, *The New Women's Theatre*, NY: Vintage, 1977
Moore, W., *Best Australian One Act Plays*, Sydney: Angus and Robertson, 1937
Morgan, Fidelis, *The Female Wits: Women Playwrights of the Restoration*, London: Virago, 1981
   The Years Between: Plays by Women on the London Stage 1900–1950, London: Virago, 1994
Moses, Montrose, *Representative Plays by American Dramatists*, NY: E. P. Dutton and Co, 1925 and Benjamin Blom, 1964, vol. 1 1765–1819
Munk, Erika, *Theater and Politics: a International Anthology*, Ubu, 1992
Nelson, Brian, *Asian American Drama*, NY: Applause, 1997
New Connections 99: New Plays for Young People, London: Faber, 1999
Nicoll, Allardyce, *Lesser English Comedies of the 18th Century*, London: Oxford UP, 1927
Nolan, Yvette, Betty Quan and George Bwanika Seremba, *Beyond the Pale: Dramatic Writings from First Nations Writers and Writers of Colour*, Toronto: Playwrights Canada Press, 1996
Ntiri, Daphne Williams, *Roots and Blossoms: African American Plays Today*, Troy, MI: Bedford, 1992
Oliver, William, *Voices of Change in the Spanish American Theatre*, Austin, TX: Texas UP, 1971
One-Act Plays for Stage and Study, NY: Samuel French, 1924 continuing
Osborn, M. Elizabeth, *On New Ground: Contemporary Hispanic-American Plays*, NY: TCG, 1987
Osborn, M. Elizabeth, *The Way We Live Now: American Plays and the AIDS Crisis*, NY: TCG, 1990
Ozieblo, Barbara, *The Provincetown Players: a Choice of the Shorter Works*, Sheffield: Sheffield Academic Press, 1994
Parr, Bruce, *Australian Gay and Lesbian Plays*, Sydney: Currency, 1996
Perkins, Kathy, *Black Female Playwrights: an Anthology of Plays Before 1960*, Bloomington, IN: Indiana UP, 1989
Perkins, Kathy A. and Roberta Uno, *Contemporary Plays by Women of Color*, London: Routledge, 1996
Perkins, Kathy A. and Judith L. Stephens, *Strange Fruit: Plays on Lynching by American Women*, Bloomington, IN: Indiana UP, 1998
Perkins, Kathy, *Black South African Women: an anthology of plays*, London: Routledge, 1999
Perkyns, Richard, *Major Plays of the Canadian Theatre 1934–1984*, Toronto: Irwin Publishing, 1984
Pfisterer, Susan, *Tremendous Worlds: Australian Women's Drama 1890–1960*, Sydney: Currency, 1999
Philbrick, Norman, *Trumpets Sounding: Propaganda Plays of the American Revolution*, NY: Blom, 1972
Poland, Albert, and Bruce Mailman, *The Off Off Broadway Book*, Indianapolis, IN: Bobbs Merrill, 1972
Pollock, Rhoda-Gale, *A Sampler of Plays by Women*, NY & Frankfurt-am-Main: Peter Lang Publishers, 1990
Potiki, Roma, *He Reo Hou: Five Plays by Maori Playwrights*, Wellington: Playmarket, 1991

Prentice, Christine and Lisa Warrington, *Playlunch: Five Short New Zealand Plays*, Dunedin, NZ: Otago UP, 1996

Press, Karen, *The World on a Hill and Other Plays*, Cape Town: Oxford UP, 1994

Quinn, Arthur Hobson, *Representative American Plays*, NY: Appleton Crofts, 1917 (revised and enlarged, 1938)

Ratcliff, Nora and John Bourne, *Six Plays*, London: Nelson Theatrecraft 3, c. 1942

Remnant, Mary, *Plays by Women vols. 5–8*, London, Methuen, 1986–90

Richardson, Willis and May Miller, *Negro History in 13 Plays*, Washington: Associated Press, 1935

Roberts, Philip, *Plays Without Wires*, Sheffield: Sheffield Academic Press, 1989

Robinson, Rony, *None of Them Knew Why I was Crying*, London: Hodder & Stoughton, 1989

Robson, Cheryl, *Female Voices, Fighting Lives: Seven Plays by Women*, London: Aurora Metro, 1991

    A Touch of the Dutch, London: Aurora Metro, 1997

Rogers, Katherine M., *The Meridian Anthology of Restoration and Eighteenth-Century Plays by Women*, NY: Meridian, 1994

Rudakoff, Judith, *Dangerous Traditions: a Passe Muraille Anthology*, Winnipeg: Blizzard, 1992

Russell, Mark, *Out of Character: Rants, Raves and Monologues from Today's Top Performance Artists*, NY: Bantam, 1997

Sainer, Arthur, *The Radical Theatre Notebook*, NY: Avon, 1975

Schiff, Ellen, *Fruitful and Multiplying: 9 Contemporary Plays from the American Jewish Repertoire*, NY: Mentor, 1996

Scullion, Adrienne, *Female Playwrights of the Nineteenth Century*, London: Dent, Everyman, 1996

Sears, Djanet, *Testifyin's: Contemporary African Canadian Drama vol. 1*, Toronto: Playwrights Canada Press, 2000

Setren, Phil, *Best of the Fest*, London: Aurora Metro, 1998

Sherman, Jason, *Solo*, Toronto: Coach House Press, 1994

Shewey, Don, *Out Front: Contemporary Gay & Lesbian Plays*, NY: Grove Press, 1988

Sinksongs: Feminist Plays, London: Feminist Books, 1986

Six Canadian Plays, Toronto: Playwrights Canada Press, DATE

Smith, Marisa, *Women Playwrights: the Best Plays of 1994*, Lyme, NH: Smith and Kraus, 1994

    Humana Festival '94: the Complete Plays (Actors' Theatre of Louisville 1994)

    Humana Festival '95 Lyme, NH: Smith and Kraus, 1995

    EST Marathon One Act Plays 1995, Lyme, NH: Smith and Kraus, 1995

Spender, Dale, *The Penguin Anthology of Australian Women's Writing* Ringwood, Va: Penguin, 1988

Spender, Dale, *Heroines: a Contemporary Anthology of Australian Women Writers*, Ringwood, Va: Penguin, 1991

Spender, Dale and Janet Todd, *Anthology of British Women Writers*, London: Pandora, 1989

Stein, Howard and Glenn Young, *The Best American Short Plays 92–96*, NY: Applause 1993–7

Studies in American Drama 1945–Present vol. 4, 1989

Sullivan, Victoria & James Hatch, *Plays By and About Women*, NY: Vintage, 1974

Tait, Peta and Elizabeth Schafer, *Australian Women's Drama: Texts and Feminisms*, Sydney: Currency, 1997

Trewin, J. C., *Plays of the Year*, London: Ungar, 1948–65

Turner, Darwin T., *Black Drama in America*, Washington, DC: Howard UP, 1994

Ubu Rep, ed., Temerson, Catherine & Francoise Kourilsky, *Plays by Women: an International Anthology*, vols 1 & 3, NY: Ubu, 1996

Uno, Roberta, *Unbroken Thread: an Anthology of Plays by Asian American Women* Amherst, MA: Massachusetts UP, 1993

Vargas, Margarita and Teresa Cajiao Salas, *Women Writing Women: an Anthology of Spanish-American Theater of the 1980s*, Albany, NY: State University of NY Press, 1997

Wagner, Anton, *Women Pioneers: Canada's Lost Plays*, vol. 2. Toronto: Canadian Theatre Review Publications, 1979

Wandor, Michelene, *Plays by Women vols. 1–4.*, London, Methuen, 1982–5

Wasserman, Jerry, *Modern Canadian Plays,* vols. 1 & 2, Vancouver: Talonbooks, 1993 & 1994

Weber, Carl, *Drama Contemporary: Germany*, Baltimore, MD: Johns Hopkins University Press, 1996

Wehle, Philippa, *Drama Contemporary: France*, NY: PAJ Publications, 1986

Wilkerson, Margaret B. *Nine Plays by Black Women*, NY: New American Library, 1986

Wilmer, S. E., *Portraits of Courage: Plays by Finnish Women*, Helsinki: Helsinki UP, 1997

Woodyard, George and Leon Lyday, *Dramatists in Revolt: the New Latin American Theatre*, Austin, TX: Texas UP, 1976

Yeo, Robert, *Prize-Winning Plays* 1, Singapore: Ministry of Culture, 1980

Zimmerman, Cynthia, *Taking the Stage: Selections from Plays by Canadian Women Playwrights*, Toronto: Canada Press, 1994

Appendix 2: Books on Women Playwrights and Women in Theatre

Anthony, Geraldine, ed., *Stage Voices: 12 Canadian Playwrights Talk About Their Work*, Toronto: Doubleday of Canada, 1978

Aston, Elaine, *An Introduction to Feminism and Theatre*, London: Routledge, 1995

Australian Drama 1920–1955, papers presented to a conference, Armidale, 1–4 Sept. 1984, Armidale: University of New England, 1986

Banks, Morwenna and Kate Swift, *The Joke's on Us: Women in Comedy from Music Hall to the Present*, London: Pandora, 1987

Betsko, Kathleen and Rachel Koenig, *Interviews with Contemporary Women Playwrights*, NY: Beech Tree Books, 1987

Bloom, Harold, ed., *Black American Women Poets and Dramatists*, NY: Chelsea House, 1996

Brask, Per, ed., *Contemporary Issues in Canadian Drama*, Winnipeg: Blizzard Publishing, 1995

Bradby, David and Annie Sparks, *Mise en Scène: French Theatre Today*, Methuen, 1997

Brater, Enoch, ed., *Feminine Focus: the New Women Playwrights*, NY: Oxford UP, 1989

Brown, Janet, *Feminist Drama: Definition and Critical Analysis*, Metuchen, NJ: Scarecrow Press, 1979

Brown, Janet, *Taking Center Stage: Feminism in Contemporary U.S. Drama*, London & Metuchen, NJ: Scarecrow Press, 1991

Brown-Guillory, Elizabeth, *Their Place on Stage: Black Women Playwrights in America*, NY: Greenwood, 1988

Canning, Charlotte, *Feminist Theaters in the U.S.A.*, London: Routledge, 1996

Carr, C., *On Edge: Performance at the End of the Twentieth Century*, Hanover and London: Wesleyan UP, 1993

Case, Sue-Ellen, *Feminism and Theatre*, Basingstoke: Macmillan, 1988

Case Sue-Ellen, ed., *Performing Feminisms: Feminist Critical Theory and Theatre*, Baltimore: Johns Hopkins UP, 1990

Chinoy, Helen Krich and Linda Walsh Jenkins, eds, *Women in American Theatre*, NY: Crown, 1981; revised edition NY: TCG, 1987

Conolly, L. W. ed., 'Modern Canadian Drama: Some Critical Perspectives' in CD 11: 1, 1985

Cotton, Nancy, *Women Playwrights in England c1363-1750*, Lewisburg: Bucknell UP, 1980

Cousin, Geraldine, *Women in Dramatic Place and Time,* London: Routledge 1993

Coven, Brenda, *American Women Dramatists of the Twentieth Century: a Bibliography*, Metuchen, NJ & London: Scarecrow Press, 1982

Christianson, Aileen and Alison Lumsden, *Contemporary Scottish Women Writers*, Edinburgh: Edinburgh UP, 2000.

Croft, Susan, 'Black Women Playwrights in Britain' in Griffiths and Llewellyn Jones, 1992 (below)

Curtin, Kaier, *We can Always Call them Bulgarians: the Emergence of Lesbians and Gay Men on the American Stage*, Boston: Alsyon Publications, 1987

Dolan, Jill, *The Feminist Spectator as Critic*, Ann Arbor, MI: Michigan UP, 1988

Donkin, Ellen, *Getting in on the Act: Women Playwrights in London 1776-1829*, London, Routledge, 1995

Donkin, Ellen and Susan Clement, eds, *Upstaging Big Daddy: Directing Theater as if Gender and Race Matter*, Ann Arbor, MI: Michigan UP, 1993

Dunton, Chris, *Make Man Talk True: Nigerian Drama in English Since 1970*, London: Hans Zell Publishers, 1992

Edgar, David (ed.), *State of Play: Playwrights on Playwriting*, London: Faber, 1999

Ferris, Leslie, *Acting Women: Images of Women in Theatre*, Basingstoke: Macmillan, 1990

France, Anna Kay and P. J. Corso, *International Women Playwrights, Voices of Identity and Transformation – Proceedings of the First International Women Playwrights Conference 1988*, Metuchen, NJ: Scarecrow Press, 1993

Freeman, Sandra, *Putting your Daughters on the Stage: Lesbian Theatre from the 1970s to the 1990s*, London: Cassell, 1987

Gale, Maggie, *West End Women: Women and the London Stage 1918–1962*, London: Routledge, 1996

Gardner, Viv and Susan Rutherford, *The New Woman and Her Sisters: Feminism and Theatre 1850–1914*, Hemel Hempstead: Harvester Wheatsheaf, 1992

Gilbert, Helen and Joanne Tompkins, *Post-Colonial Drama: Theory, Practice, Politics*, London: Routledge, 1996

Gilder, Rosamond, *Enter the Actress: the First Women in the Theatre* (1931), NY: Theatre Arts Books, 1960

Goodman, Lizbeth, *Contemporary Feminist Theatres: To Each Her Own*, London: Routledge, 1993

Griffiths, Trevor and Margaret Llewellyn Jones, eds, *British and Irish Women Dramatists Since 1958*, London: Open UP, 1992

Hart, Lynda, ed., *Making a Spectacle: Feminist Essays on Contemporary Women's Theatre*, Ann Arbor, MI: Michigan UP, 1989

Hart, Lynda and Peggy Phelan, eds, *Acting Out: Feminist Performances*, Ann Arbor, MI: Michigan UP, 1993

Hodkinson, Yvonne, *Female Parts: the Art and Politics of Female Playwrights*, Montreal/NY: Black Swan Books, 1991

Holledge, Julie, *Innocent Flowers: Women in the Edwardian Theatre*, London: The Women's Press, 1981

Howe, Elizabeth, *The First English Actress: Women and Drama 1660–1700*, Cambridge: Cambridge UP, 1992

Hull, Gloria T., *Colour, Sex and Poetry: Three Women Writers of the Harlem Renaissance*, Bloomington, IN: Indiana UP, 1987

Isser, Edward, *Stages of Annihilation: Theatrical Representations of the Holocaust*, Madison/Teaneck: Fairleigh Dickinson UP, 1997

Itzin, Catherine, *Stages in the Revolution*, London: Methuen, 1980

James, Adeola, ed., *In their Own Voices: African Women Writers Talk*, Portsmouth, NH: Heinemann, 1990

Juno, Andrea and V. Vale, eds, *Angry Women*, San Francisco: Re/Search Publications 13, 1991

Keyssar, Helene, *Feminist Theatre* Basingstoke: Macmillan, 1984

Keyssar, Helene, ed., *Feminist Theatre and Theory*, Basingstoke: Macmillan, 1996

Lamar, Celita, *Our Voices, Ourselves: Women Writing for the French Theatre*, NY: Peter Lang Publishers, 1991

Laughlin, Karen and Catherine Schuler, eds, *Theatre and Feminist Aesthetics*, Madison: Fairleigh Dickinson UP, 1995

Leavitt, Dinah Luise, *Feminist Theatre Groups*, Jefferson, NC: McFarland and Co., 1980

Malpede, Karen, *Women in Theatre: Compassion and Hope*, NY: Drama Book Publishers, 1983

Marranca, Bonnie, *Ecologies of Theater*, Baltimore: Johns Hopkins UP, 1996

Martin, Carol, ed., *A Sourcebook of Feminist Theatre and Performance*, London: Routledge, 1996

Much, Rita, ed., *Women on the Canadian Stage: the Legacy of Hrotswitha*, Winnipeg: Blizzard, 1992

Natalle, Elizabeth J., *Feminist Theatres: a Study in Persuasion*, Metuchen, NJ: Scarecrow Press, 1985

Otokunefor, Henriette C. and Obiageli C. Nwodo, eds, *Nigerian Female Writers: a Critical Perspective*, Lagos: Malthouse Press, 1989

Olauson, Judith, *The American Woman Playwright: a View of Criticism and Characterization*, Troy, NY: the Whitston Publishing Co., 1981

Osment, Philip, *Gay Sweatshop: Four Plays and a Company*, London: Methuen, 19??

Pearson, Jacqueline, *The Prostituted Muse: Images of Women and Women Dramatists 1642–1737*, NY and London: Harvester Wheatsheaf, 1988

Pfisterer, Susan and Carolyn Pickett, *Playing with Ideas: Australian Women Playwrights from the Suffragettes to the Sixties*, Sydney: Currency Press, 1999

Rees, Leslie, *The Making of Australian Drama: a Historical and Critical Survey from the 1830s to the 1970s*, Sydney: Angus and Robertson, 1973

Reynolds, Peter, *Novel Images: Literature in Performance*, London, Routledge, 1993

Roth, Moira, *The Amazing Decade: Women and Performance Art 1970-1980*, Los Angeles: Astro Artz, 1983

Savran, David, *In their Own Words: Interviews with Playwrights*, NY: TCG, 1989

Sayre, Henry M., *The Object of Performance*, Chicago: Chicago UP, 1989.

Schlueter, June, ed., *Modern American Drama: the Female Canon*, London and Toronto: Associated University Presses, 1990

Schneider, Rebecca, *The Explicit Body in Performance*, London: Routledge, 1997

Schofield, Mary Anne and Cecelia Macheski, eds, *Curtain Calls: British and American Women Playwrights 1660-1820*, OH: Ohio UP, 1991

Senelick, Lawrence, ed., *Gender in Performance: the Presentation of Difference in the Performing Arts*, Hanover, NH: Tufts UP, 1992

Shafer, Yvonne, *American Women Playwrights 1900–1950*, NY: Peter Lang Publishing, 1995

Sieg, Katrin, *Exiles, Eccentrics, Activists: Women in Contemporary German Theatre*, Ann Arbor: Michigan UP, 1994

Sierz, Aleks, *In-Yer-Face Theatre: British Drama Today*, London: Faber, 2001

Stephenson, Heidi and Natasha Langridge, *Rage and Reason: Women Playwrights on Playwriting*, London: Methuen, 1997

Stevenson, Randall and Gavin Wallace, eds, *Scottish Theatre Since the Seventies*, Edinburgh: Edinburgh UP, 1996

Stowell, Sheila, *A Stage of their Own: feminist playwrights in the suffrage era*, Manchester: Manchester UP, 1991

Tait, Peta, *Converging Realities: Feminism in Australian Theatre* Sydney: Currency, 1994

Todd, Susan, ed., *Women and Theatre: Calling the Shots*, London: Faber, 1984

Tompkins, Joanne and Julie Holledge, eds, *Performing Women/Performing Feminisms: Interviews with International Women Playwrights*, Australasian Drama Studies Association Academic Publications 2

Wandor, Michelene, *Carry on Understudies: Theatre and Sexual Politics*, Routledge and

Kegan Paul, 1981

Look Back in Gender: Sexuality and the Family in Post-War British Drama, London: Methuen, 1987

Wallace, Robert and Cynthia Zimmerman, *The Works: Conversations with English-Canadian Playwrights*, Toronto: Coach House Press, 1982

Watts, Emily Stipes, *The Poetry of American Women from 1632 to 1945*, Austin, TX and London: Texas UP, 1977

Zimmerman, Cynthia, *Female Voices in English Canada*, Toronto: Simon and Pierre, 1994

Special Issues of Newsletters or Journals

Acting Up! Women in Theater and Performance, Heresies no. 17, vol. 5, no. 1, 1984

The Drama Review, T86 vol. 24, June 1980 (NYU)

The Southern Quarterly special issue, ed. Millie S. Barranger: Southern Women Playwrights, vol. 25, no. 3, Spring 1987

Studies in American Drama 1945 to Present (SAD), ed. J. Madison Davis, Pennsylvania State University, vol. 4, American Women Playwrights (1989)

The Theatre Annual, vol. 40, 1985

Theatre Journal (Johns Hopkins UP) vol. 37, no. 3, Staging Gender (August 1985)

Themes in Drama (TiD) ed. James Redmond, Cambridge University Press, no. 7, Drama, Sex and Politics and no. 11, Women in Theatre (1989)

Theater (formerly *Yale/Theater*), Winter 1985

Journals Devoted to Women and Performance

Women and Performance (NYU)

Women and Theatre: Occasional Papers, Manchester UP

The Open Page and *Magdalena Newsletter*, The Magdalena Project, Chapter, Market Road, Canton, Cardiff CF5 1QE, Wales, UK. Fax: 01222 220552

Appendix 3: Contact Addresses

Unpublished Translations

For unpublished translations listed as LCP (Lord Chamberlain's plays) readers should contact the British Library

CEAD – Centre des auteurs dramatiques (all French-Canadian playwrights). 3450 rue Saint-Urbain, Montreal, Quebec H2X 2N5, Canada

Aliki Bacopolou-Halls (Anagonostaki). 21 Mesolongiou St, Kesariani 16122, Greece. Fax: 31 1 3612707

Donald Watson (Cixous). c/o Routledge (see below)

Meredith Oakes (Gallaire). Agent: Casarotto Ramsay Ltd, 60 Wardour St, London W1V 4ND, England

M. Feitlowitz (Gambaro). c/o Northwestern University Press, 625 Colfax, Evanston, Illinois 60201, USA

Nick Drake (Gambaro). 89 Nelson's Row, London SW4 7JW, England

Viveca Lindfors (Garpe), Folmer Hansen Teaterforlag, Lundagatan 4, S-171 63 Solna, Sweden.

Rhea Gaisner (Herzberg). John Rudge (Herzberg), both c/o Hans Verhoeven, Jac V. Lennepkade 311, Amsterdam 1054 ZW, Netherlands. Tel: 020 6160996

William Mishler (Loveid). Teater and Musik, Ceclia Onfelat, Bondegatan 46, 11633 Stockholm, Sweden

Nadia Christensen, (Loveid). Medienedition, Kerin Roth, Sterneckerstrasse 2, 8000 Munchen 2, Germany

Christine Furnival (Maraini). 33 West St, Stratford-upon-Avon, Warwickshire CV37 6DN, England

Stephen Mulrine, (Petruschevskaya, Sadur). Michael Imison Playwrights, c/o Alan Brodie Representation, 211 Piccadilly, London W1V 9LD, England. Fax: 020-7917 2872

Tinch Minter and Anthony Vivis (Reinshagen). Rosica Colin, 1 Clareville Grove Mews, London SW7 5AH, England. Fax: 020-7244 6441

David Hohkien (Ryum). Danske Dramatikeres Forbund, Klosterstrasse 22, Kobenhavn K, Denmark

Cathy Porter (Sadur). 16 Tremlett Grove, Holloway, London N19 5JX, England

Yara Arts Group (Ukrainka). 306 E. 11th St No.313, New York, NY 10007, USA

Major Drama Publishers

Australia

Currency Press, 330 Oxford Street (PO Box 452), Paddington, Sydney, NSW 2021. email: currency@magna.com.au. Fax: 61 (0) 29332 3848

Yackandandah Playscripts, 25 Buena Vista Drive, Montmorency, Victoria 3094

University of Queensland Press, St Lucia, Queensland, 4072

Canada

Blizzard Publishing, 73 Furby St, Winnipeg, Manitoba, R3C 2A2

Coach House Press, 50 Prince Arthur Ave, Suite 107, Toronto, M5R 1B5

Nuage Editions, P.O.B 206, RPO Corydon, Winnipeg, Manitoba, R3M 3S7. Fax: 204 779 7803. email: nuage@netcom.ca (formerly Montreal based)

Playwrights Canada, 54 Wolseley St 2nd flr, Toronto, Ontario, M5T 1A5. Fax: 416 703 0059. email: cdplays@interlog.com. Website: http://www.puc.ca

Simon and Pierre, 2181 Queen St E, Ste 301, Toronto, Ontario, M4E 1E5. Fax: 416 698 1102

Talonbooks, 201/1019 East Cordova St, Vancouver, British Columbia, V6A 1M8

Great Britain

Amber Lane Press, Cheorl House, Church St, Charlbury Oxon OX7 3PR. Fax: (0)1608 810024

Aurora Metro Press, 4 Osier Mews, Chiswick, London W4 2NT

John Calder Publications Ltd, 126 Cornwall Rd, London SE1 8TQ. Fax: (020) 7633 0599

Faber and Faber Ltd, 3 Queen Square, London WC1N 3AU. Fax: (020) 7465 0034, http://faber.co.uk

Samuel French, 52 Fitzroy Square, London W1P 6JR. Fax: (020) 7387 2161

Heinemann, Random House, 20 Vauxhall Bridge Road, London SW1V 2SA. Fax: (020) 7233 6129

Nick Hern Books, 14 Larden Road, London W3 7ST. Fax: (020) 8746 2006. email: orders@nickhernbooks.demon.co.uk. (Also UK distributor for TCG)

Hodder & Stoughton, 338 Euston Rd, London NW1 3BH. Fax: (020) 7873 6195

Longman, Longman House, Burnt Mill, Harlow, Essex, CM20 2JE

Macmillan, 25 Eccleston Place, London SW1W 9NF. Fax: (020) 7881 8001. email: books@macmillan.co.uk

Methuen Drama, 215 Vauxhall Bridge Road, London SW1V 1EJ. Fax: (020) 7828 2098

Oberon Books, 521 Caledonian Rd, London N7 9RH. Fax: (020) 7607 3629 email: oberon.books@btinternet.com. Website: www.oberonbooks.com

Routledge, 11 New Fetter Lane, London, EC4 4EE. Fax (020) 7842 2307

seren, Poetry Wales Press, First Floor, 2 Wyndham Street, Bridgend, Mid-Glamorgan, CF31 1EF

Virago, Brettenham House, Lancaster Place, London WC2E 7EN. Fax: (020) 7 383 4892

Warner Chappell Plays, 129 Park St, London W1Y 3FA. Fax: (020) 7499 9718 EC1 0DX. Fax: (020) 7608 1938. Website: http://www.the-womens-press.com

New Zealand

Victoria University Press, Private Bag, Wellington

Playmarket, PO Box 9767, Wellington. Fax: 64-4-382 8461. email: playmarket@org.nz.

USA

Applause Books, 211 West 71st St, New York NY 10023. Fax: 212 721 2856

Broadway Play Publishing (BPP), 357 W. 20th St, New York, NY 10011.

DPC (Dramatic Publishing Company), PO Box 129 Woodstock, Illinois 60098. Fax: 815 338 8981

DPS (Dramatists Play Service), 440 Park Ave S., New York, NY 10016. Fax: 212 213 1539. email: postmaster@dramatists.com

Faber Inc. (an affiliate of Farrer, Straus and Giroux LLC, 19 Union Square West, New York, NY 10010. Fax: 212 633 9385. email: publicityfsg@fsgee.com)

Samuel French, 45 West 25th St, New York, NY 10010. Fax: 212 206 1429

Garland Publishing, 717 Fifth Ave., 25th flr, New York NY 10022.

Greenwood Press, 88 Post Road, PO Box 5007, Westport, CT 06881-5007. Website: http://www.green-wood.com

Grove/Atlantic Inc., 841 Broadway, 4th flr, New York NY 10003. Fax: 212 614 7886

University of Michigan Press, P. O. Box 1104, Ann Arbor, MI 48106.

Minnesota University Press, Mill place, Ste 290, 113 3rd Ave, Minneapolis, MN 55401. Fax: 612 627 1980

Performing Arts Journal Publications, Johns Hopkins University Press, 2715 N. Charles St, Baltimore, MD 21218-4319 (formerly NY based)

Theatre Communications Group (TCG and formerly Plays in Process), 330 Lexington Ave., New York, NY 10017-0217. Fax: 212 938 4847

Where the publisher is Samuel French, the place of publication should be assumed to be NY for American playwrights and London for British, unless specified otherwise.

Other Contacts

New Dramatists, 424 W. 24th St, New York NY 10036 USA. email: NewDram@aol.com. Website: http://www.itp.tsoa.nyu.edu/~diana

Writernet (formerly New Playwrights Trust), Interchange Studios, Dalby St, Kentish Town, London NW5. UK. Tel: 020 7284 2818, Fax: 020 7482 5292. email:npt@easynet. co.uk. Website: http://www.writernet.org.uk

Theatre Museum, 1E Tavistock Street, London WC2E 7PA, UK. Tel: (020) 7943 4700. Fax: (020) 7943 4777. email: s.croft@vam.ac.uk.Website: http://theatremuseum.vam.ac.uk.

Playworks (the National Centre for Women Performance Writers), P. O. Box A2216, Sydney, South NSW, Australia. 1235 Fax: 02 9264 8449

The Women's Project, 7 West 63rd St, New York, NY 10023, USA. email:wpp@earthlink.net

Frauen in Theater, Dramaturgische Gesellschaft, Tempellherrenstrasse 4, 10961 Berlin, Germany Fax: 030 693 2654